THE REVELS PLAYS

Founder Editor
Clifford Leech 1958–71

General Editors
F. David Hoeniger, E. A. J. Honigmann and J. R. Mulryne

TAMBURLAINE THE GREAT

Tamburlaine
the Great.

Who, from a Scythian Shephearde,
by his rare and woonderfull Conquests,
became a most puissant and migh-
tye Monarque.

And (for his tyranny, and terrour in
Warre) was tearmed,

The Scourge of God.

Deuided into two Tragicall Dis-
courses, as they were sundrie times
shewed vpon Stages in the Citie
of London.

By the right honorable the Lord
Admyrall, his seruantes.

Now first, and newlie published.

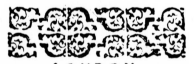

LONDON.
Printed by Richard Ihones: at the signe
of the Rose and Crowne neere Hol-
borne Bridge. 1590.

THE REVELS PLAYS

TAMBURLAINE THE GREAT

CHRISTOPHER MARLOWE

Edited by

J. S. Cunningham

MANCHESTER
UNIVERSITY PRESS

THE JOHNS HOPKINS
UNIVERSITY PRESS

© J. S. Cunningham 1981

Published by
Manchester University Press
Oxford Road, Manchester M13 9PL

ISBN 0–7190–1528–6

Published in the United States of America, 1981 by
The Johns Hopkins University Press
Baltimore, Maryland 21218

ISBN 0–8018–2669–1

Library of Congress Catalog Card Number 81 47596

British Library Cataloguing in Publication Data

Marlowe, Christopher, *b. 1564*
    Tamburlaine the Great.—(The revels plays).
    I. Title   II. Cunningham, Joseph Sandy
    III. Series
    822'.3   PR2669

    ISBN 0–7190–1528–6 (UK)
    ISBN 0–8018–2669–1 (USA)

Printed in Great Britain
by Latimer Trend & Company Ltd, Plymouth

Contents

ILLUSTRATIONS

Title-page of Part One from the 1590 octavo (courtesy
Huntington Library) *frontispiece*

Engraving of Tamburlaine in Richard Knolles, *The Generall
Historie of the Turkes* (London, 1603), p. 236 (courtesy
John Rylands University Library of Manchester). This is
claimed as 'An Unrecorded Portrait of Edward Alleyn' by
Martin Holmes, *Theatre Notebook*, 1950–2, pp. 11–13. *p. 106*

General Editors' Preface

The series known as the Revels Plays was conceived by Clifford Leech. The idea for the series emerged in his mind, as he explained in his preface to the first of the Revels Plays in 1958, from the success of the New Arden Shakespeare. The aim of the new group of texts was 'to apply to Shakespeare's predecessors, contemporaries and successors the methods that are now used in Shakespeare editing'. The plays chosen were to include well-known works from the early Tudor period to about 1700, as well as others less familiar but of literary and theatrical merit: 'the plays included,' Leech wrote, 'should be such as to deserve and indeed demand performance.' We owe it to Clifford Leech that the idea became reality. He set the high standards of the series, ensuring that editors of individual volumes produced work of lasting merit, equally useful for teachers and students, theatre directors and actors. Clifford Leech remained General Editor until 1971, supervising the first seventeen volumes to be published.

The Revels Plays are now under the direction of three General Editors, F. David Hoeniger, E. A. J. Honigmann and J. R. Mulryne. The publishers, originally Methuen, are now Manchester University Press, with Johns Hopkins University Press as co-publisher. Yet, despite these changes, the format and essential character of the series will continue, and it is hoped that its editorial standards will be maintained. Except for some work in progress, the General Editors intend, in expanding the series, to concentrate for the immediate future on plays of the period 1558–1642, and may include a small number of non-dramatic works of interest to students of drama. Some slight changes have been forced by considerations of cost. For example, in editions from 1978, notes to the introduction are placed together at the end, not at the foot of the page. Collation and commentary notes will continue, however, to appear on the relevant pages.

The text of each Revels play, in accordance with established practice in the series, is edited afresh from the original text of best authority (in a few instances, texts), but spelling and punctuation are modernised and speech headings are silently made consistent. Elisions in the original are also silently regularised, except where metre would be affected by the change; since 1968 the '-ed' form is used for non-syllabic terminations in past tenses and past participles ('-'d' earlier), and '-èd' for syllabic ('-ed' earlier). The editor emends, as distinct from modernises, his original only in instances where error is patent or at least very probable, and correction persuasive. Act divisions are given only if they appear in the original or if the structure of the play clearly points to them. Those act and scene divisions not found in the original are provided unobtrusively in small type and in square brackets. Square brackets are also used for any other additions to or changes in the stage directions of the original.

Revels Plays do not provide a variorum collation, but only those variants which require the critical attention of serious textual students. All departures of substance from 'copy-text' are listed, including any relineation and those changes in punctuation which involve to any degree a decision between alternative interpretations; but not such accidentals as turned letters, nor necessarily additions to stage directions whose editorial nature is already made clear by the use of brackets. Press corrections in the 'copy-texts' are likewise included. Of later emendations of the text, only those are given which as alternative readings still deserve serious attention.

One of the hallmarks of the Revels Plays is the thoroughness of their annotations. Besides explaining the meaning of difficult words and passages, the editor provides comments on customs or usage, text or stage business—indeed, on anything he judges pertinent and helpful. Each volume contains a Glossarial Index to the Commentary, in which particular attention is drawn to meanings for words not listed in *O.E.D.*

The Introduction to a Revels play assesses the authority of the 'copy-text' on which it is based, and discusses the editorial methods employed in dealing with it; the editor also considers his play's date and (where relevant) sources, together with its place in the work of the author and in the theatre of its time. Stage history is offered, and in the case of a play by an author not previously represented in the series a brief biography is given.

It is our hope that plays edited in this fashion will promote further scholarly and theatrical investigation of one of the richest periods in theatrical history.

F. DAVID HOENIGER
E. A. J. HONIGMANN
J. R. MULRYNE

Preface

To my regret, this edition of *Tamburlaine* is published too late for it to be seen, and no doubt perceptively criticised, by the original General Editor of the Series, Clifford Leech. He looked to the day when all the volumes comprising 'the Revels edition of Marlowe' would be available, as the up-to-date equivalent of the original Methuen Marlowe, which was published under the general direction of R. H. Case. Leech looked back with particular respect and admiration to the work of Una Ellis-Fermor; and the present edition of *Tamburlaine* was conceived, at Leech's instigation, as a re-working of her pioneer scholarly work on the play. Published in 1930, and revised in 1951, her edition has provided the working basis of many subsequent editions of the play. An editor working on *Tamburlaine* afresh finds his admiration for her work enhanced, and many of her annotations remain authoritative. He also finds, of course, that scholarship and criticism have, in the intervening years, extended and in some respects transformed our understanding of Marlowe and his context. Leech himself was among the most persistent and judicious critics of Marlowe, and he commented extensively on modern criticism of the plays. My debt to him complements my debt to Ellis-Fermor's edition of this play, and when I salute his memory I think not only of his work on Marlowe and other dramatists, but also of his generous influence and friendship over many years, beginning with his lectures to the undergraduate class at Durham University in the autumn of 1946. This edition is, at heart, for him.

Two of Leech's successors as General Editors of The Revels Plays have given me invaluable help and advice. David Hoeniger offered many wise comments and suggestions at a relatively early stage. Ernst Honigmann gave both typescript and proof his meticulous and patient attention, far beyond the routine obligation of a General Editor, and amounting to a magnanimous scholarly participation in the later stages of the work. J. C. Maxwell sent me several scholarly notes on the play, and lent me his copy of the Ellis-Fermor edition, with his own pencilled marginalia. Equally generous, two colleagues at Leicester corrected and encouraged my work at various points, and made many useful suggestions: to Gordon Campbell and Roger Warren I offer my sincere gratitude. I have, perforce, indicated only a few of the many particular places at which I am indebted to the scholars and friends named in this paragraph: such people give lustre to the banal idea of 'the community of scholars'.

Many other colleagues have offered help, or have responded generously to my requests. H. D. Purcell brought his work on Marlowe's sources to my attention, and gave me the use of his typescript. Duncan Cloud, of the Leicester Department of Classics, helped with specialist information, and he revised and extended the translations of Latin source material which Ian Ker had first helped me with at York. G. B. Shand lent me his copy of Oxberry's rare edition of *Tamburlaine*. Particular references I might well have missed were brought to my attention by Süheyla Artemel, Philip Brockbank, J. R. Coates, H. W. Crundell, Brian Gibbons, Bernard Harris, and Mervyn Jannetta. Margaret Bruce and Eithne Henson made encouraging and helpful comments on the Introduction. Several major libraries gave, as ever, the unostentatious assistance we depend upon: the British Library, the Bodleian, the Folger, and the Huntington Library. I am grateful to the Research Boards of the Universities of York and Leicester for grants in aid of library visits. John Banks, of Manchester University Press, gave the edition his close and patient supervisory attention. Jill Cunningham spent many vigilant, painstaking hours checking typescript and proofs, no stranger to the barbarous company of the Scythian.

An editor seeks, as he must, to draw discriminatingly and accurately on the work of those who, at many points, know better than he, not least the unsung compilers and authors of reference books. I hope I have more aided than impeded the right understanding of the play. The faults are mine.

University of Leicester, 1981   J. S. CUNNINGHAM

Abbreviations

Bowers
: *The Complete Works of Christopher Marlowe*, ed. Fredson Bowers (Cambridge, 1973), two volumes.

Brereton
: J. le G. Brereton, 'Notes on the text of Marlowe', *Beiblatt zur Anglia*, XVI (1905), 203-7.

Brooke
: *The Works of Christopher Marlowe*, ed. C. F. Tucker Brooke (Oxford, 1910).

Broughton
: James Broughton's notes in his copy of Robinson, now in the British Library.

Bullen
: *The Works of Christopher Marlowe*, ed. A. H. Bullen (London, 1885).

Collier
: J. P. Collier's notes in his copy of Dyce 1, now in the British Library.

Dyce 1
: *The Works of Christopher Marlowe*, ed. Alexander Dyce (London, 1850).

Dyce 2
: *The Works of Christopher Marlowe, a New Edition, Revised and Corrected*, ed. Dyce (London, 1858).

Cunningham
: *The Works of Christopher Marlowe*, ed. Francis Cunningham (London, 1870).

Ellis-Fermor
: *Tamburlaine the Great*, ed. Una Ellis-Fermor (London, 1930); second edition, revised, 1951.

Jump
: *Tamburlaine the Great*, ed. John D. Jump (London, 1967).

Kirschbaum
: *The Plays of Christopher Marlowe*, ed. Leo Kirschbaum (Cleveland, 1962).

Malone
: MS notes by Malone in Bodleian copy of *Q*.

O1
: *Tamburlaine the Great* (London, 1590). The first octavo.

O2
: *Tamburlaine the Great* (London, 1593).

O3
: *Tamburlaine the Great* (London, 1597).

Q
: *Tamburlaine the Great* (London, 1605-6). Two volumes.

Oxberry   *Tamburlaine the Great*, ed. W. Oxberry
                        (London, 1820).
Pendry–Maxwell   Marlowe, *Complete Plays and Poems*, ed. E. D.
                        Pendry and J. C. Maxwell (London, 1976).
Robinson   *The Works of Christopher Marlowe* [ed. G.
                        Robinson] (London, 1826).
van Dam   B. A. P. van Dam, 'Marlowe's *Tamburlaine*',
                        English Studies, XVI (1934), 1–17.
Woolf   *Tamburlaine the Great*, ed. Tatiana M. Woolf
                        (London, 1964).

OTHER REFERENCES

Battenhouse   Roy W. Battenhouse, *Marlowe's Tamburlaine:
                        a Study in Renaissance Moral Philosophy*
                        (Nashville, 1941).
Bevington   David M. Bevington, *From Mankind to
                        Marlowe* (Cambridge, Mass., 1962).
Bizarus   *Historia di Pietro Bizari* (Lyon, 1568).
Bonfinius   *Antonii Bonfinii Rerum Ungaricum* (Frankfurt,
                        1543).
Chalcondylas   *Laonici Chalcondylae, de origine et rebus gestis
                        Turcorum* (Basle, [1556]).
Clemen   Wolfgang Clemen, *English Tragedy Before
                        Shakespeare*, tr. T. S. Dorsch (London, 1961).
Cole   Douglas Cole, *Suffering and Evil in the Plays of
                        Christopher Marlowe* (Princeton, N.J., 1962).
Dido   Marlowe, *Dido Queen of Carthage*, ed. H. J.
                        Oliver (London, 1968). One volume with
                        Massacre at Paris.
Dr Faustus   Marlowe, *Doctor Faustus*, ed. John D. Jump
                        (London, 1962).
E.A.J.H.   E. A. J. Honigmann: suggestion to editor.
Edward II   Marlowe, *Edward II*, ed. H. B. Charlton and
                        R. D. Waller, revised F. N. Lees (London,
                        1955).
F.D.H.   F. D. Hoeniger: suggestion to editor.
L. and E. Feasey   'Marlowe and the Prophetic Dooms', *N.&Q.*,
                        CXCV (1950), 356–7, 404–7, 419–21.
Fieler   Frank B. Fieler, *Tamburlaine, Part I and its
                        Audience* (Gainesville, Fla., 1961).
Fortescue   Thomas Fortescue, *The Foreste or Collection of
                        Histories* (London, 1571).
Golding   *Shakespeare's Ovid, Being Arthur Golding's*

Translation of the Metamorphoses, ed. W. H. D. Rouse (London, 1962).

Heninger   S. K. Heninger, Jr., *A Handbook of Renaissance Meteorology* (Durham, N.C., 1960).

Hero   Marlowe, *Hero and Leander* (see *Poems*).

Jew of Malta   Marlowe, *The Jew of Malta*, ed. N. W. Bawcutt (Manchester, 1978).

Kocher   Paul H. Kocher, *Christopher Marlowe. A Study of his Thought, Learning, and Character* (New York, 1946).

Leech   Clifford Leech, 'Marlowe's Humor', in R. Hosley (ed.), *Essays on Shakespeare and Elizabethan Drama in Honor of Hardin Craig* (London, 1963), pp. 69–81.

Lonicerus   Philippus Lonicerus, *Chronicorum Turcorum . . . Tomus primus (–tertius)* (Frankfurt, 1578).

Lucan   see *Poems*.

Massacre at Paris   Marlowe, *The Massacre at Paris*, ed. H. J. Oliver (London, 1968). One volume with *Dido*.

Ortelius   Abraham Ortelius, *Theatrum Orbis Terrarum* (Antwerp, 1570).

Ovid's Elegies   see *Poems*.

Parr   Johnstone Parr, *Tamburlaine's Malady* (University, Alabama, 1953).

Perondinus   Petrus Perondinus, *Magni Tamerlanis Scytharum Imperatoris Vita* (Florence, 1553).

Poems   Marlowe, *The Poems*, ed. Millar Maclure (London, 1968).

Purcell   H. D. Purcell, doctoral thesis, University of Cambridge (1967), *Spanish Literary Influence on the English Drama to 1625*.

Revels History   J. Leeds Barroll, Alexander Leggatt, Richard Hosley, Alvin Kernan, *The Revels History of Drama in English*, III (London, 1975).

Seaton   Ethel Seaton, 'Marlowe's Map', *Essays and Studies by Members of the English Association*, X (1924), 13–35.

Seaton, 'Sources'   Ethel Seaton, 'Fresh Sources for Marlowe', *R.E.S.*, V (1929), 385–401.

Tilley   M. P. Tilley, *A Dictionary of the Proverbs in England in the Sixteenth and Seventeenth Centuries* (Ann Arbor, Mich., 1950).

Waith   Eugene M. Waith, *The Herculean Hero* (London, 1962).

Weil

Judith Weil, *Christopher Marlowe: Merlin's Prophet* (Cambridge, 1977).

Whetstone

George Whetstone, *The English Myrror* (London, 1586). Facsimile, 1973, *The English Experience*, No. 632 (Amsterdam and New York).

Wilson

F. P. Wilson, *Marlowe and the Early Shakespeare* (Oxford, 1953).

Zucker

David Hard Zucker, *Stage and Image in the Plays of Christopher Marlowe* (Salzburg, 1972).

PERIODICALS

E.H.R.	*English Historical Review*
E.L.H.	*English Literary History*
E.L.R.	*English Literary Renaissance*
J.E.G.P.	*Journal of English and Germanic Philology*
M.L.N.	*Modern Language Notes*
M.L.Q.	*Modern Language Quarterly*
M.L.R.	*Modern Language Review*
M.P.	*Modern Philology*
N.&Q.	*Notes and Queries*
P.M.L.A.	*Publications of the Modern Language Association*
R.E.S.	*Review of English Studies*
S.E.L.	*Studies in English Literature*
S.P.	*Studies in Philology*
T.D.R.	*Tulane Drama Review*
T.L.S.	*Times Literary Supplement*

Titles of Shakespeare plays are abbreviated as in Onions, *A Shakespeare Glossary* (Oxford, 1911). Shakespeare quotations are from *Works*, ed. P. Alexander (London, 1951).

Introduction

I. CHRISTOPHER MARLOWE

The known events of Marlowe's life, few in number but persistently dramatic, have been frequently retold.[1] The most notorious of them, leading up to his violent death in 1593 at the age of twenty-nine, entangle us in a web of accusation, recrimination, and speculation. As these complexities mostly emerge in the period between the publication of *Tamburlaine* in 1590 and the end of Marlowe's life, their bearing on this play is indirect. However, events and allegations which occur after 1590 relate in part to some which are met with earlier in Marlowe's career. His connection with the Privy Council, most ominous, perhaps, during the last few weeks of his life, had begun during the three years which elapsed between the award of his first and second degrees at Cambridge. The tone and the main drift of the depositions made about Marlowe in 1593 by Thomas Kyd and Richard Baines are to some extent anticipated in the terms in which he is, obliquely, described and rebuked in the earlier years by Robert Greene. It is dangerous to take these reports on trust. Both Greene and Baines, in their different ways, bore grudges against Marlowe, and Kyd wrote his statements when he had good cause to fear for his own life. After the immediate theatrical success of *Tamburlaine*, in 1587 or 1588, this play and to some extent other plays by Marlowe were readily seen as self-indulgent projections of his own convictions and his own life-style. In its less crude forms, this view of Marlowe's work can still be met.[2] It is, therefore, important to restate, however briefly, what is known about his life and what was alleged at the time about his attitudes and convictions. Scholars have recently brought more information to light to supplement the lucid biographical summary which is to be found in the Revels edition of *Doctor Faustus* (1962).[3]

Christopher Marlowe was baptised in the church of St. George the Martyr, Canterbury, on 26 February 1564, presumably within a few days of his birth. His father, John, was a shoemaker, continuing a family tradition. His mother, Catherine Marlowe (*née* Arthur), came from Dover. John Marlowe has recently been described, on evidence drawn from local records, as 'a noisy, self-assertive, improvident fellow'.[4] He was frequently embroiled in lawsuits, as were several of his near relatives. Early in 1579, Marlowe became a scholar at King's School, Canterbury. It is thought unlikely that he was a commoner at the school before that date.

Marlowe appears in the records of Corpus Christi College, Cambridge, in December 1580, and he matriculates in March 1581. His formal election to an Archbishop Parker scholarship occurs in May 1581. In Lent Term three years later, he is allowed to proceed to the degree of B.A. We learn of his visiting Canterbury in November 1585; and he was away from Cambridge for some time in the following year. These absences may have some connection with the episode in 1587 which makes us aware that Marlowe had already been covertly employed in some form of governmental service. The University authorities had shown some reluctance to confer the degree of M.A., to which Marlowe was formally entitled, and the Privy Council intervened. The Council were at pains to scotch the rumour that Marlowe intended to go to Rheims for an indefinite period—a rumour which would carry the suspicion that Marlowe was emigrating to the English seminary as a convert to Catholicism. Marlowe had, the Council affirmed, acquitted himself well on the Queen's behalf in 'matters touching the benefitt of his Countrie'.[5] The degree was conferred shortly afterwards, in July 1587.

Both parts of *Tamburlaine*, or perhaps just the single play which was subsequently redesignated Part One, may have been acted in the winter of 1587, but this date is conjectural. Certainly Robert Greene's preface to his *Perimedes the Blacke-Smith*, published on 29 March 1588, testifies all too clearly to the emergence of a new, extravagant theatrical style. He has chosen, he says, to 'speake darkely', smarting under mockery brought upon him by 'two Gentleman Poets':

> I keepe my old course, to palter up some thing in Prose, using mine olde poesie still, *Omne tulit punctum*, although latelye two Gentlemen Poets, made two mad men of Rome beate it out of their paper bucklers: & had it in derision, for that I could not make my verses jet upon the stage in tragicall buskins, everie worde filling the mouth like the faburden of Bo-Bell, daring God out of heaven with that Atheist *Tamburlan*, or blaspheming with the mad preest of the sonne: but let me rather openly pocket up the Asse at *Diogenes* hand: then wantonlye set out such impious instances of intollerable poetrie, such mad and scoffing poets, that have propheticall spirits as bred of *Merlins* race, if there be anye in England that set the end of scollarisme in an English blanck verse, I thinke either it is the humor of a novice that tickles them with self-love, or to much frequenting the hot house (to use the Germaine proverbe) swet out all the greatest part of their wits.[6]

Greene excuses this cloudy scurrility as payment in kind: 'I but answere in print, what they have offered on the Stage'. Greene may perhaps be referring to stage parodies of his attempt in *Alphonsus* to imitate the *Tamburlaine* rhetoric; alternatively, he may be reacting to criticisms that he has failed to take up writing for the stage. In the phrase '*Merlins* race', he may well be punning on Marlowe's name; but in any case, in describing the character Tamburlaine as atheistical, and in seeing him as a mere noisy extension of the play's arrogant and scoffing author, Greene anticipates much later commentary on the play. Thomas Nashe contributes a prefatory epistle to Greene's *Menaphon* in 1589, rebuking certain un-named tragedians whose blank verse is merely bombast, and Thomas Brabine's Commendatory Verses support Nashe in scorning the volubly stage-struck. Further oblique attacks by Greene culminate in his grandiloquent address to 'a famous gracer of Tragedians', atheist and Machiavellian worshipper of arbitrary power, in the posthumous *Greenes Groats-Worth of Wit* (1592). His reproachful sorrow might well be directed towards Marlowe:

Wonder not, (for with thee wil I first begin) thou famous gracer of Tragedians, that *Greene*, who hath said with thee (like the foole in his heart) There is no God, should now give glorie unto his greatnes; for penetrating is his power, his hand lies heavie upon me, he hath spoken unto mee with a voice of thunder, and I have felt he is a God that can punish enemies. Why should thy excellent wit, his gift, bee so blinded, that thou shouldst give no glorie to the giver? Is it pestilent Machivilian pollicy that thou hast studied? O peevish follie! What are his rules but meere confused mockeries, able to extirpate in small time the genera-tion of mankind. For if *Sic volo, sic iubeo*, hold in those that are able to commaund: and if it be lawfull *Fas & nefas* to do any thing that is beneficiall; onely Tyrants should possesse the earth, and they striving to exceed in tyrannie, should each to other be a slaughter man; till the mightiest outliving all, one stroke were lefte for Death, that in one age mans life should end.[7]

Clearly, Greene is overlooking Marlowe's readiness to set the cult of power or the profession of disbelief in a framework of dramatic contrast.

In 1591, and perhaps earlier, Marlowe was sharing a writing-chamber with Thomas Kyd. This fact emerges two years later when Kyd, after a period spent under arrest on suspicion of seditious libel, is hard put to explain in a letter to Lord Pucker-ing the presence among his papers of certain 'vile hereticall Conceiptes denying the deity of Jhesus Christe'.[8] These were papers, he says, which 'he had from Marlowe'. They are less inflammatory than they are made to sound in this description—transcriptions from a forty-year-old treatise of a proto-Unitarian character. Anxious to reinstate himself, Kyd offers comments on Marlowe's reputation and character. They have both professed to serve the one patron, but Marlowe's only service was 'in writing for his plaiers, ffor never cold my L[ord]. endure his name or sight, when he had heard of his conditions'. Marlowe was 'intemp[er]ate & of a cruel hart, the verie contraries to w^ch, my greatest enemies will saie by me'. On 18 May 1593, six days after the arrest of Kyd, a warrant was issued to bring Marlowe himself before the Privy Council. On 20 May, he was instructed to attend daily upon the Council. The comparative leniency with which he was treated may reflect the measure of his involvement, perhaps through Walsingham, with government matters.

A possible reason for the arrest of Kyd, which occurred on or before 12 May, has been advanced in a recent account of the unsavoury episode known as the Dutch Church Libel. Marlowe was away from London, at Sir Thomas Walsingham's country house in Kent, when scurrilous doggerel verses, threatening alien minority communities in the capital, were posted on the wall of the Dutch Church yard. These lines, it is now known, carried the words '*per* Tamberlaine' as a marginal gloss to emphasise the vindictive sentiments being expressed. It may be that the Privy Council connected Marlowe's name with this reference to the play, and in seeking Marlowe on suspicion of complicity with the libel turned their attention to Kyd. In this account, Kyd becomes a 'secondary victim', though it is not suggested that Marlowe himself was directly involved in any way in this incident. The 'hereticall' papers said to belong to Marlowe are instrumental in prolonging Kyd's imprisonment and torture.[9]

Marlowe was killed in self-defence by Ingram Frizer, among unsavoury companions, ten days after appearing before the Privy Council. Two days later, the Council was in receipt of a note from Richard Baines, 'containing the opinion of one Christopher Marly concerning his damnable judgment of religion and scorn of God's word'.[10] It has been shown recently that Marlowe had been embroiled with Baines on a previous occasion. Sir Robert Sidney, governor of Flushing, writes to Lord Treasurer Burghley on 26 January 1592, explaining why he is sending, along with a separate prisoner, three other men who are under suspicion. The three are Marlowe, 'by his profession a scholer', 'Gifford Gilbert a goldsmith taken heer for coining', and Baines, who has been sharing their lodgings and has informed on them. Marlowe and Baines are caught up in charge and counter-charge: 'The scholer sais himself to be very wel known both to the Earle of Northumberland and my lord Strang. Bains and he do also accuse one another of intent to goe to the Ennemy or to Rome, both as they say of malice one to another.'[11] Among the convictions which Baines formally attributed to Marlowe in June 1593 was one that 'he had as good right to coin as the Queen of England'.[12] It seems possible that Marlowe had tried to put this belief into practice. But perhaps he had been acting as a provocative agent.

Baines's note attributes to Marlowe a range of heterodox and iconoclastic opinions, catching a tone of scoffing debunkery and braggart defiance. Religions are conspiracies 'to keep men in awe', though Roman Catholicism, with its ceremonious observances, is to be preferred to Protestantism 'if there be any God or any good religion'. Kyd, too, driven to write a second time to Lord Puckering 'touching marlowes monstruous opinions', speaks of how frequently he would 'jest at the devine scriptures gybe at praie^rs, & stryve in argum^t to frustrate & confute what hath byn spoke or wrytt by prophets & such holie men'.[13] It seems reasonable to conclude with Jump that Marlowe at least liked to appear, among his contemporaries, as 'a bold and sceptical spirit, addicted to uninhibited iconoclastic talk'. The plays themselves offer many examples of rebellious and dismissive opinions, sometimes close in tone to Baines's report of Marlowe's conversation. Interpretation of the plays could not end here, of course, nor is it safe to trust the biographical material as a firm beginning. Why this is so might be illustrated by quoting one critic's view of the obstacles to interpretation which Marlowe himself sets up as a dramatist: 'Because Marlowe's ironic relationship with his audience varies from play to play, we probably cannot expect to infer his personal attitudes from any one work'.[14] Perhaps the reports we have of his attitudes and convictions are best received as glimpses of a similar game played by Marlowe to the life.

2. AUTHORSHIP

Oxberry's edition of the play, published in 1820, is the first to carry Marlowe's name.[15] Dyce in 1850 takes Marlowe 'confidently' to be the author.[16] Between the two, Robinson in 1826 records a doubt as to authorship.[17] He asserts that 'internal

evidence' is 'strong' against Marlowe, and finds (correctly) that
an apparent attribution to Marlowe in 1633 depends, strictly
speaking, on mere punctuation. In that year, Heywood's
'Prologue to the Stage, at the Cocke-pit', written for a production
of *The Jew of Malta*, brought together the names of Marlowe
and Alleyn in glancing at *Tamburlaine* and *Hero and Leander*:

> We know not how our Play may passe this Stage,
> But by the best of *Poets in that age   *Marlo.
> The *Malta Jew* had being, and was made;
> And He, then by the best of *Actors play'd: *Allin.
> In *Hero* and *Leander*, one did gaine
> A lasting memorie: in *Tamberlaine*,
> This *Jew*, with others many: th'other wan
> The Attribute of peerelesse, being a man
> Whom we may ranke with (doing no one wrong)
> *Proteus* for shapes, and *Roscius* for a tongue,
> So could he speake, so vary.

If, with Bawcutt and others, we read the seventh line here with
only a comma break after 'many', it is Alleyn's acting of Tamburlaine, not Marlowe's writing of the play, that Heywood is
referring to.[18] However, we may still think that the decorum
of Heywood's eulogy of the poet and the actor implies that both
men were associated in both *Tamburlaine* and *The Jew*.

Moving back in time from Heywood's Prologue, there is a
specific attribution to Marlowe in 1631. R[obert] H[enderson],
author of *The Arraignment of the Whole Creature*, published in
that year, has the marginal gloss '*Marlow* in his Poem' to a
passage of his text to do with two episodes which are prominent
in *Tamburlaine*: 'Great *Bajazet* as a Wolfe or some wilde Beast,
carried up and downe by the *Conquering Tamberlaine*, in an
Iron Cage: . . . how that *Scythian Shepheard*, had his *Coach
drawne* with the Kings of *Asia*, as though they had beene his
Coach-horses'.[19] This is the earliest unequivocal attribution.
If Robert Greene is punning on Marlowe's name in *Perimedes*
in March 1588, he is obliquely attributing the play to Marlowe
within a year or so of its composition.[20] And if Arthur Freeman
is right about the circumstances of Kyd's arrest over the Dutch
Church Libel in 1593, that episode connects Marlowe with the

play by implication.[21] Absence of direct ascription to Marlowe
among the numerous references to the play by Shakespeare,
Marston, Jonson, and others, need not imply ignorance of the
identity of its author: it may, on the contrary, indicate that
Marlowe's authorship is common knowledge.

However, Edward Phillips ascribes the play to Thomas
Newton when compiling his *Theatrum Poetarum* (1675, ii.182).
Thomas Warton is still at pains to correct this attribution in
1781. In doing so, he is depending, like others before him, on
the shaky evidence of the Heywood Prologue to *The Jew of
Malta*. We meet with a definite attribution of the play to
Marlowe in Francis Kirkman's list of printed plays in 1671; and
Kirkman is followed with conviction in 1687 by Gerard Lang-
baine and in 1691 by Anthony à Wood.[22]

Marlowe's authorship of *Tamburlaine* does not rest on the
few early attributions, nor on the weight of tradition associating
him with the play. Criticism of the plays which are taken to
constitute the Marlowe canon has, in course of time, familiarised
us with distinctive traits common to two or more of them. Of
course, the disjunctions among these plays are often sharp, even
blatant; Marlowe's brief career takes abrupt strides while
exploring, and exploiting, certain leading preoccupations in
more or less individual ways. A relish for the dramatic, often
dismissive, exposure of hypocritical professions of religious or
political principle; aspiration represented as a norm of human
feeling, seeking gratification beyond the ceiling of hyperbole—
and brought into abrupt collision with received morality and
poetic justice, and often with provocatively ambiguous results:
Marlowe's familiar insistences and themes are not peculiar to
him, nor is there an agreed chronology, which might show a
coherent development from *Tamburlaine* or *Dido* through to
(say) *Edward II*. But the reader recognises distinctive rhythmic
effects; something approaching a repertory, even a code, of
images conveying states of felicity; and the repeated collapse of
emphatic effects and sentiments through overt deflation. Were
a case for Marlowe's authorship of *Tamburlaine* called for, it
could readily be built up on such elements as these; and it

would probably emphasise his persistent imitation and capping of prominent lines and cadences within each of his plays, and from play to play:

> So looks my love, shadowing in her brows ...
> Shadowing more beauty in their airy brows ...
>
> And set black streamers in the firmament ...
> See, see, where Christ's blood streams in the firmament! ...

T. S. Eliot referred to this as Marlowe's 'economy'.[23]

Alvin Kernan's listing of the 'chief characteristics of the Marlovian heroic style' is based on a reading of *Tamburlaine*, but each of these features is easily illustrated from one or more of the other plays commonly accepted as forming the Marlowe canon:

> (1) the steady, heavy beat of 'Marlowe's mighty line', carrying authority, determination and steady onward movement; (2) the consistent use of present participles for adjectives—'shining' for 'bright', 'rising' for 'high'—expressing a mind always in movement and always aspiring; (3) frequent appearance of such 'rising' words as 'soar', 'mount' and 'climb'; (4) persistence of the rhetorical figure Hyperbole, conveying a constant striving for a condition beyond any known in this world ... (5) parataxis, the joining of several phrases and clauses by 'and'—and ... and ... and—to create a sense of endless ongoing, of constant reaching; (6) the use of the privative suffix in words which state limits—'topless', 'quenchless', 'endless'; (7) frequent use of ringing popular names and exotic geographical places to realise the sensed wideness, brightness and richness of the world.[24]

One critic, surveying Marlowe's plays, will find a regrettable tendency to artistic self-indulgence, another will find a special kind of ironic outlook and method central to his work. Some see *Tamburlaine* as an early work soon outgrown, others find that it precociously anticipates other Marlowe plays. But there is now no lack of conviction that *Tamburlaine* belongs to the Marlowe canon.

3. SOURCES

Investigation of the play's sources began effectively some ninety years ago, and has drawn the attention of many scholars since then.[25] Ellis-Fermor's comprehensive survey is indispensable.[26] It traces the descent of the staple material through two centuries, but tends to confuse the reader with a multiplicity of analogues. Over the years, it has proved relatively easy to find accounts of Tamburlaine in Western European languages, particularly in the middle and late sixteenth century, but rather more difficult to distinguish those which Marlowe almost certainly did use from those which he probably did not. The most thorough recent survey is that by H. D. Purcell.[27] Three things now seem quite clear. First, that a prototype Tamburlaine narrative was thoroughly established in Europe by the time a century or so had elapsed following Timur Khan's dramatic defeat of Bayazid I at Angora in 1402. Second, that this material was developed in Part One of *Tamburlaine* from two main sources—one in Latin by Petrus Perondinus (Pietro Perondino), and one in English by George Whetstone. Third, that a series of minor sources was also used in Marlowe's writing of the sequel. Whetstone was translating, and re-ordering, material from Claude Gruget's *Diverses Leçons* (1552), itself a version of the Spanish historian Pedro Mexia's *Silva de varia lección* (1540). Perondinus's account itself owes to Mexia, but differs from him, and therefore from Whetstone, in some ways that are significant for readers of *Tamburlaine*. It has been convincingly demonstrated that it was Whetstone's version of Mexia that Marlowe used, rather than that of Thomas Fortescue (*The Foreste*, 1571).[28] Herford and Wagner in 1883 were working from Fortescue, not Whetstone; but their conclusion stands today, that Perondinus and (in translation) Mexia are the major sources of Marlowe's play.[29]

The Tamburlaine narrative, simple in outline and legendary in scope, owed much to the work of Italian historians such as Baptista Fulgosius (Battista Fregoso), whose work Mexia, and after him Whetstone, acknowledge. This prototype narrative has been shown to have exercised a powerful influence on Machiavelli—which is to say, that it engaged thoroughly with currents of new thinking about history. For Marlowe, it called up an astonishing range of associations with historical and mythical figures. It focused questions to do with destiny and

human will, providence and history, on the career of a colossal
figure which impinged on Elizabethan thought and sensibility
at many levels.

To read George Whetstone's version of Mexia in *The English
Myrror*, not long after its publication in 1586, was to encounter a
prodigious military figure, hailed as the equal of 'the illustrous
Captaines *Romaines*, and *Grecians*'—among whom the freshest
in Marlowe's mind was perhaps Lucan's Caesar, the 'diabolical
"superman" ' to whom Tamburlaine alludes in Part One.[30]
Not the lame Timur, one of the line of Tartar Khans, but 'a
pure appearance out of nothing',[31] barely impeded by his obscure birth: '*Tamberlaine* being a poore labourer, or in the best
degree a meane souldiour, descended from the *Partians*:
notwithstanding the povertye of his parents: even from his
infancy he had a reaching & an imaginative minde, the strength
and comelinesse of his body, aunswered the hautines of his
hart'. Motivated simply by 'a ruling desire'—in Marlowe's
words 'He dares so doubtlessly resolve of rule' (*One* II.vi.13)—
Mexia's Tamburlaine is totally generous to subordinates and
ruthless to enemies. He attains the throne of Persia by astute
political opportunism, taking sides with the king's brother in a
successful struggle for power, then deposing the new king by
turning the people against him. This initiates a career of astounding conquests—'*Siria, Armenia, Babylon, Mesopotamia, Scitia,
Asia, Albania,* and other provinces, with many goodly and
invincible Cities'. In Bajazeth, Mexia's Tamburlaine confronts
a leader of equal power, courage, and military brilliance, and is
hard put to defeat him. The captured Bajazeth is used as a
mounting-block, imprisoned in an iron cage, and fed 'as a dog'
with fragments from Tamburlaine's table. Tamburlaine goes on
to invade Egypt, taking Damascus after a protracted siege, and
he defeats the Soldan of Egypt and the King of Arabia. In
Whetstone's version, the account of the siege of Damascus
precedes a description of 'Tamburlaine's order at assaults'—
the succession of white, red, and black tents over three successive
days of siege. At one siege of 'a strong city', as Whetstone has it,
the inhabitants plead for mercy 'with their wives & children

cloathed all in white, having Olive branches in their handes'. The people are slaughtered, and Tamburlaine is challenged by a merchant in his camp: 'Whom *Tamberlaine* (with a countenance fiered with fury) answered: thou supposest that I am a man, but thou art deceived, for I am no other than the ire of God, and the destruction of the world'. Marlowe does not appropriate this incident, but the conception of Tamburlaine which it embodies is crucial. The narrative rather abruptly concludes, after this episode: 'In the ende this great personage, without disgrace of fortune, after sundry great victories, by the course of nature died, & left behind him two sons, every way far unlike their father'. Whetstone then resumes his doggedly moralistic theme: the envious dissension of Tamburlaine's sons brings about the loss of his empire.

Whetstone's version of the Tamburlaine narrative afforded Marlowe a plain, clear version of these incidents, distributed rather repetitiously into three chapters of *The English Myrror*, but with marginal glosses that catch the eye. Differences of detail and emphasis emerge in Marlowe's play. The overthrow of Cosroe for the crown of Persia is not accomplished by politic plotting but by exuberant open defiance—Marlowe perhaps taking up a hint from Whetstone's mention of the 'meriment' with which Tamburlaine's youthful companions chose him as their leader. Bajazeth is in Marlowe a formidable opponent, but not Whetstone's figure of 'worthinesse'. His defeat draws from Whetstone firstly the comment 'such was Gods will'. This sentiment Marlowe's Tamburlaine appropriates for his assertive purposes, seeing himself here as a liberator of Christians and as

> the scourge and wrath of God,
> The only fear and terror of the world.
>
> (*One* III.iii.44-5)

Then Whetstone offers a brooding reflection which perhaps influences Zenocrate's lines about the fickleness of earthly Fortune (*One* V.i.355 ff.): '*Bajazet*, that in the morning was the mightiest Emperor on the earth, at night, and the residue of his life, was driven to feede among the dogs, and which might most grieve him, he was thus abased, by one that in the beginning was but a poore sheepheard'. In sum, Marlowe seizes elements of a broad conception of Tamburlaine, and brings them into emphatic relation or into sharp contrast. Both ruthless and generous; 'wise, liberall', but 'worthy the name of vengeance': Marlowe tightens the tensions between the rival aspects of Tamburlaine, in contrast with Whetstone's relatively mild 'although . . . yet': 'And in truth *Tamberlain* although he was endued with many excellencies & vertues: yet it seemed by his cruelty, that God raysed him to chasten the kings & proud people of the earth'.

Perondinus, on the other hand, also retelling the main events in the received Tamburlaine narrative, offers 'a clear and consistent picture of the central figure': 'From the pages of Perondinus's packed and pregnant Latin, the figure of Tamburlaine emerges insatiable, irresistible, ruthless, destructive, but instinct with power'.[32] Here is a figure of Destiny, the child of Fortune, elevated by Her from obscurity to accomplish worldwide devastation and the overthrow of all his enemies: 'ex adverso ab illa ipsa rerum humanarum domina fortuna'. Like the Mexia–Whetstone Tamburlaine, he is physically powerful and well-proportioned—Timur himself was lame—and Perondinus dwells on the fierceness and brooding intensity which in Marlowe is emphasised as the other face of the chivalric hero. Perondinus's Tamburlaine restrains his men from plunder, but he appropriates everything he conquers, and insatiably seeks people to fight as if that were an exercise of virtue, enslaving the free. He is a figure to excite boundless 'admiration': 'what may seem extraordinary is that this fierce veteran of wars sought indefatigably, as though it were a wonderful work of virtue, for people he might wage war on, or for people to harry constantly with tempestuous raids, or for people enjoying complete freedom, so that he could impose on them a savage yoke'.[33] Tamburlaine's assertion, fiery-eyed, that he is the wrath of God, rings with greater resonance in the context of this dynamic and barbaric self-sufficiency, heightening the impact of the concept itself: 'Memento, ait, me Dei maximis iram esse'.

Perondinus gives a dramatic elaboration to Bajazeth's humiliation, exploring his condition with vivid imaginative sympathy. In his cage, the degraded Bajazeth contemplates the faithlessness of Fortune: 'As for the rest of the time, he spent it in an iron cage, shut up like a beast, affording a wondrous and lamentable example of the fickleness of fortune in human affairs'. Through this, and the obscene treatment of his wife, Bajazeth suffers extremes of anger and grief. This Bajazeth, unlike Whetstone's, is a figure dramatised from inside. He is joined in humiliation by his wife and (again unlike Whetstone's) driven to commit suicide, beating out his brains on his cage, after praying for death, torn with anger, shame, and grief. A victim of fate or fortune, he had allowed Tamburlaine, the shepherd, to displace him.

Perondinus has also been shown to provide Marlowe with hints (more detailed than in Mexia) from which minor characters could be developed: Theridamas, Cosroe, Mycetes, the Soldan of Egypt, Calyphas.[34] The *Vita* is a piece of biography in its own right, divided into clearly distinct subjects and episodes—for instance, Tamburlaine's physique and character, his defeat of Bajazeth, his death and the portents which announced it. This distinctness would encourage Marlowe in the vigorous development of Tamburlaine as a phenomenon of awesome scale and integrity. Perondinus is, by implication, putting Marlowe in touch with Italian humanistic writing more vividly than Whetstone does. Eric Voegelin has dwelt on the *Vita Tamerlanis* as a distinct *genre*, reflecting the preoccupation of fifteenth-century Italian historians with 'the new phenomenon of power on the world scale'.[35] This biographical tradition shows Timur as a meteoric figure, embodying sheer will, 'symbolizing the naked fanaticism of expanding power, the lust and horror of destruction, the blindness of a fate which crushes one existence in its march and thereby perhaps saves another one'. He becomes, in this light, a symbol of *virtù*, favoured by Fortune, and constituting a challenge to Christian interpretations of history: 'The *virtù* of the conquering prince became the source of order; and since the Christian, transcendental order of existence had become a dead letter for the

Italian thinkers of the fifteenth century, the *virtù ordinata* of the prince, the only ordering force experienced as real, acquired human–divine, heroic proportions'.[36]

Voegelin's account of the influence of Machiavelli on the Tamburlaine *Vita* as a *genre* might lead us to find a significant, if indirect, relationship between the Italian thinker and Marlowe. This is at its clearest in Machiavelli's *Vita di Castruccio Castracani* (1520), 'a fantasy based very loosely upon the career of a real military dictator who flourished in fourteenth-century Lucca'.[37] Castruccio emerges as a charismatic, physically imposing figure, 'gracious to his friends, to his enemies terrible'. His rise to eminence is highlighted by the fact of his humble birth. Such men, Machiavelli reflects, have often 'made themselves out sons of Jove or of some other god'. He is assisted, and eventually killed, by Fortune. Unlike Marlowe's Tamburlaine, he prefers to win by fraud, not force; but an avid thirst for experience and a hubristic arrogance relate the two tyrants emphatically: 'He used to say that men ought to try everything, not to be afraid of everything; and that God is a lover of strong men, because we see that he always punished the powerless by means of the powerful.' Equally easy to match with Marlowe's play is Machiavelli's account of ambition in the *Discourses on Titus Livius*: 'nature has created men so that they desire everything, but are unable to attain it'.[39] And *The Prince*, of course, affords numerous suggestive parallels: the opportunistic overthrow of decadent *régimes*; the necessity of maintaining a strong political base; the virtue of war as a means of attaining power. Above all, there is the multiform insistence on Fortune and *virtù*. As in Marlowe's play, Fortune may be seen as 'sheer chance', or as 'an elemental force', or as 'susceptible to persuasion or to human influence', or as 'a pagan goddess who ruthlessly wields her power, and deliberately makes or breaks men in order to demonstrate her supremacy'.[40]

Clearly, Machiavelli could have exerted first-hand influence on Marlowe at many points, but no evidence has yet been found to show that Marlowe had such direct contact with his work. Machiavelli himself, to complicate matters, drew extensively on further sources, especially in Latin. It is also clear that Marlowe's Tamburlaine is in some respects very different from the image of the politically successful Prince. He is not, predominantly, a shrewdly prudent and calculating intriguer, maintaining a mask of 'mercy, faith, integrity, humanity, and religion' but ready to break faith when it is in his own interest to do so.[41] His disloyalty to Cosroe, for instance, is open and exuberant, though the Governor of Damascus is indeed treated with cynical callousness. Something is lost if we see *Tamburlaine* as 'a serious exposition of Machiavelli's actual philosophy', and still more if we take it that Machiavelli's 'doctrine' is Marlowe's own (even if allowing that Part Two shows disenchantment with it).[42] The play's central figure alone asserts many different things, and is a volatile compound of many elements, some of them remote from the portrait found in Perondinus or in Whetstone. Marlowe's Tamburlaine, in part a chivalric hero, can display an aspiration which purifies energies, an exalted religious awareness, and he can speak a poetry of tender love and sympathetic human feeling. The mythical figure of the sources activates, perhaps with assistance from Machiavelli's own broad reflections on history, a wide-ranging series of allusions to the giants of both history and myth—Jove, Dis, Atlas, Hercules, Achilles, Lucan's Caesar, Xerxes, Darius. And the play takes on the bold dimensions of a continually shifting encounter between history as the hand of Providence and as the work of the individual will, between man-as-destined and hero-as-Destiny, between aspiration as *hubris* and as a natural drive, between strife as a perversion and as a normal condition, between man as mortal and as destined for imagined immortality. The play dramatises these oppositions vividly, without fully resolving them: always within the ambience of its central figure, and conveying insistently a sense of man as himself the creator of his own world—a humanistic response to a humanistic tradition, but not reducible to creed or doctrine.[43] Marlowe will in later plays become closely concerned with Machiavellian political craft; in *Tamburlaine* he is, for the most part, responding (however indirectly) to

Machiavelli as a source of vigorous ideology: 'If a man has both *virtù* and Fortune with him he will achieve *la gloria*'.[44]

Part Two promptly effects a transition to a frame of action more directly (and notoriously) associated with Machiavelli— that of 'necessary policy', here linked with the 'scourge of God' theme in that the Christian Sigismond is persuaded to scourge the Turks at the cost of breaking an oath of truce. Marlowe had met with a Christian Sigismond overthrown by Bajazeth in Whetstone, but for this episode he turned to an account of the battle of Varna, fought some forty years after Timur's death. The Latin narrative, by Antonius Bonfinius, had been published in 1543;[45] Marlowe may also have had access to a manuscript of Knolles's version of Bonfinius, in *The General Historie of the Turkes*, which was published in 1603.[46] The Christian Vladislaus of the historical battle was persuaded to break his oath with Amurath by the Cardinal Julian. Marlowe changes the participants but echoes very closely his source's rendering of the speeches of the betrayers and the betrayed. Julian argues 'Against a perfidious enemy it is lawfull (as they say) for a man to use all cunning, force, and deceit, deluding craft with craft, and fraud with fraud'.[47] Indeed, not to take this opportunity will be to risk incurring God's wrath:

> make no conscience of the league you have made with the Infidell, but thinke it a great impietie and wickednesse to violate the holy league made with the great bishop, and the other Christian princes: thinking, that if you should doe otherwise, God (which he of his mercie forbid) would become of that your falsified faith a most severe and sharpe revenger.[48]

Marlowe's Baldwin and Frederick in their turn catch just these accents of hypocritical piety. Their sophistry is the more clearly isolated for us in that Marlowe's Sigismond is thinking only of one treaty, with the Turks, rather than weighing such a treaty with one entered into with other Christians:

> for with such infidels,
> In whom no faith nor true religion rests,
> We are not bound to those accomplishments
> The holy laws of Christendom enjoin.   (*Two* II.i.33–6)

Here, we are only a short step from the anarchy of mutual distrust and plot-counter-plot that characterises *The Jew of Malta*. As elsewhere, Marlowe gives prominence to the eloquence with which the non-Christian expresses religious feeling. Knolles reads as follows:

> Behold thou crucified Christ, this is the league thy Christians in thy name made with mee: which they have without cause violated. Now if thou bee a God, as they say thou art, and as we dreame, revenge the wrong now done unto thy name, and me, and shew thy power upon thy perjurious people, who in their deeds denie thee their God.[49]

Marlowe expands this, through a close parallel—

> Then if there be a Christ, as Christians say—
> But in their deeds deny him for their Christ
> *(Two* II.ii.39–40)

—into a moving prayer to a deity in whom Christian, classical, and Mohammedan elements meet. But possibly the most Marlovian extension of the incident is Gazellus' laconic deflation of Orcanes' interpretation of the overthrow of Sigismond as evidence of the Christian god's justice:

> 'Tis but the fortune of the wars, my lord,
> Whose power is often proved a miracle.
> *(Two* II.iii.31–2)

The Sigismond episode casts some retrospective lustre on Tamburlaine's repudiation of Cosroe in Part One. To compare the two incidents illustrates the narrowing of implications from bafflement in face of a phenomenon which Cosroe has no means of measuring—'The strangest men that ever Nature made!' *(One* II.vii.40)—to dramatising precise ethical issues which afford a full measure of the events. Part Two's reflection of Tamburlaine's eloquent address to the captive Zenocrate is Theridamas' bullying courtship of Olympia—a frustrated mimicry of imperious seduction. Marlowe drew this material episode from Ariosto's *Orlando Furioso*, in which Isabella meets her death by way of the same stratagem as Olympia employs against Theridamas.[50] He conflated this with an incident which occurred at the siege of Rhodes: the fort's governor is killed, and his lover (unlike Isabella) kills and burns her two children before going to seek her own death on the field of battle. With this second story, Marlowe had probably, as Ethel Seaton points out, found his way into Belleforest's *Cosmographie Universelle* (1557), a compilation which may also have lent him some vivid details elsewhere in *Tamburlaine*.[51]

Two English works of very recent date afforded material which Marlowe worked into Part Two, in the process of writing or revising it. Spenser's description of King Arthur's crest caught his attention:

> Upon the top of all his loftie crest,
>   A bunch of haires discolourd diversly,
>   With sprincled pearle, and gold full richly drest,
>   Did shake, and seem'd to daunce for jollity,
>   Like to an Almond tree ymounted hye
>   On top of greene *Selinis* all alone,
>   With blossomes brave bedecked daintily;
>   Whose tender locks do tremble every one
> At every little breath, that under heaven is blowne.[52]

The last five lines of this stanza, with the concluding Alexandrine, are transferred, with some alterations that weaken their effect, to form part of Tamburlaine's hyperbolic description of himself at the end of Act Four of Part Two. Although the lines chime with chivalric insistences elsewhere in the play, their elements of archaism and daintiness ('ymounted', 'quaintly decked') sound odd out of their Spenserian context; and although Marlowe has the occasional Alexandrine elsewhere in *Tamburlaine*, this one stands out as the culmination of a set-piece description. Marlowe may draw on other lines from *The Faerie Queene* in the play.[52] He is also in debt to Paul Ive's *Practise of Fortification* (1589) for an imposing, if rather self-consciously technical, account of military tactics.[53] *The Faerie Queene* (Books I–II) was entered in the Stationers' Register on 1 December 1589. We do not know whether Marlowe drew on Spenser or Ive in manuscript or in print, nor whether, when doing so, he was writing Part Two, or revising it for publication.

Ethel Seaton's demonstration of Marlowe's dependence on the atlas of Abraham Ortelius clarified several passages in the play, accounted for some apparent factual errors, and excitingly enhanced our appreciation of Marlowe's ability to confer on ultimates a local habitation and a name.[54] In Part Two, we find Marlowe constructing for Tamburlaine whole military campaigns at the whim of a finger moving across geographical boundaries redolent of history and myth. From Ortelius, he drew the names of several of his African kings. And Miss Seaton's proof that Marlowe knew the work of Philippus Lonicerus allowed her to show that this was the source of names to bestow on Tamburlaine's sons.[55] Marlowe drew on other sources, too, for names to give characters in both Parts: kings and soldiers of other periods yield names for Techelles, Mycetes, Usumcasane, Gazellus, Orcanes, and others, from Marlowe's glancing into accounts of Persian history. His ear for the blank-verse line guides this appropriation of names from remote periods of history. And perhaps the most striking extension of his source-material, the creation of the main female character, is signalled by a brilliant act of naming—'Zenocrate', a feminine metrical counterpart of 'Tamburlaine'. The imaginative stimulus afforded by Ortelius is only matched in the play by Ovid's *Metamorphoses*. This work provides, at every turn, a major source of Marlowe's lively and adroit evocation of classical mythology. Perhaps the best example of this debt is to be found in Tamburlaine's soliloquy in the last scene of Part One. Here, Marlowe is close to Golding's translation of the story of Baucis and Philemon, who welcome Jove and Mercury to their cottage and are spared from a subsequent deluge. It is a climactic moment in the attempt to resolve conflict. It has been argued that Marlowe uses the allusion to suggest that 'the poet, like the hero, competes with God'.[56]

4. FROM PERFORMANCE TO PUBLICATION

Tamburlaine the Great was first published in 1590, a black-letter octavo edition of both Parts of the play in a single volume.

This text does not carry the author's name, but it is otherwise quite elaborately—and somewhat puzzlingly—informative. The title page announces two central elements of the story of Tamburlaine—his rise from rustic obscurity to imperial grandeur, and his reputation as 'the scourge of God'. The two 'tragicall Discourses' are offered to the reader 'as they were sundrie times shewed upon Stages in the Citie of London. By the right honorable the Lord Admyrall, his servantes'.[57] However, the (nominal) printer, Richard Jones,[58] declares in a prefatory letter, addressed to discriminating readers, that he has excised from the text 'some fond and frivolous jestures' which had been present in at least some stage performances to the delight of the vulgar. To publish these comic passages would, for Jones, offend against the decorum of 'so honorable and stately a history'.[59] His author, he says, is eloquent; the matter, worthy. Indeed, the title page of Jones's reprint of *Tamburlaine* in 1593 (the year of Marlowe's death) says of the play that it was 'sundrie times most stately shewed'—an emphasis borrowed, perhaps, from the opening lines of Marlowe's original Preface to Part One:

> From jigging veins of rhyming mother-wits
> And such conceits as clownage keeps in pay,
> We'll lead you to the stately tent of War.

Scorning the farcical and the homespun by contrast with an exalted and capacious tragic style, Marlowe's Prologue is close in sentiment to the printer's Preface.

Are we right, then, to assume that the excised passages were not written by Marlowe himself? If so, what does that imply about the nature of the manuscript text with which the printer worked? Can we detect the points at which the excisions were made? Answers to these questions obviously have some bearing on what the reader or the producer will make of the varied provocations to mirth which are offered by the text as it now stands. Equally, it is true that if we read the play in the light of the disparagement of low comedy expressed by Marlowe and by the printer, we may find less to laugh at in the text we have.

Curiously, it was as comedies that the two *Tamburlaine* plays were entered by Jones in the Stationers' Register for 14 August 1590:[60]

Entred unto him for his Copye *The twooe commicall discourses of* TOMBERLEIN *the Cithian shepparde* under the handes of Master ABRAHAM HARTEWELL, and the Wardens . . . vj^d

This description is most readily accounted for as the publisher's response to the emphasis given, on the title-page of Part One, to Tamburlaine's prosperous early career; and the play had perhaps become notorious for exciting laughter. But the title-page goes on, with equal emphasis, to describe the two Parts as '*Tragicall Discourses*'.

Some two or three years separate the first performance of *Tamburlaine* from the 1590 printing. Robert Greene's reference to its impact on the stage, in March 1588, seems to imply that the play is already notorious.[61] For Greene, the impious behaviour of its central figure is matched by an absurdly extravagant tragical bearing and utterance. Some ten years before Pistol's mimicry of Marlovian (and other) declamation, Greene finds Tamburlaine a figure of histrionic excess, a character uncritically indulged by his author—though Greene may be moved to think so by envy and pique. Greene's phrase 'daring God out of Heaven with that Atheist *Tamburlan*' may be meant to characterise the whole play, and it certainly implies both that Tamburlaine himself defies God and that he (along with Marlowe) *deserves* divine retribution. There are many occasions, especially in Part Two, when divine powers are explicitly defied. But it has long seemed reasonable to assume that Greene has in mind the climactic incident in Part Two, when Tamburlaine orders the burning of the 'superstitious books' of Mohammedan scripture. This is his most emphatic and extensive invitation to divine wrath—though strictly speaking, he is defying Mahomet in the name of another God, one 'full of revenging wrath', as a self-proclaimed scourge of heretics:

> Now, Mahomet, if thou have any power,
> Come down thyself and work a miracle;

Thou are not worthy to be worshippèd
That suffers flames of fire to burn the writ
Wherein the sum of thy religion rests.

(*Two* V.i.186–90)

If Greene is indeed alluding to this incident in the play, he is
providing invaluable evidence that Part Two was written and
performed soon after Part One. The Prologue to Part Two
asserts that Marlowe wrote the second play in response to the
theatrical success of the first, and there is no reason to doubt
this. It may be that both Parts were produced before 16 November 1587, the date on which Philip Gawdy, in a letter to
his father, reported an incident which had caused a stir in
London:

> Yow shall understande of some accydentall newes heare in this
> towne thoughe my selfe no wyttnesse thereof, yet I may be bold
> to veryfye it for an assured troth. My L. Admyrall his men
> and players having a devyse in ther playe to tye one of their
> fellowes to a poste and so to shoote him to deathe, having
> borrowed their callyvers one of the players handes swerved his
> peece being charged with bullett missed the fellowe he aymed at
> and killed a chyld, and a woman great with chyld forthwith, and
> hurt an other man in the head very soore.[62]

The story has an air of circumstantial truth, and if the play in
question was *Tamburlaine*, the accident could have happened
in the last Act of Part Two, where the Governor of Babylon is
hung in chains on the 'battered wall' of the city and shot at,
first by Theridamas and then by Tamburlaine and others. But
this is very conjectural, and the Admiral's Men may have been
acting some other play, now lost. Perhaps Marlowe wrote Part
One before leaving Cambridge in 1587, and composed the sequel
in time for production later the same year or early in 1588. It is
also possible that what Greene saw in 1587 or 1588 was the play
we now know as Part One, and that Marlowe wrote the sequel
at some time between that date and the publication of the first
octavo text.[63]

We do not know on what stages *Tamburlaine* was 'sundrie
times' performed before its publication in 1590. Part Two
makes a significantly greater call on the physical resources of

the playing area than Part One, and this may reflect a transition to a public playhouse from whatever stage the first Part was meant for—inn or game house or outdoor space of some kind. The revival of both Parts in 1594–5 takes place in Henslowe's Rose, with the sequel often playing a day or two after Part One and drawing comparable audiences.[64] The Rose is not known beyond doubt to be in use before 19 February 1592, and Glynne Wickham is led to say, discussing the possible location of productions which occurred during Marlowe's lifetime, 'what we have to reckon with is a number of game-houses or playhouses'.[65] But a recent author has tentatively suggested that plays may have been presented at the Rose 'as early as 29 October 1587', the date of a Privy Council letter concerned with theatrical performances and the precise area in London where the Rose was built.[66] The minimum requirements of Part Two may include a discovery area, and an upper level which could be scaled by soldiers and used for hanging up the body of a victim.[67] Discoveries could, of course, be effected with movable properties—Zenocrate's death-bed or Calyphas' tent; and it has been argued that the sack of Babylon, and the confrontation before the walls of Balsera, two incidents in Part Two, 'could be played on that scenic property known as the "battlement" . . . which figures so frequently in the Revels Accounts of the 1590s'.[68]

As for the Rose, inference and conjecture have led Ernest L. Rhodes to suggest that it had a trap-door, two discovery spaces (one each side of the gates at centre backstage), and a gallery.[69] A discovery space could be used to represent Calyphas' tent, and Zenocrate's sick-bed might be drawn on stage from it, and drawn back into it. Rhodes comments that there is only one instance, among extant plays known to have been produced at the Rose, 'in which a scene both begins and ends with stage directions calling for a curtain to be used': this is Act II scene 4 of the second Part of *Tamburlaine*, the scene of Zenocrate's death. The scaling of the walls of Balsera or Babylon might be enacted by climbing the gallery, whose floor was some fifteen feet above the stage. The stage-directions being probably

Marlowe's own, rather than of theatre origin, we lack firm evidence from the text about how various incidents were staged; besides, methods would vary from one acting-space to another.[70] But, we can, cautiously, infer a good deal from the text about theatrical effects and properties, and about acting style.

The play's title-page and the Prologue to Part One agree to emphasise the stately. The indispensable requirement is acting of a ceremonious and imposing dignity, able to mime love, grief, anger, and terror, to achieve set groupings with promptness and fluent conviction, to strike and hold a telling pose or a speaking look, perhaps for a long time with little or nothing to say, and always under the challenge of the poetry's breadth of reference and wide imaginative scale. Sometimes, the achieved physical appearance is given a direct verbal mirror:

> Zenocrate, lovelier than the love of Jove,
> Brighter than is the silver Rhodope
>
> (*One* I.ii.87–8)

or

> With what a majesty he rears his looks!
>
> (*One* I.ii.164)

Eugene Waith rightly observes that 'Marlowe depends on unhesitating acceptance of the verbal picture'.[71] Equally, a slight ineptitude of carriage or gesture could seem comprehensively risible. But imaginary scale is repeatedly, in the poetry, transmuting the actual: stage dimensions will seem to match a geography of the spirit. And this impression of imaginative amplitude is necessary as a basis for the converse effect which shows us Tamburlaine as a tragic, near-absurd figure seeking to transcend inevitable limitations.

The *Tamburlaine* text as a whole requires carefully-orchestrated rituals of entry and departure; coronations, a banquet, the formal surrender and return of tributary crowns; a funeral march to music, 'the town burning'; a dying speech paced in sensitive concord with music played to a sounding close; the discovery of a stylised *tableau*, ending with the solemn drawing of an arras.[72] Costumes are sumptuously elaborate.[73] Dress, accoutrements, flags, perhaps tents, are colour-coded through successive days of siege. The text implies a stirring repertory of sound-effects: 'hear the clang / Of Scythian trumpets, hear the basilisks' (*One* IV.i.1–2) and 'The crack, the echo, and the soldiers' cry' (*Two* III.iii.60). Battle noises offstage are timed to occur in the intervals of speech onstage. And the play's formal speeches have to be spoken with fidelity to the impression commonly given that they develop *as they occur*, but without sacrifice of their firm rhythmical and syntactical integrity. As T. S. Eliot observed as early as 1919, Marlowe 'gets a new driving power by reinforcing the sentence period against the line period'.[74] Rhetorical address in *Tamburlaine*, by no means all declamatory, is a disciplined medium for the voice. The central figure himself shows innocent elation, mischievous verve, grief, brooding introversion, magnanimity, quiet acceptance of mortality, futile rage. The distinctions across the range of feelings are not in themselves fine, but they have to register convincingly without the support of a simple governing line of 'character development'.

The elaborateness and formality of many of the stage effects in *Tamburlaine* make it an ideal subject for discussion in the light of George Kernodle's emphasis on a central frame and background for the action: 'The façade had on some occasions the appearance of a triumphal arch; on others, with black curtains hung for tragedies, it suggested a public ceremonial of mourning'.[75] What could be accomplished in such an environment, with its range of ceremonial emphasis and the visible enforcing of dramatic ironies, has been persuasively evoked by David Zucker.[76] Cosroe dies before the triumphal arch, earlier the scene of his own coronation, now the setting for Tamburlaine's crowning of himself, to the accompaniment of a soaring eulogy of kingship. As a besieged city, the façade forms a continuous focus of attention behind the successive white, red, black, of Tamburlaine's assault. Within or before the discovery-space, it may be, Zenocrate dies in the place of her own triumphal crowning, recognising that 'I fare, my lord, as other empresses'—among them Zabina, who dies before the besieged

Damascus. Kernodle envisages theatre decoration giving comprehensive support to the dramatic rhetoric:

> When Tamburlaine and Romeo defied the stars, there were the stars, very visible to the audience in a canopy-heavens. . . . Tamburlaine could assert his individuality to the fullest because on his open platform he was backed by a colourful, banner-decked symbol of monarchical order.[77]

Zucker underlines the flexibility of this production style, and the rich diversity of engagement between theatrical impression and the poetry itself. Certainly, ironic reflections run to and fro between the poetry and the action. Theridamas imagines Olympia in heaven courted by Dis in theatrical style:

> Inventing masks and stately shows for her,
> Opening the doors of his rich treasury
> To entertain this queen of chastity.   (*Two* IV.ii.94–6)

She has contrived her own death in order to avoid rape threatened by Theridamas himself; and the words closely echo Tamburlaine's eulogy of the dying Zenocrate. Theoretical reconstructions of stage architecture and decoration are, of course, hazardous; but effects of ritual, effects of emblematic suggestion, and effects of bold ironic contrast, are germane to the *Tamburlaine* plays, however they were or are performed. Increasingly, Marlowe scholarship has emphasised the play's relation to the moral themes and allegorical conventions of earlier drama and of civic pageantry. Tamburlaine's entry in his chariot, for example, has suggestive affinities with the dumb-show of Gascoigne and Kinwelmersh's *Jocasta*, where Sesostris, representing Ambition, is drawn by four kings; and T. W. Craik refers us to the chariot-drawn figure of Fortune, in *Liberality and Prodigality*.[78] The four Virgins of Damascus can be seen as the four Daughters of God.[79] M. C. Bradbrook observes that a mounted King of the Moors, 'dressed in satin and silver paper, led the way in many street processions of the sixteenth century'.[80] Tamburlaine himself is readily cast in emblematic roles, for instance as a God of Death addressed mistakenly at Damascus as a God of Mercy.[81] To relate *Tam-*

burlaine to theatrical emblems such as these is not to allegorise
it in simple terms: it is, rather, to gain a heightened awareness
of the collisions within the play between old and new, between
sacred and profane, between allegorical type and self-willed
individual being.

Such contrasts could excite in an audience the mirth of
exhilarated partisanship, or the defensive laughter of shocked
conventionality. Those who aspire to the high style and the
stately effect are frequently exposed in *Tamburlaine* as laughable. We can recognise that the play's varied provocations to
laughter have their own association with those traditions of
pageantry on which its more elevated theatrical effects so
persistently draw.[82] When Tamburlaine distributes the Turkish
queens to his troops, he expresses the gloating which Shakespeare's Cleopatra came to fear from the Roman crowd:

> *Theridamas.* It seems they meant to conquer us, my lord,
> And make us jesting pageants for their trulls.
> *Tamburlaine.* And now themselves shall make our pageant,
> And common soldiers jest with all their trulls.
>
>   (*Two* IV.iii.88–91)

Tamburlaine's treatment of such victims as Bajazeth and Orcanes casts himself in the role of director of a pageant, inviting a
coarse response from the crowd–audience. Such moments break
the high style blatantly, but they are true to one thoroughly-
developed aspect of the Tamburlaine figure. His brutality
and his zest repeatedly find expression in gleeful or sardonic
mockery. A comedy of abrupt deflation and satiric mimicry is
readily found elsewhere in Marlowe's plays as we have them:
more persistently present in *The Jew of Malta*, it is no less
crucial, and no less disturbing, in *Tamburlaine*.

Joseph Hall, in 1597, thought the Edward Alleyn style
indiscriminately pretentious:

> The stalking steps of his great personage,
> Graced with huf-cap termes and thundring threats.[83]

And in the same context Hall writes pungently about farcical
intrusion in tragic theatre:

> mids the silent rout
> Comes leaping in a selfe-misformed lout,
> And laughes, and grins, and frames his Mimik face,
> And justles straight into the Princes place.

One critic suggests that the passages which the printer claimed
to have excised from *Tamburlaine* displayed 'some cowardly or
depraved villains in the camp of Tamburlaine or of his enemies,
whose antics showed the satiric obverse of Tamburlaine's
grandiloquent bravado'.[84] Another guess is that the censored
material featured 'not a clown like the Strumbo and Bulli-
thrumble of *Locrine* and *Selimus*, two plays much influenced by
Tamburlaine, but more speeches of scornful comedy in those
scenes in which Tamburlaine taunts Mycetes, and Zenocrate
Zabina'.[85] To Una Ellis-Fermor, the play as printed is still
disfigured by puerile and bathetic moments, which may be
variously thought of as interpolations, or prosaic contractions of
verse lines, or the remnants of indecorous passages which the
printer rightly excised.[86] These suspect elements in the text
actually promote a range of effects. There is the laughable ineptitude of Almeda's defence of his lack of royal birth:

> That's no matter, sir, for being a king,
> For Tamburlaine came up of nothing.
>
> (*Two* III.i.74–5)

There is the high-spirited banter of the Tamburlaine party
after the defeat of Bajazeth (*One* III.iii.215–27). Tamburlaine
himself toys with the absurdly gullible Mycetes:

> Are you the witty king of Persia?
> Ay, marry am I; have you any suit to me?
> I would entreat you to speak but three wise words.
>
> (*One* II.iv.23–5)

Elsewhere in the play, passages of crude threat and counter-
threat are thought suspicious. And a jocular back-reference by
Tamburlaine from the Orcanes confrontation in Part Two to
the comic episode with Mycetes in Part One is thought to read
like an actor's gag (*Two* III.v.156–7). In all, Ellis-Fermor

identifies some thirty-six lines as likely survivals of 'fond and frivolous' interpolations in Marlowe's text, possibly written by Marlowe himself, she suggests, to suit the audience. They are almost all in prose, which is felt to be an inept medium in this context (except as used to convey the mad ravings of Zabina).[87] More generally, Ellis-Fermor's editorial judgment is conditioned by her conception of Tamburlaine (especially the Tamburlaine of Part One) as a captivating, if ingenuous, projection of Marlowe's own idealistic fervour. If we do not take such a simple and subjectivist view of Marlowe's relationship to the central figure, the coarse and bathetic passages can be defended as one end of a spectrum of attitudes to him, with even the least 'comic' moments frequently courting absurdity. In so extravagant a play, the balances of seriousness and levity, admiration and mockery, are capable of sudden alteration, especially in performance. A display of exuberant cruelty— 'Holla, ye pampered jades of Asia'—might excite an astonished, nervous laughter; a passage of flat, gloating banter might freeze mirth at its source. The actors in the early productions may have taken their cue for clowning from an audience needing more relief than Marlowe had allowed for from the weight of 'stately' emphasis in language and in spectacle alike. But it is clear that Marlowe's text itself persistently subjects response and judgment to divergent pressures. Do we laugh at the caged Bajazeth, at (and with) the sardonic and effete Calyphas, at the 'pampered jades' and the violated queens? To find that we do, or that we hesitate to do so, is to register part of the stress incurred in contemplating an image of a brutal 'scourge of God'. We can argue with conviction that the 'suspect' passages are at home in such a play; but all or some of them may be additions to the play, by Marlowe or by others, or the remnants of sizeable excisions from the text.

If we return to the printer's claim that he cut out low passages from the text on his own initiative, we are faced with a possibly unique occasion. F. P. Wilson asks: 'Is there another example of an Elizabethan publisher who in the interests of good art excised from a popular drama passages which had proved successful upon the stage?'[88] Perhaps we should distrust Jones's statement. Fredson Bowers's suggestion provides the printer with a motive for making a false claim about his text:

> By 'purposely' Jones implies that he could have printed these scenes if he had wished, in which case the copy would almost necessarily have been theatrical in origin. But since it bears no sign of the playhouse, it is much more likely that Jones's copy did not contain this material; hence his virtuous defence of the omission of unsuitable scenes may very possibly be an attempt to anticipate criticism that they were not present, though acted.[89]

This is a possible interpretation of the evidence, though we should note that the 'jestures' Jones found offensive may have been little more than occasional embellishments, not whole scenes. Perhaps, after all, the excised material was brief, and was present in the manuscript text, and the printer felt encouraged by the tone of the Part One Prologue to delete it on his own initiative. Whatever the facts of the matter, it seems clear that even without all the prose passages, the play is skilfully varied in tone and effect: the 'suspect' lines are not unique breaks in a sustained grand style.

5. FROM NOTORIETY TO CRITICISM

Though deferring to Marlowe's 'mighty line' in one context, Ben Jonson was elsewhere abruptly dismissive of a complete theatrical style which he associated with *Tamburlaine*:

> The true Artificer will not run away from nature, as hee were afraid of her; or depart from life, and the likenesse of Truth; but speake to the capacity of his hearers. And though his language differ from the vulgar somewhat; it shall not fly from all humanity, with the *Tamerlanes*, and *Tamer-Chams*, of the late Age, which had nothing in them but the *scenicall* strutting, and furious vociferation, to warrant them then to the ignorant gapers.[90]

This epilogue on an archaic theatrical fashion is in tune with some prominent moments in Shakespeare which characterise extravagant acting. Ulysses, in *Troilus and Cressida*, describes Patroclus' imitation of

> a strutting player whose conceit
> Lies in his hamstring, and doth think it rich
> To hear the wooden dialogue and sound
> 'Twixt his stretch'd footing and the scaffoldage.[91]

Patroclus overtops hyperbole for comic effect with his

> terms unsquar'd,
> Which, from the tongue of roaring Typhon dropp'd,
> Would seem hyperboles.

In the name of the true imitation of life, Hamlet rebukes actors who 'neither having th'accent of Christians, nor the gait of Christian, pagan, nor man, have so strutted and bellowed that I have thought some of Nature's journeymen had made men, and not made them well, they imitated humanity so abominably'.[92] When the strutting Pistol alludes directly to *Tamburlaine* in his unsquared rant, it begins to seem likely that Shakespeare's dramatised criticism of 'high' theatre in his time is focused directly on Marlowe and on the acting of Edward Alleyn:

> Shall packhorses,
> And hollow pamper'd jades of Asia,
> Which cannot go but thirty mile a day,
> Compare with Caesars, and with Cannibals,
> And Troiant Greeks? Nay, rather damn them with
> King Cerberus; and let the welkin roar.[93]

Pistol, however, is funny for his indiscriminate theft of many styles, not simply for his mimicry of Tamburlaine—and the point may be that it is *bad* mimicry. Shakespeare's creative encounter with Marlowe as a contemporary to reckon with is diverse and intricate.[94] We cannot suppose that Marlovian heroic style seemed to him merely absurd. At the same time, the shift in taste within a few years of Marlowe's death seems clear:

> While there is every reason to believe that Alleyn was no mere barnstormer, but an excellent actor in his vein, that vein was probably looking old-fashioned by the turn of the century. No one was writing plays like *Tamburlaine* any more, and you could raise a laugh by quoting it.[95]

An interesting reference to extreme acting style is quoted by
Alexander Leggatt from a work published in 1597: 'with that
S. bent his browes and fetcht his stations up and downe the
rome, with such furious Iesture as if he had beene playing
Tamberlane on a stage'.[96] To 'play the Tamburlaine' gratified
a need for holiday thrills as late as 1654:

> on Holy dayes, when Saylers, Water-men, Shoomakers, Butchers
> and Apprentices are at leisure, then it is good policy to amaze
> those violent spirits, with some tearing Tragedy full of fights and
> skirmishes ... sometimes *Tamerlane*, sometimes *Jugurth*, some-
> times the Jew of *Malta*, and sometimes parts of all these, and at
> last, none of the three taking, they were forc'd to undresse and
> put off their Tragick habits, and conclude the day with the merry
> milke-maides.[97]

Jonson's pronouncement does not allow for an element in
Marlowe's play which has come to seem very significant—the
focusing of critical attention on 'raging' within *Tamburlaine*
itself, through the expression of overt criticism, or by demon-
strating its impotence in face of natural catastrophe. Nor does
Jonson distinguish *Tamburlaine* from its imitations. George
Peele, writing *A Farewell* to Norris and Drake in 1589, names
Tamburlaine in one line along with a reference to Greene's
Alphonsus, as a figure of high tragedy among the chief delights
of London:

> Bid Theaters and proude Tragedians,
> Bid Mahomets Poo, and mightie Tamburlaine,
> King Charlemaine, Tom Stukeley and the rest
> Adiewe.[98]

But such imitations of *Tamburlaine* as Greene and Peele
provide, following very soon on the first performances of
Marlowe's play, are metrically and tonally so insecure, so dully
derivative, that it is hard now to conceive of seeing model and
copies alike as undifferentiated fustian.[99] John Donne will
remember as a portentous image 'Bajazeth, the shepheards
scoffe', and—with a sense of apocalypse—'Tamerlins last dayes
black ensignes whose threatnings none scaped'.[100]

Discussion of Marlowe was slow to relinquish preconceptions

drawn from misleading, and at times irrelevant, sources. The early date of *Tamburlaine*, both in Marlowe's own career and in the development of major Elizabethan drama, led to its being seen as a relatively formless work, tiresomely prolix. A very tenacious critical view saw the play as an ingenuous, if energetic, projection of the poet himself into the career of Tamburlaine. A nineteenth-century editor saw it, representatively, as 'one of the most wild and extravagant productions of an imperfectly formed stage'.[101] Swinburne found a 'stormy monotony of Titanic truculence', while acknowledging (in what becomes routine, rather damning, praise) the 'exquisite excellence' of individual lines and passages.[102] For Una Ellis-Fermor, in 1930, the play 'lacks, even in the first part, that clear shaping of its material which itself constitutes a great part of the dramatist's interpretation'.[103] While variants of these judgments are still expressed, it is now much more frequently asserted that the *Tamburlaine* plays together form a carefully-controlled dramatic unity, and that Marlowe is far from allowing the central figure to become a mere mirror of his own appetites.

In 1964, Clifford Leech reviewed developments in Marlowe criticism and scholarship.[104] The 'wide differences' he observed among the published interpretations of Marlowe had effectively displaced the old-fashioned, almost unanimous view of him. *Tamburlaine* was no longer seen as a monotonous, feebly-dramatised series of episodes whose central figure was merely a mouthpiece for a 'dazzled' author. The 'intellectual quality' of Marlowe's address to the writing of his plays was now being emphasised; the complexity of the plays themselves was gaining recognition; and more was coming to be known about Marlowe's relation to the theatre of his time and to the theatre traditions on which he could draw.

Looking back towards the great scholarly achievement of Una Ellis-Fermor's edition of *Tamburlaine*, Leech emphasised several major efforts of interpretative criticism of the play. Roy W. Battenhouse, in *Marlowe's Tamburlaine* (1941), had read the play in the light of a range of received Elizabethan ideas about ethics and about human nature, especially our passional nature. Paul H. Kocher, in *Christopher Marlowe: a Study of his Thought, Learning and Character* (1946), had explored *Tamburlaine* with particular reference to theological questions. The context offered for the play in Eugene Waith's *The Herculean Hero* (1962) was the tradition of a specific kind of dramatic figure which the Renaissance had developed from classical sources. And Ethel Seaton's 'Marlowe's Map', published as early as 1924, had pioneered research into one aspect of Marlowe's groundwork preparation for the writing of *Tamburlaine*.[105]

Those who were finding complexity and subtlety in Marlowe's work—not monotony and mere display—were, Leech argued, looking back ultimately to T. S. Eliot's essay of 1919.[106] Eliot stressed Marlowe's development as a dramatist, and assumed an outline chronology for which there is little hard evidence. This development, he took it, was from the 'pretty simple huffe-snuffe bombast' of *Tamburlaine*, towards the writing of a dramatic poetry in which Marlowe turns rhetorical vice into virtue, an 'intense and serious' poetry 'which ... attains its effects by something not unlike caricature'. Within this general view of Marlowe's work, Eliot offered his deeply influential description of the dominant tone of *The Jew of Malta*: a 'powerful and mature tone' of farce, 'the farce of the old English humour, the terribly serious even savage comic humour'. For Leech Marlowe's humour was an impulse active at the heart of Marlowe's whole work, including *Tamburlaine* quite typically. It reflected 'Marlowe's recognition of the puniness of human ambition, the ludicrous gap between aspiration and any possible fulfilment'.[107] In *Tamburlaine* itself, humour in this specialised sense was seen as 'part of a predominantly tragic attitude to the world, complicating but not destroying the tragic attitude'.[108] This view emphasises Marlowe's capacity for ironic dispassion and for dramatic manipulation of his material and of audience response. It was corroborated, Leech found, in the way critics had seen the relation between the two Parts of *Tamburlaine*. Helen Gardner had argued, very influentially, that the sequel is a decisive and deliberate advance on the first play, not a lame repetition drawing on flimsy source-material.[109] G. I. Duthie, while finding Part Two 'much inferior', had asserted that each Part had a coherent dramatic structure based on a governing theme.[110] Duthie's account seemed to Leech to be 'too neat', but it marked the definitive rejection of the old view of *Tamburlaine* as an arbitrary succession of episodes which squandered dramatic emphasis uncritically.

Discussion of the relation of Marlowe's work to the stage seemed barely to have started in 1964. Leech drew attention to David M. Bevington's *From Mankind to Marlowe* (1962), which 'strengthens our idea of Marlowe's dramatic and theatrical inheritance, bringing closer to us the nature of the theatre that he found waiting for him in London'. Marlowe's dramatic practice, Leech felt, persistently sought to promote an ambivalent effect, and knowledge of dramatic tradition could inform our sense of this ambivalence. An instance he offered from *Tamburlaine* is the ending of Part One. Here, Tamburlaine himself declares a 'truce with all the world', and crowns his queen, on a stage which bears the corpses of Bajazeth, Zabina, and Zenocrate's first lover, the King of Arabia. The visual effect of the dead victims, Leech says, reinforces Tamburlaine's triumph; but 'their presence charges his words with irony'. This kind of point had been emphatically made by Douglas Cole, who found an insistent contrast between the brutal stage picture and 'the glowing words': Calyphas, for instance, is stabbed in the immediate context of 'the most aspiring speech that Tamburlaine has yet uttered'.[111]

Kocher's view of Marlowe differed at many points from that offered by Battenhouse. But each was concerned to define a 'doctrine' or an outlook which, held by Marlowe himself, constituted the basic conviction behind the *Tamburlaine* plays. Battenhouse, for instance, saw Marlowe as writing 'moralised history after the pattern of the *Mirror for Magistrates*': Tamburlaine is a tragic example of a nature readily interpreted by orthodox Elizabethan theory—impious, feverish, 'the result of uncontrolled, misdirected, and diseased passions'.[112] Similarly, Irving Ribner has read the play as a 'serious exposition of

[Machiavelli's] actual philosophy'.[113] Such interpretations may be contrasted with the view that sympathy and antipathy for Tamburlaine, struggling against each other in the play, are symptoms of a 'divided mind' in Marlowe himself: 'It is clear that, whether in pleasure or repulsion, Marlowe was attracted to cruelty; and here in *Tamburlaine*, although the mind is divided, the division is unequal and the larger part seems to rate violence and cruelty as among the enviable excitements of life'.[114] J. B. Steane's account of the play finds not one Marlowe but two; not a Marlowe in full conscious, even ironic, control of his material, but a writer whose deepest predilections are at odds with other impulses in his nature.

Since 1964, the view of Marlowe as a dramatist substantially in command of a theatre of ironic contrasts has gained many adherents and developed many variants. It is now no longer surprising to find him interpreted in a way that is wholly opposite to the traditional insistence on his uncritical partisanship with his aspiring hero-figures. This 'newer' Marlowe is dispassionate, calculating, sardonic, enigmatic: a wide range of tones is detected by this sort of critical approach, and the basic creative resource of the playwright is irony. Perhaps the most influential book for this line of Marlowe interpretation is still Eugene Waith's *The Herculean Hero* (1962), not because it emphasises irony but because it dwells on the continuous collision between opposite impressions given by the central figure of the play. Waith turned away from such discussions of *Tamburlaine* as sought to identify Marlowe's attitude to the play's hero in terms of authorial approval or disapproval. Marlowe is seeking to re-define a specific kind of heroic character which is itself a compound of opposed impulses and attitudes: 'In the depiction of the Herculean hero there is no relaxation of the tensions between his egotism and altruism, his cruelties and benefactions, his human limitations and his divine potentialities'.[115] For Waith, the dramatic display of these 'tensions' is essentially an appeal, not to ironic apprehension, but to 'the wonder aroused by vast heroic potential'. The killing of Calyphas, for example, obliges us 'to accept cruelty along with valour, pride and ambition as part of the spirit which makes this man great'. The dramatic method imposes great stress on the audience, because our conventional susceptibilities are shocked; but the strain is essentially resolved in the commanding, antithetical nature of Tamburlaine himself. Zenocrate voices an orthodox morality, in terms of the expected punishment of *hubris*, but for Waith the main point here is that such a view is seen to be inadequate for the purposes of judging Tamburlaine, the hubristic figure. A rival account of this moment in the play would give Zenocrate a different status, as the speaker of only *one* eloquent view of Tamburlaine among the many offered in the play, with Marlowe leaving us to arbitrate among them as best we can and to fit them to what happens in the play wherever we can. Waith is, by contrast, locating an authorial constant which holds good throughout the two Parts of the play: 'It is possible, of course, that Marlowe's attitude shifts from scene to scene, or from Part I to Part II, but it seems to me more likely that his conception of heroic character is sufficiently complex to include what appear to be contradictory elements and that his attitude, going beyond simple approval or disapproval, remains constant'. Specifically on the relation of Part One to Part Two, Waith adopts the now quite orthodox view that the sequel amplifies and complicates themes already firmly adumbrated, for the most part, in the first play: 'The portrait is not changed: its lines are more deeply incised'. Waith emphasises contrast and discrepancy in the picture; but a dynamic force, for him, holds the opposite elements together, to our astonishment and to the destruction of irony.

Judith Weil, on the other hand, observes the great 'dialectical vigour' of the *Tamburlaine* plays, but sees them essentially as 'tragic riddles': 'They presuppose the value of history and continuity; Tamburlaine's political conquests and family relationships equip us to regard him as a tragic figure. But at the same time the plays make Tamburlaine insensitive to the tragic elements of his own life; his imagination always gets the last triumphant word'.[116] This Tamburlaine, in some respects a figure of Folly, tries, and fails, to project his own death as a heroic combat; he is engaged in an attempt to justify himself, throughout, by way of 'shows'; he tries to give his far-reaching conceits literal existence: 'To create his reputation, he must forever be raising up new enemies who deny his myth'. This Tamburlaine, unlike Waith's, does not transcend contradictions:

> It is Tamburlaine's *own* attitude which remains constant in the plays, not the attitudes of the author or of the audience. Because the framing landscape constantly reminds us of limits, we are apt to grow sceptical of Tamburlaine's romantic trust that all the barriers in his world are permeable. Thoroughly as he may dazzle us with his poetry, Tamburlaine cannot finally outrun our perception that his power falls far short of his hopes and that it does enormous damage to other men.

A conception emerges of Marlowe as an ironist of a special kind, one who, not essentially negative, 'extends the sense of freedom from characters to audience'. The audience carries 'the burdens of inference and interpretation'—but it is positively *enabled* to do so: 'By appealing to our memories of literature and tradition, by inviting us to ponder analogies and scrutinize shows, Marlowe stimulates our imagination. By praising folly he exercises our wisdom. He invites us to use those faculties of choice and recognition which his heroes neglect.'

Clearly, interpretation of the play in this light will draw continually on the knowledge of those repositories of meaning which Marlowe brings into play explicitly or implicitly: emblems, concepts, the scriptures, works of literature. What we are to concentrate on particularly with Weil is the 'puzzling relationship' of Tamburlaine's word-magic to true wisdom. Tamburlaine himself works with material which proves increasingly recalcitrant as the two plays unfold. For Weil, this is in one light a tragedy of the consequences of human imagining. And there is scope for a sympathetic response to Tamburlaine's folly, though it is, of course, a sympathy stiffened by critical resistance to him and held back by puzzlement about what, in the end, he portends: 'Tamburlaine cannot overcome time, change, and death with his remarkable imagination. But while we use imagination ourselves, can we entirely blame him for trying?

His pride is indeed like the pride of Phaeton. We must always be dazzled by it until it dips closer to us and scorches a ground more familiar than Marlowe's land of fortune.'

The conceptual framework offered by Weil is radically different from that of Waith, and the interpretative problems are construed in ways fundamentally opposed. But it is clear that both accounts of *Tamburlaine* emphasise contrast, and both take Marlowe to be in control of his material, in its overt dramatic motion and in its deepest (for Weil, its most riddling) implications. Their strength is that they offer a theoretical position in terms of which the play may be interpreted without forfeiting attention to the ever-increasing knowledge we enjoy of the Elizabethan context. Pageant, morality play, romance; emblematic imagery; the scriptures: scholarship has extended our awareness of the possible range of Marlowe's allusions, though by no means all of these allusions are unchallengeably set up in the text. Eugene Waith has revisited the play in the light of the conviction that 'The heroic entered English drama through the door of chivalric romance'.[117] This approach yields an interesting perspective on the placing of Tamburlaine himself in relation to a given range of values: it highlights both his chivalric ideals and his diverging from them as his occasion serves. *Tamburlaine* is seen as a prototype heroic play, taking over from epic and from its successor, romance, 'a concern with the wonder of human potentiality'.

M. C. Bradbrook and Wolfgang Clemen are deeply influential figures behind the developing commentary on Marlowe's rhetoric of ear and eye. Clemen finds that 'in *Tamburlaine* Marlowe created a highly individual dramatic style in which stage-tableau and stage-business combined with the long speeches to produce a new kind of unity'.[118] He identifies the prominent influences operating on the theatrical style and manner of the play as 'those of the pageants, of the spectacular elements in the masques, and of the Italian *trionfi*'. However, he finds that Marlowe has, in *Tamburlaine*, only intermittently achieved a full co-ordination of 'the set speech and the stage-tableau, the spoken word and stage-business': 'For in many

other episodes sudden alarums and battles are scattered indiscriminately among passages of speech, or are introduced by
means of awkwardly explanatory lines of prose'.[119] It is interesting to set this qualified verdict on Marlowe's dramatic craft
alongside those accounts of the play which find discrepancies
and anomalies of tone and method to be in themselves important
vehicles of Marlowe's purpose.

Our knowledge of the architecture, properties, and methods
of the theatres in which Tamburlaine was produced will never
be exact. Nor are we sure just *where* it was played, in the years
preceding the revival at Henslowe's Rose in 1594. About its
staging in that theatre much can be cautiously inferred, as has
been shown by Ernest L. Rhodes.[120] And Glynne Wickham
has offered equally cautious 'Notes on the Staging of Marlowe's
Plays'.[121] David Hard Zucker offers an interpretation of the
kind of stage procedures and decoration which may be thought
necessary to carry the play's distinctive emphasis on ritual and
emblematic contrast.[122] His work carries, explicitly, a debt to
George Kernodle's book *From Art to Theatre* (1944).[123] A
judicious survey of this complex territory of inference, painstaking reconstruction, and educated guesswork, is given by
Richard Hosley in 'The Playhouse', Chapter III of *The Revels
History of Drama in English*, vol. 3 (1975).

What may be called the *thinking* which Marlowe brings to
bear on Tamburlaine's career was notably clarified by Jean
Jacquot in an important essay published in 1953.[124] Jacquot is
concerned mostly with the variations which Marlowe plays on
received ideas about man and the universe. He emphasises the
struggle in *Tamburlaine*, as a play, between the Platonic idea
that the soul ascends towards contemplation of the divine, and
the idea that human nature and universal nature are characterised by strife. This is one complication. Another is that
strife itself is not seen by Marlowe as the context out of which
harmony may develop. The concept of the scourge of God is
appropriated and exploited by Marlowe in a similarly un-
orthodox way: it ceases to be simply a homiletic commonplace,
whose function is to discourage rebellion and to reinforce

authority. And Marlowe omits the Elizabethan emphasis on the duties of the king and the respect for law. Tamburlaine's cult of rebellion as a godlike impulse contrasts with his own intolerance of opposition and insurrection. Jacquot is particularly concerned to define omissions or reversals or surprising extensions of traditional thinking. For instance, he shows that the ending of *Tamburlaine* Part Two omits elements which an audience might have confidently expected: a suggestion that the world of social and natural order was about to be restored, that experience has a purifying effect in a world seen as being prey to Fortune, or that the sufferings of the just have their counterpart in eternal joy. The neo-platonic ingredient is one element among others which have been interestingly invoked to define an aspect of Marlowe's treatment of aspiration. Stephen J. Greenblatt, observing that Marlowe's heroes 'could not finally desire anything for itself', comments:

> For Hooker and Bruno, this inability arises from the existence of transcendent goals—it is a proof of the existence of God; for Marlowe, it springs from the tragic fact that all objects of desire are fictions, theatrical illusions shaped by the characters. And these characters are themselves fictions, fashioned in reiterated acts of self-naming.[125]

N. W. Bawcutt has judiciously reviewed the vexed question of the extent of Marlowe's knowledge of Machiavelli, and has carried forward the painstaking process of documenting Elizabethan allusions to his work.[126] This has its bearing on *Tamburlaine*, particularly with reference to those episodes in which a formal undertaking is broken for reasons of expedience. And research into the historiographical tradition of the *vita Tamerlanis* throws light on one important aspect of the play.[127]

On the blank verse of *Tamburlaine*, T. S. Eliot offered the influential comment that 'Marlowe gets into verse the melody of Spenser, and he gets a new driving power by reinforcing the sentence period against the line period'.[127] F. P. Wilson charts the transmission of blank verse through *Gorboduc* and *Jocasta* to Marlowe and Kyd, and comments on the unstiffening of dramatic rhetoric in the two decades from 1540.[128] To one ear,

Marlowe's 'mighty line' will sound mainly like the indulgence of a 'free-flowing impetuousness'.[129] The Marlovian style in *Tamburlaine* is not wholly free from the suspicion of automatism and self-mimicry. But the play frequently makes dramatic points by way of these tendencies in the rolling pentameter: it discriminates between Tamburlaine's own range and that of many of his adversaries, and it gives us a critical grasp of the less admirable aspects of Tamburlaine's enterprise, such as egotistical fantasy, brutality and senseless rant. Our response to the pentameter rhythms has been notably refined by M. R. Ridley:

> Marlowe had an ear acute enough to perceive that though the base, the 'norm', of English blank verse was to be the five-stress 'iambic' line, and though the hearer's awareness of that norm must not be lost, yet few lines should strictly conform to the norm, and that five is, so far from being the desirable, almost the forbidden, number.[130]

Editors, scholars, and critics have significantly extended our knowledge and refined our understanding of *Tamburlaine* in the years since Leech surveyed new developments in the study of Marlowe. Any review of the play draws continually on the work of others, and such accounts as those of Waith and Weil offer a critical framework within which ostensibly minor pieces of information can play a meaningful role: a very slight allusion might be a detail in a significant pattern.[131] An editor still looks back, across successive new editions, to the authoritative work of Una Ellis-Fermor, which has remained the principal source of subsequent editorial commentary on the play. But he will also recognise that his work depends at every turn, beyond exact acknowledgement, on more recent work. Two major interpretative efforts were the professional productions of *Tamburlaine* which were seen in 1951, 1956, and 1976. The last of these, directed by Peter Hall at the National Theatre, was particularly significant in the confirmation it gave of the range of comic tones which the staging of the play can transmit without incurring the suspicion that the text is being exploited for the sake of amusement and relief.[132] Leech's conviction about the critical importance of 'Marlowe's humour' seemed thoroughly vindicated, on stage, where he would have wished it. It is also true to say that the performance interrogated the audience. Judith Weil has set out some of the questions which, in her view, we are left with:

> Will poetry and history always be at odds? Are vengeful gods bad examples for men? Does proud idealism generate religion? Is God a poem, the Bible a collection of conceits? Would Marlowe have agreed with Montaigne that men who attempt to imitate angels will only behave like devils?[133]

It is, of course, important to distinguish those questions which are explicitly enunciated in, or immediately provoked by, the play, from those which spring from a gathered consideration of what the full text *portends*.

6. THE PLAY

In the closing scene of Part One, the tragic glass which the Prologue invited us to watch reflects one of the most astounding figures in the play's rhetoric of speaking pictures. Tamburlaine, 'all in black and very melancholy', confronts the 'sun-bright' Virgins of Damascus who have come out to plead for their city on the fatal third day of the Tartar siege. His demeanour recalls the episode when, without speaking, he drove Agydas to suicide

> astonièd
> To see his choler shut in secret thoughts
> And wrapt in silence of his angry soul.
>
> (*One* III.ii.69–71)

He is again all in black when, in Part Two, he threatens to 'wake black Jove to crouch and kneel to me' (V.i.98). A Black Knight of romance, about to violate the chivalric code in allegiance to his own peremptory custom, Tamburlaine is also here a terrible inverse God. Our sense of him, focused by the white–black emblematic contrast with the Virgins, is a compound of wonder and revulsion: repellently inhuman, he is also portentously extra-human. His anger has a powerful eschatological aspect, here and at Babylon in Part Two—'wrathful planets, death, or destiny', 'his last day's dreadful siege'.[124]

The Virgins offer him symbols of the surrender of Egypt, addressing their brooding conqueror in terms which his appearance wholly contradicts:

> Most happy king and emperor of the earth,
> Image of honour and nobility,
> For whom the powers divine have made the world,
> And on whose throne the holy Graces sit.
>
> (*One* V.i.74–7)

It was 'love of honour' in one sense that led the Governor of Damascus to resist the siege so long. The 'honour' of the Virgins is now put at risk in the hope of moving Tamburlaine to pity. And equally in the name of 'honour', now in the sense of rigid observance of his ritual of siege, Tamburlaine consigns the Virgins to Death, his obedient judge. The play on the word 'honour', here and elsewhere in the play, sharpens the dramatic point. Above all, here, an appeal to one received code, the 'common rites of arms', is rejected summarily in favour of an arbitrary variant of it, 'the custom proper to his sword'. There will be a second version of this clash of codes in Part Two, when Tamburlaine ritually murders his own son. Required by 'the argument of arms', in one view, the execution of Calyphas also causes deep revulsion as a barbarism. The revulsion is expressed by some who had themselves been eager, earlier, to inflict cruelty—a characteristic Marlovian complication.

Act Four saw Tamburlaine accoutred all in white, with white plumes and a silver crest, among milk-white flags which 'reflexed' the beams of Mercy to the city. His own words persistently comment on the emblematic meaning of his appearance and his deeds. This white chivalric image is, clearly, in keeping with his general bearing towards Zenocrate. In this same costume, however, he ascends the stage throne by way of a brutally degraded human footstool, proclaiming himself a God, 'the chiefest lamp of all the earth'. He celebrates himself as a bearer of blood and fire, not of mercy, in lines which proclaim a deliberate concentration on the red of slaughter:

> Then, when the sky shall wax as red as blood,
> It shall be said I made it red myself,
> To make me think of naught but blood and war.
>
> (*One* IV.ii.53–5)

Agydas—for this reason a significant minor character—had contrasted the Romance aspect with the martial cruelty of Tamburlaine, who

> when you look for amorous discourse
> Will rattle forth his facts of war and blood.
>
> (*One* III.ii.44–5)

Bajazeth had himself prepared us for this sanguinary emphasis, invoking vengeance on Tamburlaine from the priests 'That, sacrificing, slice and cut your flesh' (*One* IV.ii.2). Now, as Tamburlaine mounts the throne, we register the abrupt narrowing of an expansive gesture—'lamp of all the earth'—to the constrictions of wilful obsession—'naught but blood and war'. Such changes of scale and focus are characteristic. In Part Two, for instance, the physical correlative of

> the figure of my dignity
> By which I hold my name and majesty
>
> (*Two* IV.iii.25–6)

is a chariot drawn by exhausted captive kings.[135] Again, at the end of Part One, Tamburlaine's magnanimous truce-taking has a stage context of brained captives and a dead rival. The footstool motif itself has Romance antecedents, and may carry a suggestion of an anti-papal nature; but Marlowe, this time expanding the scale of reference shockingly, may want us to recall Psalm 110: 'The Lord said unto my Lord, Sit thou at my right hand, until I make thine enemies thy footstool'.[136]

After the footstool scene, there is a brief episode in which others who oppose Tamburlaine set out to raise the siege, a chivalric army.

> As frolic as the hunters in the chase
> Of savage beasts amid the desert woods.
>
> (*One* IV.iii.56–7)

Then Tamburlaine comes in complete scarlet to a bloodthirsty banquet, his red flags 'reflexing hues of blood' in a context of Thyestean curses and malignant jokes about cannibalism. Scarlet is the costume of Death, in the killing of the Damascus Virgins, and of Death and the Fatal Sisters in Part Two (III. iv.54–5). In the truce that ends Part One, scarlet is to be worn by Tamburlaine's generals-turned-lawgivers. In the 'plot' of a play called *England's Joy*, acted in 1602, there appeared a figure of Justice 'And at her feete Warre, with a Scarlet Roabe of peace upon his Armour: A wreath of Bayes about his temples, and a braunch of Palme in his hand'.[137] The black figure who meets the virgins is the third in Tamburlaine's own sequence of emblematic knights—white, red, and black. His armour, bearing, and speech impose themselves as a single deliberate style, the rhetorical figures of an inflexible will to destroy. But the doomed Virgins are allowed a moving counter-eloquence of speech and gesture, bearing the gilded wreath of propitiation.

White and black, mercy and doom, pliancy and resolution, fire and dross, life and death, Jove and Hades, Heaven and Erebus. These bold opposites govern the play's visual and verbal rhetoric. They range together in sets—white, mercy, pliancy, life; black, wrath, resolution, death—but they also activate our sense of ambivalence, complicating the simple patterns of response. For instance, they dramatise the opposition between Tamburlaine and some of his victims, or between Tamburlaine's sensibility and Zenocrate's, the more powerfully because they are two faces of Tamburlaine himself:

> His lofty brows in folds do figure death,
> And in their smoothness amity and life.
>
> (*One* II.i.21–2)

As a figure of life, he may command admiration—however reluctant we are to grant it—while provoking troublesome questions about vitality's apparent dependence on egotism and on strife. As a figure of death, he excites terror and revulsion, but draws justification from the imperatives of heroic conquest and imaginative ardour, and from the supposed sanction of divine sponsorship. As a figure of both life and death, he can be felt to exemplify a daring command over extremes, stirringly defiant, bursting the doors of Janus' temple. At other times, on the contrary, this double aspect of Tamburlaine appears an exercise of perverse self-assertion, driven by whim, and based on a subjugation of the self to its own extreme proclivities—a mechanical operation of the spirit.

It has been well observed that Tamburlaine's characteristic method is that of 'sublimating an ethical conflict into an aesthetic programme'.[138] Certainly, Marlowe is preoccupied with rival aesthetics. An aesthetic of love and aspiration is opposed by one of cruelty and constriction: the 'sweet and curious harmony' of the first, learnt from a heaven that 'tunes [it] to our souls', is held against the infernal order, insistently 'loathsome', 'baneful', and 'ugly'. Each aesthetic is, of course, decisively announced by Tamburlaine himself—there is no substantial area of experience in the play to which he has not at least partial access. And such is the extremism of Marlowe's method, the face of creation alters with each major shift of emotional tone or imaginative focus. Close by

> the shining bower where Cynthia sits
> Like lovely Thetis in a crystal robe
>
> (*Two* III.iv.50–1)

we encounter Rhamnusia carrying a helmet full of blood, strewing the way 'with brains of slaughtered men', from which we ascend as abruptly to Fame's airy zenith, along

> that straight line
> Which measureth the glorious frame of heaven.
>
> (*Two* III.iv.64–5)

The two main poles in this vivid imaginative geography have ranges of imagery for themselves: evocatively, but at the risk of their becoming codified. Pearl, ivory, crystal, gold, Heaven's lightsome windows; pitchy cloud, mist, rust, standing air, the black circumference of Hell. Against both sides, Tamburlaine directs rage, threatening Jove, invading Hell. In the name of either side, he can pursue a career of conquest, either aspiring to exotic felicity or thirsting for seas of blood. In Act Five of

Part One, the pull between the two is developed as an inner conflict within Tamburlaine himself. Part Two opposes Zenocrate and Tamburlaine, gentleness and brutality, in relation to their sons. One son, Calyphas, is killed because he follows his own (debased) version of the aesthetic of peace.

The figure who confronts the Virgins is the fully conceived, and fully produced, antithesis of love and clemency. Bearing, posture, dress, the 'full and significant action of the body': he is, to use an apt expression from the play, the 'picture' of Death—in Sidney's phrase, a 'perfect picture' able to 'strike, pearce, and possesse the sight of the soule'.[139] For this black appearance, as for the white and the red before it, Marlowe has written into the text a direction for costume and properties (if we exclude the horse, and possibly the tent):

> Black are his colours, black pavilion,
> His spear, his shield, his horse, his armour, plumes,
> And jetty feathers menace death and hell.
>
> (*One* IV.i.60–2)

It is a complete and arbitrary ritual, vividly theatrical in the tradition of triumph or pageant, readily freezing into *tableau*, the player suiting his whole action with forms to his conceit. In its emphasis and its expanded scale, this prodigious figure at once demands and intimidates our efforts to comprehend and to judge. The figure expresses a glowering malevolence; melancholy rules the figure. Perhaps the competition between these two modes of apprehension lies near the heart of our fascination with stylised spectacle and symbolic acting. Seen one way, Tamburlaine's 'aspect' consummates his personality and purpose. The monolith's forehead, in the poetry's terms, 'bears figures of renown and miracle'. We can register these portents as the signs of an awesome integrity. Seen another way, the set appearance has been arbitrarily assumed or imposed: and we readily take this to constitute a concealment or obstruction of the natural self, the denial of humane impulse, affection, 'respect of pity'. What to make of Tamburlaine is a challenge borne in upon us by the stage idiom as much as by the spoken perplexity of his victims:

> What god or fiend or spirit of the earth,
> Or monster turnèd to a manly shape,
> Or of what mould or mettle he be made,
> What star or state soever govern him . . .
>
> (*One* II.vi.15–18)

The symbolic force of the monolith is imposing. The figures of renown and miracle are borne 'in the forehead of his fortune'. Destiny becomes an attribute of the man destined to wield power. Tamburlaine's fortunes, which the Prologue invites us to applaud as we please, are sometimes seen as governed by a partisan goddess of Fortune, sometimes as part of Tamburlaine's own prerogative. The wheel that should bring him misfortune, as it does to Cosroe or to Bajazeth, whether as punishment for *hubris* or in the natural sequence of felicity and misery, is said to be turned by his own hands or stopped altogether. At its most oppressive, this gives his victims the sense that

> Then is there left no Mahomet, no God,
> No fiend, no Fortune.   (*One* V.i.239–40)

The tyrant is seen here as exploding all convictions of divine or infernal control of human affairs. In this view, the world he dominates is best mirrored in madness and suicide, with Bajazeth and Zabina. In Part Two, the commanding figure is even more pointedly placed in relation to human suffering— his own. The Fatal Sisters sweat with his carnage; but they rob him of Zenocrate. Death is his menial; but in Tamburlaine's own sickness, Death is the slave come to kill the master. An insistent word is 'fatal': Tamburlaine's 'fatal chair', the Fatal Sisters, fatal steel, the 'black and fatal ravens'.

Tamburlaine's initial act of self-realisation had been expressed by a symbolic change of costume—rags into armour, shepherd into chivalric leader. This was to acknowledge, and at a stroke to fulfil, one heroic and dramatic imperative. The actor *becomes* the role. By this means, Tamburlaine enacts that perfect correspondence between the being he is and the figure he makes: as Menaphon had said of him, 'Like his desire, lift upward and divine' (*One* II.i.8). The symbolic act of transformation relates to the insistence in the play on heroism as a quality of bearing, temerity, address. It wills us to 'wear ourselves and never rest', to 'bear a valiant mind': 'Let us put on our meet encount'ring minds' (*One* II.vi.19).' To 'bear a mind courageous and invincible' associates with legendary physical prowess— to 'bear the axis of the world'. This is a boast, but also a daring conviction. And the conviction may create the world within which it can be realised. A conceived ideal of manly power and fortitude, shining in 'complete virtue', shines in 'complete armour'. In this vision, Tamburlaine's character and his figure, his prowess and his image, mirror each other, almost to the point of tautology.

For such effects, the play draws continuously upon a conception of event and appearance as making essence manifest. In this theatre, manifestation is power, and power is vested in eloquence of gesture and in the talismans of feeling and of authority. Zenocrate's picture and her statue are set up as icons in the place where she dies, to draw the stars in admiration out of their orbit. Day gives 'virtue' to our eyes. A dying lover makes a 'virtue' of the sight of his love. The 'virtues' of a crown inhere in its burnished appearance. Tributary kings render up their crowns. Crowns are served at banquets. A feeble king's only recourse in a crisis is to try to hide his crown. Kingly looks exact allegiance and accomplish victories. The stare of imperious displeasure moves an adversary to suicide, or terrorises an entire army. A black army of Moors is the fear of death incarnate. This vigorous creative centre gives force to the opposed insights—for instance, that power is blindly destructive, and inimical to pity and love. The effect is of symbolism boldly revitalised at source, remote from the docile formalities of personification. Colours take on sonority; sound has a brazen shine.

The play's specialised and heightened verbal rhetoric of assertion, protestation, and lament, can claim at best a similar kind of theatrical truthfulness. It is expressive of a psychology of emotion in which a sight or other stimulus directly generates intense feeling, and that feeling then imposes itself, peremp-

torily, as a pervasive *state* of feeling. Here again, the character
becomes figurative. Hearts weep tears of blood. Souls are
pierced. Looks 'shed influence'. We 'surfeit in conceiving joy'.
The fearful inhabitants of a besieged city

> so punished with conceit . . .
> Now wax all pale and withered to the death.
>
> *(One* V.i.87, 91)

Pain or pleasure, present or anticipated; pain suffered, or felt
in sympathy for another being; the pleasure of inflicting pain:
all are equally strongly 'conceived'. Such a rhetoric is natural to
a theatre of mask and stylised spectacle. It moves essentially
towards a surfeit of emphasis: the characteristic Marlovian
word is 'glutted'.[140] It is no vehicle for subtle gradations of
emotion, but it does carry the play's broad human themes,
along with the discriminations these require—the atrophy or
denial of sympathy or love, and the conflicts among different
impulses and different gratifications. The Virgins of Damascus
hope their words and gestures will 'convey events of Mercy'
directly to the heart. To love is to live in the light of a heavenly
presence 'In whose sweet being I repose my life' *(Two* II.iv.48).
To fear that love is unreciprocated is to find that anxiety feeds
the mind

> With ceaseless and disconsolate conceits
> Which dyes my looks so lifeless as they are,
> And might, if my extremes had full events,
> Make me the ghastly counterfeit of death.
>
> *(One* III.ii.14–17)

The sufferings of the dying are felt by others' hearts 'all
drowned in tears of blood'. We may be 'wounded and broken'
with another's pain, and the thought of his death

> daunts our thoughts
> More than the ruin of our proper souls.
>
> *(Two* V.iii.181–2)

The dying can themselves achieve adroit conceits within this
extreme rhetoric. For instance, the wounded Arabia sees
Zenocrate

Whose sight with joy would take away my life,
As now it bringeth sweetness to my wound,
If I had not been wounded as I am.   (*One* V.i.420–2)

For Amyras, quite as complexly, to think of finding any delight in succeeding his dying father is to think of his own grief's 'mortified lineaments' moving a hardened heart. Olympia, too, can allow no thought but mourning, and her would-be lover can feel nothing for her but love. Torment, for Bajazeth, strikes at the source of energy and love:

> gripes the root
> From which the issues of my thoughts do break.
>
> (*One* V.i.273–4)

Given this, Bajazeth has nothing to look forward to but his own death's extreme sensation and the savour of an after-life in which he can inflict torture on his torturer.

The intensity and extremism of this rhetoric is not gratuitous. It draws support from the persistent stylization of gesture, and from the sense that we are witnessing events which typify elemental human experiences. It is not, of course, a naturalistic language; but it can prove strikingly impressive when spoken, conveying the drama of a human search for an appropriate idiom in which to convey primary feelings. We have to ask whether Marlowe is always sure of the ease with which conventions and habits of style turn to self-mimicry, and through self-mimicry to unwitting parody. But Marlowe is certainly resourceful in exposing such a style to various correctives. There is the tacit criticism of Tamburlaine which can be heard in Zenocrate's hurt silences. There is Theridamas' explicit protest against voluble excess:

> If words might serve, our voice hath rent the air;
> If tears, our eyes have watered all the earth;
> If grief, our murdered hearts have strained forth blood.
> Nothing prevails, for she is dead, my lord.
>
> (*Two* II.iv.121–4)

Not that such correctives expose the 'high astounding terms' as comprehensively hollow. We can't, for instance, reject their use to convey deep personal grief as mere ridiculous excess. They are sometimes stilted and prolix. They are frequently pronounced arrogant and indulgent in the play itself. But they are, in principle, indispensable to the play's scope and pitch, and to the boldness of its human canvas.

The early Tamburlaine of Part One is a compound of ideal forms drawn from classical myth and romantic chivalry—though he will deviate widely from these ideals. He demands, excites, and returns loyalty, in contrast to the effete Damon-and-Pythias cult of Mycetes. He is true to, and respectful of, Zenocrate—though this heightens the impact of her distress at his brutality, and the prospect of his cruelty to her father:

> Ah Tamburlaine, wert thou the cause of this,
> That term'st Zenocrate thy dearest love?
>
> (*One* V.i.336–7)

He is also, as Bajazeth's opponent in Part One, and again (fleetingly) in Part Two, a liberator of enslaved Christians from the scourge of Islam. He enters on the heroic role with zest, acting up to it. There is an exuberant opportunism, not the dour craft of a Machiavel, in the early encounters with Theridamas and Cosroe. The rhetorical command does not burst on us ready made. Tamburlaine jovially evolves it:

> Then shall we fight courageously with them,
> Or look you I should play the orator?
>
> (*One* I.ii.128–9)

The verve and invention of Tamburlaine's *acting*, like the distinctive delight he takes in evolving his style, are defined partly by way of carefully graded contrasts. There are, for example, Mycetes' daintily-rhymed mimicries of kingship, Cosroe's public-spirited acceptance of empire, quick to concede moral dominance to Tamburlaine, and there is Bajazeth's hieratic and scornful pomp. But each of these victims also focuses critical questions about Tamburlaine's motives. So do Calyphas, Callapine, Orcanes, and Olympia, in Part Two. In Part One, Marlowe takes pains to emphasise Tamburlaine's generosity and his probity:

> Not all the gold in India's wealthy arms
> Shall buy the meanest soldier in my train.
>
> (*One* I.ii.85–6)

This dooms to failure Meander's plan to trap Tamburlaine by an appeal to greed. More generally, Tamburlaine's career is not characterised by cupidity. But his refusal of a ransom for Bajazeth is motivated primarily by an impulse to inflict humiliation on him. And generosity on the part of a continual victor progressively loses moral credit. In Tamburlaine's career, the gratuitous exercise of will is often creative, and can even seem nobly disinterested. But it can also come over as a perverse wilfulness.

That the slaughter of the Virgins is an atrocity is painfully registered by Zenocrate, and the Soldan of Egypt has already reacted with disgust to the reports of Tamburlaine's indiscriminate killing of stubborn victims:

> Merciless villain, peasant ignorant
> Of lawful arms or martial discipline!
> Pillage and murder are his usual trades—
> The slave usurps the glorious name of war.
>
> (*One* IV.i.65–8)

But the play will not allow us simply to endorse this judgment, however ringing it sounds. Tamburlaine is in part an example of heroic irruption out of a low social background—though the Soldan himself is by no means a corrupt emperor ripe for overthrow. Then again, Marlowe shows Tamburlaine's own impulse to slaughter being moderated in the course of Act Five—short of silencing his vaunts about killing, which are, indeed, the more blatant by contrast. And the Soldan himself comes to moderate his verdict, rather conveniently, on learning that Tamburlaine has used Zenocrate with 'honour': does the dramatist's wish for a harmonious close here blunt his critical recognition of a specious tidiness?

One means by which Marlowe prevents our taking a settled view of Tamburlaine himself is the persistent diversity of interpretation and purpose in the play's invocations of myth. It purges 'allusions to mythology' of the academicism and fixed moralising that perennially threaten them. They cease to be merely the docile illustrations of orthodox lessons such as the punishment of pride. They expand the physical and temporal scale. And they collectively enhance our awareness of the malleability of myth in the hands of human interpreters. Myth is, so to speak, reinstated as a ground of human invention. Tamburlaine is likened, by himself and by others, to a range of figures—Jove, black Jove, Mars, Hercules, Achilles, Phaethon— and the scale of such references is, in one view, validated by the scope of his own enterprise. He intimidates Jove; equally, he imitates Jove as an archetypal rebel. He rejoices in Jove's protection, as he rejoices also in being the *protégé* of Nature, Fortune, 'fates and oracles of Heaven', and his uniquely propitious stars. He proclaims himself Jove's scourge, his 'wrathful messenger'. At his death, he boasts that Jove snatches him to heaven, esteeming him 'much too good for this disdainful earth'. We give some imaginative assent to the claim—which is in other respects outrageous—that the death of Tamburlaine is the overturning of heavenly honour. To see him die is, in this view, 'To see the devils mount in angels' thrones, And angels dive into the pools of hell' (*Two* V.iii.32–3)—though these very lines could stand as one description of his disruptive life, not his death. Those who merely expect that aspiration will suffer the nemesis reserved for pride will find ample support at intervals in the text, from Zenocrate most tellingly, appealing to Jove as a power beyond Tamburlaine's province:

> Ah mighty Jove and holy Mahomet,
> Pardon my love, O pardon his contempt
> Of earthly fortune and respect of pity.

(*One* V.i.364–6)

Marlowe is, however, true to the play in refusing us the reassurance to be gained from seeing Tamburlaine's death in simple retributive terms.

For a play so concerned with extremes, *Tamburlaine* depends to a surprising extent on control. Measure, discipline, form, associate with pride of carriage and bearing, by way of the *manège*. The management of arms and that of words are seen,

in the idealised view, as cognate skills. We may move from
Zenocrate's description of the beauty of her son 'Trotting the
ring, and tilting at a glove' (*Two* I.iii.39) through one account of
Tamburlaine's cavalry

> Upon their prancing steeds, disdainfully
> With wanton paces trampling on the ground
> (*One* IV.i.23–4)

to the assertion that

> every warrior that is rapt with love
> Of fame, of valour, and of victory,
> Must needs have beauty beat on his conceits.
> (*One* V.i.180–2)

In these last lines, the pacing and balancing of stress carry and
authenticate the insight we are being offered. Metre and syntax,
repeatedly in the play, become analogues of other kinds of
capability. They are the media through which various kinds of
schooled energy may beat on our conceits. Syntax maintains a
clear purpose and lucidity, for the most part, seeking to conclude
decisively in the sentence and the verse paragraph. Metre
achieves, almost unfailingly, an integrity of pace and rhythm
through successive lines, with memorable announcements enabled to spring naturally from the firm metrical context. As
Marlowe, in *Tamburlaine*, seldom elides a syllable (even at the
beginning or the end of a speech) and seldom introduces an
Alexandrine, the iambic pentameter is the controlling metrical
paradigm. But the 'mighty line' has three or four stresses as
often as five, and our hearing learns to recognise the beat of
several distinct kinds of stress pattern.[141] Readers will 'scan' the
lines variously, but perhaps some broad distinctions will stand.

Three-stress lines persistently terminate on the mitigating
cadences of dactyls, which are apt to convey a savoured elation,
or a dancing verve, or a lingering poignancy:

> To Babylon, my lords, to Babylon!   (*Two* IV.iii.133)
> Now Hell is fairer than Elysium.   (*Two* IV.ii.87)
> And ride in triumph through Persepolis.
> (*One* II.v.49, 50, 54)
> Usumcasane and Theridamas.   (*One* II.v.52)

Four-stress lines often offer a more emphatic variant of this:

> For Will and Shall best fitteth Tamburlaine.
> *(One* III.iii.41)
> That nobly must admit necessity.   *(Two* V.iii.201)
> To entertain divine Zenocrate.
> *(Two* II.iv.17, 21, 25, 29, 33)
> Behold the Turk and his great emperess!
> *(One* V.i.355, 358)

Sometimes four-stress lines with a similar ending begin with a strong syllable:

> Wanders about the black circumference.
> *(Two* IV.ii.90)
> Warring within our breasts for regiment.
> *(One* II.vii.19)

Again, the third of four stresses may be deferred by a trip of light syllables:

> Their minds and muses on admirèd themes.
> *(One* V.i.164)
> Whose beams illuminate the lamps of heaven.
> *(Two* I.iii.2)

There are also, of course, five-stress lines of regular iambic pattern:

> The strangest men that ever Nature made!
> *(One* II.vii.40)
> The golden ball of heaven's eternal fire.   *(Two* II.iv.2)
> Whose scourge I am, and him will I obey. *(Two* V.i.184)
> The scum of men, the hate and scourge of God.
> *(One* IV.iii.9)

Or there are five-stress lines with two stresses opening the line, and the fifth held back to the end:

> Blush, heaven, that gave them honour at their birth.
> *(One* V.i.351)
> Must needs have beauty beat on his conceits.
> *(One* V.i.182)

And perhaps the play's most deviant metrical line—some six stresses:

> Stoop, villain, stoop, stoop, for so he bids.
>
> (*One* IV.ii.22)

The play draws extensively on a mystique of naming and of number. A sonorous roll-call of proper names, or their chiming returns in positions of metrical emphasis, can be felt as the primal poetic act. The name 'Tamburlaine' itself seeks the place of stress at line-endings, even in the mouths of his detractors. 'Zenocrate', similarly, recapitulates the accents of that softer music which is one (often denied) mode of feeling open to Tamburlaine himself. 'Triple world', 'triple moat', threefold stage groupings, a choric lament with three speakers: the play's mystique works for speech and for stage spectacle, for celestial, infernal, and terrestrial worlds. It has, of course, very important things to say about knowing and imagining. Conquest is, in one view, a means of knowing what has, in anticipation, already been vividly imagined. It seeks in the discoverable world what, as a dream landscape, is without spatial boundaries. The play does not tell us that what is found disappoints expectation; but clearly, the quest for the actual embodiment of an infinite possibility is at once admirable and self-contradictory. Conquest is celebrated as a means of making clear the newly known:

> I will confute those blind geographers
> That make a triple region in the world,
> Excluding regions which I mean to trace,
> And with this pen reduce them to a map.
>
> (*One* IV.iv.77–80)

In Tamburlaine's conceit, the sword is the cartographer's true pen, the arbiter of meridians, refuting the boundaries and timidity of our extant maps, correcting ignorance, bestowing names. Known and yet-unknown, the world is of our own making (if also of our 'unpeopling'). Conquest, impelled (in the favourable account) by a thirst to verify the splendours of the undiscovered, is creatively inquisitive—to search 'all corners of the new-found world'. Tamburlaine's fleet is to circumnavigate the globe, pioneering canals, trading and policing. A map is to terrestrial wonder what an image is to imagined worlds. And thirst for experience can, in this play, be at once amply gratified and insatiable: attainment feeds and 'famishes the craving'. The play excites disdain of limits but brings them, in conclusion, poignantly to bear: 'And shall I die, and this unconquered?' (*Two* V.iii.150, 158).

The insistent characterisation of enterprise through the be-haviour of metre and rhythm matches the explicit assertion of the aspiring will. When Theridamas remarks 'You see, my lord, what working words he hath' (*One* II.iii.25) we have been hearing Tamburlaine say

> And with our sun-bright armour as we march
> We'll chase the stars from heaven and dim their eyes
> That stand and muse on our admirèd arms.
>
> (*One* II.iii.22–4)

The lines have a sustained rhythmic impulse, but only the second has a thoroughly iambic feel. Each of the lines ends on a masculine stress, but the syntax builds up an expectation of climax which is answered to in the slowed four stresses of the last line. It is easy to multiply examples of such control. For instance, open vowels offering a chime of assonance which feels true to the general impression of dilated awareness and ecstatic homage:

> The crystal springs whose taste illuminates
> Refinèd eyes with an eternal sight,
> Like trièd silver runs through Paradise
> To entertain divine Zenocrate   (*Two* II.iv.22–5)

Such things characterise Tamburlaine, however, without silencing dissenting voices. He *can* seem no more than his style. The impression is sometimes given that his rhythms take their cue from *any* stimulus, that his enterprise is wordy. Tambur-laine himself, we may feel, not just the stars, gazes at his fantasy image.

The Virgins killed, and their 'slaughtered carcasses' reported hoisted on the city walls (a barbarism that will be *staged* in Part

Two), Tamburlaine sends his army in to sack the city. He is now for the first time absenting himself from the military action, a dramatic moment matched in significance in Part Two when he first kills on stage with his own hands. His long and unique soliloquy gives a further dimension to that 'very melancholy' aspect with which this long scene began. Zenocrate is offstage until later in the scene, when she will herself cry out against the murder of the Virgins and the desecration of Damascus:

> Thy streets strowed with dissevered joints of men
> And wounded bodies gasping yet for life. (*One* V.i.323-4)

But it is not such thoughts as these that provoke Tamburlaine's soliloquy, even in the immediate context of his being told that the slaughter is under way. He is moved by the sense of Zenocrate's grief—or, rather, of her beauty in grief. The attention he pays to mortal beauty as a source of delight able to turn away anger, even assuaging the wrath of the gods, recalls Tamburlaine's own eulogy of Zenocrate in Act Three as one

> Whose eyes are brighter than the lamps of heaven,
> And speech more pleasant than sweet harmony;
> That with thy looks canst clear the darkened sky
> And calm the rage of thund'ring Jupiter.
>
> (*One* III.iii.120-3)

When Tamburlaine spoke these lines—to register another discrepancy—Zenocrate was about to be left to exchange insults with Zabina. She was, later, a ready enough participant in the malignant mirth at the banquet, until moved to express her grief and fear in lines that carry the true voice of feeling in a context of jokes about the rival aesthetics of torture and music. Her plea is prefaced by a line that, with startling simplicity, clarifies our consternation at Tamburlaine's callousness: 'If any love remain in you, my lord . . .' (*One* IV.iv.70). His reply is that her father's life is not worth the loss of another conquest—but that if the Soldan surrenders he may live.

Tamburlaine's soliloquy affirms 'virtue' or manliness as the faculty which fashions true nobility. The rival claims of beauty are acknowledged, ultimately inexpressible though beauty may be. The warrior's love of valiance is fed by his apprehension of the beautiful; but because thoughts of the beautiful are 'effeminate', the warrior must subdue them as well as conceive them. The argument is perplexing, and this may be because the thinking behind it is necessarily intricate, or because the text is corrupt at this point, or because we are faced here with 'a vain effort on Marlowe's part to make some sense of the countervailing forces he has found in his account of Tamburlaine's mind and deeds' (Pendry–Maxwell, p. xvi). The speech is a very necessary attempt by Tamburlaine to reappraise his life of conquest in face of the grief of Zenocrate. As such, it has a direct bearing on our understanding of the truce which ends the bloodshed of Part One. Marlowe returns to some of the issues it raises in Part Two, when Tamburlaine and Zenocrate express different views about his protracted career of slaughter. In that such a career can itself be seen as driven by aspiration, the play has related it to Nature. We aspire not just towards some object, but because aspiration is natural; and the physiology behind this is a condition of conflict, of

> four elements
> Warring within our breasts for regiment.
>
> (*One* II.vii.18–19)

Plainly, Tamburlaine's conception of his enterprise alternately emphasises the existential and the ultimate, the turbulent and the serene. 'Climbing after knowledge infinite', the imagination has already 'comprehended' it, in the movingly constant frame of heaven itself, lit by the lamps of human beauty and intelligence. An earthly crown can be celebrated as an ultimate in itself, a 'perfect bliss and sole felicity'. This affirmation is given one placing by contrast with the phrase that looks towards higher glory, 'both our souls aspire celestial thrones'. It also becomes clear that the pursuit of felicity through earthly rule is the pursuit of an endless succession of crowns, not a final majestic fulfilment. There is, further, an opposed eloquence in Zenocrate's lines about the folly of setting store by 'slippery crowns' (*One* V.i.357). But Tamburlaine is consistent in claiming, at the approach of death, that he is merely changing one throne for another, being 'much too high for this disdainful earth'. And if his career illustrates in extreme form the clash between aspiration and fulfilment in human designs, the cautionary moralist is unlikely to read Tamburlaine's tragic folly with sufficiently resilient understanding.

Judgment of Tamburlaine reaches a climax late in Part One. To Zenocrate, the sack of Damascus calls in question nothing less than his love of her:

> Ah Tamburlaine, wert thou the cause of this,
> That term'st Zenocrate thy dearest love?
>
> (*One* V.i.336–7)

Words may be all he amounts to. For Bajazeth, earth had become hell: love and 'ruth', the springs of human sympathy ('effeminate' in Tamburlaine's terms, partly), are the victims of 'wrath and hate'. Destructive anger, fire, and the colours of Tamburlaine's siege ritual, find a disturbing reflection in the mad language of Zabina:

> give me the sword with a ball of wild-fire upon it. Down with him, down with him! Go to my child, away, away, away. Ah, save that infant, save him, save him. I, even I, speak to her. The sun was down. Streamers white, red, black, here, here, here. Fling the meat in his face. Tamburlaine, Tamburlaine! Let the soldiers be buried. Hell, death, Tamburlaine, hell. Make ready my coach, my chair, my jewels, I come, I come, I come!
>
> (*One* V.i.311–19)

What emerges most powerfully in the suicide scene is the grotesque despair of two human beings morally disfigured by the brutality they have seen and suffered. Its bearing on Tamburlaine's soliloquy is underlined by the contrast we are now offered between his and Zenocrate's response to the sight of the suicide victims.

In victory, being magnanimous to Zenocrate's father, Tamburlaine declares that she has

> calmed the fury of my sword,
> Which had ere this been bathed in streams of blood
> As vast and deep as Euphrates or Nile.   (*One* V.i.438–40)

The effect is curious: abstention from killing affirmed in lines

which convey a deep longing for bloody satiety. Zenocrate's
first lover has just died in her arms, and Bajazeth and Zabina
lie obscenely dead on the stage. Within a few lines, Tamburlaine
is boasting about the vast scale of his killing, keeping Charon
busy with his victims—an image that recalls Zabina's feeling
that earth itself has been turned into the Stygian terror:

> A hell as hopeless and as full of fear
> As are the blasted banks of Erebus,
> Where shaking ghosts with ever-howling groans
> Hover about the ugly ferryman
> To get a passage to Elysium.   (*One* V.i.243–7)

To Tamburlaine, the corpses of such victims are not objects of
pity, nor mementos of the slipperiness of crowns. They reflect
the true nature of (once again) his 'honour':

> And such are objects fit for Tamburlaine,
> Wherein as in a mirror may be seen
> His honour, that consists in shedding blood
> When men presume to manage arms with him.
>   (*One* V.i.476–9)

There could hardly be a more provocative climax to the attention Marlowe has paid in Part One to the mirror which the
conqueror holds up to reflect himself. And these very lines recall
closely Tamburlaine's soliloquy at its most aspiringly eloquent,
in its celebration not of the image of dead enemies but of poetry
itself as a medium in which men seek to express the beauty
which is ultimately ineffable:

> Wherein as in a mirror we perceive
> The highest reaches of a human wit.
>   (*One* V.i.167–8)

Part One ends with a sonorous *coda*, conducted with dignity
by Tamburlaine himself. Zenocrate, so recently eloquent about
earthly vanity, is crowned. Tamburlaine will bury 'with honour'
the broken 'Turk and his great emperess'—his phrase repeating
the refrain of Zenocrate's lament over them. We are left applaud-
ing, in some perplexity . . . Tamburlaine himself, or the play?
His followers are to don the scarlet robes of Peace: the colour

has oppressed us within the play as the emblem of blood and cruelty. Anomaly, or a stirring command over the necessarily opposed aspects of martial grandeur? Zenocrate had called for a 'league of honour', and this has been achieved. The diverse views of Tamburlaine himself—hero, barbarian, liberator, scourge of God, torturer, Hell-figure, favourite of Jove, rival of Jove—all hold some truth about him. He has affirmed strife as a norm of human living, within moments of Meander's baffled speculation about Tamburlaine as a monstrous incoherence:

> Some powers divine, or else infernal, mixed
> Their angry seeds at his conception:
> For he was never sprung of human race.
>
> (*One* II.vi.9–11)

Tamburlaine's conception of strife outdoes Meander's, but does not eclipse it. The dying Cosroe's words, a little later, offer a variant on the theme of what is natural, and what unnatural:

> The strangest men that ever Nature made!
> I know not how to take their tyrannies.
>
> (*One* II.vii.40–1)

Nor, at the end of Part One, do *we* know. But our doubts struggle to register themselves. The closing music is that of ritual celebration.

Part One was completed, it seems clear, as a self-sufficient play. This fact throws the sequel into relief as a creative and critical response by Marlowe himself to the way in which he had, for five acts, interpreted the Tamburlaine story. If he had not written Part Two, the first play might have seemed an evasive and short-sighted work which raised questions about tyrannical self-assertion without satisfactorily following them through; or it might have stood as a powerful enigma, ending true to itself; or as a bold invitation to admire a frighteningly capacious heroic image, rightly issuing in victory. Such alternative ways of reading it need a much more complex appraisal in the light of the five Acts of the sequel. Part One is the major 'source' of Part Two, not simply because Marlowe had already used up the main elements in the biographical material he was

using. The sequel pursues themes and relationships (especially
the relationship of Tamburlaine and Zenocrate) in a sustained,
deliberate response to the first play. The poetry of Part One, for
instance, had repeatedly thrown attention on to dissolution, that
of the world and that of the individual life, when 'our bodies
turn to elements'. Bajazeth and Alcidamus had afforded us
powerful emblems of death visited on a tyrant and on a heroic
lover. Tamburlaine's own encounter with death is dramatised
at the end of Part Two in relation to other deaths, in both Parts
of the play, and with particular reference to the developed theme
of the scourge of God, which had been announced in Part One.
Is punishment for hubris—a concept already present in Part
One—the right reading of Tamburlaine's death? Do the laws of
Providence, or of Fortune, or of poetic justice, or of all three,
require the scourging of the scourge? This question, too, requires Part One as well as Part Two for an attempt to answer
it.

Effects of mirroring being germane to the *Tamburlaine* theatre,
it is appropriate that episodes and characters in one Part are
mirrored pointedly in the other. Tamburlaine's early attack on
Cosroe, breaking their league, was not so much a betrayal as a
piece of overt opportunism. In sharp contrast we are now shown
Sigismond's 'Machiavellian' treachery towards Orcanes. Mycetes
finds a counterpart in Almeda, with his fussy ineffectuality,
eventually crowned as a mock-king, and he is also reflected in
Calyphas, effete like Mycetes and like him a trenchant critic of
warfare. Callapine's tempting of Almeda from his responsibility
to Tamburlaine contrasts with Tamburlaine's own winning of
Theridamas from Mycetes. The torture of Bajazeth finds a
counterpart in the bridling of the captive Turkish kings. Each
Part features a siege. The siege of Babylon in the sequel includes
the callous treatment of the Governor of the city, a casual oath-
breaking by Tamburlaine not matched by anything in Part One.
The courtship of Zenocrate by Tamburlaine in Part One is
reflected in the pursuit of Olympia by Theridamas. Within Part
Two, Olympia's noble killing of her own son stands as a striking
contrast to Tamburlaine's murder of his son, Calyphas.

Tamburlaine's first words in Part Two, heralded by 'drums and trumpets', movingly celebrate

> Zenocrate, the world's fair eye
> Whose beams illuminate the lamps of heaven,
> Whose cheerful looks do clear the cloudy air
> And clothe it in a crystal livery. (*Two* I.iii.1–4)

She and her sons form a *tableau* for this eulogy. But she herself protests against the martial element in this theatrical moment. The polarities of Part One have been promptly restated. Within a few lines, Tamburlaine is recalling Bajazeth's imprisonment, in the process of exhorting his sons to 'shine in complete virtue'. In doing so, he sets against Zenocrate's delight in their chivalric horsemanship and beauty—'Trotting the ring, and tilting at a glove' (*Two* I.iii.39)—the scowling rhetoric of blood thirst:

> sprinkled with the brains of slaughtered men,
> My royal throne of state shall be advanced;
> And he that means to place himself therein
> Must armèd wade up to the chin in blood.
>
> (*Two* I.iii.81–4)

This announces the mood in which ritual blood-letting, the murder of Calyphas, and the feeding of raw flesh to the 'pampered jades' can occur (recalling the gloating banquet of Part One).

Before his first battle in Part Two (the delay is telling), the 'scourge of God' faces severe suffering himself, in the death of Zenocrate:

> Proud fury and intolerable fit
> That dares torment the body of my love
> And scourge the scourge of the immortal God!
>
> (*Two* II.iv.78–80)

His experience here parallels that of the would-be scourge of the Turks, Sigismond. However, Sigismond dies on a noble recognition of the justice of his fall, seen as divine punishment of perjury. Tamburlaine's rage at Zenocrate's death contrasts sharply with her own dignified calm, though the perspective changes when, at the approach of his own death, he recognises that

he too 'nobly must admit necessity'. His raging over bereave
ment is aptly rebuked by Theridamas. But his lament at her
dying carries us beyond the reach of criticism based on mere
moderation.

'Black is the beauty of the brightest day.' This extravagant
figure carries a simple truth about the emotional life. Encounter-
ing a death, we encounter Death, and such feeling eclipses the
sun. This rhetoric has as its visible context the scenic 'discovery'
of Zenocrate dying at the centre of stage light and attention.
Celebrating the 'sweet and curious harmony' that greets Zenocrate in Paradise, Tamburlaine's words, with their limpid refrain—'To entertain divine Zenocrate' (*Two* II.iv.17 ff.)—
achieve in themselves a skilled and noble euphony. It is the
poetry of a grieving meditative ecstasy, a chiming clarity and
metrical firmness, lucidly articulate. Drayton's praise of Marlowe provides us with apt terms:

> Neat Marlow bathed in the Thespian springs
> Had in him those brave translunary things
> That the first poets had, his raptures were,
> All ayre, and fire, which made his verses cleere,
> For that fine madness still he did retaine,
> Which rightly should possesse a poets braine.[142]

Tamburlaine's 'impassionate fury' over the death of Zenocrate,
in the title-page's phrase, has perhaps two aspects: the Platonic
rapture or *furor*, and the Herculean rage which leads him to
devastate the place where Zenocrate dies.

Zenocrate calls for a consort of instruments: 'Some music
and my fit will cease, my lord' (*Two* II.iv.77). We may find
ourselves recalling, from Part One, the moment when Tamburlaine's taunting of Bajazeth broke against Zenocrate's sadness:

> How now, Zenocrate, doth not the Turk and his wife make
> a goodly show at a banquet?
> Yes, my lord.
> Methinks 'tis a great deal better than a consort of music.
> Yet music would do well to cheer up Zenocrate. Pray thee tell,
> why art thou so sad? If thou wilt have a song, the Turk shall
> strain his voice. But why is it?

> (*One* IV.iv.59–66)

And Bajazeth is likely to be in our minds, because Zenocrate's line 'I fare, my Lord, as other empresses' (*Two* II.iv.42) recalls her lament in Part One: 'Behold the Turk and his great emperess!' (*One* V.i.355 ff.). Zenocrate dies to music, composing herself to its harmonious close. Tamburlaine is left to try to evade recognition of the event—'let me think she lives'—and to seek an ample commemorative gesture. 'The arras is drawn' . . . but not until he has broken the scene's decorum with a violent outburst. High lament and impotent rage collide again in the funeral scene of the next Act, 'the drums sounding a doleful march, the town burning'. The fire of grief, that causes Amyras to say

> As is that town, so is my heart consumed
> With grief and sorrow for my mother's death,
> (*Two* III.ii.49–50)

is close in context to the vindictive fire of the scourge:

> Over my zenith hang a blazing star
> That may endure till heaven be dissolved,
> Fed with the fresh supply of earthly dregs,
> Threat'ning a death and famine to this land.
> (*Two* III.ii.6–9)

Part of that supply of dregs will be Tamburlaine's son Calyphas, 'Created of the massy dregs of earth' (*Two* IV.i.123), who had asked permission to renounce arms and follow Zenocrate.

'Let there be a fire presently' (*Two* V.i.177): Tamburlaine is about to burn the Koran. Throughout the two plays, fire runs from literal to metaphorical, from action to speech. Wildfire erupts in the derangement of Zabina. Basilisks flash. A burning town kindles portentous fiery dragons. Fiery impressions joust in air. The fires of Hell are borne by the Furies. Auster and Aquilon strike lightning from cloudy chariot clashes. A fatal illness extinguishes the sun, 'golden ball of heaven's eternal fire'. The death of a fiery spirit exhausts the living fire of heaven. Burnt scriptures dare God from Heaven—or Mahomet from Hell. Boötes drives oxen through the sky; Phaethon the sun's chariot; Tamburlaine his captive kings, scourging them with a metaphor turned all too literal, on the brink of absurdity. The correspondences (and the discrepancies) thrive on the vividness and scope of Renaissance meteorology as it moves from the sublunary to the celestial, impregnated with classical legend and myth. And above the zones of tumult, the 'glorious frame of heaven' offers a sanction for fiery aspiration—we take on the restiveness of the 'restless spheres' which we contemplate. Tumult and serenity are mutually dependent aspects of the natural creation.

To 'joy the fire of this martial flesh' is to burn, burn others, and be burned. Consuming passion is a norm of feeling in this theatre. Flesh is 'martial' both by nature (strife), and in the specially intense life of 'the jealousy [zeal] of wars'. In the name of this 'natural' energy, ironically, Tamburlaine sees fit to kill his own son. The fiery prodigy, seen one way, dignifies and clarifies ('illustrates') the norm, purging our humanity of the drossy 'earth' which clouds vision and clogs aspiration. Seen another way, he outrages nature, a 'monster' whose only distinction is an appalling elemental imbalance. Relatedly, the astrological and airy marvels of fire, which prefigure and reflect careers of conquest, are eccentric, yet they are phenomena of nature. They threaten the stable order and announce apocalypse, yet they behave according to observed patterns by which we know the nature of fire—and part of its nature confirms aspiration, ascending, associating aspiration with the high sphere of fire itself. In fire, the spiritual and the physical meet, the normal and the perverted, creation and destruction, the intensities of energetic living and the ultimates to which 'virtue' aspires. These contrasts and correspondences mark the poetry from page to page. Heroic zeal thirsts for imagined heavens; equally, it bears the fires of Hell, savouring the delights of the torturer. The disastrous career of Phaethon, 'Clymen's brainsick son', may be invoked to sanction a career that will 'think of naught but blood and war', and this bears a relation to the sense of Tamburlaine in Part Two as a madman—'the poisoned brains of this proud Scythian'. Alternatively, Tamburlaine can draw from the Phaethon story the lesson that what

was wrong was merely the upstart's failure to drive the chariot
well. Conquest requires that the charioteer thrive

> full of thoughts
> As pure and fiery as Phyteus' beams.
>
> (*Two* V.iii.236–7)

If health is here seen as a product of fire, we come full circle
from delight in power to delight in beauty when Tamburlaine
relates beauty to health through fire: Zenocrate's eyes

> shot fire from their ivory bowers
> And tempered every soul with lively heat.
>
> (*Two* II.iv.9–10)

In dying, Tamburlaine consumes his own body with a fever
which is expressive of his entire insatiable career. But his
dying is also seen as the breaking free of the fiery spirit from the
body which tried to contain it. His furious killing of Calyphas
had been aptly cursed:

> May never spirit, vein, or artier feed
> The cursed substance of that cruel heart,
> But, wanting moisture and remorseful blood,
> Dry up with anger and consume with heat!
>
> (*Two* IV.i.178–81)

But we also see Tamburlaine's death as fire's apotheosis. The
play could conclude aptly, as does *Dido Queen of Carthage,* with
a funeral pyre.[143]

An emblematic figure representing St Ambrose bears a
scourge in one hand, and a thunderbolt in the other. Dressed in
red, he expels the Arians from Italy, acting as God's arm against
heresy. Tamburlaine, to some extent comparably, is alternately
Jove and Jehovah, thunder and scourge. Driving the chariot
pulled by conquered Turks, he wields a literal scourge, and
declares this composite image of himself to be his emblem or
'figure'. Marlowe's sources report Tamburlaine's declaration
that he is the wrath of God.[144] The play carries many variants
of this, chiefly in Part Two, among them 'the scourge and wrath
of God' (*One* III.iii.44), 'the scourge of the immortal God'
(*Two* II.iv.80), 'the scourge of God and terror of the world'

(*Two* IV.i.154), 'the scourge of highest Jove' (*Two* IV.iii.24),

> The wrathful messenger of highest Jove,
> That with his sword hath quailed all earthly kings,
>
> (*Two* V.i.92–3)

and the scourge of

> a God full of revenging wrath,
> From whom the thunder and the lightning breaks.
>
> (*Two* V.i.182–3)

This last God Tamburlaine declares he will 'obey'. But the characteristic assertion of his role as scourge emphasises not his obedience to God, but rather his own peremptory will as a destroyer and avenger. Noting this, we are made aware of the distinction between the scourge seen as one who, inflicting suffering on God's people, is the unwitting instrument of God's purpose, and the scourge seen as one who identifies God's enemies and punishes them on His behalf. Often, Tamburlaine is not punishing or avenging a known fault, but inflicting punishment as an activity in its own right.

The ideas of the scourge and the wrath of God have a varied and emphatic presence in the Old Testament and the New. They afford signs of God's purpose at moments of acute human suffering. Within Marlowe's play, they provide images of the central figure, but many other conceptions of him compete for our credence. The God invoked varies in name and nature from passage to passage, as does man's conceived relationship to Him. Secondary characters also complicate our response to the image of Tamburlaine as God's scourge. Not only do they challenge it directly. They also become implicated themselves in dramatic events which have an explicit bearing on the idea that one God or another superintends human conflict in order to work His justice, however alarming the chosen circumstances and the means, and however resistant to our understanding His mystery may be.

An exchange between Tamburlaine and the vanquished Turks, early in Act Four of the sequel, demonstrates the complexity of the dramatic context. Tamburlaine executes his

own son, in the name of military justice. Calyphas is a dis-
honourable 'shame of nature'. But the 'Jove' whom Tamburlaine invokes here is not simply a God of honour and justice,
but the archetypal rebel whom Tamburlaine emulates with a
vengeance:

> valiant, proud, ambitious,
> Ready to levy power against thy throne,
> That I might move the turning spheres of heaven.
>
> *(Two* IV.i.116–18)

God, who might scourge impiety, is Himself celebrated as an
impious rebel. This is a characteristically abrupt change of
perspective on divine sanctions for human conduct. Tamburlaine swears by Mahomet, Jove's 'mighty friend', that he will
war on Jove in revenge for sending him such a decadent son as
Calyphas. Within a few lines, Tamburlaine is declaring, with
outrageous inconsistency, that he is Jove's regent, the manifestation of heavenly power and majesty:

> Villains, these terrors and these tyrannies
> (If tyrannies war's justice ye repute)
> I execute, enjoined me from above,
> To scourge the pride of such as Heaven abhors—
> Nor am I made arch-monarch of the world,
> Crowned and invested by the hand of Jove,
> For deeds of bounty and nobility:
> But since I exercise a greater name,
> The scourge of God and terror of the world,
> I must apply myself to fit those terms,
> In war, in blood, in death, in cruelty,
> And plague such peasants as resist in me
> The power of heaven's eternal majesty.
>
> *(Two* IV.i.146–58)

He will persist 'a terror to the world' until

> by vision or by speech I hear
> Immortal Jove say 'Cease, my Tamburlaine'.
>
> *(Two* IV.i.199–200)

The self-styled scourge both invokes and repudiates divine
authority, imitating God even in rebelling against Him.

It may be that the phrase 'such . . . as resist in me' is meant to set us thinking of one of the New Testament *loci* for the idea of God's righteous agents:

> Let everie soule be subject unto the higher powers: for there is no power but of God: & the powers that be, are ordeined of God.
>
> Whosoever therefore resisteth the power, resisteth the ordinance of God: and they that resist, shal receive to themselves judgement.
>
> For princes are not to be feared *for* good workes, but *for* evil. Wilt you be without fears of the power? do wel: so shalt thou have praise of the same.
>
> For he is the minister of God to thee for thy wealth: but if thou do evil, feare: for he beareth not the sworde for noght for he is the minister of God to take vengeance on him that doeth evil.
>
> (Rom. xiii.1–4)[145]

This essentially Stoic view counsels complete submission to earthly power, which is conceived of as the God-ordained wielding of justice. Good is rewarded, evil retributively scourged. The element of correspondence between this Biblical text and Tamburlaine's defence of his killing of Calyphas throws into relief the contrast between them. Magnanimous rule Tamburlaine in many cases repudiates—though he does display, at intervals, some respect for equity and mercy. Justice, for him, takes on an increasingly tyrannous and bloody aspect, though persistently in God's name. This illustrates the difficulties which a doctrine of absolute submission might lead to in face of an arbitrary and incoherent iron rule.

Scourging, not by the indigenous civil power, but by pestilence or other adversity, is frequently stressed in the Old Testament. God punishes dissidents with fire: 'When the people became "murmurers", it displeased the Lord: and the Lord heard it, therefore his wrath was kindled, and the fire of the Lord, burnt among them, and consumed the utmost parte of the hoste' (Num. xi.1). Jehovah's anger is continually imaged as flame:

> Beholde, the Name of the Lord cometh from farre, his face burning, and the burden thereof is heavie: his lippes are ful of indignacion, and his tongue *is* as a devouring fyre.

And his Spirit *is* a river that overfloweth up to the necke: it divideth asondre, to fanne the nations with the fanne of vanitie, and there *shal be* a bridle to cause them to erre in the chawes of the people.

And the Lord shal cause his glorious voyce to be heard, & shal declare the lighting downe of his arme with the angre of *his* countenance, and flame of a devouring fyre, with scattering & tempest, and haile stones.

(Isa. xxx.27–8, 30)

Isaiah carries the announcement of hostile invasion as the scourging decreed by God against his people:

O Asshur, the rodde of my wrath: and the staffe in their hands is mine indignation.

I will send him to a dissembling nation, and I will give him a charge against the people of my wrath to take the spoile & to take the praie, and to treade them under fete like the myre in the strete.

(Isa. x.5–6)

Tamburlaine facing the Turks, one might say, sees himself at times as the Assyrian might if he had read Isaiah and understood his own role in God's eyes. But which God?

With the extension of the 'scourge' theme into the secondary action of Part Two, we enter a thoroughly confusing territory of conflicting conceptions of God and of ethics, fought over by Turks and Christians. These secondary episodes provide a context for the consideration of Tamburlaine himself as scourge, and in particular for his experience of the scourging of the scourge. They provide a parallel confusion and, to some extent, criteria by which we may seek to judge Tamburlaine. The theme carries us forward to God's promise, later in the same chapter of Isaiah, to scourge the enemies of Israel in their turn:

Therefore thus saith the Lord God of hostes, O my people, that dwellest in Zion, be not afraied of Asshur: he shal smite thee with a rod, and shal lift up his staffe against thee after the maner of Egypt:

But yet a very little time, and the wrath shalbe consumed, and mine angre in their destruction.

And the Lord of hosts shal raise up a scourge for him, according to the plague of Midian in the rocke Oreb: and *as* his staffe was upon the Sea, so he wil lift it up after the maner of Egypt.

And at that day shal his burden be taken away from of thy shulder, & his yoke from of thy necke: & the yoke shalbe destroyed because of the anointing.

(Isa. x.24–7)

For Isaiah, God's anger is a measure of His mercy and love. Here, we might look towards Hebrews xii.6—'whom the Lorde loveth, he chasteneth: and he scourgeth everie sonne that he receiveth'. Within the Old Testament, we may turn to the occasion when God stays His arm after sending Satan as His scourge: 'And God sent the Angel into Jerusalem to destroy it. And as he was destroying, the Lord behelde, and repented of the evil, and said to that Angel that destroyed, it is now ynough, let thine hand cease' (1 Chron. xxi.15). 'Cease, my Tamburlaine' bears no such implication of divine pity and forbearance: the contrast with God's restraining of the angel is marked. But the notion of the scourger scourged, present in Isaiah, is vigorously explored by Marlowe, both in the second-ary action and in the two episodes when Tamburlaine himself suffers. The exploration is provocative and mischievous, informed by Marlowe's taste for the spectacle of human confusion and deceit, and his sharp ear for the accents of casuistry and hypocrisy.

Turks and Christians, equally enemies of Tamburlaine, meet to conclude a peace in the opening Act of Part Two. Sigismond swears by Christ, Orcanes by Mahomet. Our predispositions are engaged, and implicitly questioned. Sigismond is, reluc-tantly, persuaded by his allies that he should treacherously take advantage of a weakness in the Turkish forces. To do so would be to avenge previous massacres of Christians, acting in Christ's name to 'scourge their foul blasphemous paganism'. Confronted with this shock, Orcanes in his turn calls on the God of the Christians to punish their treachery: this would, as it were, cast the Turk in the role of Isaiah's Assyrian. Orcanes' invoca-tion of God's vengeance carries a true note of limpid religious

feeling for an immanent Godhead who is above the quarrel of
rival faiths:

> That he that sits on high and never sleeps
> Nor in one place is circumscriptible,
> But everywhere fills every continent
> With strange infusion of his sacred vigour,
> May in his endless power and purity
> Behold and venge this traitor's perjury!
>
> (*Two* II.ii.49–54)

This God is aligned, in the dramatic confrontation, with a
simple ethical principle. Sigismond himself interprets his own
immediate defeat as divine punishment. The episode stabilizes,
for the moment, as an emphatic demonstration of a congenial
broad principle, integrity. But Marlowe leaves a loophole, as so
often, for laconic dissent from the general assertion:

> 'Tis but the fortune of the wars, my lord,
> Whose power is often proved a miracle.
>
> (*Two* II.iii.31–2)

Orcanes, his probity established, looks for the defeat of
Tamburlaine himself. He conceives this as the working of two
metaphysical principles which are, to us but not to Orcanes,
strikingly incompatible. First, the 'old inconstancy' of Fortune,
distributing her favours by whim, and then the righteous anger
of a pitying Jove, 'Scourging the pride of cursèd Tamburlaine'
(*Two* III.i.38). In a drily perceptive line, Orcanes recognises
that Tamburlaine's career depends heavily on self-description:
he 'calls himself the scourge of God'. In this light, Tamburlaine
is a second (non-Christian) Sigismond, setting himself up in
God's name as an avenger. The battle between him and the
Turks is, therefore, expected by the audience to resolve the
questions of ethics and belief which the secondary plot has
generated and elucidated. The arrogant Scythian 'rails' and is
defied. He defeats the Turks, executes his son, and draws from
Orcanes yet another of the play's appeals to divine retribution:

> Revenge it, Rhadamanth and Aeacus
> And let your hates, extended in his pains,
> Expel the hate wherewith he pains our souls!
>
> (*Two* IV.i.172–4)

Divine hatred is here invoked as an antidote to the hatred induced in man by man. Tamburlaine sees in the victory a vindication of him as the scourge of those whom Heaven abhors. These are not specifically infidels here, but arrogant obstacles to Tamburlaine's career as God's minister. He claims that he scourges 'pride'. But the ethical demarcations between Scythian and Turk are confused. If anything, the ethical criteria favour the Turks, and Orcanes in particular carries a weight of audience approval and sympathy. The central issues were clear, if not unambiguously resolved, in the Orcanes–Sigismond episode. In this scene of the defeat of the Turks and the killing of Calyphas, clarity turns to belligerent confusion, principle into the hubbub of obsession and random assertion.

If Orcanes' lines of transcendent religious feeling are matched anywhere in the play, it is in the lines Tamburlaine himself speaks shortly afterwards at the death-bed of Zenocrate. And the context is, once again, the scourging of the scourge:

> Proud fury and intolerable fit
> That dares torment the body of my love
> And scourge the scourge of the immortal God!
>
> (*Two* II.iv.78–80)

The onset of his own sickness, in Act Five, occurs after Tamburlaine's own breaking of his word, given to the Governor of Babylon. The occurrence in itself recalls Sigismond's perjury, but only to enforce a contrast: nothing at all is made of this occasion as a case of perjury. It merely occurs. In the burning of the Koran, Mahomet is defied in the name of a generalised God of revenge, whose scourge Tamburlaine claims to be. This is not vengeance lighting on a specific offence, though of course we are anxious to gain some clear ground for moral judgment. Within minutes, Tamburlaine is desperately looking to wage war against the gods themselves. And he interprets his own death in conflicting ways. Now, it is seen as his elevation to a higher throne; now, as the triumph over him of an 'eyeless monster'. It is not shown clearly as the final scourging of the scourge. After all, one of the play's strongest intimations is that men's role in history may be no more—and for some, terribly, no less—than they assert it to be, including the assertion that they act on behalf of a God. Where Tamburlaine's 'Will and Shall' are imposed in God's name, we experience a frightening sense of the collapse of divine mystery into human arbitrariness —but without the confidence that God is there at all, other than in the words which different people use of Him.

Frequently, Tamburlaine's assertion of his wrath has the character of apocalypse. This moves us away from the context of historiography and the prophecies of Israel, towards the idea of the ultimate wrath. It is as if Tamburlaine were to bring each of his victims to face the two questions drawn from Kent and Edgar by the sight of Lear with the dead Cordelia in his arms:

> Is this the promis'd end?
> Or image of that horror?[146]

The wrath of God in the present prefigures His final wrath, which will precede the coming of grace. It is wielded by the armies of the Lamb in Revelation:

And I saw heaven open, and beholde a white horse, and he that sate upon him, was called, Faithful & True & he judgeth and fighteth righteously.

And his eyes *were* as a flame of fyre, & on his head *were* manie crownes: and he had a name written, that no man knewe but him self.

And he was clothed with a garment dipte in blood, and his name is called, THE WORD OF GOD.

And out of his mouth went out a sharpe sworde, that with it he shulde smite the heathen: and he shal rule them with a rodde of yron: for he it is that treadeth the wine press of the fiercenes and wrath of almightie God.

(Rev. xix.11-15)

For a tyrant to announce himself as the bearer of this eschatological terror does, of course, strain to breaking-point our tolerance of the idea that God avails himself of human scourges for His own high purposes. No redemptive consequence of his tyranny is offered by Tamburlaine. Indeed, the God associated with him as an apocalyptic figure is often, quite simply, the God of War. Alternatively, he is described as himself a God, with his own subordinate scourges:

> That treadeth Fortune underneath his feet
> And makes the mighty God of arms his slave;
> On whom death and the Fatal Sisters wait
> With naked swords and scarlet liveries;
> Before whom, mounted on a lion's back,
> Rhamnusia bears a helmet full of blood
> And strows the way with brains of slaughtered men;
> By whose proud side the ugly Furies run,
> Hearkening when he shall bid them plague the world.
>
> *(Two* III.iv.52–60)

The obscenity of this picture is emphasised by its being spoken in praise of Tamburlaine to a character whose humanity is outraged by his cruelty.

Battenhouse helpfully cites several examples of Renaissance interpretations of history which draw upon the idea of the scourge.[147] Calvin's *Commentary upon Isaiah* is particularly apt:

> Wherefore wee must not marvell if he lets loose the bridle to tyrants, and suffreth them still to exercise their crueltie against his Church: for the consolation is readie, to wit, *having used them as his vassals to correct his people, he will visit their pride and arrogancie.*

The victories of the Turks are, for Knolles and others, susceptible of explanation in the same terms:

> the just and secret judgement of the Almightie, who in justice delivereth into the hands of these mercilesse miscreants, nation after nation, and kingdome upon kingdome, as unto the most terrible executioners of his dreadful wrath, to be punished for their sinnes.

Marlowe has subjected this received idea to intense dramatic pressure, increasing the audience's need to embrace orthodox homiletic and apologetic convictions, but denying us the clear grounds of true belief, and the clear ethical criteria, which we would require. The need for such an explanation increases in ratio to the scale of human suffering which we contemplate, and this in its turn subjects the explanation to great strain. Marlowe has imposed on his audience a turbulent dramatisation of the chaos of human claims and counter-claims, acted out with explicit reference to the idea of God's scourge. The pressure upon the audience of this chaos becomes, for them, the rod.

Divine power is, in the play, very variously imaged; and this diversity itself appears sometimes as a chaos, sometimes as testimony to the vitality of man's mythologising of his world. The range is striking, even given the allowance we must make for some slackness of usage (such as 'Jove', on occasion, for the Christian God). Fortune, Nemesis, Fate, astrological determinants, the will of Jove, Mahomet, a sleepless God of righteous anger, a God of seemingly indiscriminate wrath. Such powers man might variously pray to, swear by, imitate, or defy. He might declare one or more of them his propitious guides, or his slaves, or the distant symbols of his thirst for knowledge and felicity. The focus shifts from tyrant to tyrant, from conqueror to victim, and from mood to mood within a single dramatic figure. Hell, Elysium, Helicon, Heaven, and Olympus have equal imaginative potency. An authentic poetry of visionary faith shares the stage with a blustering impiety and with a zestful assertion of the superiority of earthly joys to heavenly. Faith in Providence holds a mirror to a despairing conviction of doom. What may be Christian immortality to Olympia is immortality of pain to Bajazeth. The Tamburlaine party may be doomed to torment. Above all, the play shows how workable in human hands are religious sanctions—and how readily distorted, though we lack stable criteria for judging this.

Late in Act Four of the sequel, Tamburlaine seems secure in his arrogant gratifications. His speeches rise with an astonishing volatility from the context of his 'infernal cruelty' through the names of alluring earthly places, through broad self-projection —'I'll ride in golden armour like the sun' (*Two* IV.iii.115)—into total fantasy:

> Then in my coach like Saturn's royal son,
> Mounted his silver chariots, gilt with fire,
> And drawn with princely eagles through the path
> Paved with bright crystal and enchased with stars,
> When all the gods stand gazing at his pomp—

> So will I ride through Samarcanda streets
> Until my soul, dissevered from this flesh,
> Shall mount the milk-white way and meet him there.
>   (*Two* IV.iii.125–32)

The onset of Tamburlaine's illness is marked by a totally
different tone: to the incredulous question 'What is it dares
distemper Tamburlaine?' he can only reply 'Something,
Techelles, but I know not what' (*Two* V.i.218–19). Marlowe
has provoked us to read the event as a demonstration of divine
retribution incurred by an act of impiety and, on a longer view,
by a lifetime of brutal conquest. He has also, characteristically,
impeded our impulse to establish a simple, definitive interpretation. The next scene shows Tamburlaine's last opponents
vainly imploring Mahomet—whom Tamburlaine had impiously
defied—to give them victory. The varying modes and moods of
man's relation to such powers as may control his destiny have
been kept in active competition throughout the two Parts of the
play. But for the supervening eloquence (and rant) of *Tamburlaine*, there is little distance between these layered complexities and the anarchic world of 'profession' and expedience
in *The Jew of Malta*.

At Tamburlaine's death, as at the end of Part One, we are left
with a powerful current of (here, grieving) celebration in a context which offers powerful checks to the simple response. His
successor stands, overawed by the occasion, in the coveted but
untransferable chariot. We are left to reflect on what is implied
by the play as a whole about the nature of poetic justice, as that
may relate to conceptions of human destiny and to varieties of
religious belief and moral conviction. These questions are acti-
vated by a highly-charged theatrical style, and they will not stay
for an answer. To the end, Tamburlaine is living his own story
with his eyes on the great heroic and religious narratives of
Europe, history and myth. The curtain comes down on an expansive eulogy to which we are able to give some imaginative
assent, while feeling discomfited by the sense that the figure it
celebrates was a brutal, arrogant, and self-obsessed tyrant:

Meet heaven and earth, and here let all things end,
For earth hath spent the pride of all her fruit,
And heaven consumed his choicest living fire.
Let earth and heaven his timeless death deplore,
For both their worths will equal him no more.

(Two V.iii.249–53)

Only words, and misleading words. Alternatively, eloquent words in fitting response to a momentous occasion. We are no strangers, by the end of the play, to the conflict of opposed feelings about what we have been offered. But it will not do to meet this challenge merely by turning such feelings to account as a judicious wavering that reflects well on our open-mindedness.

7. STAGE REVIVALS

Tamburlaine waited some three hundred years for its revival in the professional theatre, after dropping out of the repertoire at some time in the mid seventeenth century.[148] Tyrone Guthrie produced an abridged and conflated version of both Parts at the Old Vic and at Stratford in 1951: Donald Wolfit played Tamburlaine, and Jill Balcon Zenocrate.[149] This version was staged again in 1956 at Stratford, Ontario, and in New York, with Anthony Quayle in the central role. There had been amateur productions of the play before 1951: at Yale in 1919, a condensed version of the text put together by Edgar Woolley and the poet Stephen Vincent Benet; at Oxford, Part Two on its own, in 1933; and another conflation of both Parts at Yale in 1946. Adaptations of the play have been produced more recently, by O.U.D.S. at Oxford in 1960, by the Tavistock Repertory Company at the Tower Theatre, London, in 1964, and at a Season of Elizabethan Drama in the Marlowe Theatre, Canterbury, in 1966. Glasgow Citizens' Theatre brought to the Edinburgh Festival in 1972 a production in which three separate actors shared the part of Tamburlaine in the course of each performance.

The implications which some of these productions held for our understanding of the play have been interestingly discussed by

Nancy T. Leslie, who finds in the range of theatre style and in the divergent principles of adaptation a rich source of critical material: 'At issue, of course, is whether *Tamburlaine* glorifies Machiavellian *virtù*, denigrates it, or asks us to suspend moral judgment; is the play immoral, moral, or amoral? No two *Tamburlaine* productions have pointed this question in the same way.'[150] Her account of the versions she concentrates on leads Miss Leslie to conclude that only Robert Pennant Jones's production of 1964 'asked for or expected a complex intellectual response' to the play.

In 1976, the National Theatre production of *Tamburlaine* convincingly established the integrity of the play, presenting at each performance a virtually complete text of both Parts.[151] Peter Hall directed the play in a production style essentially true to the many indications the text itself carries of Marlowe's conception of it. Pageantry, effects of *tableau*, formal groupings, firm and measured utterance, echoed and assisted the poetry at every point. Most significantly, the stage set and the visual style evoked emblematic and symbolic meanings boldly, not as a pious revival but as living theatre. A circular lighting grid picked out a matching area on the stage below it, on which a map of the world was projected before the play began, shading off into *terra incognita*. A red stain flooded the stage circle at moments of horrific conquest. A trap at the centre of this stage circle served a range of purposes, concentrating our attention on the ways in which extremes of experience impinge on each other: a raised plinth for Zenocrate in grief, a pit for cremations and the burning of the Koran, a tomb for Tamburlaine and Zenocrate as the chariot backed off stage at the end of Part Two. The white–red–black colour coding of Tamburlaine's three-day sieges was thoroughly observed; and it was supplemented by the adoption of a symbolic or evocative colour-scheme for each dramatic group—Turks, Christians, Egyptians. The text rings with 'triples', both literal and metaphorical, and the production responded with formal stage-groupings: three sons, three physicians, three followers of Tamburlaine, all grouped at the death of Zenocrate, and equally bold and simple groupings at other times. Maximum symbolic impact was achieved at such peak moments as the sack of Babylon: the governor hanging in cruciform posture formed a background to Tamburlaine pulled in his coach by vanquished kings wearing crowns of thorns.

These bold contrasts and expansive evocations provided a vivid context within which the play's human implications were explored. Here, the single most surprising discovery was the diversity of engagement among the characters and between those characters and the audience. Crucial, of course, is the response to Tamburlaine himself. Albert Finney drew his followers, and often the audience, into a delighted and mirthful partisanship with his rise to power. That rise was itself conceived of as an opportunistic and daring development by Tamburlaine of a style for himself, based partly on perceptive and irreverent mimicry of the grandeur he observes in others, such as Bajazeth. The more the audience is drawn into sympathetic alignment with Tamburlaine, the more embarrassing is their realisation that this is, in effect, complicity with a spirit of gloating atrocity and hubristic pride. Zenocrate, played by Susan Fleetwood, emerged as a fully conceived figure whose relation to Tamburlaine is complex and painful. Her entry during the battle for Damascus was closely parallel to the entries of Tamburlaine's victims themselves at the successive moments of hideous conquest. The production allowed no compromise with such painful implications as these. It confirmed how continually in Marlowe's play the grotesque impinges on the beautiful, the true heroic coarsens into ranting automatism, and mirth is chastened by our being brought to acknowledge the dark side of the joke.

8. THE TEXT

There are four early editions of *Tamburlaine*, published in 1590, 1593 (the year of Marlowe's death), 1597, and 1605–6.[152] Each carries a full text of both Parts of the play, printed in black letter. The first three are single-volume editions, and are in octavo form; the fourth, a quarto, has a separate volume for each Part, dated 1605 and 1606 respectively.[153] Ellis-Fermor's survey of the four early editions was particularly indebted to the work of Albrecht Wagner. She, unlike Wagner, had access to the one surviving copy of the 1597 edition, but she was able to confirm his conclusion that only the 1590 text had any substantive authority.[154] Subsequent study of the 1590 text has established beyond reasonable doubt that the manuscript from which it was printed was not of theatre origin. It may, indeed, have been a manuscript in Marlowe's own hand. The evidence for these two conclusions can be briefly summarised.

The printer named on the title-page of the first octavo declares in his Prefatory address that he has excised from the text some passages of low comedy which had enjoyed theatrical success.[155] These might have been written by Marlowe himself; but it is clear that the manuscript which the printer is working with fails to give precise and exact instructions at many points where a prompter, or those involved in staging and acting, would need them. The author himself would know what he had in mind; but an alert reader of the first edition might find himself puzzled at many points. These (not by any means all necessarily significant) include the following:

1. *Misnumbered scenes.* In One, the text reads IV.v for IV.iv; in Two, II.ii for III.ii, III.i for III.iii, IV.iii for IV.ii, and IV.iv for IV.iii. Also in Two, there is a false division 'II.i' at our III.v.57.

2. *Omission of scene divisions required by the divisions we are given.* We lack II.iv and II.v in Part One, and III.iv in Part Two. An editor will also feel justified in supplying the division II.vii to close Act Two in Part One, where characters enter after the stage has been cleared, and again, for the same reason II.iii in Part Two (which is followed not by a numbered scene but the 'Scaena ultima' of the Act). These scene divisions all occur at points where rival armies join battle, and in most cases we are told, or can reasonably infer, that the battle occurs wholly, or mostly, offstage: for instance, '*Sound trumpets to the battle, and he* [Mycetes] *runs in*' precedes Tamburlaine's triumphant entry where we supply the division at *One* II.v. In the other cases

where we supply scene-divisions, we also have to direct *Exeunt* before the battle. Omission of *Exit* or *Exeunt* is not at all uncommon in the 1590–1606 texts; but perhaps in these particular examples, there is scope for variation in the balance of onstage and offstage action. The fight for Balsera that precedes *Two* III.iv is heralded by an impressive volume of military noise, as indicated by the speeches just before it, and it may be that *they scale the walls* here as they are directed to do at the siege of Babylon at *Two* V.i.62.1. Curiously, where we divide for *One* II.vii, a despairing speech by Cosroe, including a direction in his lines to 'strike up drum' is followed by '*Enter to the Battell, and after the battell, enter* Cosroe *wounded,* Theridamas', etc. We could read '*Enter*' here as a simple error for '*Exeunt*', as Bowers does (i.105) after Oxberry, but perhaps Marlowe was thinking of battle being joined onstage and moving off before the defeated Cosroe is to re-enter. Marlowe uses offstage action, and action flowing across the stage, very tellingly in both Parts: battle noises hush while Zenocrate and Zabina, on stage, insult each other: Bajazeth is pursued across the stage before their eyes, and re-enters defeated. A supreme instance of such suspense is found in Part Two, when the dying Tamburlaine goes off stage to meet his last adversaries, leaving only the Physicians, it seems, to await the outcome with us, silently.

3. *Scene division according to two different principles.* The 1590 text offers divisions at five places on the principle that new characters are joining those already on. These occur at *One* V.i.63, and *Two* I.i.77, I.iii.111, I.iii.127, and III.v.57. These are entries of great dramatic impact and flourish—Tamburlaine coming in black to meet the Virgins of Damascus, his generals entering from victorious campaigns, and Tamburlaine surprising the Turkish kings on stage. The impact is not lessened, of course, if in the name of consistency a modern editor omits these divisions in which, it seems, Marlowe turns to the French system of scene division. We might perhaps suppose that a theatre manuscript would apply one principle of division throughout.

4. *Omission of required entry directions.* These concern both major and minor characters, and occur both in mid-scene and

at the beginning of scenes. Instances are: a Messenger at *One* II.iii.48, at *Two* V.iii.101, and at the opening of *One* IV.i and *Two* III.5; a Spy at *One* II.ii.38; citizens at *Two* V.i.23 and 37; soldiers and pioneers at the opening of *Two* III.iii; a captain and soldiers to open *Two* V.ii; Menaphon in the very first scene of Part One; a Basso at the opening of *One* III.i; Magnetes and Agydas at the start of *One* I.ii; Anippe, Zenocrate's maid, at the start of *One* III.iii; Zabina and Ebea at *One* III.iii.60; Zenocrate, Zabina, and Bajazeth in the notorious cage, at the start of *One* IV.iv; Almeda is not named at the beginning of *Two* III.i; Zabina at *One* V.i.202; Perdicas at *Two* IV.i.59; Maximus at the opening of *Two* V.i; Theridamas at *Two* V.i.147; Techelles at *Two* V.i.201.

5. *Omission of required exit directions.* We are left to infer the exit of Tamburlaine at *One* II.iv.39; of all the characters at the end of *One* II.iii, II.vi, II.vii, *Two* II.ii, and *One* IV.iv (perhaps envisaged as a *tableau* ending to the fourth Act); of all except Agydas at *One* III.ii.65; of all except the Virgins, left on stage to face Tamburlaine at *One* V.i.63, and all except Tamburlaine himself at *One* V.i.134; of all the characters except Bajazeth and Zabina at *One* V.i.213; of the Attendants at *One* V.i.195; of soldiers carrying the body of Calyphas at *Two* IV.i.168; of those who have stormed the city walls at *Two* V.i.62; of the Governor of Damascus, taken out for execution at *Two* V.i.126; and of Theridamas with the doomed Trebizond and Soria at *Two* V.i.135.

6. *Omission of directions for necessary stage action.* The reader of the 1590 text has to supply directions implied, more or less clearly, in the text: for the actual moment of death for Cosroe (*One* II.vii.52), Arabia (*One* V.i.433), the Captain (*Two* III.iv.10), and Tamburlaine himself (*Two* V.iii.248); for the caging of Bajazeth (*One* IV.ii.82); for the kneeling of Techelles and Usumcasane to Tamburlaine (*Two* IV.i.98); for the stabbing of Olympia (*Two* IV.ii.81); for the appearance of the hanging body of the Governor of Babylon (*Two* V.i.147); and for the bridling and unharnessing of Tamburlaine's human jades (*Two* IV.iii.52, V.i.130). It might be that Olympia's claim

to have burnt the bodies of her husband and son should be mirrored in stage fire (*Two* III.iv.36).

7. *Omission of speech prefix*. Orcanes is not named at *Two* I.i.25, nor Theridamas at *Two* V.i.49.

8. *Omission of names*. We supply the name 'Philemus' from Zenocrate's greeting to the 'Messenger' who is directed on stage at *One* V.i.377; and the name 'Magnetes' is Oxberry's conjecture for the character who appears in the octavo text merely as the prefix '*Mag.*' in *One* I.ii, where his entry at the beginning of the scene is unannounced in the stage direction.

9. *Omission of directions for entries or speeches 'aside', and for the speaking of lines to selected characters*. Examples will be found at *One* I.ii.106–8, 154–65, *One* III.ii.24 (the highly dramatic entry by Tamburlaine and others to overhear the treacherous words of Agydas), *One* IV.iv.94, and *Two* V.iii.177.

10. *Variable naming of characters in stage directions*. Bajazeth is directed on stage as 'the Turk' at the opening of *One* IV.iv. Orcanes (King of Natolia) is at times indicated as 'Natolia' or 'Nat', and Usumcasane varies between 'Vsum' and 'Cas'.

11. *Inexplicit directions*. Such expressions occur as 'He' for Tamburlaine (*One* II.vii.52, *One* III.iii.211, *Two* IV.i.90), or for Theridamas (*One* III.iii.224) or Bajazeth (*One* IV.iv.41), 'They' for Tamburlaine's followers (*One* III.iii.267, *One* V.i.120), 'his wife' for Zabina (opening of *One* IV.ii), and Tamburlaine's 'three sons' (*Two* III.v.57). At *Two* V.i.62, the phrase 'the two spare kings' occurs, perhaps the most striking example of vagueness.[156]

There is, then, general agreement that the printer in 1590 was not working from a theatre manuscript.[157] Perhaps he had Marlowe's original manuscript, or a transcript by Marlowe or another hand, or the manuscript of Marlowe's possible revision of the plays for publication. N. W. Bawcutt notes that the existence of intermediate transcripts has been questioned in general, but holds that 'the text of *Tamburlaine*, which obviously derives from a very neat and carefully written manuscript, might lend support to the theory'.[158] The text has the look of the writing-desk, not the theatre, not least in its Latin announcements of Act and Scene divisions. When we reach the end of the first play with the words '*Finis Actus quinti & ultimi huius primae partis*', we recognise that the author is decidedly concerned to emphasise the classical structure of the play—something which might well have disappeared in the process of annotation for the purposes of the playhouse.[159] Those few places in the text where we encounter minor omissions, or obscurity, or words which resist explanation, are not susceptible of explanation in terms of corruption through some process connected with the theatre, and may, as Pendry–Maxwell suggest, 'be the fault of Marlowe himself'.[160] And if the nominal printer, Richard Jones, is to be trusted in his assertion that he excised from the text some passages of inelegant low comedy, we must, it seems, suppose that these very passages were written by Marlowe himself.

Jones appears on the title page as the printer, but it has been conjectured that the 1590 text was printed for him by Thomas Orwin.[161] The style of punctuation maintained fairly consistently in this edition has attracted some attention. As Bowers remarks, 'the compositor with some frequency placed a full stop before the second Part of a compound sentence beginning with 'and' or 'or', before a relative clause, and sometimes even before participial clauses'.[162] This punctuation may, of course, be Marlowe's. It is described by Ellis-Fermor as 'an example of judicious rhythmical pointing', and Ethel Seaton identified in *Two* I.i.69–76 a particularly clear instance of rhetorical punctuation—one which had proved misleading to interpreters of Marlowe's geography in the play.[163] Admiring this mode of punctuation, Ellis-Fermor regretfully discarded it in favour of 'modern conventions of grammatical punctuation' (p. vi), and in doing so she could be said to have drawn too much attention to the (often light) line-ending pauses, and to Marlowe's parenthetical syntax. I have sought to keep the punctuation light, often allowing the integrity of the line and the building of the verse sentence to make their impact with minimal pointing. I have tried to find inoffensive modern equivalents for the original rhetorical stopping, as opportunity arose. Reading Marlovian blank verse, the ear seeks an appropriate tact of pace, breath-interval, and emphasis: which syllable to accent; whether a proper name has one syllable, or two, or three; what balance should be struck between the excitement of feeling articulation taking shape under rhythmic stress, and the recognition of conventional rhetorical figures being carefully worked out. 'Cosroe' sometimes, it seems, asks for two syllables, sometimes three; 'Fesse' two or one. I have supplied marks of accentuation not to suggest ponderous fidelity to scansion, but simply to assist the ear: it is irritating to have to repeat a line, even in silent reading, when one discovers that one has missed out a required syllable or placed an accent awry. I have retained contractions (e.g., 'flow'ry', 'thund'ring') where the metre seemed clearly to require them. I have modernised 'renowmed', treating it as a variant spelling of 'renowned', though at the cost of one etymological signal back to the Latin.

Extending the work of Albrecht Wagner, by consulting the newly available third octavo (1597), Ellis-Fermor established that the 1593 text and that of 1597 derived, independently of each other, from the first edition, and that the two-volume text of 1605–6 took the 1597 text as its copy. O2 (1593) corrects manifest errors in O1 at several places: examples will be found at *One* I.ii.67, *One* IV.ii.49, and *Two* V.iii.231. Much more often, O3 corrects errors in O1 which are missed by O2: for example, at *One* II.v.32, *One* V.i.300, *Two* II.iv.51, *Two* III.iii.13. On a few occasions, Q (traditionally referred to as O4) finds an error that has stood in all three previous texts: we may note *Two* II.iv.56 and *Two* III.ii.58. At one point, Q seeks to make sense of a line by conjectural emendation: finding 'snowy' in O3 as a description of Tamburlaine's arms and fingers, the printer felt constrained to try 'snowy-white' (*One* II.i.27); Dyce, editing the play in 1850, recognised in 'snowy' a word lacking only an 'i' to make an acceptable Elizabethan spelling of 'sinewy'.

Among the items of evidence establishing that Q was printed from O3, we may note: at *One* IV.iv.44, O1–2 read 'slice', but O3 misprinted 'flice', leading to the absurd 'fleece' of Q; at

One V.i.187, the 'cottages' of O1 and O2 appears as 'cottges' in O3, to which Q responds by printing 'coatches'; and Q leaves out altogether the puzzling 'insty' which is O3's error for 'lusty' at *One* IV.iii.4. Ellis-Fermor gives a statistical analysis of the relationship between the four early texts, as well as offering such examples as these.[164]

A modern editor will, of course, accept the common-sense corrections made in the successive octavo editions, even though O2, O3, and Q have no independent authority. I have not recorded minor variants, for which readers may be referred to the annotated old-spelling edition by Fredson Bowers. In establishing the present text, I have been reluctant to adopt an alternative reading from O2-3-Q even when it offers an arguably superior sense to the reading given in O1. I have not followed Ellis-Fermor's adoption of the O3 'apeece' for 'apace' at *One* II.v.86; for a similar reason, I have not followed most modern editors in their preference for Oxberry's emendation 'continent' for the O1-3, Q 'content' at *Two* IV.iii.81 (noting, by the way, that 'continent' gives the line eleven syllables, unusual with Marlowe in this play). I have collated the two surviving copies of O1, the British Library copy of O2, the Huntington Library's O3, and the Bodleian Library copy of Q.[165] As is usual in Revels editions, the textual footnotes record substantive editorial departures from the 1590 octavo, the copy-text. The editions of 1593, 1597, and 1605-6 have no independent authority. Where they provide the earliest correction of a copy-text error, this is recorded, and some other features of interest are noted, in particular those variant readings which have a bearing on the discussion of the descent of the text through the first four editions. The significant emendations and conjectures of editors in the nineteenth and twentieth centuries are noted. I have modernised i/j and u/v throughout, except when entering variant readings in the textual notes.

H. J. Oliver's discovery of the Oxberry editions of Marlowe means that we now date modern editing of *Tamburlaine* from 1820, rather than from the edition by George Robinson which was published six years later.[166] Oxberry, a vigilant reader of the text, began a process of making good deficiencies in the octavo texts which has been continued until the most recent editions. He supplied, for the first time, a list (albeit incomplete) of Dramatis Personae. He corrected manifest errors that had persisted through O1–3–Q for instance, at *One* I.i.15, *One* IV.iv.129, *One* V.i.243, *Two* Prologue 8, *Two* I.ii.19, and *Two* IV.i.108. He supplied the name 'Magnetes' conjecturally for the character known to us only by the speech-prefix 'Mag.'. He added directions for exit and entry at many points, supplied speech-prefixes here and there (e.g. *One* III.ii.1, *Two* I.i.25), supplemented the lists of characters needed on stage (*One* I.i.106.1, *One* IV.i.0.1, *One* V.i.377.1), and added other necessary stage directions (*One* II.iii.48.1, *One* II.vii.52, *One* IV.ii.82. He also conjecturally made good the lack of a word in some lines (e.g., *One* I.i.87, *One* II.iii.7, and *Two* III.iii.33).

Oxberry was followed most notably in the nineteenth century by Robinson (1826), Alexander Dyce (1850 and 1858), and Albrecht Wagner, whose work has already been noted. Robinson corrected more errors from the early texts (e.g., *One* I.ii.88 and *One* II.v.100). He also added necessary stage directions and names of characters required on stage. Alexander Dyce thought Robinson's edition full of 'the grossest errors' when he made use of it, and of some annotations in it by James Broughton, in preparing his own 1850 edition. Once again, we find necessary stage-directions being supplied: examples, among many, may be found at *One* II.ii.38.1, *One* II.v.104, *One* V.i.120.1, *Two* IV.i.59.1, and *Two* V.i.177. Dyce also finds more omissions of names from stage-directions: e.g., at *One* III.iii.0.2 and *One* IV.iv.0.2–4. And Dyce offers several influential conjectural readings, sometimes after Broughton: examples occur at *One* III.iii.158 (a much-discussed, possibly corrupt, line), *One* III.iii.213, and *Two* II.i.47. Manuscript notes by J. P. Collier in his copy of the 1850 Dyce edition of the play are also of interest.[167]

Stringent study of the descent of the text through the four octavo editions begins with Wagner, and is supplemented most effectively by Ellis-Fermor, whose scholarly text, extensive annotation, and ranging study of Marlowe's sources and his allusions have provided the working basis of most subsequent editions, including the present one. Any editor avails himself, properly enough, of the scholarly work of his predecessors and contemporaries; he does so with a continuous awareness of indebtedness. Perhaps the editions which have been most helpful for my particular purpose have been, after Ellis-Fermor's, those by Leo Kirschbaum (1962), Tatiana M. Woolf (1964), Fredson Bowers (1973), and E. D. Pendry and J. C. Maxwell (1976).[168] A fuller acknowledgment of the work of J. C. Maxwell may be found in the Preface.

NOTES TO INTRODUCTION

1 See, for instance, J. L. Hotson, *The Death of Christopher Marlowe* (London, 1925), C. F. Tucker Brooke, *The Life of Marlowe and The Tragedy of Dido Queen of Carthage* (London, 1930), F. S. Boas, *Christopher Marlowe: a Biographical and Critical Study* (Oxford, 1940, rev. 1953). Pendry–Maxwell provide a very useful Chronology of Documents, pp. xxvii–xxix.

2 E.g. L. C. Knights, 'The Strange Case of Christopher Marlowe', *Further Explorations* (London, 1965), pp. 75–98.

3 Marlowe, *Doctor Faustus*, ed. John D. Jump (London, 1962), pp. xix–xxiii.

4 William Urry, 'Marlowe and Canterbury', *T.L.S.*, 13 February 1964, p. 136.

5 For the full text, see *Dr Faustus*, pp. xix–xx.

6 *Perimedes The Blacke-Smith* (London, 1588), A3–A3v, 'To the Gentlemen readers, *Health*'. On the context of the passage, see Greene, *The Scottish History of James the Fourth*, ed. N. Sanders (London, 1970), p. xxi. Variant spellings of Marlowe's name include Marlen, Marlin, and Merling.

7 *Greenes Groatsworth of Wit* (London, 1592), fols. D4v–E1. The passage veers characteristically from regretful admonishment to grandiose self-abasement.

8 The 'hereticall' document is Harleian MS. 6848, fols. 187–9: it is endorsed '12 May 1593 vile hereticall Conceiptes denyinge the deity of Jhesus Christe or Savior fownd emongst the paprs of Thos Kydd prisoner' and 'wch he affirmethe that he had from Marlowe'. Kyd's letter, written after Marlowe's death, is Harleian MS. 6849, fols. 218–219. For a fuller account of these documents, and a transcript of Kyd's two letters to Puckering, see Arthur Freeman, *Thomas Kyd: Facts and Problems* (Oxford, 1967), pp. 26–37, 181–3. Freeman sees Henry Radcliffe, fourth Earl of Sussex, as the likely patron common

to Kyd and Marlowe; another possibility he discusses is Lord Strange, and we find Marlowe in January 1592 professing himself to be 'very well known both to the Earle of Northumberland and my Lord Strang' (see n. 11 below). 'From 1588 to 1594 the Admiral's Men operated in an amalgamation, the exact nature of which is unclear, with Lord Strange's Men' (Alexander Leggatt, *Revels History*, p. 101). The theatres were closed for much of the time because of plague in 1592–4.

9 Arthur Freeman, 'Marlowe, Kyd, and the Dutch Church Libel', *E.L.R.*, III (1973), 44–52. L. and E. Feasey, p. 421, refer to Gabriel Harvey's sonnet '*Gorgon, or the Wonderfull yeare*', which may be alluding to a conflation of Marlowe's and Tamburlaine's reputation in the line '*Weepe Powles, thy* Tamberlaine *voutsafes to dye*': the 'yeare' is 1593.

10 For a discussion and transcript of the Baines note, see Pendry–Maxwell, pp. 511–14.

11 R. B. Wernham, 'Christopher Marlowe at Flushing in 1592', *E.H.R.*, XCI (1976), 344–5. Marlowe may, of course, have been involved in this episode, as in others, as an undercover agent.

12 Pendry–Maxwell, p. 514. This note by Baines offers details about how Marlowe learned about coining.

13 See Freeman, *Thomas Kyd*, pp. 182–3.

14 Judith Weil, *Christopher Marlowe: Merlin's Prophet* (Cambridge, 1977), p. 171.

15 See n. 166 below. Much material relevant to this Introduction will be found in *Marlowe: The Critical Heritage 1588–1896* (London, 1979), ed. Millar Maclure.

16 Dyce 1, p. viii.

17 Robinson, I.xx.

18 *The Famous Tragedy of The Rich Jew of Malta* (London, 1633), fol. A4v. See *Jew of Malta*, ed. Bawcutt, p. 193.

19 *The Arraignement of the Whole Creature, At the Barre of Religion, Reason, and Experience*, p. 240. Noted by Hallett Smith, 'Tamburlaine and the Renaissance', *Elizabethan Studies and Other Essays in Honor of George F. Reynolds* (Boulder, Colo., 1945), pp. 130–1.

20 See p. 3 above.

21 See p. 5 above.

22 See Warton, *History of English Poetry* (London, 1778–81), iii.392; F. Kirkham, *A True, perfect and exact Catalogue of all [the plays] that were ever yet Printed and Published, till this present year 1671*. Anthony à Wood, *Athenae Oxonienses* (London, 1691), II.7; Langbaine, *Momus Triumphans* (London, 1687), p. 17. Much of the evidence is discussed in John Bakeless, *The Tragicall History of Christopher Marlowe* (Cambridge, Mass., 1942), i. 190–7.

23 'Christopher Marlowe', 1919, *Selected Essays* (London, 1932), ed. 1951, p. 121.

24 Alvin Kernan, *Revels History*, pp. 255–6.

25 C. H. Herford and A. Wagner, 'The Sources of Marlowe's *Tamburlaine*', *Academy*, XXIV (1883), 265–6. On the danger of assuming

that Marlowe saw copies of his source books for the play in the Matthew Parker collection at Cambridge, see R. I. Page, *N.&Q.*, XXIV (1977), 510–14.

26 Ellis-Fermor, pp. 17–61.

27 Cambridge University doctoral thesis, *Spanish Literary Influence on the English Drama to 1625* (Cambridge University Library Ph.D. 6099).

28 See Purcell, pp. 47–58; T. C. Izard, 'The Principal Source for Marlowe's *Tamburlaine*', *M.L.N.*, LVIII (1943), 411–17. As early as 1891, Emil Koeppel had noted the presence of the Tamburlaine narrative in *The English Myrror*: see J. C. Maxwell, *M.L.N.*, LXIII (1948), 436.

29 For extracts from Perondinus (*Magni Tamerlanis Scytharum Imperatoris Vita*, 1553) and Whetstone (*The English Myrror*, 1586) see Appendix. Wagner's 1885 edition of *Tamburlaine* (see n. 154 below) carried extracts from Perondinus and Fortescue.

30 III.iii.152–5. See *Poems*, p. xxxv.

31 A phrase from Eric Voegelin. See n. 35 below.

32 Ellis-Fermor, p. 31.

33 I give a working translation. For the Latin, see p. 327 below.

34 Ellis-Fermor, p. 40. Other local debts to Perondinus may be Marlowe's emphasis on astrological portents, and on Tamburlaine's being Scythian, and the references to Samarcand as his birthplace, the city he beautified and enriched, placed (inaccurately in both Perondinus and Marlowe) on, not near, the Jaxartes. See Purcell, pp. 53–4.

35 'Machiavelli's Prince: Background and Formation', *Review of Politics*, XIII (1951), 142–68.

36 Voegelin, *op. cit.*, p. 165.

37 Sydney Anglo, *Machiavelli: a Dissection* (London, 1969), p. 158.

38 *The Life of Castruccio Castracani*, tr. Allan Gilbert: Machiavelli, *The Chief Works and Others* (Durham, N.C., 1965), ii.555.

39 *Discourses*, I.xxxvii, tr. Christian E. Detmold, Modern Library (New York, 1940), p. 208.

40 Anglo, *op. cit.*, pp. 222–3. The whole of Chapter 8, '*Fortuna* and *Virtù*', has indirect interest for students of *Tamburlaine*.

41 *The Prince*, ch. xviii, tr. Luigi Ricci, Modern Library (New York, 1940), pp. 64–5.

42 See Irving Ribner, 'Marlowe and Macchiavelli', *Comparative Literature*, VI (1954), 348–56. Claude J. Summers, 'Tamburlaine's Opponents and Machiavelli's *Prince*', *E.L.H.*, XI (1974), 256–8, argues that Marlowe models successive kings opposed to Tamburlaine on *The Prince*. Whetstone mentions Machiavelli prominently.

43 Michael Quinn finds in *Tamburlaine* 'the essence of a new morality in which the obligation is not to any external law, but to one's own stated intentions': 'The Freedom of Tamburlaine', *M.L.Q.*, XXI (1960), 315–20.

44 Grattan Freyer, 'The Ideas of Machiavelli', *Scrutiny*, VIII (1939), 20. See also Moelwyn Merchant, 'Marlowe the Orthodox', in

Christopher Marlowe, ed. Brian Morris (London, 1968), pp. 179–92.

45 *Antonii Bonfinii Rerum Vngaricum* (Basle, 1543), ed. 1581, pp. 457–460. For an argument that Marlowe was influenced by Protestant apologetics in conflating Sigismond and the Varna episode, see Roy W. Battenhouse, 'Protestant Apologetics and the Subplot of *2 Tamburlaine*', *E.L.R.*, III (1973), 30–43.

46 Richard Knolles, *The General Historie of the Turkes* (London, 1603). See Hugh G. Dick, '*Tamburlaine* sources once more', *S.P.*, XLVI (1949), 154–66.

47 Knolles, *op. cit.*, p. 291.

48 Knolles, *op. cit.*, p. 292.

49 Knolles, *op. cit.*, p. 297. The presence of the phrase 'if thou bee a God' ('Christe, si Deus es') in Bonfinius is taken by F. P. Wilson to lend support to his protest against those who find in Orcanes' 'if there be a Christ' a disclosure of Marlowe's own scepticism: *Marlowe and the Early Shakespeare* (Oxford, 1953), p. 47.

50 First noted by J. P. Collier, *English Dramatic Poets and Annals of the Stage* (London, 1879), ii.496. Marlowe's version does not seem close to Sir John Harington's translation of Ariosto (published in 1591).

51 Seaton, 'Sources', pp. 395–6. See notes to *One* III.iii.164 and *One* IV.ii.2–3.

52 *The Faerie Queene*, I.vii.32. It was for some time thought likely that Spenser, not Marlowe, was the borrower; but the internal evidence seems conclusive the other way. See T. W. Baldwin, 'The Genesis of Some Passages which Spenser borrowed from Marlowe', *E.L.H.*, IX (1942), 157. For other possible echoes of *The Faerie Queene*, see notes to *One* V.i.259–62, 290–3, 302–3, and *Two* IV.i.188. More (sometimes tenuous) echoes are listed by Battenhouse, pp. 178–92. See also John D. Jump, *N.&Q.*, XI (1964), 261–2. Comparing Marlowe and Spenser in this specific borrowing, see R. Freeman, *The Faerie Queene: A Companion* (London, 1970), pp. 102–3.

53 The debt was noticed by F. C. Danchin, *Revue Germanique*, 1912. See Ellis-Fermor, pp. 8–10, noting that Ive's connection with the Walsingham family may encourage us to suppose that Marlowe saw the work in manuscript.

54 Seaton, pp. 13–35.

55 Seaton, 'Sources', pp. 385–401.

56 Weil, pp. 131–3.

57 See ii. F. P. Wilson observes that this is the first printed play text to name the company who played it: *The English Drama 1485–1642* (Oxford, 1969), p. 51.

58 On the probable identity of the actual printer, see Introduction, section 8.

59 See p. 111 below.

60 *A Transcript of the Registers of the Company of Stationers*, ed. E. Arber (London, 1875–94), ii.558.

61 See p. 2 above.

62 See E. K. Chambers, *The Elizabethan Stage* (Oxford, 1923), ii.135. On the possible link with *Tamburlaine*, see Chambers, *T.L.S.*, 28 August 1930, p. 684. See also George F. Reynolds, *The Staging of Elizabethan Plays* (New York and London, 1940), p. 47 n.

63 See p. 65 above. On the chronology of Marlowe's plays, note Louis Ule, *A Concordance to the Works of Christopher Marlowe* (New York, 1979).

64 *Henslowe's Diary*, ed. R. A. Foakes and R. T. Rickert (Cambridge, 1961), pp. 23 ff., records performances of the two Parts from 28 August 1594 to 13 November 1595.

65 *Shakespeare's Dramatic Heritage* (London, 1969), p. 122. Brooke, pp. 44–5, says *Tamburlaine* 'evidently got its start in the old inn-yards'. On inn-yards and game houses as outdoor playhouses accommodating booth stages, see Hosley, *Revels History*, pp. 124–30.

66 Ernest L. Rhodes, *Henslowe's Rose* (Lexington, Ky., 1976), especially pp. 68, 82, 134–5. Roger Warren suggests to me that early productions might have made use of hobby-horse frames and surcoats, such as were later used in masques.

67 On the 'now generally discarded concept' of the 'inner stage', see Hosley, *Revels History*, pp. 234–5.

68 *Shakespeare's Dramatic Heritage*, p. 127.

69 See n. 66.

70 See p. 41 above.

71 Waith, p. 66. On acting style, see John Russell Brown, 'Marlowe and the Actors', *T.D.R.*, VIII (1964), 155–73. Brown argues that here the actors 'must be prepared, after the exhausting demands of such powerful and simplified playing, to allow the audience to view the whole, to transcend every character's consciousness, to respond to Marlowe's world not that of his heroes. The "violent, stalking, astounding" performances must, in the last resort, be self-effacing' (p. 173).

72 See Thomas B. Stroup, 'Ritual in Marlowe's Plays', *Comparative Drama*, VII (1973), 198–221. The 'town burning' effect may have been achieved by means of a painted backdrop (Zucker, p. 68) or with fireworks (Wickham, *Early English Stages*, London, 1959, vol. II, part 2, pp. 286 ff., 296, 339–40). Pinnacles, mentioned by Tamburlaine, are typical of stage cities.

73 'Tamberlyne brydell', 'Tamberlynes cotte with coper lace', and 'Tamberlanes breches of crymson vellvet' are recorded among the possessions of the Lord Admiral's Men, 10 March 1598: *Henslowe's Diary*, ed. Foakes and Rickert, pp. 320–2.

74 'Christopher Marlowe', 1919, *Selected Essays* (London, 1932), ed. 1951, p. 122.

75 Kernodle, *From Art to Theatre* (Chicago, Ill., 1944), p. 151.

76 For full reference, see p. xiv above. On ironic contrasts between speech and the stage spectacle, see Douglas Cole, *Suffering and Evil in the Plays of Christopher Marlowe* (Princeton, N.J., 1962), p. 102 and elsewhere, and Nicholas Brooke, 'Marlowe the Dramatist', *Elizabethan Theatre*, Stratford-upon-Avon Studies 9 (1966), pp. 89–90.

77 G. Kernodle, 'The Open Stage: Elizabethan or Existentialist?', *Shakespeare Survey* 19 (London, 1959), pp. 2–3.

78 The Gascoigne analogue was first noted in Dyce's edition of 1850. See also T. W. Craik, *The Tudor Interlude* (Leicester, 1958), p. 96, M. C. Bradbrook, *Themes and Conventions in Elizabethan Tragedy* (Cambridge, 1935), ed. 1966, p. 96, and Dieter Mehl, *The Elizabethan Dumb-Show* (London, 1965), p. 43. On the possible driving of the chariot *alongside* the stage, see Zucker, p. 73, n. 19. Hallett Smith quotes a reference in Nashe, *Strange Newes* (London, 1592), to 'Tamberlaine drawne in a chariot by foure [not two] Kings': *Elizabethan Studies and Other Essays in Honor of George F. Reynolds* (Boulder, Colo., 1945), pp. 130–1. See further Wilson, p. 7, and Weil, pp. 137–41. On precise details of staging, see Felix Bosonnet, *The Function of Stage Properties in Christopher Marlowe's Plays* (Bern, 1978).

79 Zucker, p. 46.

80 'The Inheritance of Christopher Marlowe—I', *Theology*, LXVII (1964), 298–305. Other parallels suggested in this essay are between Tamburlaine and the image of Henry VIII making a footstool of the Pope, and between the crowning of Zenocrate and the coronation of the Virgin.

81 Zucker, p. 48. G. B. Shand refers me to Dekker, *The Wonderfull Yeare* (London [1603]), fol. D1: 'Imagine then that all this while, Death (like a Spanish Leagar, or rather like stalking *Tamberlaine*) hath pitcht his tents'.

82 Cf. 'triumphs, masks, lascivious shows', *Edward II*, II.ii.155. Eugene Waith finds in this Tamburlaine episode a 'burlesque rape of the Sabine women': 'Marlowe and the Jades of Asia', *S.E.L.*, V (1965), 229–45. Ulysses complains that Patroclus 'pageants us' in *Troil.*, I.iii.151. See *Ant.*, V.ii.206 ff.

83 *Virgidemiarum*, I.iii.16–17, 33–6. *Collected Poems*, ed. A. Davenport (London, 1949), pp. 14–15.

84 Bevington, p. 200.

85 Wilson, p. 28.

86 See Ellis-Fermor, notes to pp. 67, 104, 134, 149, 193, 222, 239, 241.

87 Ellis-Fermor, p. 170 n. F. P. Wilson notes that the only use of prose in *The Rare Triumphs of Love and Fortune* (1589), acted in 1582, is 'to represent the incoherence of madness': *The English Drama 1485–1585* (Oxford, 1969), pp. 124–5.

88 Wilson, pp. 26–7.

89 Bowers, i.75.

90 'To the Memory of my Beloved, the Author, Mr. William Shakespeare', 30; and *Discoveries*, ed. G. B. Harrison, Bodley Head Quartos (London, 1923), p. 33.

91 *Troil.*, I.iii.153–6, 159–61.

92 *Ham.*, III.ii.29–34.

93 *2H4*, II.iv.154–9. Cf. Marston, *Eastward Ho*, II.i.86.

94 Cf. Wilson, and Nicholas Brooke, 'Marlowe as Provocative Agent

        in Shakespeare's Early Plays', *Shakespeare Survey*, 14 (1961), 34–44.
 95 Alexander Leggatt, 'The Companies and Actors', *Revels History*,
        p. 115.
 96 E.S., *The Discouerie of the Knights of the Poste* (London, 1597), fol.
        C2v: Leggatt, *op. cit.*, p. 115.
 97 Edmund Gayton, *Pleasant Notes upon Don Quixot* (London, 1654),
        p. 271.
 98 *The Life and Minor Works of George Peele*, ed. David H. Horne
        (New Haven, Conn., 1952), p. 221. 'Poo', meaning 'poll', refers to
        the brazen head episode in *Alphonsus*.
 99 For a specialised account of them, see Clifford Leech, 'The Two-
        Part Play: Marlowe and the Early Shakespeare', *Shakespeare-
        Jahrbuch*, XCIV (1958), 90–106. See also Christopher G. Fanta,
        Marlowe's 'Agonists' (Cambridge, Mass., 1970), esp. pp. 12–13.
100 'The Calme', 33, and (a letter conjecturally dated 1608 or 1609),
        Evelyn M. Simpson, *A Study of the Prose Works of John Donne*
        (Oxford, 1924), rev. ed. 1948, p. 332.
101 Robinson, p. xix.
102 Swinburne, *Contemporaries of Shakespeare* (London, 1919), p. 9.
103 Ellis-Fermor, p. 55.
104 Leech, Introduction to his anthology *Marlowe: a Collection of
        Critical Essays* (Englewood Cliffs, N.J., 1964), pp. 1–11.
105 For full reference, see Abbreviations.
106 *Selected Essays* (London, 1932), ed. 1951, pp. 118–25.
107 Leech, *op. cit.*, p. 5.
108 For full reference, see Abbreviations.
109 Gardner, 'The Second Part of *Tamburlaine the Great*', *M.L.R.*,
        XXXVII (1942), 18–24.
110 Duthie, 'The Dramatic Structure of Marlowe's "Tamburlaine the
        Great", Parts I and II', *English Studies 1948*, pp. 101–26. See also
        Fieler, p. 80; Cole, pp. 107–8; G. K. Hunter, '*Henry IV* and the
        Elizabethan Two-Part Plays', *R.E.S.*, V (1954), 236–48. On struc-
        ture in relation to theatre practice, see Bevington, p. 206, arguing that
        each Part of *Tamburlaine* is of 'tripartite construction . . . upon which
        is superimposed the nominal division of the text into five acts'.
111 Cole, pp. 106–8.
112 Battenhouse, p. 16. See also Johnstone Parr, *Tamburlaine's Malady
        and Other Essays* (University, Alabama, 1953).
113 Ribner, 'Marlowe and Macchiavelli', *Comparative Literature*, VI
        (1954), 355. See Introduction, section 3.
114 J. B. Steane, *Marlowe: a Critical Study* (Cambridge, 1964), pp. 82 ff.
115 Waith, p. 86. Further references are to pp. 87, 62–3, 79.
116 Weil, p. 175. Tamburlaine 'is less like Hercules than he wishes he
        were': Weil, p. 108. Further references are to pp. 111, 107–8, 172
        (thrice), 142.
117 *Ideas of Greatness* (London, 1971), pp. 5, 64.
118 Clemen, p. 125. See Bradbrook, *Themes and Conventions of Eliza-
        bethan Tragedy* (Cambridge, 1935), ch. 6.
119 Clemen, p. 129.

120 Rhodes, *Henslowe's Rose* (Lexington, Ky., 1976). See Introduction, section 4.

121 Wickham, *Shakespeare's Dramatic Heritage* (London, 1969), pp. 121–31 (reprinted from *T.D.R.*, VIII, 1964).

122 For full reference, see Abbreviations.

123 George Riley Kernodle, *From Art to Theatre: Form and Conventions in the Renaissance* (Chicago, Ill., 1944).

124 'La Pensée de Marlowe dans Tamburlaine The Great', *Études Anglaises*, VI (1953), 332–45.

125 'Marlowe and Renaissance Self-Fashioning', *Two Renaissance Myth-Makers* (Baltimore, Md., 1977), p. 62.

126 *Jew of Malta*, pp. 11–15; 'Some Elizabethan Allusions to Machiavelli', *English Miscellany*, XX (Rome, 1969), 53–74.

127 See pp. 14–15 above. Eliot's essay ' "Rhetoric" and Poetic Drama' (1919) finds that '*Tamburlaine* is bombastic because it is monotonous, inflexible to the alterations of emotion' (*Selected Essays*, ed. 1951, p. 39).

128 F. P. Wilson, *The English Drama 1485–1585* (Oxford, 1969), pp. 133–50.

129 L. C. Knights, 'The Strange Case of Christopher Marlowe', p. 83 (see n. 2 above). Knights finds 'instances of increasing objectivity and critical detachment' in the play (p. 88), but his basic indictment is that Marlowe's work 'does not only enlist, it is partly at the mercy of, unconscious drives'. Cf. Steane, quoted on p. 37 above.

130 *Marlowe's Poems and Plays*, ed. M. R. Ridley (London, 1955), p. xiv.

131 Cf., for example, M. C. Bradbrook, 'The Inheritance of Christopher Marlowe—I', *Theology*, LXVII (1964), 298–305; L. and E. Feasey, 'Marlowe and the Prophetic Dooms', *N.&Q.*, CXCV (1950), 356–9, 404–7, 419–21. On a possible association of Tamburlaine with 'the apocalyptic Christ with flaming eyes' in Rev. xix, see Weil, p. 201.

132 See pp. 84–5 above.

133 Weil, p. 141. For a useful listing of recent work, see *Elizabethan Bibliographies Supplements*, VI, compiled by Robert C. Johnson (London, 1967). See also Jonathan F. S. Post, 'Recent Studies in Marlowe (1968–1976)', *E.L.R.*, VII (1977), 382–99, and T. P. Logan and D. S. Smith, ed., *The Predecessors of Shakespeare* (Lincoln, Nebraska, 1973), pp. 47–9.

134 On the colour sequence, relating it to Rev. vi.6–8, see John P. Cutts, 'The Ultimate Source of Tamburlaine's White, Red, Black, and Death?', *N.&Q.*, V (1958), 146–7.

135 For analogues and possible sources for the chariot emblem, see Robert Cockcroft, 'Emblematic Irony: Some Possible Significances of Tamburlaine's Chariot', *Renaissance and Modern Studies*, XII (1968), p. 49. About Tamburlaine's appearance at the siege of Babylon in *Two* V.i, Clifford Leech notes that there are references to 'vermilion' and 'bloody' tents although it is the last day of siege, and black is the ritual colour. 'This could be Marlowe's forgetfulness of his own symbolism; it could be a sign of incipient disorder in

Tamburlaine's arrangements': 'The Structure of *Tamburlaine*', *T.D.R.*, VIII (1964), p. 44.

136 Weil, p. 202. Ethel Seaton, 'Marlowe's Light Reading', *Elizabethan and Jacobean Studies* (Oxford, 1959), p. 34. M. C. Bradbrook, *Shakespeare's Primitive Art*, Proceedings of the British Academy, LI (1965), p. 216.

137 See *One* V.i.525 n.

138 Weil, p. 131.

139 Sidney, *Defence of Poesie*, ed. A. Feuillerat (Cambridge, 1963), p. 14.

140 See *One* III.iii.164 n.

141 See n. 130.

142 'To Henery Reynolds Esquire', 105–10. On *eroici furori*, as derived by Giordano Bruno from a Platonic background, see Paul Eugene Memmo, Jr., *Giordano Bruno's The Heroic Frenzies* (Chapel Hill, N.C., 1964). On Ficino, opening another element of affinity between neoplatonism and *Tamburlaine*, see P. O. Kristeller, *Renaissance Concepts of Man* (New York, 1972): 'The soul tends to know all truth and to attain all goodness; it tries to become all things and is capable of living the life of all beings higher and lower. In this way the soul tries to become God, and this is its divinity. It is, however, inferior to God, since God is all things, whereas the soul merely tends to become all things' (p. 10). Setting such convictions alongside *Tamburlaine* also helpfully isolates discrepancies. See, particularly for the relation to Bruno, J. R. Howe, *Marlowe, Tamburlaine, and Magic* (Athens, Ohio, 1976).

143 See J. P. Brockbank, *Marlowe: Dr Faustus* (London, 1962), p. 25.

144 See Appendix.

145 Biblical quotations from the Genevan Bible, 1520. I have modernised u/v, i/j, and expanded contractions. On the possible echo of Paul here, relating this and other passages in the play to the homilies, see L. and E. Feasey, *N.&Q.*, CXCV (1950), 8 ff. For more extensive discussion of Marlowe's echoing of passages from the Prophetic Books and from Revelation, seen as evidence of a burlesque intention, see L. and E. Feasey (as cited in Abbreviations). Imagery of hail and earthquakes, Tamburlaine's bridle and his staring appearance, is among the material related to the Scriptures, often with close verbal reference. 'Sometimes Tamburlaine appears to be not so much the Wrath of God, as the God of Wrath himself' (*op. cit.*, p. 420).

146 *Lr.*, V.iii.263–4. The 'scourge' concept is persistently present, perhaps in part through Marlowe's influence, in *H6*. Joan la Pucelle declares herself to be 'the English scourge' (*1H6*, I.ii.129). Talbot is the scourge of France, sometimes described in terms whose extremism may recall *Tamburlaine*:

> Is Talbot slain—the Frenchmen's only scourge,
> Your kingdom's terror and black Nemesis?   (IV.vii.77–8)

> Thou ominous and fearful owl of death,
> Our nation's terror and their bloody scourge!   (IV.ii.15–16)

The Countess of Auvergne mocks Talbot as a failed Colossus:

Is this the Scourge of France? . . .
I thought I should have seen some Hercules,
A second Hector, for his grim aspect
And large proportion of his strong-knit limbs. (II.iii.15–21)

Hamlet considers himself punished by Heaven in his role as Heaven's
'scourge and minister' (III.iv.172–5). The warring families in *Rom.*
are rebuked in lines that extend the dramatic force of the 'scourge'
concept:

See what a scourge is laid upon your hate,
That heaven finds means to kill your joys with love! (V.iii.291–2)

147 Battenhouse, pp. 108–13. The scourge concept 'serves to explain
historical calamities by showing that they are chastisements of sin
. . . and it assures tyrants that God is not helpless before their power
but that He will, when He has used them, destroy them utterly'
(p. 113).

148 Bakeless interprets an allusion to *Tamburlaine* by Abraham Cowley
to mean that it was performed at the Bull Theatre in, or a little
before, the year 1641; and he quotes Charles Saunders's Preface to
his own play *Tamerlane the Great* (1681) to the effect that the old
'Cock-Pit play' of this name is 'a thing, not a Bookseller in *London*,
or scarce the Players themselves, who Acted it formerly, cou'd call
to Remembrance'. Saunders does not know who wrote the Marlowe
play. See J. Bakeless, *The Tragicall History of Christopher Marlowe*
(Cambridge, Mass., 1942), ii.203, 244.

149 The text for this production was published in 1951 (London), with
Introductions by Guthrie and Wolfit. This edition carried a full
cast list, and such comments by Guthrie as his description of the
play as 'an orgy of sadism in the light of meteors, in the inflamed
power-dream of this genius that never reached maturity'. Comments
on this production may be found in John Russell Brown, 'Marlowe
and the Actors', *T.D.R.*, VIII (1964), 155–73.

150 '*Tamburlaine* in the Theater: Tartar, Grand Guignol, or Janus?',
Renaissance Drama, IV (1971), 105–20.

151 Text, edited by Peter Hall and John Russell Brown, published by
Rex Collings (London, 1976): full cast list included. For fuller discussion of this production, reference may be made to J. S. Cunningham and Roger Warren, '*Tamburlaine the Great* Re-discovered',
Shakespeare Survey, 31 (1978), 155–62.

152 There are two extant copies of the 1590 edition, one in the Bodleian,
and one in the Huntington Library. Two leaves (fol. A1–2) of a third
copy are pasted into the Huntington (Bridgewater) copy of the first
volume of Q (1605–6). In consequence, it was long thought that there
were two 1590 versions, an error corrected when Albrecht Wagner
demonstrated in 1885 that these leaves 'were no other than fragments
of the already known 1590 8vo' (Ellis-Fermor, p. 4).

The only surviving copy of the 1593 octavo belongs to the British
Library, and has been published as a Scolar Press Facsimile (1973),

with an Introductory Note by Roma Gill which states succinctly the reason for there having been, over the years, some who took its date to be 1592: 'There has been some tampering with the date on the titlepage, the last figure being blotted and partly erased. If it is a "2" it lacks the serif common to other 2s in this fount; if a "3" it lacks the lower lobe. Langbaine and bibliographers until the nineteenth century speak of a 1593 edition and make no mention of one in 1592, so it would seem that the later date is to be preferred.' See also Ellis-Fermor, p. 2.

153 Bowers, i.74, suggests: 'It is probable that no real interval separated the publication of the two parts; very likely the second came out near the end of 1605 and so was pre-dated'. Long referred to as an octavo, the edition of 1605–6 is correctly identified as a quarto by Katharine F. Pantzer, *A Short-Title Catalogue of Books . . . 1475–1640*, London, 1976. Pantzer lists the extant copies.

154 See Ellis-Fermor, pp. 5–6, 281–2. *Marlowes Werke*, ed. H. Breymann and Albrecht Wagner, vol. i (*Tamburlaine*), Heilbronn, 1885.

155 See pp. 28–31 above.

156 This has been thought a possible stage-manager's usage: see Wilfred T. Jewkes, *Act Division in Elizabethan and Jacobean Plays* (Hamden, Conn., 1958), p. 113.

157 e.g., Bowers, i.74; Jewkes, *op. cit.*, p. 113; *Tamburlaine*, ed. John D. Jump (London, 1967), p. xxv; Pendry–Maxwell, p. xxxvi.

158 *Jew of Malta*, p. 46.

159 See *Jew of Malta*, p. 47, referring to Jewkes, *op. cit.*

160 Pendry–Maxwell, p. xxxvi.

161 See Robert Ford Welsh, *The Printing of the Early Editions of Marlowe's Plays* (University Microfilms, Ann Arbor, Mich., 1964), for full bibliographical description. The collation is A–K^8, L^2. Part Two opens with a half-title on F3, prefaced on F2v by a woodcut figure of a man in armour, headed 'Tamburlaine, the great'. It is thought that a single compositor set both Parts of this 1590 edition, composing by formes from cast-off copy (Welsh, *op. cit.*, pp. 16–31; Bowers, i.73). Welsh gives details of press-corrections, which are not very material for this edition.

162 Bowers, i. 73.

163 Ellis-Fermor, p. viii; Seaton, pp. 31–2. See *Two* I.i.71–6 n.

164 Ellis-Fermor, pp. 281–2.

165 For three passages in the text, the Huntington copy is our sole primary authority. *One* IV.iii.43–6 and *One* IV.iv.0.1–2 are missing from the Bodleian Library copy because the lower part of D6 is torn away, and *Two* V.i.56–112 because K3 is missing. The margins of the Bodleian copy are trimmed very close, at the cost of some words and whole lines. The Bodleian copy has a corrected outer forme of B; the Huntington a corrected outer forme of A. The Bodleian Library holds a facsimile print of the Huntington Library copy.

166 See *Dido and Massacre at Paris*, p. 1. The title-page reads: 'Tamburlaine the Great, a Tragedy; By Christopher Marlowe. Part the First. With Prefatory Remarks, Notes, Critical and Explanatory. By

W. Oxberry, Comedian. London. Published for the Proprietors, by W. Simpkin, and R. Marshall, Stationers' Court, Ludgate-Street; and C. Chapple, 66, Pall-Mall. 1820.' A volume in the possession of G. B. Shand has the two Parts of *Tamburlaine* in this edition bound together with several other plays, clearly all separately published, under the general title 'The Dramatic Works of Christopher Marlowe, with Prefatory Remarks, Notes, Critical and Explanatory. By W. Oxberry, Comedian. London . . .', [n.d.]. The other plays are *The Jew of Malta*, *Edward II*, *Dr Faustus*, *Lust's Dominion*, *The Massacre at Paris*, and *Dido Queen of Carthage*.

167 See N. W. Bawcutt, 'James Broughton's Edition of Marlowe's Plays', *N.&Q.*, XVIII (1971), 449–52, discussing, among other things, the likelihood that Broughton caused to be printed, but did not publish, an edition of *Tamburlaine* in 1818. The annotated copies of Robinson and Dyce 1 are in the British Library.

168 On the Bowers edition, see Roma Gill, *R.E.S.*, XXV (1974), 464; *T.L.S.* correspondence, 8 February, 26 April, 3, 10, 17 May 1974; Lester E. Barber, 'A Recent Edition of Marlowe', *Research Opportunities in Renaissance Drama*, XVII (1974), 17–24. Among J. C. Maxwell's published contributions to the establishing of the *Tamburlaine* text are: *N.&Q.*, XXII (1975), 274–7, *The Yearbook of English Studies*, VI (1976), p. 234.

TAMERLANES TARTARORVM IMPER. POTENTISS. IRA DEI ET TERROR ORBIS APPELLATVS OBIIT ANº 1402

LAWRANCE IOHNSONN SCVLP:

The two tragical Discourses
of mighty Tamburlaine
the Scythian shepherd, &c.

PART ONE

[DRAMATIS PERSONAE

The Prologue.

MYCETES, *King of Persia.*

COSROE, *his brother.*

MEANDER ⎤
THERIDAMAS ⎥   5
MENAPHON ⎬ *Persian lords.*
ORTYGIUS ⎥
CENEUS ⎦

TAMBURLAINE, *a Scythian shepherd.*

TECHELLES, *his follower.*   10

Part One DRAMATIS PERSONAE] *not in O1–3, Q; first listed, in incomplete form, in Oxberry.*

---

2. *Mycetes*] not in history a king of Persia. Marlowe may be adapting the name 'Mesithes' found by chance in Bizarus' *Persicarum Rerum Historia*.

3. *Cosroe*] name of a Persian king of later date.

8. *Ceneus*] See *One* I.i.135.1 n.

9. *Tamburlaine*] The Tartar ruler Timur (1336–1405) was lame in his right leg—and had a damaged right hand and arm—perhaps through wounds received in 1363. In consequence, he was known as Timur-i-Lenk (Timur the Lame), a term used in contempt by his enemies. The western version of the name, Tamburlaine or Tamerlane, is often used in apparent ignorance of its derivation: Marlowe's hero has no physical disability. Timur came to real prominence about 1360, taking over Samarcand in 1366. After years of military campaigning, in India, Persia, Moghulistan, and elsewhere, including the sacking of Damascus, Timur's ascendancy reached its peak—to western eyes—when he caused Bayazid, the Ottoman Sultan of Turkey, to raise the siege of Constantinople. This was a dramatic intervention in the struggle between the Turkish and the Christian powers. In the crucial battle, at Angora in 1402, Bayazid was captured; and he died in captivity, perhaps by suicide, in 1403. Timur was a devout Mahometan; he took many wives. Marlowe's hero professes, and disavows, many allegiances; he is monogamous. Except for the scale of Timur's conquests—and Marlowe exaggerates these—there is little correspondence between historical fact and the 'heroic romances' of the western Tamburlaine tradition. Timur himself died, old and ill but still campaigning, at Otrar on the Jaxartes, in February 1405. See Hilda Hookham, *Tamburlaine the Conqueror* (London, 1962).

10. *Techelles*] name of a warrior of later date.

USUMCASANE, *his follower*.

MAGNETES
AGYDAS *Median lords attending Zenocrate*.

BAJAZETH, *Emperor of the Turks*.

KING OF FESSE   15
KING OF MOROCCO *tributary kings to Bajazeth*.
KING OF ARGIER

SOLDAN OF EGYPT.

CAPOLIN, *an Egyptian*.

ALCIDAMUS, *King of Arabia*.   20

GOVERNOR OF DAMASCUS.

A Spy, Messengers (including PHILEMUS), Lords, Soldiers,
   Bassoes, Moors, Citizens, Attendants.

ZENOCRATE, *daughter of the Soldan of Egypt*.

ANIPPE, *her maid*.   25

ZABINA, *Empress of the Turks*.

EBEA, *her maid*.

FOUR VIRGINS OF DAMASCUS.]

---

11. *Usumcasane*] a Persian king of later date, mentioned ('Usancasan')
by Whetstone.

12. *Magnetes*] conjectural name (see *One* I.ii.0.2 n.).

14. *Bajazeth*] See l. 9 n. above.

15. *Fesse*] Fez.

17. *Argier*] Algiers.

18. *Soldan*] Sultan.

20. *Alcidamus*] Given this name by Marlowe, the King of Arabia occurs
in his major sources, as does the Soldan of Egypt.

23. *Bassoes*] bashaws, pashas.

24. *Zenocrate*] Evidently Marlowe invented the name. There are some
inessential hints for her character in Chalcondylas. The Greek source of
this word, *zenokratos*, means 'the might of Zeus'.

26. *Zabina*] The name may be an adaptation of 'Despina', the title of
Bajazeth's wife.

To the Gentlemen Readers and others that take
pleasure in reading Histories.

Gentlemen and courteous readers whosoever: I have here
published in print for your sakes the two tragical discourses of
the Scythian shepherd Tamburlaine, that became so great a
conqueror and so mighty a monarch. My hope is, that they
will be now no less acceptable unto you to read after your   5
serious affairs and studies than they have been, lately, delight-
ful for many of you to see, when the same were showed in
London upon stages. I have purposely omitted and left out
some fond and frivolous jestures, digressing and, in my poor
opinion, far unmeet for the matter, which I thought might   10
seem more tedious unto the wise than any way else to be regarded—though, haply, they have been of some vain con-
ceited fondlings greatly gaped at, what times they were
showed upon the stage in their graced deformities. Never-
theless, now to be mixtured in print with such matter of   15
worth, it would prove a great disgrace to so honourable and
stately a history. Great folly were it in me to commend unto
your wisdoms either the eloquence of the author that writ
them or the worthiness of the matter itself; I therefore leave
unto your learned censures both the one and the other, and   20
myself the poor printer of them unto your most courteous

---

2. the two . . . discourses] *O1–3;* this . . . discourse *Q.*   4. they]
O1–3; it *Q.*   6. they have] *O1–3;* it hath *Q.*   7. were] *O1–3;*
was *Q.*   13. times] *O1, O3, Q;* time *O2.*   15. mixtured] *O1–2;*
mingled *O3, Q.*   19. them] *O1–3;* it *Q.* leave] *O1–3;* leaue it *Q.*
20. both . . . other] *O1–3; not in Q.*   21. of them] *O1–3;* thereof *Q.*

---

2. *discourses*] narratives, tales (*O.E.D. sb.* 4); process of actions or
events (*O.E.D. sb.* 1).

9. *jestures*] clearly associated with 'jest', though *O.E.D.* records this
form only as a variant spelling of our 'gestures'. On the nature of this
material which the printer claims to have excised, see Introduction,
section 4.

13. *fondlings*] fools.

14. *graced*] favoured, applauded (by the vulgar); closer to *O.E.D.* grace,
vb. 2, than to graced, *ppl. adj.*

III

and favourable protection: which if you vouchsafe to accept,
you shall evermore bind me to employ what travail and
service I can to the advancing and pleasuring of your excellent
degree.   25

Yours, most humble at commandment,

R. J.

Printer.

22. protection] *O1–2;* protections *O3, Q.* accept] *O1–2;* doo *O3, Q.*
26. humble] *O1–3; not in Q.*

---

22. *which*] i.e., the printer's dedicatory gesture.
25. *degree*] rank, station.
27–8. *R. J. Printer*] Richard Jones is named in the Stationers' Register
entry for the play (see p. 22 above), but the play was probably printed
for him by Thomas Orwin. See R. F. Welsh, *The Printing of the Early
Editions of Marlowe's Plays,* University Microfilms (Ann Arbor, Mich.,
1964).

Part One

The Prologue

From jigging veins of rhyming mother-wits
And such conceits as clownage keeps in pay,
We'll lead you to the stately tent of War,
Where you shall hear the Scythian Tamburlaine
Threat'ning the world with high astounding terms   5

---

1. *jigging*] may serve here generally for doggerel metre; more precisely, it could allude to the farcical 'jigs' used as interludes or end-pieces, in which the 'extemporall wit' of clowns like Tarlton or Kempe could be kept in pay. Marlowe's disparaging words anticipate many later attacks, but his own work includes, or is infiltrated by, scenes of farce and horseplay. See Andrew Gurr, *The Shakespearean Stage 1574–1642* (Cambridge, 1970), pp. 66, 113–14. Alexander Leggatt points out that the Admiral's Men, who acted *Tamburlaine* and other Marlowe plays, developed 'a vein of native comedy to balance the exotic heroics of Marlowe' (*Revels History*, p. 102). McKerrow suggests that this Prologue 'may well have been intended for a performance of *Tamburlaine* which succeeded an entertainment of a lighter sort, or the phrase may be merely a hit at a rival company of players'. He adds: 'The word "riming", though often used in its present sense, had also, more frequently, perhaps, a depreciatory meaning, being indeed simply equivalent to crude or bad verse' (R. B. McKerrow, ed., *The Works of Thomas Nashe*, London, 1910, iv.446). The early scenes of *Tamburlaine* dramatise the contrast between effete jingling and true eloquence. Cf. Nashe, *The Anatomie of Absurditie* (c. 1587–8): 'Nowe whether ryming be Poetry, I referre to the judgment of the learned: yea, let the indifferent Reader divine, what deepe misterie can be placed under plodding meeter. Who is it, that reading Bevis of Hampton, can forbeare laughing, if he marke what scrambling shyft he makes to ende his verses a like?' (McKerrow, i.26). For a different, equally explicit, declaration of artistic purpose, see Prologue to *Dr Faustus*, 1–8. On the Prologue to *The Wars of Cyrus*, written perhaps before *Tamburlaine*, perhaps later, announcing a similar break with theatrical fashion, see F. P. Wilson, *The English Drama 1485–1585* (Oxford, 1969), p. 148.

2. *conceits*] fanciful actions, tricks (*O.E.D.* 8b).

3. *tent*] The metaphor finds a literal equivalent in *Two* IV.i, and possibly elsewhere in the staging of both Parts.

And scourging kingdoms with his conquering sword.
View but his picture in this tragic glass
And then applaud his fortunes as you please.

---

6. *scourging*] an early hint of the 'scourge of God' theme (see Introduction, section 6).

7. *tragic glass*] The sense of Tamburlaine as a mirror, whether for rulers or tyrants or common men, is continually present in the play.

8. *fortunes*] for the plural form, see Glossarial Index.

Act I

Scene i

[*Enter*] MYCETES, COSROE, MEANDER, THERIDAMAS,
ORTYGIUS, CENEUS, [MENAPHON], *with others*.

Mycetes. Brother Cosroe, I find myself aggrieved
    Yet insufficient to express the same,
    For it requires a great and thund'ring speech:
    Good brother, tell the cause unto my lords;
    I know you have a better wit than I.   5
Cosroe. Unhappy Persia, that in former age
    Hast been the seat of mighty conquerors
    That in their prowess and their policies
    Have triumphed over Afric, and the bounds
    Of Europe where the sun dares scarce appear   10
    For freezing meteors and congealèd cold—

0.1. Enter] Oxberry; *not in* O1–3, Q.   0.2. MENAPHON] Oxberry; *not in* O1–3, Q.

Act I Scene i.] Scene divisions are in Latin throughout both Parts in
O1–3, Q.

2. *insufficient*] not competent, unfit. Mycetes' coy recognition of his
own inadequacy is apter than he knows.

5. *wit*] wisdom, good judgment. The word clings ironically to Mycetes,
both in this sense and in others, linking his lack of sense with his effete
relish of frilly effects ('a pretty toy to be a poet'). Cf. his regrettable (unwitting?) wordplay at l. 22, and Tamburlaine's taunting 'Are you the
witty king of Persia?' at *One* II.iv.23.

7. *mighty conquerors*] Cosroe invokes the memory of Cyrus the Great,
who founded the Persian Empire and established its boundaries from the
Indus and the Jaxartes to the Aegean and the borders of Egypt, and
Darius his successor, who encountered the freezing 'bounds of Europe'
in war against the Scythians.

9.] Cambyses 'triumphed over Afric', i.e. conquered Egypt.

11. *freezing ... cold*] sleet and snow. 'In Elizabethan usage the term
[meteor] included all atmospheric phenomena—that is, all natural processes that occurred in the region of Air: clouds, dew, winds, lightning,
comets, rainbows, and associated weather processes' (Heninger, pp. 3–4).

Now to be ruled and governed by a man
At whose birth-day Cynthia with Saturn joined,
And Jove, the Sun, and Mercury denied
To shed their influence in his fickle brain!   15
Now Turks and Tartars shake their swords at thee,
Meaning to mangle all thy provinces.

Mycetes. Brother, I see your meaning well enough,
And through your planets I perceive you think
I am not wise enough to be a king;   20
But I refer me to my noblemen
That know my wit, and can be witnesses:
I might command you to be slain for this—
Meander, might I not?

Meander. Not for so small a fault, my sovereign lord.   25

Mycetes. I mean it not, but yet I know I might.
Yet live, yea, live, Mycetes wills it so.
Meander, thou my faithful counsellor,
Declare the cause of my conceivèd grief
Which is, God knows, about that Tamburlaine,   30
That like a fox in midst of harvest time
Doth prey upon my flocks of passengers,
And, as I hear, doth mean to pull my plumes.
Therefore 'tis good and meet for to be wise.

Meander. Oft have I heard your majesty complain   35
Of Tamburlaine, that sturdy Scythian thief,

---

15. their] *Oxberry;* his *O1–3, Q.*   19. through] *O3, Q;* thorough *O1–2.*

13–15.] Saturn, 'the most powerful of the malefic planets', joins Luna's
vacillation. Jupiter 'would have mitigated more than any other planet
the evil influence of a malignant conjunction', and the lack of beneficence
from Sol and Mercury robs Mycetes of kingly stature and of wise eloquence (Parr, pp. 26 ff.).

16. *thee*] i.e., Persia.

19. *your planets*] your citing of astrology.

22. *wit . . . witnesses*] the inept wordplay contributes to the characterisation of Mycetes and helps prepare us for Tamburlaine's own imperious
command over words.

29. *conceivèd*] thought of, registered in the mind (*O.E.D. ppl. adv. 2:*
earliest entry). 'Conceit' and 'conceiving' become dynamic in Tamburlaine's enterprise: cf. *One* I.ii.64 n.

32. *passengers*] travellers. See *One* I.ii.70, and Shakespeare, *2 H6,*
III.i.129.

36. *Scythian*] 'The Scythians were actually at this time a branch of

That robs your merchants of Persepolis
Trading by land unto the Western Isles,
And in your confines with his lawless train
Daily commits incivil outrages,   40
Hoping, misled by dreaming prophecies,
To reign in Asia, and with barbarous arms
To make himself the monarch of the East.
But ere he march in Asia, or display
His vagrant ensign in the Persian fields,   45
Your grace hath taken order by Theridamas,
Charged with a thousand horse, to apprehend
And bring him captive to your highness' throne.

Mycetes. Full true thou speakest, and like thyself, my lord,
Whom I may term a Damon for thy love.   50
Therefore 'tis best, if so it like you all,
To send my thousand horse incontinent
To apprehend that paltry Scythian.
How like you this, my honourable lords?
Is it not a kingly resolution?   55

Cosroe. It cannot choose, because it comes from you.

Mycetes. Then hear thy charge, valiant Theridamas,
The chiefest captain of Mycetes' host,

---

38. Trading] *O2;* Treading *O1, O3, Q.*

---

the Tartar race. Scythia for Ortelius is the district along the north shores
of the Euxine (Black) Sea, just west of the Chersonese (Crimea), but was
also frequently used, as in classical cartography, of the whole of Central
and North-Eastern Asia' (Ellis-Fermor, p. 72).

38. *Western Isles*] possibly Britain, or the West Indies (as perhaps at
l. 166 n. below).

39. *confines*] border regions (*O.E.D. sb.*[2] 1).

40. *incivil*] barbarous (*O.E.D. adj.* 3: sole entry).

43. *monarch of the East*] The phrase returns with Cosroe's usurpation
of Mycetes' titles (l. 161), and becomes a focus for Tamburlaine's
ambition (*One* I.ii.184). Cf. *Two* III.ii.22.

45. *vagrant*] moving hither and thither (*O.E.D.* 5).

46.] On this and other alexandrines, see Introduction, p. 19. *Taken
order by*, for 'ordered', is an unusual construction.

50. *Damon*] The classical model of heroic friendship is ill suited to
Mycetes' decadent empire. The contrast is with Tamburlaine's sense of
collective loyalty and generosity: he invokes 'the love of Pylades and
Orestes' at *One* I.ii.242 n. In Mycetes' tone and sentiment there is an
anticipation of *Edward II.*

52. *incontinent*] immediately (*O.E.D. adv.*[2]).

The hope of Persia, and the very legs
Whereon our state doth lean, as on a staff   60
That holds us up and foils our neighbour foes:
Thou shalt be leader of this thousand horse,
Whose foaming gall with rage and high disdain
Have sworn the death of wicked Tamburlaine.
Go frowning forth, but come thou smiling home,   65
As did Sir Paris with the Grecian dame;
Return with speed, time passeth swift away,
Our life is frail, and we may die today.

Theridamas. Before the moon renew her borrowed light
Doubt not, my lord and gracious sovereign,   70
But Tamburlaine and that Tartarian rout
Shall either perish by our warlike hands
Or plead for mercy at your highness' feet.

Mycetes. Go, stout Theridamas, thy words are swords,
And with thy looks thou conquerest all thy foes.   75
I long to see thee back return from thence,
That I may view these milk-white steeds of mine
All loaden with the heads of killèd men,
And from their knees even to their hoofs below
Besmeared with blood, that makes a dainty show.   80

Theridamas. Then now, my lord, I humbly take my leave.

Exit.

Mycetes. Theridamas, farewell ten thousand times.
Ah, Menaphon, why stayest thou thus behind
When other men press forward for renown?
Go, Menaphon, go into Scythia,   85

---

66. *Sir Paris*] Sir was 'applied retrospectively to notable personages of ancient, especially sacred or classical history' (*O.E.D.*). Helen is 'the peerless dame of Greece' in *Dr Faustus*, xviii.23; and cf. *P.M.L.A.*, LII (1937), 904.

67–8.] banal proverbial sentiments (Tilley T323, 327).

71. *Tartarian*] Asiatic; became 'a cant word for a thief' (*O.E.D. sb.* A. b.); ?hellish (earliest *O.E.D.* entry 1623).

rout] attendant company; disorderly, tumultuous, or disreputable crowd (*O.E.D. sb.* 1, 5: E.A.J.H.).

74. *thy words are swords*] intensifying the proverbial 'Words hurt (cut) more than swords' (Tilley W839). The praise of Theridamas in these terms is part of Marlowe's studied preparation for Tamburlaine's entry; it is capped at *One* I.ii.227. At *One* I.ii.132, swords themselves are to 'play the orators'.

And foot by foot follow Theridamas.

Cosroe. Nay, pray you let him stay, a greater task
 Fits Menaphon, than warring with a thief:
 Create him prorex of Assyria,
 That he may win the Babylonians' hearts,   90
 Which will revolt from Persian government
 Unless they have a wiser king than you.

Mycetes. Unless they have a wiser king than you!
 These are his words, Meander, set them down.

Cosroe. And add this to them, that all Asia   95
 Lament to see the folly of their king.

Mycetes. Well, here I swear by this my royal seat—

Cosroe. You may do well to kiss it then.

Mycetes. —Embossed with silk as best beseems my state,
 To be revenged for these contemptuous words.   100
 O where is duty and allegiance now?
 Fled to the Caspian or the Ocean main?

---

87. task] *conj. Oxberry;* feat *conj. Malone;* charge *conj. Pendry–Maxwell;*
not in O1–3, Q. 89. Assyria] *conj. van Dam;* Affrica *O1–3;* all Affrica
Q, Oxberry.

---

87. *task*] Most editors adopt this suggested replacement for the word
presumably omitted from the 1590–1606 texts: the line lacks a syllable—
though 'greater' *can* have substantive status.

89. *prorex*] viceroy; first entry in *O.E.D.*

Assyria] The line as it stands in O1–3 is metrically just tolerable, and
compares with other nine-syllable lines in the play; Q makes the scansion
regular; but it becomes regular if one adopts, with Bowers, the emendation 'Assyria' suggested by B. A. P. van Dam ('Marlowe's *Tamburlaine*',
English Studies, XVI (1934), 97). He argues that there would be no sense
in creating a viceroy of Africa to placate Babylonians, observes that
Babylon was once under Assyrian rule, and adds 'Marlowe seems to
have had this period in his mind, for when writing about Babylon [*Two*
V.i.63 ff.] he mentions "th'Assirians bones" and "braue Assirian
Dames" '. The doubt lingers, however, because 'Africa' could, it seems,
include for Marlowe territories we now think of as part of Asia. (F.D.H.)
See l. 164, and *One* I.ii.16.

90–1.] Babylon and the Babylonian provinces in Syria fell to Cyrus the
Great in 539 B.C.

98.] Kirschbaum's stage direction '*aside*' is possible, though the line
has most point if it is heard by Mycetes without his registering its scornful
pointing of his unintended pun on 'seat'.

99. *state*] rank; and also, assisting the wordplay, the theatrical throne
on its dais (*O.E.D. sb.* 15, 20).

What, shall I call thee brother? No, a foe,
Monster of Nature, shame unto thy stock,
That darest presume thy sovereign for to mock.   105
Meander, come, I am abused, Meander.

Exit [*with* MEANDER *and others.*]

Manent COSROE *and* MENAPHON.

Menaphon. How now my lord, what, mated and amazed
    To hear the king thus threaten like himself?
Cosroe. Ah Menaphon, I pass not for his threats:
    The plot is laid by Persian noblemen   110
    And captains of the Median garrisons
    To crown me emperor of Asia.
    But this it is that doth excruciate
    The very substance of my vexèd soul:
    To see our neighbours that were wont to quake   115
    And tremble at the Persian monarch's name
    Now sits and laughs our regiment to scorn;
    And that which might resolve me into tears,
    Men from the farthest equinoctial line
    Have swarmed in troops into the Eastern India,   120
    Lading their ships with gold and precious stones,
    And made their spoils from all our provinces.
Menaphon. This should entreat your highness to rejoice,
    Since Fortune gives you opportunity

106.1. with . . . others] after Oxberry [All go out but Cosroe and Menaphon];
not in O1–3, Q.

106.2. Manent] They remain.

107. *mated*] abashed, daunted. Cf. *Mac.*, V.i.76: 'My mind she has
mated, and amaz'd my sight'.

109. *pass*] care. Cf. *Edward II*, I.iv.142, V.i.78.

113. *excruciate*] torment (*O.E.D.* 2, first entry).

114. *substance*] essence (*O.E.D.* 13): E.A.J.H.

117. *regiment*] rule, royal authority.

118. *resolve me into*] reduce me to, dissolve me into.

119. *equinoctial line*] the equator. Men from the southern districts
around the equator have advanced north into Eastern India, 'long the
wealthiest province of any Oriental nation that held supremacy over it'
(Ellis-Fermor, p. 74).

121. *Lading*] Loading.

123. *entreat*] persuade.

124.] With this sense of Fortune as giving political opportunity which

To gain the title of a conqueror   125
By curing of this maimèd empery:
Afric and Europe bordering on your land
And continent to your dominions,
How easily may you with a mighty host
Pass into Graecia, as did Cyrus once,   130
And cause them to withdraw their forces home
Lest you subdue the pride of Christendom!

Cosroe. But Menaphon, what means this trumpet's sound?
Menaphon. Behold, my lord, Ortygius and the rest,
    Bringing the crown to make you emperor.   135

Enter ORTYGIUS *and* CENEUS, *bearing a crown, with others.*

Ortygius. Magnificent and mighty prince Cosroe,
    We in the name of other Persian states
    And commons of this mighty monarchy,
    Present thee with th'imperial diadem.
Ceneus. The warlike soldiers and the gentlemen   140
    That heretofore have filled Persepolis
    With Afric captains taken in the field—
    Whose ransom made them march in coats of gold,
    With costly jewels hanging at their ears
    And shining stones upon their lofty crests—   145
    Now living idle in the wallèd towns,

---

134. lord, Ortygius] *Oxberry;* Lord Ortigius *O1–3, Q.*   135.1 CENEUS]
Oxberry; Conerus *O1–3, Q.*   139. th'imperial] *This ed.;* th'Emperiall
O1–3, Q.   140. *Ceneus*] *O1–3;* Cone. *Q.*

---

must be seized, compare *Two* II.i.11–13. The commoner insistences in
the play are on Fortune as chance ('the fortune of the wars'), or on her
being Tamburlaine's sponsor, or his slave. Cf. *One* I.ii.174 n., and
Introduction, p. 15.

126. *empery*] territory ruled by an emperor.

128. *continent to*] connected to, continuous with. *O.E.D.* first entry
from *Dr Faustus*, iii.110.

130.] Cyrus 'subdued the Greek cities of Asia Minor, but it is Darius
[I] who is associated with the invasion of Greece and the defeat at
Marathon in 490 B.C.' (Ellis-Fermor, pp. 74–5, suggesting a source for
the confusion).

135.1.] It is clearly sensible to emend to Ceneus with Oxberry: the
speech heading at l. 140 is 'Cene.' in O1 (Q emends it ineptly to 'Cone.').

137. *states*] persons of high estate.

139. *th'imperial*] See *One* II.vii.15 n.

> Wanting both pay and martial discipline,
> Begin in troops to threaten civil war
> And openly exclaim against the king.
> Therefore, to stay all sudden mutinies,   150
> We will invest your highness emperor;
> Whereat the soldiers will conceive more joy
> Than did the Macedonians at the spoil
> Of great Darius and his wealthy host.

Cosroe. Well, since I see the state of Persia droop   155
> And languish in my brother's government,
> I willingly receive th'imperial crown
> And vow to wear it for my country's good,
> In spite of them shall malice my estate.

Ortygius. And in assurance of desired success   160
> We here do crown thee monarch of the East,
> Emperor of Asia and of Persia,
> Great lord of Media and Armenia,
> Duke of Assyria and Albania,
> Mesopotamia and of Parthia,   165
> East India and the late-discovered isles,
> Chief lord of all the wide vast Euxine Sea

---

157. th'imperial] *This ed.;* th'Emperiall *O1–3, Q.*   164. Assyria] *van Dam; Affrica O1–3, Q.*

---

152. *conceive*] 'become possessed with' (Pendry–Maxwell).

153–4.] Alexander the Great defeated Darius III (not the Darius of ll. 7 and 130) at the battle of Issus in 333 B.C. and in 331 B.C. at Arbela.

155. *state*] 'commonweal' (Pendry–Maxwell).

157. *th'imperial*] See *One* II.vii.15 n.

159. *them shall malice*] those who may seek to injure, or regard with malice.

162 ff.] The colouring of Ortelius' atlas would vividly define Marlowe's sense of these regions, as Ellis-Fermor points out. Persia extends 'from the western extremity of the Caspian Sea, due south to the Persian Gulf and eastward to include a large portion of the modern Afghanistan'; Media lies 'between the northern reaches of the Tigris and the Caspian Sea', its extreme northern part being called Armenia. 'The Parthia of the ancients was the district south-east of the Caspian, while Albania lay between the Black Sea and the Caspian' (Ellis-Fermor, p. 76). On 'Assyria', see l. 89 n. above.

163. *Media*] on the Caspian Sea, adjacent to Persia.

166. *the late-discovered isles*] 'possibly the West Indies' (Jump). Perhaps more probably islands in the region of Indonesia, discovered by Drake during his circumnavigation (F.D.H.).

And of the ever-raging Caspian Lake.
Long live Cosroë, mighty emperor!

Cosroe. And Jove may never let me longer live   170
Than I may seek to gratify your love
And cause the soldiers that thus honour me
To triumph over many provinces;
By whose desires of discipline in arms
I doubt not shortly but to reign sole king,   175
And with the army of Theridamas,
Whither we presently will fly, my lords,
To rest secure against my brother's force.

Ortygius. We knew, my lord, before we brought the crown,
Intending your invention so near   180
The residence of your despisèd brother,
The lords would not be too exasperate
To injure or suppress your worthy title.
Or if they would, there are in readiness
Ten thousand horse to carry you from hence   185
In spite of all suspected enemies.

Cosroe. I know it well, my lord, and thank you all.

Ortygius. Sound up the trumpets, then; God save the
        King!   *Exeunt.*

SCENE ii

[*Enter*] TAMBURLAINE *leading* ZENOCRATE; TECHELLES,
USUMCASANE, *other* Lords [*among them* MAGNETES *and*
AGYDAS] *and* Soldiers *loaden with treasure.*

169. Long] *O1–2; All.* Long *O3, Q.*   182. lords] *O3, Q;* Lord *O1–2.*
188. God] *O1–2; All.* God *O3, Q.*   0.1. *Enter*] Oxberry; not in *O1–3, Q.*
0.2. among . . . AGYDAS] *after* Oxberry (ARGYDAS [*sic*], MAGNETES, Lords);
not in O1–3, Q.

169.] The insertion of '*All*' as a speech-heading *O3, Q,* seems unnecessary, though commonly adopted by editors: it is only apparently
necessary for metrical regularity, as 'Cosroe' is frequently trisyllabic.

170. *Jove may*] may Jove.

171. *gratify*] requite.

180. *investion*] investiture; earliest *O.E.D.* instance.

182. *too exasperate*] so exasperated as; earliest *O.E.D.* instance 1601.
Cf. *Edward II*, I.iv.182.

188.] On the needless insertion of '*All*'. in *O3, Q,* cf. l. 169 above.

I.ii.0.2. MAGNETES] Oxberry's conjectural expansion of the speech-
heading *Mag.* at ll. 17 and 80; by analogy with 'Mycetes'.

Tamburlaine. Come, lady, let not this appal your thoughts;
          The jewels and the treasure we have ta'en
          Shall be reserved, and you in better state
          Than if you were arrived in Syria,
          Even in the circle of your father's arms,   5
          The mighty Soldan of Egyptia.
Zenocrate. Ah shepherd, pity my distressèd plight
          (If, as thou seemest, thou art so mean a man)
          And seek not to enrich thy followers
          By lawless rapine from a silly maid   10
          Who, travelling with these Median lords
          To Memphis, from my uncle's country of Media,
          Where all my youth I have been governèd,
          Have passed the army of the mighty Turk,
          Bearing his privy signet and his hand   15
          To safe conduct us thorough Africa.
Magnetes. And, since we have arrived in Scythia,
          Besides rich presents from the puissant Cham
          We have his highness' letters to command
          Aid and assistance if we stand in need.   20
Tamburlaine. But now you see these letters and commands
          Are countermanded by a greater man,
          And through my provinces you must expect
          Letters of conduct from my mightiness
          If you intend to keep your treasure safe.   25
          But since I love to live at liberty,
          As easily may you get the Soldan's crown
          As any prizes out of my precinct:

---

3. *reserved*] kept intact, preserved; cf. *Dr Faustus*, ix.47.

better state] 'greater splendour' (Jump).

10. *silly*] helpless; cf. l. 47 n. below.

13. *governèd*] cared for; cf. *Two* V.iii.25.

15. *privy ... hand*] a document signed and sealed; cf. *Edward II*, I.ii.71: 'Confirms his banishment with our hands and seals'.

16. *Africa*] See *One* I.i.89 n. Pendry–Maxwell suggest 'i.e. (full extent of) Turkish Empire'.

18. *Cham*] emperor of Tartary.

22. *countermanded*] revoked by a contrary command; for a different sense, see *One* III.i.63. Similar verbal repetitions are at *Two* III.v.27, *Two* V.iii.7, 170.

24. *conduct*] permission 'granted to ensure safe passage' (*O.E.D. sb.*[1] 2).

28. *precinct*] sphere of control.

For they are friends that help to wean my state
Till men and kingdoms help to strengthen it,   30
And must maintain my life exempt from servitude.
But tell me, madam, is your grace betrothed?
Zenocrate. I am, my lord—for so you do import.
Tamburlaine. I am a lord, for so my deeds shall prove,
And yet a shepherd by my parentage.   35
But lady, this fair face and heavenly hue
Must grace his bed that conquers Asia
And means to be a terror to the world,
Measuring the limits of his empery
By east and west as Phoebus doth his course.   40
Lie here, ye weeds that I disdain to wear!
This complete armour and this curtle-axe
Are adjuncts more beseeming Tamburlaine.
And madam, whatsoever you esteem
Of this success, and loss unvalued,   45
Both may invest you empress of the East;
And these that seem but silly country swains
May have the leading of so great an host
As with their weight shall make the mountains quake,

---

29. *wean my state*] assist the growth of my power. 'Wean' in this sense is not recorded in *O.E.D.*, though it bears comparison with recorded expressions which emphasise weaning *to*, rather than *from*, something.

33. *import*] imply (i.e., that he is a lord).

39. *empery*] dominion. Its extent, Tamburlaine here asserts, will be boundless.

42. *complete*] 'frequently accented, as here, upon the first syllable' (Ellis-Fermor, p. 79).

curtle-axe] cutlass, as at *One* II.iii.55 (where the O1 form is the common enough 'Cutle-axe').

45. *success*] outcome.

unvalued] inestimable (earliest instance in *O.E.D.*). J. C. Maxwell (*Yearbook of English Studies*, VI (1976), p. 234) suggests that 'loss unvalued' means 'loss of what is invaluable'.

47. *silly*] lowly, simple.

48–9.] Seaton, 'Marlowe's Light Reading' (*Elizabethan and Jacobean Studies Presented to F. P. Wilson*, ed. H. Davis and Helen Gardner, Oxford, 1959, pp. 21–2), cites Romance analogues for this hyperbole and those at *One* III.i.50–5.

49–51.] 'It was generally agreed that earthquakes were the natural results of vapors and exhalations compressed within subterranean caverns. As they struggled for escape, these evaporations disturbed the

    Even as when windy exhalations,   50
    Fighting for passage, tilt within the earth.
Techelles. As princely lions when they rouse themselves,
    Stretching their paws and threat'ning herds of beasts,
    So in his armour looketh Tamburlaine:
    Methinks I see kings kneeling at his feet,   55
    And he with frowning brows and fiery looks
    Spurning their crowns from off their captive heads.
Usumcasane. And making thee and me, Techelles, kings,
    That even to death will follow Tamburlaine.
Tamburlaine. Nobly resolved, sweet friends and followers.   60
    These lords, perhaps, do scorn our estimates,
    And think we prattle with distempered spirits;
    But since they measure our deserts so mean
    That in conceit bear empires on our spears,
    Affecting thoughts coequal with the clouds,   65
    They shall be kept our forcèd followers
    Till with their eyes they view us emperors.
Zenocrate. The gods, defenders of the innocent,
    Will never prosper your intended drifts
    That thus oppress poor friendless passengers.   70
    Therefore at least admit us liberty,
    Even as thou hopest to be eternised
    By living Asia's mighty emperor.
Agydas. I hope our lady's treasure and our own

67. they] *O2–3, Q;* thee *O1.*

---

earth's surface' (Heninger, p. 128). See *One* V.i.348 n. Characteristically, Tamburlaine stresses not the abnormality of such violence, but its heroic verve.

    51. *tilt*] used of thunder at *One* III.ii.79.

    61. *estimates*] attributed, or asserted, value.

    62. *distempered*] intemperate (*O.E.D. ppl. adj.*); or, perhaps, deranged (*O.E.D.* 4, from 1605).

    64. *conceit*] 'imagination, but imagination seeking to express itself in action' (Ellis-Fermor, p. 80). But 'conceiving' (of love and beauty) opposes 'subduing' in some respects: cf. *One* V.i.174–90.

    65. *Affecting*] drawn to, aspiring to.

    coequal] cf. *1H6*, V.i.33.

    69. *drifts*] purposes.

    70. *passengers*] travellers.

    72. *eternised*] made perpetually famous, immortalised. First *O.E.D.* instance 1603.

May serve for ransom to our liberties: 75
Return our mules and empty camels back,
That we may travel into Syria,
Where her betrothèd lord, Alcidamus,
Expects th'arrival of her highness' person.

Magnetes. And wheresoever we repose ourselves   80
We will report but well of Tamburlaine.

Tamburlaine. Disdains Zenocrate to live with me?
Or you, my lords, to be my followers?
Think you I weigh this treasure more than you?
Not all the gold in India's wealthy arms   85
Shall buy the meanest soldier in my train.
Zenocrate, lovelier than the love of Jove,
Brighter than is the silver Rhodope,
Fairer than whitest snow on Scythian hills,
Thy person is more worth to Tamburlaine   90
Than the possession of the Persian crown,
Which gracious stars have promised at my birth.
A hundred Tartars shall attend on thee,
Mounted on steeds swifter than Pegasus;
Thy garments shall be made of Median silk,   95
Enchased with precious jewels of mine own,

---

80. *Magnetes*] conj. *Oxberry;* Mag. *O1–3, Q.*   88. Rhodope] *Robinson;*
Rhodophe *Oxberry;* Rhodolfe *O1–3, Q.*

---

75. *ransom to our liberties*] 'by metonymy, for "ransom restoring us to
liberty" ' (Ellis-Fermor, p. 80, citing *Cor.,* V.iii.178).

79. *Expects*] awaits.

87. *the love of Jove*] Juno.

88. *Rhodope*] 'See Nicholas Nicholay, *The Navigations . . . made into
Turkey,* chap. i.: "the height and sharpness of the mount *Rhodope,*
vulgarly called the mounts of *silver,* because of the silver mines that are
there found" ' (Ellis-Fermor, p. 81).

92.] the 'happy stars' of *One* V.i.359, and the 'gracious aspect' of *Two*
III.v.80; emphasised in Perondinus's account, among others.

94. *Pegasus*] winged horse of classical mythology, later represented as
the favourite steed of the Muses (*O.E.D.*).

96. *Enchased*] adorned. No instance of the word's application to
embroidery in *O.E.D.* Marlowe uses the word elsewhere of jewelled
crowns, thrones, and canopies, and (by a characteristic extension) of
the night sky; cf. *One* II.v.60, *One* IV.ii.9, *Two* I.ii.49, *Two* III.ii.120,
Two IV.iii.128. *Dido,* I.i.101, has 'azur'd gates, enchased with his
name'.

More rich and valurous than Zenocrate's;
With milk-white harts upon an ivory sled
Thou shalt be drawn amidst the frozen pools
And scale the icy mountains' lofty tops,   100
Which with thy beauty will be soon resolved;
My martial prizes, with five hundred men,
Won on the fifty-headed Volga's waves,
Shall all we offer to Zenocrate,
And then my self to fair Zenocrate.   105

Techelles. [*Aside to Tamburlaine.*] What now? in love?
Tamburlaine [*Aside*] Techelles, women must be flatterèd.
But this is she with whom I am in love.

Enter a Soldier.

Soldier. News, news!
Tamburlaine. How now, what's the matter?   110
Soldier. A thousand Persian horsemen are at hand,
Sent from the king to overcome us all.
Tamburlaine. How now, my lords of Egypt and Zenocrate!
Now must your jewels be restored again,
And I that triumphed so be overcome?   115
How say you lordings, is not this your hope?
Agydas. We hope yourself will willingly restore them.
Tamburlaine. Such hope, such fortune, have the thousand
        horse.
Soft ye, my lords and sweet Zenocrate:
You must be forcèd from me ere you go.   120

---

106. *Aside to Tamburlaine*] Oxberry; not in *O1–3, Q.*   107. *Aside*] Oxberry; not in *O1–3, Q.*

---

97. *valurous*] valuable; sole instance in *O.E.D.*

101. *resolved*] melted; cf. *Lucan,* l.221: 'And frozen Alps thaw'd with
resolving winds'.

103. *fifty-headed Volga*] Ortelius's maps emphasise the Volga's
numerous major tributaries.

104. *Shall all we*] all of these we shall; cf. 'Both we', *One* I.ii.196.

111.] 'The exact number of horsemen sent against Tamburlaine is
specified by ... Mexia [and] Perondinus' (Ellis-Fermor, p. 82). See
p. 321 for Whetstone (deriving from Mexia), and see Perondinus; on
these two main sources, see Introduction, pp. 9–15.

118. *Such hope, such fortune*] i.e., as Zenocrate and her train are
experiencing.

119. *Soft ye*] gently, steady.

A thousand horsemen! We five hundred foot!
An odds too great for us to stand against.
But are they rich? And is their armour good?
Soldier. Their plumèd helms are wrought with beaten gold,
Their swords enamelled, and about their necks   125
Hangs massy chains of gold down to the waist:
In every part exceeding brave and rich.
Tamburlaine. Then shall we fight courageously with them,
Or look you I should play the orator?
Techelles. No: cowards and faint-hearted runaways   130
Look for orations when the foe is near.
Our swords shall play the orators for us.
Usumcasane. Come, let us meet them at the mountain top,
And with a sudden and an hot alarm
Drive all their horses headlong down the hill.   135
Techelles. Come, let us march.
Tamburlaine. Stay, Techelles, ask a parley first.

The Soldiers [*of Tamburlaine*] *enter.*

Open the mails, yet guard the treasure sure;
Lay out our golden wedges to the view,
That their reflections may amaze the Persians.   140
And look we friendly on them when they come;
But if they offer word or violence
We'll fight five hundred men at arms to one
Before we part with our possession.
And 'gainst the general we will lift our swords   145
And either lance his greedy thirsting throat
Or take him prisoner, and his chain shall serve

133. top] *Q;* foot *O1–3.*

127. *brave*] showy, fine.
133. *top*] Q's (unauthoritative) emendation to 'top' was adopted by some editors; to some, 'foot' is anomalous. *O.E.D.* does not support the sense of 'foothill', and in any event Usumcasane is speaking with surging bravado.
137. *parley*] Spelt 'parlee' in O1 here, elsewhere 'parle', and 'parlie', the word seems to be a disyllable for Marlowe throughout: cf. *Two* I.i.11, 50, 117.
138. *mails*] bags or vehicles containing Tamburlaine's booty.
139. *wedges*] ingots (*O.E.D. sb.* 3).
146. *lance*] slit open (*O.E.D. vb.* II.6).
147. *chain*] i.e., of office.

For manacles, till he be ransomed home.

Techelles. I hear them come; shall we encounter them?

Tamburlaine. Keep all your standings, and not stir a foot;   150
    Myself will bide the danger of the brunt.

Enter THERIDAMAS *with others.*

Theridamas. Where is this Scythian Tamburlaine?

Tamburlaine. Whom seekest thou, Persian? I am
    Tamburlaine.

Theridamas. [*Aside.*] Tamburlaine? A Scythian shepherd,
    so embellishèd
    With nature's pride and richest furniture?   155
    His looks do menace heaven and dare the gods;
    His fiery eyes are fixed upon the earth,
    As if he now devised some stratagem,
    Or meant to pierce Avernus' darksome vaults
    And pull the triple-headed dog from hell.   160

Tamburlaine. [*Aside to Techelles.*]
    Noble and mild this Persian seems to be,

160. And] *O1 catchword, Bowers;* To *O1–3, Q text.*

---

148. *home*] to the full.

150. *standings*] stations.

151. *brunt*] attack, onset (*O.E.D.* 2).

154.] lineation as in O1–3, Q; some editors print 'Tamburlaine' on a
separate line.

157–8.] J. C. Maxwell pointed out to me classical instances of a
brooding rhetorical posture that merges here with this Herculean image
of heroic anger: e.g., Odysseus in *Iliad*, III.216, and Ajax and Ulysses
in Ovid, *Metam.*, xiii.124–6 and 2–4: 'Aiax, / utque erat inpatiens irae,
Sigeia torvo / litora respexit classemque in litore vultu' ('Ajax . . . With
uncontrolled indignation he let his lowering gaze rest awhile on the
Sigean shores and on the fleet', Loeb Classical Library). The relation
of looks to feelings and to words is often emphasised in the play: cf.
Two IV.i.175–7.

159–60.] Hercules' descent into Hades to fetch Cerberus may have
been in Marlowe's mind from his reading of Ovid, *Metam.*, vii.409 ff.,
or iv.450–1. Avernus: the lake near Naples closely associated with
Aeneas's descent into the underworld, gave its name to that world.

160.] This line begins sheet B1 in O1; the catchword on A8v is 'And'.
Bowers (i.221) argues persuasively that we should allow the catchword
greater authority than the text's 'To', which might be owing to memorial
contamination from 'to pierce' in l. 159. The emended construction has
a more Marlovian look.

If outward habit judge the inward man.
Techelles. [*Aside to Tamburlaine.*]
    His deep affections make him passionate.
Tamburlaine. [*Aside to Techelles.*]
    With what a majesty he rears his looks!
[*To Theridamas.*]
    In thee, thou valiant man of Persia,   165
I see the folly of thy emperor:
Art thou but captain of a thousand horse,
That by characters graven in thy brows,
And by thy martial face and stout aspect,
Deservest to have the leading of an host?   170
Forsake thy king and do but join with me,
And we will triumph over all the world.
I hold the Fates bound fast in iron chains,
And with my hand turn Fortune's wheel about,
And sooner shall the sun fall from his sphere   175
Than Tamburlaine be slain or overcome.
Draw forth thy sword, thou mighty man-at-arms,
Intending but to raze my charmèd skin,
And Jove himself will stretch his hand from heaven

---

162. *habit*] bearing, demeanour (*O.E.D.* 4).

163.] 'His deep feelings (declared in his face) betoken a passionate nature'.

164 ff.] For the bare source account of this episode, cf. Appendix.

168. *characters*] distinctive mark, stamp (figuratively); second syllable stressed.

168–70.] Cf. the celebration of Tamburlaine at *One* II.i.3–4, and insistently the declaration of personality through *aspect*—expression, face: *O.E.D.* 10, first entry (cf. *One* IV.ii.37). For astrologial 'aspect' see *Two* III.v.80, and on 'aspect' generally Introduction, p. 49.

173. *the Fates*] Clotho, Atropos, and Lachesis; as in *Two*, Prologue l. 5. Cf. the 'Fatal Sisters' of *Two* II.iv.98–100 and *Two* III.iv.54, and see Introduction, p. 50.

174.] Tamburlaine is said to have made Fortune stop her wheel, at *One* V.i.374–5. At *Two* III.iv.52, he treads her under his feet. Cf. *Edward II*, V.ii.55: 'Who now makes Fortune's wheel turn as he please'. An alternative insistence is that Fortune is actively partisan with Tamburlaine: cf. *One* II.ii.73, *Two* I.i.60, etc.

175.] Marlowe's astronomy is Ptolemaic, as in Mephistophilis's disappointingly orthodox resolution of such 'slender questions' (*Dr Faustus*, vi.35–68 and notes). 'Hence the orbit of the sun around the earth, believed to be a circle, is conceived as the generating circle of a sphere'. (Ellis-Fermor, pp. 85–6). See *One* II.i.15–17 n.

To ward the blow and shield me safe from harm.   180
See how he rains down heaps of gold in showers
As if he meant to give my soldiers pay;
And as a sure and grounded argument
That I shall be the monarch of the East,
He sends this Soldan's daughter rich and brave   185
To be my queen and portly emperess.
If thou wilt stay with me, renownèd man,
And lead thy thousand horse with my conduct,
Besides thy share of this Egyptian prize
Those thousand horse shall sweat with martial spoil   190
Of conquered kingdoms and of cities sacked;
Both we will walk upon the lofty clifts,
And Christian merchants that with Russian stems
Plough up huge furrows in the Caspian Sea
Shall vail to us as lords of all the lake.   195
Both we will reign as consuls of the earth,
And mighty kings shall be our senators.
Jove sometimes maskèd in a shepherd's weed,

---

192. clifts] *O1, O3, Q;* cliffes *O2.*

185. *brave*] fine, splendid.

186. *portly*] stately.

187. *renownèd*] The 1590–1606 texts read 'renowmed', a spelling reflecting the word's Latin derivation.

188. *with my conduct*] under my leadership; as at *One* III.i.3. Second syllable of 'conduct' stressed.

192. *clifts*] 'A by-form of CLIFF, due to confusion between that word and *clift*, CLEFT, a fissure' (*O.E.D.*).

193. *merchants*] merchant ships.

stems] prows, 'here used, by metonymy, for the whole ship' (Ellis-Fermor).

194. *Caspian Sea*] 'One of the most convenient trade routes to the east involved a passage across the Caspian from the Russian to the Persian side' (Ellis-Fermor, p. 86).

195. *vail*] salute by lowering sail; cf. *Jew of Malta*, V.ii.1, and *Edward II*, I.iv.276.

198. *Jove*] Elsewhere in the play a model of revolt against authority, Jove is here taken not as the disguised abducter of mortals but as a mirror for aspiration from a lowly estate. The love of shepherds is celebrated as capable of stopping divine wrath at *One* V.i.183–7. For *maskèd*, 'disguised himself' (for example, in courting Mnemosyne), cf. *One* IV.ii.108, *One* IV.iv.17, and *Two* III.ii.12. Golding, p. 121, tells of Jove appearing as 'A sheepeherd to *Mnemosyne*'.

And by those steps that he hath scaled the heavens
May we become immortal like the gods.   200
Join with me now in this my mean estate
(I call it mean, because, being yet obscure,
The nations far removed admire me not),
And when my name and honour shall be spread
As far as Boreas claps his brazen wings   205
Or fair Boötes sends his cheerful light,
Then shalt thou be competitor with me
And sit with Tamburlaine in all his majesty.

Theridamas. Not Hermes, prolocutor to the gods,
   Could use persuasions more pathetical.   210

Tamburlaine. Nor are Apollo's oracles more true
   Than thou shalt find my vaunts substantial.

Techelles. We are his friends, and if the Persian king
   Should offer present dukedoms to our state,
   We think it loss to make exchange for that   215
   We are assured of by our friend's success.

Usumcasane. And kingdoms at the least we all expect,
   Besides the honour in assured conquests
   Where kings shall crouch unto our conquering swords
   And hosts of soldiers stand amazed at us,   220
   When with their fearful tongues they shall confess
   'These are the men that all the world admires.'

---

199. *that*] by which.

203. *admire*] marvel at.

205–6.] The furthest northern distances: *Boreas* is the north wind,
Boötes or Arcturus the Bear a northern constellation. Cf. *One* II.iv.5 and
Two I.iii.160. *O.E.D.* earliest entry for Boötes is 1656.

207. *competitor*] partner.

209. *Hermes*] messenger of the gods, and himself the god of eloquence;
his influence (as Mercury) regrettably absent from Mycetes' horoscope
(*One* I.i.14).

prolocutor] can mean both 'messenger' and 'advocate'.

210. *pathetical*] emotive.

212. *vaunts*] brags (*O.E.D. sb.*² 3: earliest instance 1597).

substantial] firmly based (*O.E.D. adj.* 10).

214. *present*] immediate.

to our state] to exalt our standing; cf. *One* I.ii.29 n.

221. *fearful*] awed, full of fear.

confess] acknowledge.

Theridamas. What strong enchantments tice my yielding
  soul?
  Are these resolvèd noble *Scythians*?
  But shall I prove a traitor to my king?   225
Tamburlaine. No, but the trusty friend of Tamburlaine.
Theridamas. Won with thy words and conquered with thy looks,
  I yield myself, my men and horse to thee:
  To be partaker of thy good or ill
  As long as life maintains Theridamas.   230
Tamburlaine. Theridamas my friend, take here my hand,
  Which is as much as if I swore by heaven
  And called the gods to witness of my vow:
  Thus shall my heart be still combined with thine
  Until our bodies turn to elements   235
  And both our souls aspire celestial thrones.
  Techelles and Casane, welcome him.
Techelles. Welcome renownèd Persian to us all.
Usumcasane. Long may Theridamas remain with us.
Tamburlaine. These are my friends, in whom I more rejoice 240
  Than doth the king of Persia in his crown;

223. soul?] *Q;* soule *O1–3.* 224. Are] *O1–3, Q;* To *Oxberry;* Ah *Brooke,*
conj. *Brereton.* Scythians] *ital. this ed.;* Scythians *O1–3, Q.*

---

223. tice] entice.

223–4. soul? | Are] Oxberry and others emend 'Are' to 'To', finding
l. 224 obscure; there is no punctuation after 'soule' in O1. Brooke emended to 'Ah', a word which frequently opens exclamatory lines in
Marlowe. Bowers argues that there was little room for the compositor to
punctuate after 'soule', and points out that the catchword preceding
this line is 'Are', corroborating the octavo reading. Defending the O1
'Are' on these grounds, Bowers takes the sense to be that Theridamas is
asking if these are not mere shepherds, but noble and resolved Scythian
warriors (Bowers, i.221–2). What is expressed is rather, I take it, astonishment that, of all people, *Scythians* should prove dignified and resolute:
this echoes Theridamas' surprise at *One* I.ii.154–5. The argument that
the compositor lacked space seems questionable.

227.] See *One* I.i.74 n.

235–6.] The body disintegrating at death into its four constituent
elements: Ellis-Fermor remarks the basically orthodox Aristotelianism
of this physiology, together with an allusion to Ecclesiastes xii.7. Cf.
One II.vi.26–7, and *Dr Faustus,* xix.177–8.

236. aspire] Cf. *Hero,* 'The Argument of the Second Sestiad', ll. 7–8:
'Whose suit he shuns, and doth aspire / Hero's fair tow'r and his desire'.
Aspire may mean *achieve* (*O.E.D.* 8; suggestion by J. C. Maxwell).

And by the love of Pylades and Orestes,
Whose statues we adore in Scythia,
Thyself and them shall never part from me
Before I crown you kings in Asia.   245
Make much of them, gentle Theridamas,
And they will never leave thee till the death.

Theridamas. Nor thee nor them, thrice-noble Tamburlaine,
Shall want my heart to be with gladness pierced
To do you honour and security.   250

Tamburlaine. A thousand thanks, worthy Theridamas.
And now, fair madam, and my noble lords,
If you will willingly remain with me
You shall have honours as your merits be—
Or else you shall be forced with slavery.   255

Agydas. We yield unto thee, happy Tamburlaine.

Tamburlaine. For you then, madam, I am out of doubt.

Zenocrate. I must be pleased perforce, wretched Zenocrate!

                                        Exeunt.

[*Finis Actus primi.*]

243. statues *O3, Q;* statutes *O1–2.*   258.2. *Finis Actus primi.*] This
ed.; not in *O1–3, Q.*

242.] Pylades and Orestes, loyal to each other through the events
which followed Agamemnon's death, became archetypes of friendship.
The crucial episode here is perhaps their readiness to die for each other
at Tauris (in 'Scythia'). Cf. *Ovid's Elegies*, II.vi.15–16, and contrast
Mycetes' relatively precious appeal to a similar model at *One* I.i.50.

243.] *O.E.D.* records the *O1–2* form 'statute' (*sb.* III.7) as a spelling of
'statue', though not citing this line as an instance. Cf. *One* IV.ii.105 n.,
and *Two* II.iv.140 n.

244.] Cf., as Elizabethan grammar, *John*, IV.ii.50–1: 'Your safety, for
the which myself and them / Bend their best studies'.

256. *happy*] fortunate; an insistent word for Tamburlaine: cf. 'in
conduct of thy happy stars', *One* V.i.359.

Act II

SCENE i

[*Enter*] COSROE, MENAPHON, ORTYGIUS, CENEUS, *with other* Soldiers.

Cosroe. Thus far are we towards Theridamas
  And valiant Tamburlaine, the man of fame,
  The man that in the forehead of his fortune
  Bears figures of renown and miracle.
  But tell me, that hast seen him, Menaphon,   5
  What stature wields he, and what personage?
Menaphon. Of stature tall, and straightly fashionèd,
  Like his desire, lift upwards and divine;
  So large of limbs, his joints so strongly knit,
  Such breadth of shoulders as might mainly bear   10
  Old Atlas' burden; 'twixt his manly pitch
  A pearl more worth than all the world is placed,
  Wherein by curious sovereignty of art
  Are fixed his piercing instruments of sight,

0.1. *Enter*] *Oxberry; not in O1–3, Q.*   11. burden] *This ed.;* burthen
O1–3, Q.

II.i.3–4.] recalling the 'characters graven in thy [Theridamas'] brows'
at *One* I.ii.168. Ellis-Fermor (p. 92) finds an allusion to 'the secret signs
of destiny which Allah writes upon every man's forehead', and also cites
as a possible reference the seal of Rev. vii.3. More generally, the image
assists our sense of Tamburlaine as a figure of Destiny.

8. *lift*] *O.E.D.* cites instances of this obsolete version of the past
participle from 1413 onwards. The word associates strongly with Tamburlaine's enterprise: cf. *One* II.iii.52, 'lift thy lofty arm into the clouds'—
words spoken to Tamburlaine, with unconscious dramatic irony, by
Cosroe.

10. *mainly*] by main force.

11. *Atlas' burden*] the stars of heaven.

pitch] breadth of shoulders: *O.E.D. sb.*[2] 16, first entry.

12. *pearl*] i.e., his head.

Whose fiery circles bear encompassèd   15
A heaven of heavenly bodies in their spheres
That guides his steps and actions to the throne
Where honour sits invested royally;
Pale of complexion—wrought in him with passion,
Thirsting with sovereignty, with love of arms;   20
His lofty brows in folds do figure death,
And in their smoothness amity and life;
About them hangs a knot of amber hair
Wrappèd in curls, as fierce Achilles' was,
On which the breath of heaven delights to play,   25
Making it dance with wanton majesty;
His arms and fingers long and sinewy,
Betokening valour and excess of strength:
In every part proportioned like the man
Should make the world subdued to Tamburlaine.   30

Cosroe. Well hast thou portrayed in thy terms of life
The face and personage of a wondrous man:
Nature doth strive with Fortune and his stars

---

27. and fingers long and sinewy] *Dyce 1;* and fingers long and snowy
O1–3; long, his fingers snowy-white *Q;* and fingers, long, and snowy-
white *Oxberry.*

15–17.] Tamburlaine's fiery eyes are planetary spheres which pro-
pitiously guide his career of aspiration. Possibly associated with the
apocalyptic Christ of Rev. xix (Weil, p. 201).

19.] 'This pallor of genius is Marlowe's own addition' (Ellis-Fermor,
p. 93).

20. *Thirsting with sovereignty*] closely echoed at *One* II.vi.31. This
theme holds right through the play to Tamburlaine's dying fever.

21. *figure*] prefigure, foreshadow (*O.E.D.* 5, earliest instance 1593).

23. *amber hair*] Ellis-Fermor (p. 93) notes the affinities with Homer's
descriptions of Achilles (*Iliad* I.197 and XXIII.141), and also cites Ovid,
Metam., xiii. 162 ff., and Statius, *Achilleid,* i.611.

27.] It seems plain that O1's 'snowy' is a simple error for 'sinowy' in
the printer's copy: 'sinews' is spelt 'sinowes' in O1 at *One* IV.iv.97,
Two II.ii.9, and *Two* III.i.10 (though 'sinewes' at *Two* I.i.156). Q attemp-
ted to make sense of the line by working 'snowy-white' into the line, and
was followed by Oxberry and others. Marlowe uses 'sinewy' in *Hero*,
Sest. I.371 (Q1 spells 'sinowie'), and *Ovid's Elegies*, i.27 ('sinewy').

31. *terms of life*] lively terms; if 'lifelike terms' (Pendry-Maxwell), not
in *O.E.D.*

33.] 'Familiar terms from three different systems are here combined,
as often with Marlowe: Nature, the Natura Dei of the Middle Ages, . . .

To make him famous in accomplished worth,
And well his merits shew him to be made   35
His fortune's master and the king of men
That could persuade at such a sudden pinch,
With reasons of his valour and his life,
A thousand sworn and overmatching foes.
Then, when our powers in points of swords are joined   40
And closed in compass of the killing bullet,
Though strait the passage and the port be made
That leads to palace of my brother's life,
Proud is his fortune if we pierce it not.
And when the princely Persian diadem   45
Shall overweigh his weary witless head
And fall like mellowed fruit, with shakes of death,
In fair Persia noble Tamburlaine
Shall be my regent and remain as king.

Ortygius. In happy hour we have set the crown   50
Upon your kingly head, that seeks our honour
In joining with the man ordained by heaven
To further every action to the best.

Ceneus. He that with shepherds and a little spoil
Durst, in disdain of wrong and tyranny,   55
Defend his freedom 'gainst a monarchy—
What will he do supported by a king,
Leading a troop of gentlemen and lords,
And stuffed with treasure for his highest thoughts?

Cosroe. And such shall wait on worthy Tamburlaine.   60
Our army will be forty thousand strong
When Tamburlaine and brave Theridamas

Fortune, the Roman deity of chance, ... and the stars of medieval
(and ultimately Oriental) astrology' (Ellis-Fermor, p. 94).

38.] i.e., by means of Tamburlaine's courage and under threat of
sudden death.

40. *powers*] armies (as constantly in the play).

41. *compass*] range.

42-3.] The recall of Matt. vii.14 seems to carry no irony: 'Strait is the
gate and narrow is the way which leadeth unto life'. The 'palace of my
brother's life' is Mycetes' heart.

59. *stuffed*] well-provided (cf. the insistent Marlovian word 'glutted'
and *One* III.iii.164 n.).

for] to the measure of; or, as a stimulus to.

Have met us by the river Araris,
And all conjoined to meet the witless king
That now is marching near to Parthia,   65
And with unwilling soldiers faintly armed,
To seek revenge on me and Tamburlaine.
To whom, sweet Menaphon, direct me straight.

Menaphon. I will, my lord.   *Exeunt.*

SCENE ii

[*Enter*] MYCETES, MEANDER, *with other* Lords *and* Soldiers.

Mycetes. Come, my Meander, let us to this gear;
I tell you true, my heart is swoll'n with wrath
On this same thievish villain Tamburlaine,
And of that false Cosroe, my traitorous brother.
Would it not grieve a king to be so abused   5
And have a thousand horsemen ta'en away?
And, which is worst, to have his diadem

0.1. *Enter*] Oxberry; *not in O1–3, Q.*

63. *Araris*] In Marlowe's *Lucan*, 'swift Rhodanus / Drives Araris to sea' (ll. 434–5). Various attempts have been made to identify this river: e.g. the Araxes in Armenia, clearly marked by Ortelius (Ellis-Fermor, p. 95), the Ararus in Scythia (D. C. Allen, *T.L.S.*, 24 September 1931). J. O. Thomson persuasively argues that Marlowe was led to invent this form by his memory of a line from Virgil, *Ecl.*, i.61–2: ' "Ante pereratis amborum finibus exsul / Aut Ararim Parthus bibet aut Germania Tigrim" ... that is, people at the opposite ends of the earth will change places and drink the wrong rivers, the Germans drinking the Tigris, while the Parthians will drink the Arar' (i.e., the Saône): *M.L.R.*, XLVIII (1953), 323. See also *One* II.iii.16 n. The Araxes, with a recollection of Virgil's words, seems likeliest.

65. *near to Parthia*] 'The Persian army is described as moving north towards the territory about the Caspian Sea. Marlowe is intentionally vague about the actual site of this unhistorical battle' (Ellis-Fermor, p. 95).

II.ii.1. *gear*] business. The colloquial word is an apt agent of deflation here. Cf. *Edward II*, V.v.37–8: 'So now / Must I about this gear'.

3, 4. *On ... of*] 'The two prepositions are used interchangeably to signify the direction or the object of the emotion' (Ellis-Fermor, p. 96).

5.] With its indecisive rhythm and expletive syllable, the line is the weak counterpart of Tamburlaine's 'Is it not passing brave to be a king', *One* II.v.53.

Sought for by such scald knaves as love him not?
I think it would; well then, by heavens I swear,
Aurora shall not peep out of her doors   10
But I will have Cosroë by the head
And kill proud Tamburlaine with point of sword.
Tell you the rest, Meander, I have said.

Meander. Then, having passed Armenian deserts now
And pitched our tents under the Georgian hills,   15
Whose tops are covered with Tartarian thieves
That lie in ambush waiting for a prey,
What should we do but bid them battle straight,
And rid the world of those detested troops?
Lest, if we let them linger here a while,   20
They gather strength by power of fresh supplies.
This country swarms with vile outrageous men
That live by rapine and by lawless spoil,
Fit soldiers for the wicked Tamburlaine.
And he that could with gifts and promises   25
Inveigle him that led a thousand horse,
And make him false his faith unto his king,
Will quickly win such as are like himself.
Therefore cheer up your minds, prepare to fight.
He that can take or slaughter Tamburlaine   30
Shall rule the province of Albania.
Who brings that traitor's head, Theridamas',
Shall have a government in Media,
Beside the spoil of him and all his train.
But if Cosroë (as our spials say,   35
And as we know) remains with Tamburlaine,

---

15. pitched] *O2–3, Q;* pitch *O1.*

---

8. *scald*] low, contemptible.

11. *Cosroë*] a trisyllable here, but (as with other proper names in the play) more or less elided elsewhere to suit the metre (e.g. l. 4 above).

14–15.] Mycetes, 'marching near to Parthia' (south-east of the Caspian) has crossed Armenia and reached the foothills of the Caucasus. Parthia and Armenia are now both ruled by Cosroe (*One* I.i.163, 165).

22. *outrageous*] fierce, violent (Ellis-Fermor). Cf. *Edward II*, II.ii.55.

27. *false*] break, violate.

32. *Theridamas'*] 'a genitive in apposition to "traitor's" ' (Ellis-Fermor, p. 97).

35. *spials*] spies.

His highness' pleasure is that he should live
And be reclaimed with princely lenity.

[*Enter a* Spy.]

Spy. An hundred horsemen of my company,
    Scouting abroad upon these champion plains,   40
    Have viewed the army of the Scythians,
    Which make report it far exceeds the king's.
Meander. Suppose they be in number infinite,
    Yet being void of martial discipline,
    All running headlong after greedy spoils   45
    And more regarding gain than victory,
    Like to the cruel brothers of the earth
    Sprung of the teeth of dragons venomous,
    Their careless swords shall lance their fellows' throats
    And make us triumph in their overthrow.   50
Mycetes. Was there such brethren, sweet Meander, say,
    That sprung of teeth of dragons venomous?
Meander. So poets say, my lord.
Mycetes. And 'tis a pretty toy to be a poet.
    Well, well, Meander, thou art deeply read,   55
    And having thee I have a jewel sure.
    Go on, my lord, and give your charge I say,
    Thy wit will make us conquerors today.
Meander. Then, noble soldiers, to entrap these thieves
    That live confounded in disordered troops,   60

38.1. *Enter a* Spy] *Dyce 1; not in O1–3, Q.*   45. after greedy] *O1–3,*
Q; greedy after *Dyce 1 (conj.).*

---

40. *champion*] level and open.
42. *which*] i.e., the horsemen.
45. *after greedy spoils*] a striking, and for Marlowe unusual, trans-
ference. Dyce 1 conjectures 'greedy after spoils'. For 'greedy' used to
sharpen a tonal effect, cf. *One* II.vii.48–9. Meander's trick intended to
distract Tamburlaine's army is a futile counterpart of Tamburlaine's
own display of gold to assist his winning over of Theridamas.
47–8.] Armed men sprang up from the dragon's teeth sowed by
Cadmus, and attacked each other.
52. *dragons venomous*] Cf. *One* III.iii.105 n.
58. *wit*] intelligence, inventiveness.
59–67.] a stratagem much praised in military manuals of Marlowe's
day (Kocher, p. 247).

If wealth or riches may prevail with them,
We have our camels laden all with gold
Which you that be but common soldiers
Shall fling in every corner of the field,
And while the base-born Tartars take it up,   65
You, fighting more for honour than for gold,
Shall massacre those greedy-minded slaves.
And when their scattered army is subdued
And you march on their slaughtered carcasses,
Share equally the gold that bought their lives   70
And live like gentlemen in Persia.
Strike up the drum and march courageously:
Fortune herself doth sit upon our crests.
Mycetes. He tells you true, my masters, so he does.
Drums, why sound ye not when Meander speaks?   75

                     Exeunt.

Scene iii

[*Enter*] COSROE, TAMBURLAINE, THERIDAMAS, TECHELLES,
USUMCASANE, ORTYGIUS, *with others.*

Cosroe. Now, worthy Tamburlaine, have I reposed
In thy approvèd fortunes all my hope.
What thinkest thou, man, shall come of our attempts?
For even as from assurèd oracle,
I take thy doom for satisfaction.   5
Tamburlaine. And so mistake you not a whit, my lord,
For fates and oracles of heaven have sworn

0.1. *Enter*] *Oxberry; not in O1–3, Q.*   7. oracles of heaven] *Oxberry;*
Oracles, heauen *O1–3, Q.*

75.1. *Exeunt*] Oxberry adds *Flourish of drums*, but perhaps Mycetes
fails to rouse martial noise.
    II.iii.2. *approvèd*] 'proved or established by experience' (*O.E.D.*);
perhaps with a colour, here, of 'sanctioned' (by divine powers), though
the *O.E.D.*'s first instance of this sense is 1667.
    fortunes] On the plural, see Prologue to Part One, l. 8 n.
    5. *doom*] judgment, opinion—though these synonyms lack the appro-
priate portentousness.
    7.] The O1 reading makes sense, indeed produces an emphatic line;
but Oxberry's emendation gives a Marlovian construction. On Marlowe's
mingling of pagan and Christian concepts, cf. *One* II.i.33 n.

To royalise the deeds of Tamburlaine
And make them blest that share in his attempts.
And doubt you not but, if you favour me   10
And let my fortunes and my valour sway
To some direction in your martial deeds,
The world will strive with hosts of men at arms
To swarm unto the ensign I support.
The host of Xerxes, which by fame is said   15
To drink the mighty Parthian Araris,
Was but a handful to that we will have.
Our quivering lances shaking in the air
And bullets like Jove's dreadful thunderbolts
Enrolled in flames and fiery smouldering mists   20
Shall threat the gods more than Cyclopian wars;
And with our sun-bright armour as we march
We'll chase the stars from heaven and dim their eyes
That stand and muse at our admirèd arms.
Theridamas. You see, my lord, what working words he hath.   25
But when you see his actions top his speech,
Your speech will stay, or so extol his worth
As I shall be commended and excused
For turning my poor charge to his direction.

26. top] *conj. Oxberry;* stop *O1–3, Q.*

---

8. *royalise*] render famous, celebrate (first instance, *O.E.D.* 1b.).

11–12. *sway / To some direction*] 'prevail so as to give me some degree of control' (Ellis-Fermor, p. 100).

16. *Parthian Araris*] See *One* II.i.63 n. Ellis-Fermor (p. 100) refers to Herodotus vii.21 for the legendary drinking of the 'Araxes', and she also quotes Haytoun's comparison of Xerxes' army with Tamburlaine's in this regard: ' "Les gens et les chevaulx de son ost en beuvant ont mys plusieurs grans fleuves a sec tant estoyt la nombre grant. Il estoyt plus puissant que iamais ne furent xerses ne darius et se nommoit lire de dieu" (*Les Fleurs des hystoires de la terre Dorient*, Part V. ch. vii. sig. Piv).'

18–21.] The Cyclopes, imprisoned by their brother Cronus, were freed by Zeus and made in return the thunder and lightning of his wrath (cf. 'the Cyclops' hammers', *Edward II*, I.iv.312). They are here merged with the Titans who made war on Zeus. For the portentous 'fiery meteors' of burning lances, cf. *One* IV.ii.51–2, *Two* IV.i.202–5, *Lucan* 529–30, *Dido* IV.iv.117–18; and Heninger, pp. 91–4. For the 'giants', cf. *One* V.i.511–12, *Lucan* 35–6, *Ovid's Elegies*, II.i.15–16. Cf. 'bullets wrapped in smoke and fire', *Jew of Malta*, II.iii.54 n.

And these his two renownèd friends, my lord,   30
Would make one thrust and strive to be retained
In such a great degree of amity.

Techelles. With duty and with amity we yield
Out utmost service to the fair Cosroe.

Cosroe. Which I esteem as portion of my crown.   35
Usumcasane and Techelles both,
When she that rules in Rhamnus' golden gates
And makes a passage for all prosperous arms
Shall make me solely emperor of Asia,
Then shall your meeds and valours be advanced   40
To rooms of honour and nobility.

Tamburlaine. Then haste, Cosroë, to be king alone,
That I with these my friends and all my men
May triumph in our long-expected fate.
The king your brother is now hard at hand;   45
Meet with the fool and rid your royal shoulders
Of such a burden as outweighs the sands
And all the craggy rocks of Caspia.

[*Enter a* Messenger.]

Messenger. My lord, we have discovered the enemy
Ready to charge you with a mighty army.   50

Cosroe. Come, Tamburlaine, now whet thy wingèd sword
And lift thy lofty arm into the clouds,
That it may reach the king of Persia's crown
And set it safe on my victorious head.

Tamburlaine. See where it is, the keenest curtle-axe   55
That e'er made passage thorough Persian arms.
These are the wings shall make it fly as swift

---

33. and] *Q;* not *O1–3.*   48.1. *Enter a* Messenger] Oxberry [*A* MESSEN-
GER *enters.*]; *not in O1–3, Q.*

---

35. *portion of my crown*] part of my kingly estate.

37. *she*] i.e., Nemesis, whose temple stood at Rhamnus in Attica. Cf.
'Rhamnusia' at *Two* III.iv.57. Ellis-Fermor (p. 101) cites Ovid, *Tristia*
v.8, 9, and *Metam.,* iii.406.

38. *makes . . . for*] assists the progress of.

40. *meeds*] merit, excellence; cf. 'merits' at *One* I.ii.254.

41. *rooms*] positions, offices.

48. *Caspia*] the Caspian Sea.

55. *curtle-axe*] cutlass.

57. *wings*] literally, the cross-piece to his cutlass.

As doth the lightning or the breath of heaven,
And kill as sure as it swiftly flies.

Cosroe. Thy words assure me of kind success.   60
Go, valiant soldier, go before and charge
The fainting army of that foolish king.

Tamburlaine. Usumcasane and Techelles, come:
We are enough to scare the enemy,
And more than needs to make an emperor.   [*Exeunt.*] 65

[SCENE iv]

To the battle, and MYCETES *comes out alone with his
crown in his hand, offering to hide it*

Mycetes. Accurst be he that first invented war!
They knew not, ah, they knew not, simple men,
How those were hit by pelting cannon shot
Stand staggering like a quivering aspen leaf

---

65. *Exeunt*] Oxberry [*They go out to the battle.*]; not in O1–3, Q.
Heading. SCENE iv] Dyce 1; not in O1–3, Q.

59–60. *sure . . . assure*] 'Marlowe apparently scans these as disyllabic
and trisyllabic words' (Ellis-Fermor, p. 102).

64. *scare*] The spelling in O1 is 'scarre'; cf. the O1 spelling 'scar' at
Two IV.i.19. At *Two* V.i.114, O1 has 'scard' in the sense of 'scarred'.
'Scar' is an alternative reading here.

SCENE iv] O1–3, Q, omit scene divisions here and II.v, but resume at
II.vi, where modern editions correspond. See Introduction p. 86.

II.iv.0.2. *offering to*] trying to.

1–5.] An elegy of Tibullus (I.10) castigates the same cursed inventor—
'Quis fuit horrendos primus qui protulit enses?' ('Tell me, who invented
the terrifying sword?')—and develops the theme of the madness of war
by means of that contrast with primeval felicity which is brought to bear
elsewhere on human inventions (e.g. Elegy I.3.47: 'non acies, non ira
fuit, non bella, nec ensem / immiti saevus duxerat arte faber' ('Anger and
armies and war were not yet known: / no blacksmith's cruel craft had
forged the sword': Tibullus, *Elegies*, ed. and trans. G. Lee, Cambridge,
1975). I owe this reference to J. C. Maxwell, who also drew attention to
Sophocles, *Ajax*, 1192 ff., and F. Leo, *Plautinische Forschungen*, 1895,
136 ff.). See also Ovid, *Metam.*, xv.96 ff., on the origin of killing with the
'non utilis auctor' who first ate flesh.

3. *were*] i.e., who were.

4–5. *aspen leaf . . . Boreas*] Marlowe has Golding's Ovid in mind,
perhaps for the (commonplace) 'stout blustring Boreas' and 'sturdie

Fearing the force of Boreas' boist'rous blasts.   5
In what a lamentable case were I
If nature had not given me wisdom's lore!
For kings are clouts that every man shoots at,
Our crown the pin that thousands seek to cleave;
Therefore in policy I think it good   10
To hide it close: a goodly stratagem,
And far from any man that is a fool.
So shall not I be known, or if I be,
They cannot take away my crown from me.
Here will I hide it in this simple hole.   15

Enter TAMBURLAINE.

Tamburlaine. What fearful coward straggling from the camp
    When kings themselves are present in the field?
Mycetes. Thou liest.
Tamburlaine. Base villain, darest thou give the lie?
Mycetes. Away, I am the king, go, touch me not.   20
    Thou breakest the law of arms unless thou kneel
    And cry me 'Mercy, noble king!'
Tamburlaine. Are you the witty king of Persia?
Mycetes. Ay, marry, am I; have you any suit to me?
Tamburlaine. I would entreat you to speak but three wise   25
    words.
Mycetes. So I can when I see my time.
Tamburlaine. Is this your crown?
Mycetes. Ay, didst thou ever see a fairer?

---

blasts' (i.73) of Boreas, the north wind, but more definitely for 'trembling
like an Aspen leaf' (iii.46), where the figure describes fear, in Golding
but not in the original: Mary M. Wills, 'Marlowe's Role in Borrowed
Lines', *P.M.L.A.*, LII (1937), 903. For Boreas, cf. *One* I.ii.205, *Two*
I.iii.160. Perhaps Marlowe's lines reminded Shakespeare of Golding's:
see *Titus*, II.iv.44–5 (note from Roger Warren).

    8–9. *clouts . . . pin*] metaphors from archery. 'The clout is the central
mark of the butts, to hit which is the aim of the archer; the pin is the
nail in its centre that fastens it in place. "To cleave the pin" is, of course,
a triumph achieved only by the highest skill' (Ellis-Fermor, p. 103).

    10. *policy*] Mycetes is availing himself of an (infamously) impressive
word to dignify an effete purpose. Cf. *Two* II.i.38 n.

    23. *witty*] wise, intelligent. Mycetes has prized this quality persistently,
and has been distinguished for lacking it (except, notably, for the speech
which has opened this scene).

Tamburlaine. You will not sell it, will ye?   30
Mycetes. Such another word, and I will have thee executed.
    Come, give it me.
Tamburlaine. No, I took it prisoner.
Mycetes. You lie, I gave it you.
Tamburlaine. Then 'tis mine.   35
Mycetes. No, I mean, I let you keep it.
Tamburlaine. Well, I mean you shall have it again.
    Here, take it for a while, I lend it thee,
    Till I may see thee hemmed with armèd men.
    Then shalt thou see me pull it from thy head: 40
    Thou art no match for mighty Tamburlaine.   [*Exit.*]
Mycetes. O gods, is this Tamburlaine the thief?
    I marvel much he stole it not away.
            Sound trumpets to the battle, and he runs in.

[SCENE V]

[*Enter*] COSROE, TAMBURLAINE, THERIDAMAS,
MENAPHON, MEANDER, ORTYGIUS, TECHELLES,
USUMCASANE, *with others.*

Tamburlaine. Hold thee, Cosroe, wear two imperial crowns.
    Think thee invested now as royally,
    Even by the mighty hand of Tamburlaine,
    As if as many kings as could encompass thee
    With greatest pomp had crowned thee emperor.   5
Cosroe. So do I, thrice-renownèd man-at-arms,
    And none shall keep the crown but Tamburlaine:
    Thee do I make my regent of Persia,
    And general lieutenant of my armies.
    Meander, you that were our brother's guide   10
    And chiefest counsellor in all his acts,
    Since he is yielded to the stroke of war,
    On your submission we with thanks excuse
    And give you equal place in our affairs.

41. *Exit.*] Oxberry; not in *O1–3, Q.*   Heading. SCENE v] *Dyce 1; not
in O1–3, Q.*   O.I. *Enter*] Oxberry; not in *O1–3, Q.*

43.1. *Sound . . . to*] give the signal to resume (*O.E.D. vb.* 9).

Meander. Most happy emperor, in humblest terms   15
    I vow my service to your majesty,
    With utmost virtue of my faith and duty.
Cosroe. Thanks, good Meander; then, Cosroë, reign,
    And govern Persia in her former pomp.
    Now send embassage to thy neighbour kings   20
    And let them know the Persian king is changed—
    From one that knew not what a king should do,
    To one that can command what 'longs thereto.
    And now we will to fair Persepolis
    With twenty thousand expert soldiers: 25
    The lords and captains of my brother's camp
    With little slaughter take Meander's course
    And gladly yield them to my gracious rule.
    Ortygius and Menaphon, my trusty friends,
    Now will I gratify your former good   30
    And grace your calling with a greater sway.
Ortygius. And as we ever aimed at your behoof
    And sought your state all honour it deserved,
    So will we with our powers and our lives
    Endeavour to preserve and prosper it.   35
Cosroe. I will not thank thee, sweet Ortygius:
    Better replies shall prove my purposes.
    And now, Lord Tamburlaine, my brother's camp
    I leave to thee and to Theridamas,
    To follow me to fair Persepolis.   40
    Then will we march to all those Indian mines

32. aimed] *O3, Q;* and *O1–2.*

II.v.17. *virtue*] force, active commitment.
  20. *embassage*] ambassadorial message (*O.E.D.* 2); or, ambassador and retinue (*O.E.D.* 4, earliest entry 1621).
  25. *expert*] tried, proved in battle.
  26. *camp*] '(campaigning) army' (Pendry–Maxwell).
  29.] an alexandrine: cf., for instance, *One* I.i.46 n.
  30. *gratify*] requite.
  31. *calling*] allegiance, vocation.
  32. *behoof*] advance, benefit.
  33. *sought your state*] sought for your rank, standing.
  34. *powers*] armies, perhaps, or an equivalent of 'virtues' (cf. l. 17 n. above).
  40. *to follow me*] i.e., to follow me later.
  41. *Indian mines*] cf. *Jew of Malta*, I.i.19 n.

My witless brother to the Christians lost,
And ransom them with fame and usury.
And till thou overtake me, Tamburlaine,
Staying to order all the scattered troops,   45
Farewell lord regent, and his happy friends:
I long to sit upon my brother's throne.
Menaphon. Your majesty shall shortly have your wish,
And ride in triumph through Persepolis.   *Exeunt.*

Manent TAMBURLAINE, THERIDAMAS, TECHELLES,
USUMCASANE.

Tamburlaine. And ride in triumph through Persepolis!   50
Is it not brave to be a king, Techelles?
Usumcasane and Theridamas,
Is it not passing brave to be a king,
And ride in triumph through Persepolis?
Techelles. O my lord, 'tis sweet and full of pomp.   55
Usumcasane. To be a king is half to be a god.
Theridamas. A god is not so glorious as a king.
I think the pleasure they enjoy in heaven
Cannot compare with kingly joys in earth:
To wear a crown enchased with pearl and gold,   60
Whose virtues carry with it life and death;
To ask, and have; command, and be obeyed;
When looks breed love, with looks to gain the prize—
Such power attractive shines in princes' eyes.
Tamburlaine. Why, say, Theridamas, wilt thou be a king? 65
Theridamas. Nay, though I praise it, I can live without it.
Tamburlaine. What says my other friends, will you be kings?
Techelles. Ay, if I could, with all my heart, my lord.
Tamburlaine. Why, that's well said, Techelles, so would I.
And so would you, my masters, would you not?   70
Usumcasane. What then, my lord?
Tamburlaine. Why then, Casane, shall we wish for ought
The world affords in greatest novelty,

---

43. *with . . . usury*] 'to our renown and profit' (Jump).
53. *passing brave*] surpassingly glorious.
58–9.] The Matthew text (vi.10) may be faintly present: 'Thy will be done even in earth, as *it is* in heaven.'
60. *enchased*] set.
73. *in greatest novelty*] 'no matter how new and rare' (Jump).

And rest attemptless, faint and destitute?
Methinks we should not: I am strongly moved   75
That if I should desire the Persian crown
I could attain it with a wondrous ease.
And would not all our soldiers soon consent
If we should aim at such a dignity?
Theridamas. I know they would, with our persuasions.   80
Tamburlaine. Why then, Theridamas, I'll first essay
To get the Persian kingdom to myself;
Then thou for Parthia, they for Scythia and Media.
And if I prosper, all shall be as sure
As if the Turk, the Pope, Afric and Greece   85
Came creeping to us with their crowns apace.
Techelles. Then shall we send to this triumphing king
And bid him battle for his novel crown?
Usumcasane. Nay, quickly then, before his room be hot.
Tamburlaine. 'Twill prove a pretty jest, in faith, my friends.   90
Theridamas. A jest to charge on twenty thousand men?
I judge the purchase more important far.
Tamburlaine. Judge by thyself, Theridamas, not me,
For presently Techelles here shall haste
To bid him battle ere he pass too far   95
And lose more labour than the gain will quite.

86. apace] *O1–2;* apeece *O3, Q.*

---

74. *attemptless*] without attempting, inert (sole entry in *O.E.D.*).
85.] 'Tamburlaine names the four potentates whose submission would virtually make him emperor of the world: the Turkish emperor representing Anatolia, some of the western Black Sea coast, the Levant, and several African provinces; the Pope being the spiritual head of Christendom; the Soldan of Egypt standing for the chief empire of the African continent; the Emperor of Greece the surviving eastern Roman or Byzantine Empire with its seat at Constantinople' (Ellis-Fermor, p. 108).
86. *apace*] 'apiece', the *O3, Q,* reading, was adopted by Oxberry and other editors. It occurs ('apeece') in a similarly scornful context, at *Two* IV.iii.70; but we find 'apace' used scornfully in *Edward II,* IV.iii.12: 'they bark'd apace a month ago'.
89. *before his room be hot*] before he has established his authority by wielding it eagerly ('hot', *O.E.D. adj.* 6, 7).
92. *purchase*] undertaking, enterprise; perhaps with an implication of 'loot' (Pendry–Maxwell).
important] momentous.
96. *quite*] repay, requite.

Then shalt thou see the Scythian Tamburlaine
Make but a jest to win the Persian crown.
Techelles, take a thousand horse with thee
And bid him turn him back to war with us   100
That only made him king to make us sport.
We will not steal upon him cowardly,
But give him warning and more warriors.
Haste thee, Techelles, we will follow thee.   [*Exit.*]
What saith Theridamas?   105
Theridamas. Go on, for me.   *Exeunt.*

SCENE vi

[*Enter*] COSROE, MEANDER, ORTYGIUS, MENAPHON,
with other Soldiers.

Cosroe. What means this devilish shepherd, to aspire
With such a giantly presumption,
To cast up hills against the face of heaven,
And dare the force of angry Jupiter?   '
But as he thrust them underneath the hills   5
And pressed out fire from their burning jaws,
So will I send this monstrous slave to hell
Where flames shall ever feed upon his soul.
Meander. Some powers divine, or else infernal, mixed

100. him back] *Robinson;* his back *O1–3, Q.*   104. *Dyce 1 adds Exit
Techelles.*   *Heading.* SCENE vi] *O1–3, Q.*   0.1. Enter] *Robinson; not
in O1–3, Q.*

---

100. *him back*] Robinson's emendation gives a commoner usage,
though at the cost of yet another 'him' in this congested passage.

102–3.] These lines establish the contrast with the betrayal of Orcanes
by Sigismond in Part Two: cf. *Two* II.ii.24–6.

106. *for me*] 'as far as I'm concerned' (Ellis-Fermor, p. 108; though
ll. 57–64 tell against her sense of its tone as indicating that Theridamas
'has not yet caught to the full the exaltation of Tamburlaine and his
followers').

II.vi.2–6.] Ovid's lines on the presumptuous Titans seem influentially
present here (*Metam.*, i.151–3). 'One of the Titans, Enceladus, was
trapped by Zeus under Mount Etna, from which he continued to belch
out fire and smoke. He is sometimes identified with Typhon or Typhoeus,
who was a giant' (Woolf, p. 231).

9–10.] Tamburlaine himself recasts this diagnosis of perversion,
seeing elemental strife as natural, at *One* II.vii.18–20.

Their angry seeds at his conception: 10
For he was never sprung of human race,
Since with the spirit of his fearful pride
He dares so doubtlessly resolve of rule
And by profession be ambitious.

Ortygius. What god or fiend or spirit of the earth, 15
Or monster turnèd to a manly shape,
Or of what mould or mettle he be made,
What star or state soever govern him,
Let us put on our meet encount'ring minds,
And in detesting such a devilish thief 20
In love of honour and defence of right,
Be armed against the hate of such a foe,
Whether from earth, or hell, or heaven he grow.

Cosroe. Nobly resolved, my good Ortygius:
And since we all have sucked one wholesome air, 25
And with the same proportion of elements
Resolve, I hope we are resembled,
Vowing our loves to equal death and life.
Let's cheer our soldiers to encounter him,
That grievous image of ingratitude, 30
That fiery thirster after sovereignty,
And burn him in the fury of that flame
That none can quench but blood and empery.

---

13. *doubtlessly*] without misgiving (cf., possibly, *John*, IV.i.130: 'And, pretty child, sleep doubtless and secure').

resolve of] determine firmly to achieve (*O.E.D.* 23c: first entry).

14. *by profession*] by vocation, professedly (*O.E.D.* 6c, earliest entry 1606–7). To 'profess' ambition contrasts with the sense of avowing religious belief.

17. *mettle*] disposition, temperament (*O.E.D.* 1); ? substance (punning on 'metal').

25. *sucked*] inhaled (*O.E.D.* I.6, earliest instance 1590).

25–8.] 'As we, being men, have all lived by breathing the same vital air, and shall all dissolve at death into the same proportions of the elements of which we are made, I hope we will also resemble each other in vowing, out of mutual love, to meet death or life resolutely together' (cf. Ellis-Fermor, p. 110). See also *One* I.ii.235–6 n., and *Dr. Faustus*, xix.117–8. Pendry–Maxwell suggest that *some proportion of elements* may include the idea of the body returning to earth in death.

31.] Cosroe presents the malign version of the fire and thirst which Menaphon had idealised in describing Tamburlaine to him at *One* II.i.19–20.

Resolve, my lords and loving soldiers now
To save your king and country from decay;   35
Then strike up drum, and all the stars that make
The loathsome circle of my dated life,
Direct my weapon to his barbarous heart
That thus opposeth him against the gods
And scorns the powers that govern Persia.   [*Exeunt.*]   40

[SCENE vii]

Enter to the battle, and after the battle enter COSROE
wounded, THERIDAMAS, TAMBURLAINE, TECHELLES,
USUMCASANE, *with others.*

Cosroe. Barbarous and bloody Tamburlaine,
Thus to deprive me of my crown and life!
Treacherous and false Theridamas,
Even at the morning of my happy state,
Scarce being seated in my royal throne,   5
To work my downfall and untimely end!
An uncouth pain torments my grievèd soul,
And death arrests the organ of my voice,
Who, entering at the breach thy sword hath made,
Sacks every vein and artier of my heart.   10

---

40. *Exeunt*] Oxberry [*All go out to the battle*]; not in *O1–3, Q.*   Heading. SCENE vii] Dyce *1; not in O1–3, Q.*

35. *decay*] overthrow, fall (*O.E.D.* 1).
37. *circle*] 'full extent of time [? + weary, changeless repetition;
confinement]' (Pendry–Maxwell).
dated] having a predetermined end (*O.E.D.* 2: first entry); cf. *Two*
II.iv.45. Cosroe's defeatism, which is held by Marlowe dramatically
alongside his resolution, reflects his constant conviction that Tamburlaine is invincible.
II.vii.0.1. *Enter . . . enter*] Modern editors have, if they wish, to supply
'*Exeunt*' at the end of II.vi, and the scene division above this direction.
We may suppose that in practice Cosroe first remains on stage and is
encountered in battle which moves offstage, after which he re-enters with
his victorious adversaries. Bowers chooses to read 'Exeunt to the Battell,
and . . . enter', after Oxberry. See Introduction, p. 87.
7. *uncouth*] unpleasant, strange (*O.E.D.* 4).
10. *vein and artier*] the arteries being distinguished, before Harvey, as
containing an ethereal fluid, the 'vital spirits'.

    Bloody and insatiate Tamburlaine!

Tamburlaine. The thirst of reign and sweetness of a crown,
    That caused the eldest son of heavenly Ops
    To thrust his doting father from his chair
    And place himself in th'empyreal heaven,   15
    Moved me to manage arms against thy state.
    What better precedent than mighty Jove?
    Nature, that framed us of four elements
    Warring within our breasts for regiment,
    Doth teach us all to have aspiring minds: 20

12–29.] Kocher (p. 84) notes the relation this passage bears to the assertion, at *Two* IV.i.111–20, of the divine nature of the warring spirit, and finds a transition in emphasis from love of infinite knowledge to love of infinite power. Jove is the exemplary figure in both contexts; he is described as 'usurper of his father's seat' in *Hero*, First Sestiad, 1.452. Marlowe's startling shift of emphasis to an ethic of conflict from one in whose terms man seeks to achieve a harmonious natural balance of energies, and abstains from aspiration beyond his ordained sphere, is sustained by the continual mutual mirroring in the play of human and divine. Strife and aspiration characterise gods (and also threaten them); human energy, raised to its highest power, seeks godly status as much in strife's exercise as in aspiration's rewards: the activity is firmly celebrated as an end—the ardency of a continuous heroic present. The culminating stress on 'The sweet fruition of an earthly crown' is not, as it has been thought, bathetic: its 'virtues' are already too brightly established for that. There is an element of impiety, felt in the contrast with Zenocrate's moving rebuke of *hubris* (*One* V.i.353–63); note also Tamburlaine's 'aspire celestial thrones' (*One* I.ii.236), and 'A god is not so glorious as a king' of *One* II.v.57. Pendry–Maxwell note that it is inept, or ironic, to call the goddess of earthly plenty *heavenly Ops*. Jove, son of Ops, overthrew his father Saturn (cf. l. 36).

15. *empyreal heaven*] the empyrean, 'the immovable heaven lying just beyond the outermost moving sphere (the *primum mobile*) and enclosing within its concavity all the movable celestial spheres. The throne of God and the abode of the angels lay in this steadfast empyreal heaven, a region which shone perpetually with the purest light': F. R. Johnson, 'Marlowe's "Imperial Heaven"', *E.L.H.*, XII (1945), 35–44. The spelling in O1, for this phrase and 'th'empyreal orb', varies between 'emperiall' and 'imperiall'. It seems best, as Johnson argues (p. 36), to use 'empyreal' throughout: the word associates readily and properly with 'empery' and 'imperial', especially when, as here, human enterprise looks to divine sanctions, while primarily conveying the special astronomical sense. See *Dr Faustus*, vi.60: 'the seven planets, the firmament, and the empyreal heaven'. In phrases like 'th'Emperiall Diadem' (*One* I.i.139), 'imperial' is obviously the preferable modern spelling.

19. *regiment*] control.

Our souls, whose faculties can comprehend
The wondrous architecture of the world
And measure every wand'ring planet's course,
Still climbing after knowledge infinite
And always moving as the restless spheres,   25
Wills us to wear ourselves and never rest
Until we reach the ripest fruit of all,
That perfect bliss and sole felicity,
The sweet fruition of an earthly crown.

Theridamas. And that made me to join with Tamburlaine,   30
For he is gross and like the massy earth
That moves not upwards, nor by princely deeds
Doth mean to soar above the highest sort.

Techelles. And that made us, the friends of Tamburlaine,
To lift our swords against the Persian king.   35

Usumcasane. For as, when Jove did thrust old Saturn down,
Neptune and Dis gained each of them a crown,
So do we hope to reign in Asia
If Tamburlaine be placed in Persia.

Cosroe. The strangest men that ever Nature made!   40
I know not how to take their tyrannies.
My bloodless body waxeth chill and cold,
And with my blood my life slides through my wound.
My soul begins to take her flight to hell,
And summons all my senses to depart: 45
The heat and moisture, which did feed each other,

---

25. *restless spheres*] Cf. the 'turning spheres' of *One* IV.ii.39.

31–3.] Cf. *Two* IV.i.123–6, describing Calyphas: 'Created of the massy dregs of earth . . .'; and *Two* III.ii.8. The sense is 'he that moves not upwards . . . is gross, *etc.*', not (as in Battenhouse, p. 186) 'he [Tamburlaine] is gross, *etc.*'.

36–7.] Neptune and Dis ruled with Jove after the overthrow of Saturn. Cf. the 'infernal Dis' of *Two* IV.ii.93, and the account of Techelles' black army at *Two* I.iii.141–7. This couplet and the following one may be redeemed from bathos by jocularity.

40.] For Nature as making prodigies or monsters, cf. *One* I.i.104, and *Lucan* 560–1 and 588–9.

46–8.] 'Blood, the element which combines the properties of moisture and heat, being removed, the balance of the "temperament" or constitution is destroyed and only the properties of cold and dryness, those of the melancholy humour in the constitution of man, and of the earth in the material universe, remain' (Ellis-Fermor, p. 114).

For want of nourishment to feed them both
Is dry and cold, and now doth ghastly death
With greedy talons gripe my bleeding heart
And like a harpy tires on my life.   50
Theridamas and Tamburlaine, I die,
And fearful vengeance light upon you both!

                                            [*He dies.*]

    He [TAMBURLAINE] *takes the crown and puts it on.*

Tamburlaine. Not all the curses which the Furies breathe
    Shall make me leave so rich a prize as this.
    Theridamas, Techelles, and the rest,   55
    Who think you now is king of Persia?
All. Tamburlaine! Tamburlaine!
Tamburlaine. Though Mars himself, the angry god of arms,
    And all the earthly potentates conspire
    To dispossess me of this diadem,   60
    Yet will I wear it in despite of them
    As great commander of this eastern world,
    If you but say that Tamburlaine shall reign.
All. Long live Tamburlaine, and reign in Asia!
Tamburlaine. So, now it is more surer on my head,   65
    Than if the gods had held a parliament,
    And all pronounced me king of Persia.   [*Exeunt.*]

               Finis Actus secundi.

---

49. talons] *This ed.;* talents *O1–3, Q.*   50. harpy] *O2;* Harpyr *O1, O3;*
Harper *Q.*   52.1. *He dies*] *Oxberry; not in O1–3, Q.*   67. *Exeunt*]
Oxberry; not in O1–3, Q.   67.1. secundi] *This ed.;* 2. *O1–3, Q.*

---

48. *Is*] 'A singular verb with two cognate subjects is good Elizabethan
English' (Ellis-Fermor, p. 114).

49. *talons*] (*O.E.D.* 2d.: first instance of figurative use cited). Pendry–
Maxwell suggest connotations of 'appetite', 'anger'.

50. *harpy*] One of the clawed and winged monsters of legend. Ellis-
Fermor refers to *Aeneid*, iii.210 ('uncaeque manus'), *Metam.*, vii.4, and
Fasti, vi.132 ('avidae volucres' said here to be descended from the harpies).
    tires] grips and tears—a term from falconry; disyllabic.

53. *Furies*] also at *One* IV.iv.17 (an appeal to their poison), *One* V.i.94
(Tamburlaine dreaded *by* the Furies), *One* V.i.218, *Two* I.iii.146, *Two*
III.ii.12, *Two* III.iv.59.

Act III

Scene i

[Enter] BAJAZETH, *the Kings of* FESSE, MOROCCO, *and*
ARGIER, [Basso], *with others, in great pomp.*

Bajazeth. Great kings of Barbary, and my portly bassoes,
 We hear the Tartars and the eastern thieves,
 Under the conduct of one Tamburlaine,
 Presume a bickering with your emperor
 And thinks to rouse us from our dreadful siege   5
 Of the famous Grecian Constantinople.
 You know our army is invincible:
 As many circumcisèd Turks we have
 And warlike bands of Christians renied
 As hath the ocean or the Terrene sea   10
 Small drops of water when the moon begins
 To join in one her semicircled horns.
 Yet would we not be braved with foreign power,

0.1. *Enter*] Dyce 1; *not in* O1–3, Q. Basso] *Kirschbaum; not in* O1–3, Q.

III.i.0.1–2. FESSE, MOROCCO, *and* ARGIER] 'These kingdoms are all
marked by Ortelius along the north coast of Africa; together they make
up, as Marlowe notes, the district known generally as Barbary' (Ellis-
Fermor, p. 116).
 1. *portly*] stately.
 bassoes] bashaws, pashas.
 4. *bickering*] skirmish, or altercation (*O.E.D. vbl. sb.*, 1, 2): either sense
implying scorn of Tamburlaine's pretensions.
 5. *dreadful*] fear-inspiring.
 9. *renied*] apostate.
 10–12.] The conceit has a basis in received science: Kocher (pp. 288–9)
cites Galen as an ultimate source of the idea that there is more water in
the sea at full moon than at other times. The *Terrene* is, as for Ortelius,
the Mediterranean. For the 'horns' metaphor, cf. *Two* I.iii.14, *Two*
III.i.66–7.
 13. *braved ... power*] menaced ... army.

157

     Nor raise our siege before the Grecians yield
     Or breathless lie before the city walls.   15
Fesse. Renownèd emperor and mighty general,
     What if you sent the bassoes of your guard
     To charge him to remain in Asia,
     Or else to threaten death and deadly arms
     As from the mouth of mighty Bajazeth?   20
Bajazeth. Hie thee, my basso, fast to Persia:
     Tell him thy lord the Turkish emperor,
     Dread lord of Afric, Europe and Asia,
     Great king and conqueror of Graecia,
     The ocean Terrene, and the coal-black sea,   25
     The high and highest monarch of the world,
     Wills and commands (for say not I entreat)
     Not once to set his foot in Africa
     Or spread his colours in Graecia,
     Lest he incur the fury of my wrath.   30
     Tell him I am content to take a truce
     Because I hear he bears a valiant mind.
     But if, presuming on his silly power,
     He be so mad to manage arms with me,
     Then stay thou with him, say I bid thee so;   35
     And if before the sun have measured heaven
     With triple circuit thou regreet us not,

23–6.] That the scope of this vaunt exceeds historical fact matters less than that it collides with other dispositions of power in the play: cf. Cosroe's proclamation at *One* I.i.161 ff., and *One* II.v.83–6. The internal sickness of Persia, from which Cosroe and Tamburlaine profited, is set in a spacious and wordy context of self-proclaimed rulers of vast territories, with claims overlapping confusingly, and large general titles rising out of the drum-roll of continents and countries.

27.] Tamburlaine's equally peremptory assertion of will recalls this at *One* III.iii.41.

29.] The apparent lack of a syllable has been conjecturally made good by some editors; but 'Graecia' can, like other proper names, gain a lightly-stressed syllable where scansion requires.

32. *bears a valiant mind*] For this significant description of martial character, cf. *Two* I.iii.72–3, *Two* III.ii.143, and Introduction, section 6.

33. *silly power*] feeble, rustic army (? sorry, scanty: *O.E.D.* first entry 1593).

34. *mad to*] mad as to.

37. *regreet*] greet anew (*O.E.D.* 1, first entry).

We mean to take his morning's next arise
For messenger he will not be reclaimed,
And mean to fetch thee in despite of him.   40
Basso. Most great and puissant monarch of the earth,
    Your basso will accomplish your behest
    And shew your pleasure to the Persian,
    As fits the legate of the stately Turk.   *Exit* Basso.
Argier. They say he is the king of Persia—   45
    But if he dare attempt to stir your siege
    'Twere requisite he should be ten times more,
    For all flesh quakes at your magnificence.
Bajazeth. True, Argier, and tremble at my looks.
Morocco. The spring is hindered by your smothering host,   50
    For neither rain can fall upon the earth
    Nor sun reflex his virtuous beams thereon,
    The ground is mantled with such multitudes.
Bajazeth. All this is true as holy Mahomet,
    And all the trees are blasted with our breaths.   55
Fesse. What thinks your greatness best to be achieved
    In pursuit of the city's overthrow?
Bajazeth. I will the captive pioners of Argier
    Cut off the water that by leaden pipes
    Runs to the city from the mountain Carnon;   60

49. tremble] *O1–3, Q;* trembles *Oxberry.*

---

38. *arise*] arising (*O.E.D.*, first entry 1590).

39.] i.e., to signify that he (Tamburlaine) will not be cured of error.

46. *stir*] disturb, molest.

49. *tremble*] Oxberry tidies up the grammar; but 'tremble' may deserve to stand, as it carries an apt imperative tone.

50 ff.] Marlowe seems to take a hint from the proverb 'Where the Turk's horse once treads the grass never grows' (Tilley, T610: earliest reference 1639); see S. Artemel, *N.&Q.,* XVIII (1971), 216–23. Cf. *One* I.ii.48–9 n.

52. *reflex*] cast (*O.E.D. vb.* 2 b.).

virtuous] powerful, life-giving. For 'virtue', cf. Introduction, p. 51. Cf. *Paradise Lost,* III.608–9: 'with one virtuous touch, / Th'archchemic Sun'.

58. *will*] command that.

pioners] sappers.

60. *Carnon*] perhaps 'a confusion of the famous aqueduct of Constantinople with its equally famous Golden Horn, seeing that Carnon represents adequately the Turkish for horn' (Seaton, p. 393).

Two thousand horse shall forage up and down,
That no relief or succour come by land—
And all the sea my galleys countermand.
Then shall our footmen lie within the trench,
And with their cannons mouthed like Orcus' gulf   65
Batter the walls, and we will enter in:
And thus the Grecians shall be conquerèd.   *Exeunt.*

SCENE ii

[*Enter*] AGYDAS, ZENOCRATE, ANIPPE, *with others.*

Agydas. Madam Zenocrate, may I presume
To know the cause of these unquiet fits
That work such trouble to your wonted rest?
'Tis more than pity such a heavenly face
Should by heart's sorrow wax so wan and pale,   5
When your offensive rape by Tamburlaine
(Which of your whole displeasures should be most)
Hath seemed to be digested long ago.
Zenocrate. Although it be digested long ago,
As his exceeding favours have deserved,   10
And might content the Queen of Heaven as well
As it hath changed my first conceived disdain,
Yet since a farther passion feeds my thoughts
With ceaseless and disconsolate conceits
Which dyes my looks so lifeless as they are,   15
And might, if my extremes had full events,

---

67. *Exeunt*] *O1–2, not in O3, Q.*   0.1. *Enter*] *Dyce 1; not in O1–3, Q.*
1. *Agydas*] *Oxberry; not in O1–3, Q.*

---

63. *countermand*] control, keep under command (*O.E.D.* 8, first entry).
A different sense occurs at *One* I.ii.22.
65. *Orcus' gulf*] Hell; as at *Two* II.iii.25.
III.ii.6. *rape*] seizure, abduction.
7. *displeasures*] sorrows, troubles.
8. *digested*] endured, got over.
11. *the Queen of Heaven*] Juno. Cf. ll. 53–5 below.
13. *since*] i.e., since then.
14. *conceits*] fancies.
16–17.] 'And might, if what I imagine at worst came to pass, make me
the very picture of death.' The sense is developed in her next speech.

Make me the ghastly counterfeit of death.
Agydas. Eternal heaven sooner be dissolved,
    And all that pierceth Phoebe's silver eye,
    Before such hap fall to Zenocrate!   20
Zenocrate. Ah, life and soul still hover in his breast
    And leave my body senseless as the earth,
    Or else unite you to his life and soul,
    That I may live and die with Tamburlaine!

    Enter [aside] TAMBURLAINE *with* TECHELLES *and others.*

Agydas. With Tamburlaine? Ah, fair Zenocrate,   25
    Let not a man so vile and barbarous,
    That holds you from your father in despite
    And keeps you from the honours of a queen—
    Being supposed his worthless concubine—
    Be honoured with your love, but for necessity.   30
    So now the mighty Soldan hears of you,
    Your highness needs not doubt but in short time
    He will, with Tamburlaine's destruction,
    Redeem you from this deadly servitude.
Zenocrate. Agydas, leave to wound me with these words,   35
    And speak of Tamburlaine as he deserves:
    The entertainment we have had of him
    Is far from villainy or servitude,
    And might in noble minds be counted princely.
Agydas. How can you fancy one that looks so fierce,   40
    Only disposed to martial stratagems?
    Who when he shall embrace you in his arms
    Will tell how many thousand men he slew;
    And when you look for amorous discourse
    Will rattle forth his facts of war and blood,   45

24.1. *aside*] after Oxberry [*Enter* TAMBURLAINE, TECHELLES, *and others,
behind.*]; *not in* O1–3, Q.   35. Agydas] *conj. Dyce 1; not in* O1–3, Q.

   19.] 'All that the moon beholds' (Jump).
   21–4.] Zenocrate addresses her own 'life and soul', the 'you' of l. 23.
   27. *despite*] contemptuous defiance.
   30. *but for necessity*] except for what you are obliged to affect.
   38. *villainy*] indignity, insult.
   40. *fancy*] fall in love with. Cf. *Dido*, III.i.61.
   45. *facts*] exploits—perhaps with a colour of the common Elizabethan sense, 'evil deed, crime'; cf. *Ovid's Elegies*, II.ii.63, III.xii.32.

Too harsh a subject for your dainty ears.
Zenocrate. As looks the sun through Nilus' flowing stream,
   Or when the morning holds him in her arms,
   So looks my lordly love, fair Tamburlaine;
   His talk much sweeter than the Muses' song   50
   They sung for honour 'gainst Pierides,
   Or when Minerva did with Neptune strive;
   And higher would I rear my estimate
   Than Juno, sister to the highest god,
   If I were matched with mighty Tamburlaine.   55
Agydas. Yet be not so inconstant in your love,
   But let the young Arabian live in hope
   After your rescue to enjoy his choice.
   You see, though first the king of Persia,
   Being a shepherd, seemed to love you much,   60
   Now in his majesty he leaves those looks,
   Those words of favour, and those comfortings,
   And gives no more than common courtesies.
Zenocrate. Thence rise the tears that so distain my cheeks,
   Fearing his love through my unworthiness.   65

   TAMBURLAINE *goes to her, and takes her away lovingly*
   by the hand, looking wrathfully on AGYDAS, *and says*
                     nothing.

                     [*Exeunt all except* AGYDAS.]

Agydas. Betrayed by fortune and suspicious love,
   Threatened with frowning wrath and jealousy,
   Surprised with fear of hideous revenge,
   I stand aghast; but most astonièd

65.3. *Exeunt ...* AGYDAS] Oxberry [*All follow but Agydas*]; *not in* O1–3, Q.

---

47. *Nilus'*] the Nile's.

50–2.] Ellis-Fermor (p. 122) suggests Ovid, *Metam.*, v.302 ff., as the likely direct source for Marlowe's allusions to the contest of the Muses with the daughters of Pierus, and that of Athena and Poseidon for the government of Athens.

53. *estimate*] sense of my own worth; as at *One* I.ii.61.

60–1.] i.e., when first made King of Persia, Tamburlaine was close enough to his humble origins to show her love. The point is not to be lightly discounted: cf. *One* IV.iv.70, etc.

64. *distain*] stain. The form 'stained' is used of weeping at *Two* IV.ii.4.

65. *Fearing*] doubting.

69. *astonièd*] dismayed, astounded.

To see his choler shut in secret thoughts   70
And wrapt in silence of his angry soul.
Upon his brows was portrayed ugly death,
And in his eyes the fury of his heart
That shine as comets, menacing revenge,
And casts a pale complexion on his cheeks.   75
As when the seaman sees the Hyades
Gather an army of Cimmerian clouds
(Auster and Aquilon with wingèd steeds
All sweating, tilt about the watery heavens
With shivering spears enforcing thunderclaps,   80
And from their shields strike flames of lightning),
All fearful folds his sails, and sounds the main,
Lifting his prayers to the heavens for aid
Against the terror of the winds and waves:
So fares Agydas for the late-felt frowns   85
That sent a tempest to my daunted thoughts
And makes my soul divine her overthrow.

Enter TECHELLES *with a naked dagger.*

Techelles. See you, Agydas, how the king salutes you.
    He bids you prophesy what it imports.   *Exit.*

87.1. *Enter* TECHELLES] O1–3, Q; *Enter* USUMCASANE, *and* TECHELLES
Oxberry.   89. *Exit*] O1–2; not in O3, Q.

72.] As iconography of Tamburlaine, cf. *One* II.i.21. With *ugly death*,
cf. *Two* III.iv.16; 'ugly' associates insistently with Marlowe's 'Virgilian'
imagery of Hell.

74–5. *shine ... casts*] i.e. his eyes shine with fury, a passion which
brings pallor to his face.

76–9.] The *Hyades*, seven stars in the forehead of Taurus, were traditionally seen as causing bad weather; they rise and set at rainy times of
the year. The *Cimmerii* in classical fable lived in perpetual darkness: cf.
One V.i.234, *Two* V.iii.8.

78. *Auster and Aquilon*] the south wind and the north-east wind. The
conflict of these winds is described in Ovid, *Metam.*, v.285 (Ellis-Fermor,
p. 123). The collision of clouds was one commonly-offered explanation
of thunder (see Heninger, p. 74).

79. *tilt*] joust, ride with lances. Cf. (used of earthquakes) *One* I.ii.51.

87. *divine*] have presentiment of (*O.E.D.* 3).

89–107.] O3, Q, omit '*Exit*'; and as O1–3, Q, have no entry direction
at 106.1, Robinson and others direct both Techelles and Usumcasane to
enter at 87.1 and remain on stage (presumably aside) during Agydas's

Agydas. I prophesied before and now I prove   90
　　The killing frowns of jealousy and love.
　　He needed not with words confirm my fear,
　　For words are vain where working tools present
　　The naked action of my threatened end.
　　It says, Agydas, thou shalt surely die,   95
　　And of extremities elect the least:
　　More honour and less pain it may procure
　　To die by this resolvèd hand of thine
　　Than stay the torments he and heaven have sworn.
　　Then haste, Agydas, and prevent the plagues   100
　　Which thy prolongèd fates may draw on thee:
　　Go wander free from fear of tyrant's rage,
　　Removèd from the torments and the hell
　　Wherewith he may excruciate thy soul;
　　And let Agydas by Agydas die—   105
　　And with this stab slumber eternally.   [*Stabs himself.*]

　　　　　[*Enter* TECHELLES *and* USUMCASANE.]

Techelles. Usumcasane, see how right the man
　　Hath hit the meaning of my lord the king.
Usumcasane. Faith, and, Techelles, it was manly done;
　　And since he was so wise and honourable   110
　　Let us afford him now the bearing hence
　　And crave his triple-worthy burial.
Techelles. Agreed, Casane, we will honour him.
　　　　　　　[*Exeunt, bearing out the body.*]

---

106. *Stabs himself*] *Q; not in O1–3.*   106.1. *Enter* . . . USUMCASANE]
Ellis-Fermor; not in O1–3, Q.   113.1. *Exeunt* . . . *body*] *Oxberry; not
in O1–3, Q.*

---

soliloquy. Techelles, entering alone, might merely walk aside, to be
joined by Usumcasane at 107. Again, some editors have Techelles and
Usumcasane enter together at l. 87 and leave two lines later, then re-
enter at l. 106.
　　90. *prove*] find by experience, suffer.
　　91. *jealousy*] suspicion.
　　96.] proverbial: Tilley, E207.
　　99. *stay*] await.
　　104. *excruciate*] torture.
　　112.] 'And call for the noble funeral he has amply merited'.

Scene iii

[*Enter*] TAMBURLAINE, TECHELLES, USUMCASANE,
THERIDAMAS, Basso, ZENOCRATE, [ANIPPE,] *with others.*

Tamburlaine. Basso, by this thy lord and master knows
 I mean to meet him in Bithynia—
 See how he comes! Tush, Turks are full of brags
 And menace more than they can well perform.
 He meet me in the field and fetch thee hence!   5
 Alas, poor Turk, his fortune is too weak
 T'encounter with the strength of Tamburlaine.
 View well my camp, and speak indifferently:
 Do not my captains and my soldiers look
 As if they meant to conquer Africa?   10
Basso. Your men are valiant but their number few,
 And cannot terrify his mighty host:
 My lord, the great commander of the world,
 Besides fifteen contributory kings
 Hath now in arms ten thousand janizaries   15
 Mounted on lusty Mauritanian steeds
 Brought to the war by men of Tripoly;
 Two hundred thousand footmen that have served
 In two set battles fought in Graecia;
 And for the expedition of this war,   20
 If he think good, can from his garrisons

0.1. *Enter*] Oxberry; *not in* O1–3, Q. 0.2. ANIPPE] *Dyce 1; not in*
O1–3, Q.

III.iii.1. *this*] this time.
 2. *Bithynia*] Ellis-Fermor (p. 125) notes a deliberate vagueness in
Marlowe's placing of this battle; it was given varying locations in works
he may have used as sources.
 3. *See how he comes!*] i.e. he has not appeared.
 8. *indifferently*] without bias.
 11. *their number few*] 'A deliberate departure from the records' (Ellis-
Fermor, p. 125).
 14. *contributory*] tributary.
 15. *janizaries*] Turkish troops, Sultan's guardsmen; strictly, they were
infantry (Kocher, p. 242).
 16. *Mauritanian steeds*] 'A district of North-west Africa famous for its
horses and horsemen. Tripoly is further east, on the coast of Barbary'
(Ellis-Fermor, p. 126). Cf. the 'Barbarian steeds' of *Two* I.ii.47.
 20. *expedition*] 'speedy waging' (Jump).

Withdraw as many more to follow him.

Techelles. The more he brings the greater is the spoil:
For when they perish by our warlike hands,
We mean to seat our footmen on their steeds   25
And rifle all those stately janizars.

Tamburlaine. But will those kings accompany your lord?

Basso. Such as his highness please, but some must stay
To rule the provinces he late subdued.

Tamburlaine. Then fight courageously, their crowns are
     yours: 30
This hand shall set them on your conquering heads
That made me emperor of Asia.

Usumcasane. Let him bring millions infinite of men,
Unpeopling Western Africa and Greece,
Yet we assure us of the victory.   35

Theridamas. Even he, that in a trice vanquished two kings
More mighty than the Turkish emperor,
Shall rouse him out of Europe and pursue
His scattered army till they yield or die.

Tamburlaine. Well said, Theridamas, speak in that mood,   40
For Will and Shall best fitteth Tamburlaine,
Whose smiling stars gives him assurèd hope
Of martial triumph ere he meet his foes.
I that am termed the scourge and wrath of God,
The only fear and terror of the world,   45

---

26. *rifle*] plunder.

30.] Oxberry introduces the accurate direction *'To his officers'* midway through the line.

34.] recalling the Basso's reference to Bajazeth's conquests in ll. 16–19 above.

Unpeopling] Cf. *Two* I.iii.134, 149.

35. *assure us*] feel certain (*O.E.D. vb.* 9b.).

38. *rouse*] cause (game) to rise from cover (*O.E.D. vb.*[1] 2: first figurative entry 1589).

41.] recalling Bajazeth in *One* III.i.27.

44.] The first reference in the play to Tamburlaine as the scourge of God identifies him as inflicting Christian vengeance on the Turks; a concept recalled at *Two* II.i.53. (Cf. also *Two* I.ii.32.) Ellis-Fermor (p. 127) finds a likely source for this passage in Nicholay, describing the 'Christians renied' of the pirate galleys, their cruelty to slaves, and so on (*A Collection of Voyages*, ed. 1745, p. 560).

Will first subdue the Turk, and then enlarge
Those Christian captives which you keep as slaves,
Burdening their bodies with your heavy chains
And feeding them with thin and slender fare
That naked row about the Terrene sea;   50
And when they chance to breathe and rest a space
Are punished with bastones so grievously
That they lie panting on the galley's side
And strive for life at every stroke they give:
These are the cruel pirates of Argier,   55
That damnèd train, the scum of Africa,
Inhabited with straggling runagates,
That make quick havoc of the Christian blood.
But, as I live, that town shall curse the time
That Tamburlaine set foot in Africa.   60

Enter BAJAZETH *with his* Bassoes *and contributory* Kings
[*of* FESSE, MOROCCO, *and* ARGIER], [ZABINA *and* EBEA].

Bajazeth. Bassoes and janizaries of my guard,
    Attend upon the person of your lord,
    The greatest potentate of Africa.
Tamburlaine. Techelles and the rest, prepare your swords:
    I mean t'encounter with that Bajazeth.   65
Bajazeth. Kings of Fesse, Moroccus, and Argier,
    He calls me Bajazeth, whom you call lord!
    Note the presumption of this Scythian slave.
    I tell thee, villain, those that lead my horse
    Have to their names titles of dignity—   70
    And darest thou bluntly call me Bajazeth?

60.2. ZABINA *and* EBEA] *Dyce 1; not in O1–3, Q.*

---

46. *enlarge*] set free.

47–55. *you keep . . . they give: These are*] Tamburlaine's anger generates
a vivid picture of cruelty, in the course of which the Turks change
grammatical identity from 'you' to 'These', perhaps by way of an ambi-
guity in 'every stroke they give', which can refer equally to the galley
oarsmen and to their captors.

50. *Terrene*] Mediterranean.

52. *bastones*] cudgels; disyllabic.

55. *Argier*] as commonly, Algiers.

57. *runagates*] vagabonds, apostates; cf. l. 225 below, and the 'Christians renied' of *One* III.i.9.

66. *Fesse*] Fez.

Tamburlaine. And know thou, Turk, that those which lead
   my horse
   Shall lead thee captive thorough Africa—
   And darest thou bluntly call me Tamburlaine?
Bajazeth. By Mahomet my kinsman's sepulchre   75
   And by the holy Alcaron I swear
   He shall be made a chaste and lustless eunuch
   And in my sarell tend my concubines;
   And all his captains that thus stoutly stand
   Shall draw the chariot of my emperess,   80
   Whom I have brought to see their overthrow.
Tamburlaine. By this my sword that conquered Persia,
   Thy fall shall make me famous through the world.
   I will not tell thee how I'll handle thee,
   But every common soldier of my camp   85
   Shall smile to see thy miserable state.
Fesse. What means the mighty Turkish emperor
   To talk with one so base as Tamburlaine?
Morocco. Ye Moors and valiant men of Barbary,
   How can ye suffer these indignities?   90
Argier. Leave words and let them feel your lances' points,
   Which glided through the bowels of the Greeks.
Bajazeth. Well said, my stout contributory kings:
   Your threefold army and my hugy host
   Shall swallow up these base-born Persians.   95
Techelles. Puissant, renowned, and mighty Tamburlaine,
   Why stay we thus prolonging all their lives?
Theridamas. I long to see those crowns won by our swords,
   That we may reign as kings of Africa.
Usumcasane. What coward would not fight for such a prize?   100
Tamburlaine. Fight all courageously and be you kings:
   I speak it, and my words are oracles.
Bajazeth. Zabina, mother of three braver boys
   Than Hercules, that in his infancy

---

76. *Alcaron*] the Koran; an established English form in Marlowe's day.
78. *sarell*] seraglio, harem.
92. *glided through*] pierced (*O.E.D. vb.* 4b.).
94. *hugy*] huge.
104–5.] Among the many allusions to Herculean exploits in the play;
cf. Ovid, *Metam.*, v.136 ff. and 182 ff., Ellis-Fermor, p. 129, and Waith,
passim.

Did pash the jaws of serpents venomous,   105
Whose hands are made to grip a warlike lance,
Their shoulders broad, for complete armour fit,
Their limbs more large and of a bigger size
Than all the brats y-sprung from Typhon's loins;
Who, when they come unto their father's age,   110
Will batter turrets with their manly fists—
Sit here upon this royal chair of state
And on thy head wear my imperial crown,
Until I bring this sturdy Tamburlaine
And all his captains bound in captive chains.   115
Zabina. Such good success happen to Bajazeth!
Tamburlaine. Zenocrate, the loveliest maid alive,
Fairer than rocks of pearl and precious stone,
The only paragon of Tamburlaine,
Whose eyes are brighter than the lamps of heaven,   120
And speech more pleasant than sweet harmony;
That with thy looks canst clear the darkened sky
And calm the rage of thund'ring Jupiter—
Sit down by her, adornèd with my crown,
As if thou wert the empress of the world.   125
Stir not, Zenocrate, until thou see
Me march victoriously with all my men,
Triumphing over him and these his kings
Which I will bring as vassals to thy feet.
Till then, take thou my crown, vaunt of my worth,   130

---

105. *pash*] dash to pieces. On the 'Gallic inversion' *serpents venomous*, citing a precedent in Henryson, see Harold F. Brooks, 'Marlowe and Early Shakespeare', *Christopher Marlowe*, ed. Brian Morris (Mermaid Critical Commentaries), 1968, p. 81. Cf. 'dragons venomous', *One* II.ii.52.

109. *y-sprung*] Cf. the archaic 'ymounted' at *Two* IV.iii.119, a passage owing directly to Spenser, with whom such forms are as common as they are rare in Marlowe, who uses neither of these elsewhere.

Typhon] or Typhoeus, born to Earth by Tartarus; Echidna bore him Orthrus, the Nemean lion, Cerberus, the Lernaean Hydra, the Chimaera and the Sphinx; cf. l. 140 n. below.

116. *success*] fortune.

119. *paragon*] consort; with an implication of matchless excellence.

122-3.] Cf. *Ovid's Elegies*, II.v.51-2: 'She laugh'd, and kiss'd so sweetly as might make / Wrath-kindled Jove away his thunder shake'. See *One* V.i.178-90 n., and *One* V.i.438.

130. *vaunt of*] proclaim proudly, extol.

And manage words with her as we will arms.
Zenocrate. And may my love, the king of Persia,
    Return with victory, and free from wound!
Bajazeth. Now shalt thou feel the force of Turkish arms
    Which lately made all Europe quake for fear.   135
    I have of Turks, Arabians, Moors and Jews,
    Enough to cover all Bithynia:
    Let thousands die, their slaughtered carcasses
    Shall serve for walls and bulwarks to the rest;
    And as the heads of Hydra, so my power,   140
    Subdued, shall stand as mighty as before.
    If they should yield their necks unto the sword,
    Thy soldiers' arms could not endure to strike
    So many blows as I have heads for thee.
    Thou knowest not, foolish-hardy Tamburlaine,   145
    What 'tis to meet me in the open field,
    That leave no ground for thee to march upon.
Tamburlaine. Our conquering swords shall marshal us the
      way
    We use to march upon the slaughtered foe,
    Trampling their bowels with our horses' hoofs—   150
    Brave horses, bred on the white Tartarian hills.
    My camp is like to Julius Caesar's host,
    That never fought but had the victory;
    Nor in Pharsalia was there such hot war
    As these my followers willingly would have.   155
    Legions of spirits fleeting in the air

145. foolish-hardy] *Broughton, Dyce 1;* foolish hardy *O1–3, Q.*

---

131. *manage*] wield; a variant of the chivalric phrase 'manage arms'
(at *One* III.i.34, *Two* V.iii.36).

137. *Bithynia*] see l. 2 n. above.

140. *Hydra*] one of Typhon's brats (l. 109 above), the many-headed
monster.

   power] army.

148. *marshal us the way*] guide (*O.E.D.* 6, first entry). Cf. *Mac.*,
II.i.42: 'Thou marshall'st me the way that I was going'.

152–5.] The glance towards Lucan strengthens the inference that
Marlowe's knowledge of the *Pharsalia* contributed to the tonalities of
violence in *Tamburlaine*; but we do not know when he translated Book I
(see *Poems*, pp. xxxiv–v).

156. *fleeting*] gliding; cf. *Edward II*, IV.vi.104: 'Spenser, I see our
souls are fleeted hence'.

Direct our bullets and our weapons' points
And make your strokes to wound the senseless air;
And when she sees our bloody colours spread,
Then Victory begins to take her flight,   160
Resting herself upon my milk-white tent.
But come, my lords, to weapons let us fall.
The field is ours, the Turk, his wife and all.

Exit, with his followers.

Bajazeth. Come, kings and bassoes, let us glut our swords
That thirst to drink the feeble Persians' blood.   165

Exit, with his followers.

Zabina. Base concubine, must thou be placed by me
That am the empress of the mighty Turk?
Zenocrate. Disdainful Turkess and unreverend boss,
Callest thou me concubine, that am betrothed
Unto the great and mighty Tamburlaine?   170
Zabina. To Tamburlaine the great Tartarian thief!

---

158. your] *Dyce 1;* our *O1–3, Q.*   air] *conj. Dyce 2;* lure *O1, O3, Q,*
Ellis-Fermor; lute *O2;* light *Oxberry.*

158.] Bowers (i.222–3) defends the Dyce 2 emendation of 'lure' to 'air'
but resists his 'your' for 'our' on the grounds that the speech as a whole
does not proceed by developing contrasts between what the opposed
armies can achieve: ' "Our" is the consistent point of view'. This is not
in itself decisive, and Bowers' interpretation of the line as a climactic
threat—'the strokes against Bajazeth's men will be so vehement as even
to wound the air, which being senseless is not easily wounded'—runs
against the immediate grasp of the sense which most readers would take
(a stroke that wounds the air being a miss): this is its meaning in the
line which George Peele perhaps models on this one—'And makes their
weapons wound the senseless winds' (Bakeless, p. 261). Dyce himself
noted the unfortunate clash, if we emend to 'air', with l. 156; 'lure'
resists explanation, but 'air' is lamely repetitive. 'Lure' as the imitation
bird made of feathers and leather (cf. *Ven.*, 1027) is distantly possible.
Note also 'hit the woundless air', *Ham.*, IV.i.44.

159–61. *bloody . . . milk-white*] colours later ritualised in Tamburlaine's
three-day sieges (cf. *One* IV.ii.111 ff., *Two* V.i.86).

164. *glut*] used of killing, as here, at *Two* I.i.14 and *Two* IV.i.88: these
examples having to do with surfeit or unpleasant excess, as in 'glutted
with these grievous objects' at *One* V.i.342. Cf. *Lucan*, l. 39: 'Carthage
souls be glutted with our bloods'. Seaton, 'Sources', p. 397, notes from
Belleforest's *Cosmographie*, probably known to Marlowe, the very
relevant 'Toute la nation Scythienne a este gloute du sang humain'.
Used of pleasanter objects of desire at *Two* I.iii.220, V.iii.227 n.

168. *boss*] fat woman.

Zenocrate. Thou wilt repent these lavish words of thine
        When thy great basso-master and thyself
        Must plead for mercy at his kingly feet
        And sue to me to be your advocates.   175
Zabina. And sue to thee? I tell thee, shameless girl,
        Thou shalt be laundress to my waiting-maid.
        How likest thou her, Ebea, will she serve?
Ebea. Madam, she thinks perhaps she is too fine,
        But I shall turn her into other weeds   180
        And make her dainty fingers fall to work.
Zenocrate. Hearest thou, Anippe, how thy drudge doth talk,
        And how my slave, her mistress, menaceth?
        Both for their sauciness shall be employed
        To dress the common soldiers' meat and drink,   185
        For we will scorn they should come near ourselves.
Anippe. Yet sometimes let your highness send for them
        To do the work my chambermaid disdains.
            They sound [to] the battle within, and stay.
Zenocrate. Ye gods and powers that govern Persia
        And made my lordly love her worthy king,   190
        Now strengthen him against the Turkish Bajazeth
        And let his foes, like flocks of fearful roes
        Pursued by hunters, fly his angry looks,
        That I may see him issue conqueror.
Zabina. Now, Mahomet, solicit God himself,   195
        And make him rain down murd'ring shot from heaven
        To dash the Scythians' brains, and strike them dead
        That dare to manage arms with him

173. basso-master] *O2–3, Q;* Bassoe, maister *O1.*   175. advocates]
O1–2; Aduocate *O3, Q.*   182–3.] *Q repeats ll. 181–2 between 182, 183.*
188.1. *to] O3, Q; not in O1–2.*

173. *basso-master*] Introducing the hyphen, after O3, yields a convincing term of derision obscured by O1's punctuation, and one that is in
line with the derisive 'king of bassoes', l. 212 below.

175. *your advocates*] advocate for you both. The feminine form
'advocatess' seems only distantly possible.

185. *To dress . . . drink*] 'the fate assigned to Bajazeth's empress by
Perondinus and others' (Ellis-Fermor, p. 132): see Appendix.

188.1. *sound to*] give the trumpet-signal to begin (*O.E.D. vb.*[1] 9); cf.
One II.iv.42.1.

stay] stop sounding.

That offered jewels to thy sacred shrine
When first he warred against the Christians.   200
        [They sound] to the battle again.

Zenocrate. By this the Turks lie welt'ring in their blood,
  And Tamburlaine is lord of Africa.
Zabina. Thou art deceived—I heard the trumpets sound
  As when my emperor overthrew the Greeks
  And led them captive into Africa.   205
  Straight will I use thee as thy pride deserves:
  Prepare thyself to live and die my slave.
Zenocrate. If Mahomet should come from heaven and swear
  My royal lord is slain or conquerèd,
  Yet should he not persuade me otherwise   210
  But that he lives and will be conqueror.

    BAJAZETH *flies [across the stage], and he* [TAMBURLAINE]
    pursues him [offstage]. The battle short, and they [re-] enter.
             BAJAZETH *is overcome.*

Tamburlaine. Now, king of bassoes, who is conqueror?
Bajazeth. Thou, by the fortune of this damnèd foil.
Tamburlaine. Where are your stout contributory kings?

      Enter TECHELLES, THERIDAMAS, USUMCASANE.

Techelles. We have their crowns, their bodies strow the
    field.   215
Tamburlaine. Each man a crown? Why, kingly fought,
    i'faith.
  Deliver them into my treasury.
Zenocrate. Now let me offer to my gracious lord
  His royal crown again, so highly won.
Tamburlaine. Nay, take the Turkish crown from her,
    Zenocrate,   220
  And crown me emperor of Africa.
Zabina. No, Tamburlaine, though now thou gat the best,

211.1–2. *across the stage . . . offstage . . . re*-] *This ed.; not in O1–3, Q.*
battle short] *O1–2; Battel is short O3, Q.*   213. foil] *Dyce 2;* soile *O1–3,*
Q; Dyce 1 (but conj. foil).

---

  201. *this*] this time.
  213. *foil*] defeat: Dyce's 'almost irresistible emendation' (Ellis-Fermor,
p. 134). Cf. l. 235 below.

Thou shalt not yet be lord of Africa.

Theridamas. Give her the crown, Turkess, you were best.

He [THERIDAMAS] *takes it from her, and gives it* [*to*]
                    ZENOCRATE.

Zabina. Injurious villains, thieves, runagates,   225
How dare you thus abuse my majesty?

Theridamas. Here, madam, you are empress, she is none.

Tamburlaine. Not now, Theridamas, her time is past:
The pillars that have bolstered up those terms
Are fall'n in clusters at my conquering feet.   230

Zabina. Though he be prisoner, he may be ransomed.

Tamburlaine. Not all the world shall ransom Bajazeth.

Bajazeth. Ah fair Zabina, we have lost the field,
And never had the Turkish emperor
So great a foil by any foreign foe.   235
Now will the Christian miscreants be glad,
Ringing with joy their superstitious bells
And making bonfires for my overthrow.
But ere I die, those foul idolaters
Shall make me bonfires with their filthy bones—   240
For though the glory of this day be lost,
Afric and Greece have garrisons enough
To make me sovereign of the earth again.

Tamburlaine. Those wallèd garrisons will I subdue,
And write myself great lord of Africa: 245
So from the east unto the furthest west
Shall Tamburlaine extend his puissant arm.
The galleys and those pilling brigandines
That yearly sail to the Venetian gulf
And hover in the straits for Christians' wrack,   250

225.] among the play's very effective displacements of pentameter norms by speaking stress.

runagates] vagabonds, apostates.

229. *terms*] Jump identifies a metaphorical sense here from 'a statuary bust supported by a pillar out of which it seems to spring' (first *O.E.D.* instance 1604).

235. *foil*] defeat.

236. *miscreants*] misbelievers, heretics; see *Two* II.iii.36 n.

242. *Afric and Greece*] Cf. *One* III.i.23 ff.

248. *pilling brigandines*] plundering pirate craft (brigantines); cf. *One* III.iii.55.

250. *straits*] '? i.e. of Otranto' (Pendry–Maxwell).

Shall lie at anchor in the Isle Asant
Until the Persian fleet and men-of-war,
Sailing along the oriental sea,
Have fetched about the Indian continent,
Even from Persepolis to Mexico,   255
And thence unto the Straits of Jubalter,
Where they shall meet and join their force in one,
Keeping in awe the Bay of Portingale
And all the ocean by the British shore:
And by this means I'll win the world at last.   260

Bajazeth. Yet set a ransom on me, Tamburlaine.

Tamburlaine. What, thinkest thou Tamburlaine esteems thy
    gold?
I'll make the kings of India, ere I die,
Offer their mines, to sue for peace, to me,
And dig for treasure to appease my wrath.   265
Come, bind them both, and one lead in the Turk.
The Turkess let my love's maid lead away.

                They bind them.

Bajazeth. Ah villains, dare ye touch my sacred arms?
O Mahomet, O sleepy Mahomet!

Zabina. O cursèd Mahomet that makest us thus   270
The slaves to Scythians rude and barbarous!

Tamburlaine. Come, bring them in, and for this happy
    conquest
Triumph, and solemnise a martial feast.

                           Exeunt.

    Finis Actus tertii.

---

251. *Asant*] Zacynthus in antiquity, Zante to the Venetians who held
it for several centuries from the fourteenth onwards; modern Zacinthos
(note from Gordon Campbell).

252 ff.] 'Tamburlaine's Persian fleet is to follow approximately the
route of the Portuguese and Italian traders from Ormuz to southern
China. He then sees them strike across the Pacific to the western coast of
Mexico and appears to anticipate the Panama canal, bringing them
straight through the isthmus to Gibraltar, where they are to be joined by
the Mediterranean fleet and control the shipping in Biscay and the Channel' (Ellis-Fermor, p. 135). The *oriental sea* is the Pacific.

254. *fetched about*] sailed round.

258. *Bay of Portingale*] Bay of Biscay ('Portugal').

269.] anticipating Tamburlaine's call to Mahomet, *Two* V.i.186–98.

273. *Triumph*] hold a triumphal procession.

Act IV

[*Enter*] SOLDAN *of* EGYPT *with three or four* Lords,
CAPOLIN, [Messenger].

Soldan. Awake, ye men of Memphis, hear the clang
　　Of Scythian trumpets, hear the basilisks
　　That, roaring, shake Damascus' turrets down!
　　The rogue of Volga holds Zenocrate,
　　The Soldan's daughter, for his concubine,　　　　　　5
　　And with a troop of thieves and vagabonds
　　Hath spread his colours to our high disgrace
　　While you faint-hearted base Egyptians
　　Lie slumbering on the flow'ry banks of Nile,
　　As crocodiles that unaffrighted rest　　　　　　10
　　While thund'ring cannons rattle on their skins.
Messenger. Nay, mighty Soldan, did your greatness see
　　The frowning looks of fiery Tamburlaine,
　　That with his terror and imperious eyes
　　Commands the hearts of his associates,　　　　　　15
　　It might amaze your royal majesty.
Soldan. Villain, I tell thee, were that Tamburlaine

0.1. Enter] *Oxberry; not in O1–3, Q.*　　0.2. Messenger] *Oxberry; not in
O1–3, Q.*

IV.i.1 ff.] Cf. *Two* III.iii.58 ff. as a suggestive supplementary stage
direction. There is a debt to the characteristic sonorousness of Lucan,
as Marlowe's version illustrates: 'There spread the colours, with confused
noise / Of trumpet's clange, shrill cornets, whistling fifes' (ll. 239–40).

　2. *basilisks*] brazen cannons; as in *Jew of Malta*, III.v.31.

　4. *Volga*] 'Marlowe's references suggest that he associates Tamburlaine
with the district north and west of the Caspian Sea, though at other
times he follows the tradition which makes him a native of Samarcand
or its neighbourhood' (Ellis-Fermor, p. 137).

As monstrous as Gorgon, prince of hell,
The Soldan would not start a foot from him.
But speak, what power hath he?

Messenger.   Mighty lord,   20
Three hundred thousand men in armour clad
Upon their prancing steeds, disdainfully
With wanton paces trampling on the ground;
Five hundred thousand footmen threat'ning shot,
Shaking their swords, their spears and iron bills,   25
Environing their standard round, that stood
As bristle-pointed as a thorny wood;
Their warlike engines and munition
Exceed the forces of their martial men.

Soldan. Nay, could their numbers countervail the stars,   30
Or ever-drizzling drops of April showers,
Or withered leaves that Autumn shaketh down,
Yet would the Soldan by his conquering power
So scatter and consume them in his rage
That not a man should live to rue their fall.   35

Capolin. So might your highness, had you time to sort
Your fighting men and raise your royal host.
But Tamburlaine by expedition
Advantage takes of your unreadiness.

Soldan. Let him take all th'advantages he can.   40
Were all the world conspired to fight for him,
Nay, were he devil, as he is no man,

---

18. *monstrous*] unnatural, grotesque; frequently trisyllabic, and sometimes spelt 'monstruous' (cf. Introduction, p. 6).

Gorgon] Demogorgon, a prince of Hell, invoked with Lucifer and Beelzebub in *Dr Faustus*, III.iii.18–20.

20–1.] an exception to Marlowe's usual practice in this play of beginning and ending speeches with a full pentameter line.

21–9.] Marlowe describes not an authentic Tartar horde but a typical European army of his own times.

23. *wanton*] frisky.

25. *bills*] halberds: their long handles suggesting the apt image of l. 27; cf. *Two* I.i.23.

26–7.] On two more of the few couplets in *Tamburlaine*, cf. *One* II.vii.36–7 n.

28. *engines*] instruments of assault (*O.E.D. sb.* 5).

munition] shot (*O.E.D. sb.* 2); four syllables.

30. *countervail*] equal, match.

38. *expedition*] speed.

    Yet in revenge of fair Zenocrate
    Whom he detaineth in despite of us,
    This arm should send him down to Erebus   45
    To shroud his shame in darkness of the night.
Messenger. Pleaseth your mightiness to understand,
    His resolution far exceedeth all:
    The first day when he pitcheth down his tents,
    White is their hue, and on his silver crest   50
    A snowy feather spangled white he bears,
    To signify the mildness of his mind
    That, satiate with spoil, refuseth blood;
    But when Aurora mounts the second time,
    As red as scarlet is his furniture—   55
    Then must his kindled wrath be quenched with blood,
    Not sparing any that can manage arms;
    But if these threats move not submission,
    Black are his colours, black pavilion,
    His spear, his shield, his horse, his armour, plumes,   60
    And jetty feathers menace death and hell—
    Without respect of sex, degree, or age,
    He razeth all his foes with fire and sword.
Soldan. Merciless villain, peasant ignorant
    Of lawful arms or martial discipline!   65
    Pillage and murder are his usual trades—
    The slave usurps the glorious name of war.
    See Capolin, the fair Arabian king
    That hath been disappointed by this slave
    Of my fair daughter and his princely love,   70
    May have fresh warning to go war with us
    And be revenged for her disparagement.   *[Exeunt.]*

---

72. disparagement] *O3, Q;* dispardgement *O1–2.*   *Exeunt] Oxberry;*
not in O1–3, Q.

---

45. *Erebus*] The gloomy region on whose 'blasted banks' ghosts wait
for 'the ugly ferryman' (*One* V.i.243–7).

49 ff.] Tamburlaine's ritual of siege is an accretion of European origin
to the eastern historians' accounts of Timur. See Appendix for examples
of the source descriptions, which Marlowe much expands.

55. *furniture*] armour, accoutrements (listed in ll. 59–61 below).

61. *jetty*] jet-black.

62. *degree*] rank.

72. *disparagement*] indignity, disgrace.

SCENE ii

[*Enter*] TAMBURLAINE [*all in white*], TECHELLES, THERIDAMAS,
USUMCASANE, ZENOCRATE, ANIPPE, *two* Moors *drawing*
BAJAZETH *in his cage, and his wife* [ZABINA] *following him.*

Tamburlaine. Bring out my footstool.
                They take him out of the cage.
Bajazeth. Ye holy priests of heavenly Mahomet,
        That, sacrificing, slice and cut your flesh,
        Staining his altars with your purple blood,
        Make heaven to frown and every fixèd star   5
        To suck up poison from the moorish fens
        And pour it in this glorious tyrant's throat!
Tamburlaine. The chiefest God, first mover of that sphere
        Enchased with thousands ever-shining lamps,

0.1. *Enter*] Oxberry; *not in O1–3, Q.*   *all in white*] *This ed.; not in*
O1–3, Q.

IV.ii.0.1. *in white*] We may infer that Tamburlaine is wearing a silver
crest and white feather, and that other accoutrements, pennons, perhaps
his tent, are brought on stage: it is the first day of the siege of Damascus,
as we are reminded at ll. 111–12, and IV.i.49–51 provides a producer with
clear instructions.

1. *footstool*] On the sources for this humiliation of Bajazeth, see
Introduction, pp. 12–14. Ethel Seaton, 'Marlowe's Light Reading',
Elizabethan and Jacobean Studies, ed. H. Davis and Helen Gardner
(Oxford, 1959), pp. 33–4, finds an analogue in William of Tyre, and other
romance parallels in the play. Ellis-Fermor (p. 140) quotes Sir Walter
Raleigh's recall of this event in his *History.*

2–3.] Seaton, ('Sources', p. 396) cites Belleforest, *Cosmographie
Universelle*, ii.597, as one possible source for Marlowe's allusion to
Mahometan rituals. In the banquet scene, Tamburlaine invites Bajazeth
to 'slice the brawns of thy arms into carbonadoes, and eat them' (*One*
IV.iv.44–5).

5–6. *star | To suck up poison*] Vapours sucked up by sun or stars from
fens would carry the infections thought to lie there (Kocher, pp. 237–8).
Bajazeth's curse precisely anticipates Caliban's (*Tp.*, II.ii.1–2).

7. *glorious*] boastful: Tamburlaine opposes another sense of the word
three lines later. Bajazeth's sense offers to class Tamburlaine with the
miles gloriosus of early theatre.

8. *first mover*] primum mobile: for Aristotle, the firmament, sphere of
the fixed stars, gave motion to the spheres within it (cf. Kocher, p. 217);
as at *Two* IV.i.118. Cf. *Jew of Malta*, I.ii.165, 'thou great Primus Motor'.

9. *Enchased*] set with stars as jewels in a setting; cf. the metaphorical
use at *Two* IV.iii.128.

Will sooner burn the glorious frame of heaven   10
Than it should so conspire my overthrow.
But, villain, thou that wishest this to me,
Fall prostrate on the low disdainful earth
And be the footstool of great Tamburlaine,
That I may rise into my royal throne.   15

Bajazeth. First shalt thou rip my bowels with thy sword
And sacrifice my heart to death and hell,
Before I yield to such a slavery.

Tamburlaine. Base villain, vassal, slave to Tamburlaine,
Unworthy to embrace or touch the ground   20
That bears the honour of my royal weight,
Stoop, villain, stoop, stoop, for so he bids
That may command thee piecemeal to be torn,
Or scattered like the lofty cedar trees
Struck with the voice of thund'ring Jupiter.   25

Bajazeth. Then, as I look down to the damnèd fiends,
Fiends, look on me, and thou dread god of hell,
With ebon sceptre strike this hateful earth
And make it swallow both of us at once!

He [TAMBURLAINE] *gets up upon him to his chair.*

Tamburlaine. Now clear the triple region of the air   30
And let the majesty of heaven behold
Their scourge and terror tread on emperors.
Smile, stars that reigned at my nativity
And dim the brightness of their neighbour lamps—
Disdain to borrow light of Cynthia,   35

34. their] *O1–3, Q;* your *conj. Dyce 1.*

---

10. *glorious frame of heaven*] The phrase returns at *Two* III.iv.65; cf. the 'starry frame' of *Dido,* V.i.302.

14. *footstool*] may recall Psalm 110. See pp. 45–6 above, and *Two* V.iii.29 n.

27. *god of hell*] Pluto; cf. 'infernal Jove' at *Two* I.iii.143, and 'black Jove' at *Two* V.i.98.

30. *triple region of the air*] the received division: 'The highest region was heated by proximity to the sphere of Fire and by the friction of the rotating spheres of Heaven. The lowest region was warmed by reflection of the Sun's radiation from the earth's surface . . . The middle region . . . having no direct source of heat, was consequently cold' (Heninger, p. 41).

33.] The line finds a close echo in *Dr Faustus,* xix.157 (and see Jump's note); its antitype opens the laments over Tamburlaine's fatal sickness, in *Two* V.iii.2: 'Fall, stars that govern his nativity'.

For I, the chiefest lamp of all the earth,
First rising in the east with mild aspect
But fixèd now in the meridian line,
Will send up fire to your turning spheres
And cause the sun to borrow light of you.   40
My sword struck fire from his coat of steel
Even in Bithynia, when I took this Turk:
As when a fiery exhalation
Wrapt in the bowels of a freezing cloud,
Fighting for passage, makes the welkin crack,   45
And casts a flash of lightning to the earth.
But ere I march to wealthy Persia
Or leave Damascus and th'Egyptian fields,
As was the fame of Clymen's brain-sick son
That almost brent the axletree of heaven,   50
So shall our swords, our lances and our shot
Fill all the air with fiery meteors;

---

45. makes] *Oxberry;* make *O1–3, Q.*   49. Clymen's] *O2 [Clymenes];*
Clymeus *O1, O3, Q.*   50. brent] *O1–2;* burnt *O3, Q.*

---

37. *aspect*] The word neatly combines auspicious astrological disposition with human appearance (cf. 'stout aspect', *One* I.ii.169).

38. *meridian line*] 'The great circle (of the celestial sphere) which
passes through the celestial poles and the zenith of any place on the earth's
surface' (*O.E.D.*). Tamburlaine claims to have attained a perpetual noon.

39. *turning spheres*] cf. the 'restless spheres' of *One* I.vii.25.

43–6.] Heninger (p. 174) refers us to 'the technical belief that lightning
results from the conflict between a compacted exhalation and an enclosing
cloud'. Cf. Aristotle, *Met.*, ii.369a; and *One* III.ii.78 n.

49. *Clymen's brain-sick son*] Phaethon, child of Clymene and Apollo,
described in these terms again in *Two* V.iii.231. Cf. Golding, p. 42,
where the sun's chariot has a 'fierie axeltree', and Phaethon, *'Clymens
sonne'*, is 'hairbrainde'.

50. *brent*] burned.

the axletree of heaven] the celestial diameter, running through the earth
at its centre. See also *Two* I.i.90, I.iii.12, and the 'straight line' of *Two*
III.iv.64 n.; *Dr Faustus*, 'the heavens . . . jointly move upon one axletree' (vi.38–41).

51–2.] Among the fiery impressions known to Renaissance meteorology
were 'burning spears', which are perhaps suggested here as specific
meteors caused by the shining weapons of Tamburlaine's army. Cf.
Heninger, p. 95, and *Two* IV.i.202–5 n.

52. *fiery meteors*] covering a multitude of phenomena associated with
exhalations—lightning, fiery impressions, blazing stars. 'Perhaps a

Then, when the sky shall wax as red as blood,
It shall be said I made it red myself,
To make me think of naught but blood and war.   55
Zabina. Unworthy king, that by thy cruelty
Unlawfully usurpest the Persian seat,
Darest thou, that never saw an emperor
Before thou met my husband in the field,
Being thy captive, thus abuse his state,   60
Keeping his kingly body in a cage
That roofs of gold and sun-bright palaces
Should have prepared to entertain his grace?
And treading him beneath thy loathsome feet
Whose feet the kings of Africa have kissed?   65
Techelles. You must devise some torment worse, my lord,
To make these captives rein their lavish tongues.
Tamburlaine. Zenocrate, look better to your slave.
Zenocrates. She is my handmaid's slave, and she shall look
That these abuses flow not from her tongue.   70
Chide her, Anippe.
Anippe. Let these be warnings for you then, my slave,
How you abuse the person of the king,
Or else I swear to have you whipped stark naked.
Bajazeth. Great Tamburlaine, great in my overthrow,   75
Ambitious pride shall make thee fall as low
For treading on the back of Bajazeth
That should be horsèd on four mighty kings.
Tamburlaine. Thy names and titles and thy dignities
Are fled from Bajazeth and remain with me,   80
That will maintain it against a world of kings.
Put him in again.
        [*They put* BAJAZETH *into the cage.*]

82.] *after Oxberry* [He is put in the cage.]; *not in O1–3, Q.*

reference is intended to the belief held in antiquity that missiles flying
through the air caught fire and melted' (Kocher, p. 234).

53.] Cf. the imagery of apocalypse in Joel ii.30, 31, Rev. vi.12, including
the turning of the moon to blood (L. and E. Feasey, p. 357).

63. *entertain*] receive.

67. *rein ... tongues*] The metaphor is exploited in the taunting of the
captive kings, *Two* IV.iii.43 ff.

78.] anticipating Tamburlaine's triumphal entry in *Two* IV.iii.

Bajazeth. Is this a place for mighty Bajazeth?
   Confusion light on him that helps thee thus.
Tamburlaine. There, whiles he lives, shall Bajazeth be kept,   85
   And where I go be thus in triumph drawn;
   And thou, his wife, shalt feed him with the scraps
   My servitors shall bring thee from my board.
   For he that gives him other food than this
   Shall sit by him and starve to death himself.   90
   This is my mind, and I will have it so.
   Not all the kings and emperors of the earth,
   If they would lay their crowns before my feet,
   Shall ransom him or take him from his cage.
   The ages that shall talk of Tamburlaine,   95
   Even from this day to Plato's wondrous year,
   Shall talk how I have handled Bajazeth.
   These Moors that drew him from Bithynia
   To fair Damascus, where we now remain,
   Shall lead him with us wheresoe'er we go.   100
   Techelles and my loving followers,
   Now may we see Damascus' lofty towers,
   Like to the shadows of Pyramides
   That with their beauties graced the Memphian fields:
   The golden statue of their feathered bird   105
   That spreads her wings upon the city walls
   Shall not defend it from our battering shot.
   The townsmen mask in silk and cloth of gold,

---

105. statue] *O3, Q;* stature *O1–2.*

---

96. *Plato's wondrous year*] when time would be consummated in the return of the planets to their original positions in the celestial cycle: cf. *Timaeus,* 39D.

103. *Like to the shadows*] like copies or counterparts ('shadow', *O.E.D.* 6e, earliest instance 1693); or like reflections, semblances (*O.E.D.* 5a, 6a), ?mirages.

Pyramides] evidently four syllables here.

105–6.] Seaton, 'Marlowe's Light Reading', p. 18 (see *One* IV.ii.1 n.), notes the Damascus 'egull of gold' from *Bevis of Hampton.* Ellis-Fermor (p. 145) identifies the 'bird' as the ibis (see *One* IV.iii.37 n.). *O.E.D.* records the O1–2 spelling *stature* for *statue* as early as 1390 and as late as 1653. Cf. *One* I.ii.243 n., *Two* II.iv.140 n.

108. *mask*] take part in masquerades; not 'hide' or 'lurk' as at *Two* III.ii.12.

And every house is as a treasury:

The men, the treasure, and the town is ours.   110

Theridamas. Your tents of white now pitched before the
     gates,

And gentle flags of amity displayed,

I doubt not but the governor will yield,

Offering Damascus to your majesty.

Tamburlaine. So shall he have his life, and all the rest.   115

But if he stay until the bloody flag

Be once advanced on my vermilion tent,

He dies, and those that kept us out so long.

And when they see me march in black array,

With mournful streamers hanging down their heads,   120

Were in that city all the world contained,

Not one should 'scape, but perish by our swords.

Zenocrate. Yet would you have some pity for my sake,

Because it is my country's, and my father's.

Tamburlaine. Not for the world, Zenocrate, if I have sworn.   125

Come, bring in the Turk.   *Exeunt.*

Scene iii

[*Enter*] SOLDAN, ARABIA, CAPOLIN, *with streaming
colours, and* Soldiers.

Soldan. Methinks we march as Meleager did,

Environèd with brave Argolian knights,

To chase the savage Calydonian boar;

Or Cephalus with lusty Theban youths,

0.1. *Enter*] *Robinson 1; not in O1–3, Q.   streaming*] *O3, Q; steaming O1–2.*
3. Calydonian] *O2;* Caldonian *O1;* Calcedonian *O3, Q.*   4. lusty]
O1–2; insty *O3; not in Q.*

---

115. *all the rest*] i.e. all the rest will have theirs.

120. *streamers*] pennons.

IV.iii.1–3.] Meleager, a prince of Calydon, joined with the heroes of
Greece in hunting the wild boar sent by Artemis to ravage the land, and
he himself killed it. See *Metam.*, viii.270 ff. Ironically for the present
context, the episode led to his death.

Argolian] from Argolis, the district round Argos (hence a synecdoche
for 'Greek'): note from Gordon Campbell.

4–6.] Cephalus was implicated in the hunting of the Teumessian Fox

Against the wolf that angry Themis sent   5
To waste and spoil the sweet Aonian fields.
A monster of five hundred thousand heads,
Compact of rapine, piracy, and spoil,
The scum of men, the hate and scourge of God,
Raves in Egyptia, and annoyeth us.   10
My lord, it is the bloody Tamburlaine,
A sturdy felon and a base-bred thief
By murder raisèd to the Persian crown,
That dares control us in our territories.
To tame the pride of this presumptuous beast,   15
Join your Arabians with the Soldan's power:
Let us unite our royal bands in one
And hasten to remove Damascus' siege.
It is a blemish to the majesty
And high estate of mighty emperors,   20
That such a base usurping vagabond
Should brave a king or wear a princely crown.
Arabia. Renownèd Soldan, have ye lately heard
The overthrow of mighty Bajazeth
About the confines of Bithynia?   25
The slavery wherewith he persecutes
The noble Turk and his great emperess?
Soldan. I have, and sorrow for his bad success.
But, noble lord of great Arabia,
Be so persuaded that the Soldan is   30
No more dismayed with tidings of his fall
Than in the haven when the pilot stands
And views a stranger's ship rent in the winds
And shiverèd against a craggy rock.
Yet, in compassion of his wretched state,   35
A sacred vow to heaven and him I make,

---

sent by Themis in revenge for the death of the sphinx. His hound and the
fox were turned to marble by Zeus. See *Metam.*, vii.762 ff.
  Aonian fields] the district of Thebes and Mount Helicon.
  10. *Raves*] rages, roves (*O.E.D. vb.*[1], *vb.*[2]): E.A.J.H.
  annoyeth] molests.
  14. *control*] hold sway over; perhaps with a colour of 'challenge'.
  25. *confines*] borders.
  27.] A line which will, with minor changes, resound in *One* V.i.355 ff.

Confirming it with Ibis' holy name,
That Tamburlaine shall rue the day, the hour,
Wherein he wrought such ignominious wrong
Unto the hallowed person of a prince,   40
Or kept the fair Zenocrate so long
As concubine, I fear, to feed his lust.

Arabia. Let grief and fury hasten on revenge,
Let Tamburlaine for his offences feel
Such plagues as heaven and we can pour on him.   45
I long to break my spear upon his crest
And prove the weight of his victorious arm,
For Fame I fear hath been too prodigal
In sounding through the world his partial praise.

Soldan. Capolin, hast thou surveyed our powers?   50

Capolin. Great emperors of Egypt and Arabia,
The number of your hosts united is
A hundred and fifty thousand horse,
Two hundred thousand foot, brave men-at-arms,
Courageous and full of hardiness,   55
As frolic as the hunters in the chase
Of savage beasts amid the desert woods.

Arabia. My mind presageth fortunate success;
And, Tamburlaine, my spirit doth foresee
The utter ruin of thy men and thee.   60

Soldan. Then rear your standards, let your sounding drums
Direct our soldiers to Damascus' walls.
Now, Tamburlaine, the mighty Soldan comes
And leads with him the great Arabian king
To dim thy baseness and obscurity,   65
Famous for nothing but for theft and spoil,
To raze and scatter thy inglorious crew
Of Scythians and slavish Persians.   *Exeunt.*

43–6. *Torn away in Bodleian copy of O1.*

----

37. *Ibis*] sacred bird of the Egyptians (cf. *One* IV.ii.105–6 n.).
47. *prove*] try, test.
49. *partial praise*] praise founded on prejudice in Tamburlaine's favour.
56. *frolic*] sportive, mirthful.
58. *success*] outcome.

Scene iv

The banquet, and to it cometh TAMBURLAINE *all in scarlet,*
[ZENOCRATE], THERIDAMAS, TECHELLES, USUMCASANE, *the*
Turk [BAJAZETH *drawn in his cage,* ZABINA], *with others.*

Tamburlaine. Now hang our bloody colours by Damascus,
    Reflexing hues of blood upon their heads
    While they walk quivering on their city walls,
    Half dead for fear before they feel my wrath.
    Then let us freely banquet and carouse   5
    Full bowls of wine unto the god of war
    That means to fill your helmets full of gold
    And make Damascus' spoils as rich to you
    As was to Jason Colchos' golden fleece.
    And now, Bajazeth, hast thou any stomach?   10
Bajazeth. Ay, such a stomach, cruel Tamburlaine, as I could
    willingly feed upon thy blood-raw heart.
Tamburlaine. Nay, thine own is easier to come by, pluck out
    that, and 'twill serve thee and thy wife. Well, Zenocrate,
    Techelles, and the rest, fall to your victuals.   15
Bajazeth. Fall to, and never may your meat digest!
    Ye Furies, that can mask invisible,
    Dive to the bottom of Avernus' pool
    And in your hands bring hellish poison up
    And squeeze it in the cup of Tamburlaine!   20

Heading.] SCENE iv. *Oxberry;* Actus: 4. Scaena. 5. *O1–3, Q.*
0.2. ZENOCRATE] *Dyce 1; not in O1–3, Q.*   0.3. *drawn in his cage*] *Dyce*
1; not in O1–3, Q.   ZABINA] *Oxberry ; not in O1–3, Q.*   1–2.] *Torn*
away in Bodleian copy of O1.   17. mask] *O1–2;* walke *O3, Q.*

IV.iv.0.1–2. *all in scarlet*] Henslowe has an inventory item 'Tamerlanes
breches of crymson vellvet': see Introduction, n. 73.

9.] Ovid is again a likely direct source for the allusion here: *Metam.*,
vii.1 ff., *Her.*, vi.1 ff., xii.1 ff. (Ellis-Fermor, p. 149).

10. *stomach*] The word taunts Bajazeth to register not just hunger, but
resistance to cruelty.

11–15.] We need not feel, with Ellis-Fermor, that wherever prose
occurs we are probably faced with non-Marlovian material.

16. *digest*] undergo digestion.

17. *mask*] lurk in darkness; cf. *Two* III.ii.12, 'where the Furies
mask'.

18–19.] obliquely recalls *One* I.ii.159–60 n. *Avernus' pool*: see I.ii.159–
160 n.

Or, wingèd snakes of Lerna, cast your stings,
And leave your venoms in this tyrant's dish.

Zabina. And may this banquet prove as ominous
As Procne's to th'adulterous Thracian king
That fed upon the substance of his child!   25

Zenocrate. My lord, how can you suffer these outrageous
curses by these slaves of yours?

Tamburlaine. To let them see, divine Zenocrate,
I glory in the curses of my foes,
Having the power from th'empyreal heaven   30
To turn them all upon their proper heads.

Techelles. I pray you give them leave, madam, this speech is a
goodly refreshing to them.

Theridamas. But if his highness would let them be fed, it
would do them more good.   35

Tamburlaine. Sirrah, why fall you not to? Are you so daintily
brought up you cannot eat your own flesh?

Bajazeth. First, legions of devils shall tear thee in pieces.

Usumcasane. Villain, knowest thou to whom thou speakest?

Tamburlaine. O let him alone: here, eat, sir, take it from my   40
sword's point, or I'll thrust it to thy heart.

He [BAJAZETH] *takes it and stamps upon it.*

Theridamas. He stamps it under his feet, my lord.

Tamburlaine. Take it up, villain, and eat it, or I will make

26–7.] *O3,Q ; as verse* [curses / By] *in O1–2; as verse* [these / Outrageous]
in Oxberry.   suffer] *O1–3, Q;* tamely suffer *conj. Dyce 1.*

---

21. *Lerna.*] Hercules' arrows bore poison from the gall of the Lernean
hydra: cf. *One* III.iii.140 n.; 'the blood of Hydra, Lerna's bane', *Jew of
Malta,* III.iv.100; 'Hydra, Lerna's bane', *Dr Faustus,* iv.100.

24–5.] Tereus, married to Procne, seduced her sister Philomela and
tried to conceal it by cutting out her tongue. In revenge, Procne killed
her son Itys and served up his flesh to Tereus. Marlowe probably had
Ovid's account in mind: *Metam.,* vi.433 ff.

26–7.] Dividing into two verse lines at 'these / Outrageous', Ellis-
Fermor notes former editors' attempts to supply two syllables which are
then apparently missing from a pentameter line 26. But the octavos print
as prose, and the lines gain impact from that, as (for various reasons) do
many passages in this scene.

30. *empyreal*] see *One* II.vii.15 n.

31. *proper*] own.

thee slice the brawns of thy arms into carbonadoes, and
eat them.   45

Usumcasane. Nay, 'twere better he killed his wife, and then
she shall be sure not to be starved, and he be provided
for a month's victual beforehand.

Tamburlaine. Here is my dagger, despatch her while she is fat,
for if she live but a while longer, she will fall into a con-   50
sumption with fretting, and then she will not be worth
the eating.

Theridamas. Dost thou think that Mahomet will suffer this?

Techelles. 'Tis like he will, when he cannot let it.

Tamburlaine. Go to, fall to your meat; what, not a bit?   55
Belike he hath not been watered today; give him some
drink.

They give him water to drink, and he flings it on the
ground.

Fast and welcome, sir, while hunger make you eat. How
now, Zenocrate, doth not the Turk and his wife make a
goodly show at a banquet?   60

Zenocrate. Yes, my lord.

Theridamas. Methinks 'tis a great deal better than a consort
of music.

Tamburlaine. Yet music would do well to cheer up Zenocrate.
Pray thee tell, why art thou so sad? If thou wilt have a   65
song, the Turk shall strain his voice. But why is it?

Zenocrate. My lord, to see my father's town besieged,
The country wasted where myself was born—
How can it but afflict my very soul?

---

44. slice] *O1–2;* flice *O3;* fleece *Q.*

---

44. *slice*] On the significance of the variant readings here in O3 and Q,
see Introduction, p. 91.

carbonadoes] strips of meat (first instance in *O.E.D.*). Similarly used
in *Cor.*, IV.v.186: 'he scotched him and notched him like a carbonado'.

54. *let*] hinder.

56. *watered*] i.e., like an animal (E.A.J.H.).

58. *while*] until; cf. *Mac.*, III.i.44.

62. *consort*] harmonious combination of voices or instruments (*O.E.D.*
3b, earliest entry).

64–6.] The prose here is highly expressive—at once of Tamburlaine's
chastened concern, meeting Zenocrate's brooding silence, and of his
attempt to persist with the taunting of Bajazeth.

If any love remain in you, my lord,   70
Or if my love unto your majesty
May merit favour at your highness' hands,
Then raise your siege from fair Damascus' walls
And with my father take a friendly truce.

Tamburlaine. Zenocrate, were Egypt Jove's own land,   75
Yet would I with my sword make Jove to stoop.
I will confute those blind geographers
That make a triple region in the world,
Excluding regions which I mean to trace,
And with this pen reduce them to a map,   80
Calling the provinces, cities, and towns
After my name and thine, Zenocrate.
Here at Damascus will I make the point
That shall begin the perpendicular.
And wouldst thou have me buy thy father's love   85
With such a loss? Tell me, Zenocrate.

Zenocrate. Honour still wait on happy Tamburlaine.
Yet give me leave to plead for him, my lord.

Tamburlaine. Content thyself, his person shall be safe

77–84.] The *triple region* probably indicates Asia, Europe, and Africa. 'Marlowe trusts his audience to realize that the new world is yet undiscovered, and that his [Tamburlaine's] ambitions stretch that far'; J. C. Maxwell, *N.&Q.*, CXVII (1952), 444. Reference may be intended to the T-in-O maps, archaic but still familiar in Marlowe's day, in which the 'T' 'divides the Old World into three continents: the top half of the "O" is Asia; the lower left-hand quarter, Africa'. In Tamburlaine's vision of the consequence of his exploration, Damascus replaces Jerusalem as the *point* (l. 83) at the junction of the *perpendicular*, the Mediterranean (l. 84), with the horizontal bar of the 'T', the river Nile and the Tanais (Don). See Donald K. Anderson, Jr., *N.&Q.*, XXI (1974), 284–6. Marlowe frequently refers to the world as comprising three continents, e.g. *Two* IV.iii.63, 118. It has a suggestive correspondence with 'the triple region of the air' (*One* IV.ii.30). If Marlowe is not thinking of the T-in-O maps, the *perpendicular* is the meridian: 'Marlowe knew that the cartographer of his time had a wide choice for his initial meridian of longitude' (Seaton, p. 14).

80. *this pen*] 'i.e., his sword' (Jump); the word-play carries through to 'the point', l. 83.

reduce them to] bring them to the form of (*O.E.D.* 15, first entry 1592 [*sic*], *Massacre at Paris*, I.vii.46); subjugate (pun), Pendry–Maxwell (*O.E.D.* 20, first entry 1612).

87. *still*] always, for ever.

89–92.] See *One* V.i.203–8 n.

And all the friends of fair Zenocrate,   90
If with their lives they will be pleased to yield
Or may be forced to make me emperor:
For Egypt and Arabia must be mine.
                    [*To Bajazeth.*]
Feed, you slave; thou mayst think thyself happy to be
    fed from my trencher.   95
Bajazeth. My empty stomach, full of idle heat,
    Draws bloody humours from my feeble parts,
    Preserving life by hasting cruel death.
    My veins are pale, my sinews hard and dry,
    My joints benumbed; unless I eat, I die.   100
Zabina. Eat, Bajazeth, let us live in spite of them, looking
    some happy power will pity and enlarge us.
Tamburlaine. Here, Turk, wilt thou have a clean trencher?
Bajazeth. Ay, tyrant, and more meat.
Tamburlaine. Soft, sir, you must be dieted; too much eating 105
    will make you surfeit.
Theridamas. So it would, my lord, specially having so small a
    walk, and so little exercise.

            Enter a second course of crowns.

Tamburlaine. Theridamas, Techelles and Casane, here are the
    cates you desire to finger, are they not?   110
Theridamas. Ay, my lord, but none save kings must feed with
    these.
Techelles. 'Tis enough for us to see them, and for Tam-
    burlaine only to enjoy them.

93.1. *To Bajazeth*] *This ed.; not in O1–3, Q.*   101–2.] *As prose in Ellis-*
Fermor; as verse [them, / Looking] *O1–3, Q.*

---

90. *friends*] kinsmen, near relatives (*O.E.D.* 3).
95. *trencher*] plate, platter.
97. *bloody humours*] one of the four chief fluids of the body—blood,
phlegm, choler, melancholy—whose relative proportion determined a
man's constitution and character.
101. *looking*] expecting; ?hoping.
105. *Soft*] steady, not so fast.
108.1. *of crowns*] Perhaps the banquet itself included crowns made
of sweetmeats. 'It seems quite possible that the gold crowns are brought
to Tamburlaine and food in the shape of crowns set on the table before
the guests' (Waith, *Ideas of Greatness*, London, 1971, p. 54).
110. *cates*] dainties.

Tamburlaine. Well, here is now to the Soldan of Egypt, the
    King of Arabia, and the Governor of Damascus. Now 115
    take these three crowns, and pledge me, my contributory
    kings.
       I crown you here, Theridamas, King of Argier,
    Techelles, King of Fesse, and Usumcasane, King of
    Moroccus. How say you to this, Turk—these are not 120
    your contributory kings!
Bajazeth. Nor shall they long be thine, I warrant them.
Tamburlaine. Kings of Argier, Moroccus, and of Fesse,
    You that have marched with happy Tamburlaine
    As far as from the frozen plage of heaven 125
    Unto the wat'ry morning's ruddy bower,
    And thence by land unto the torrid zone,
    Deserve these titles I endow you with,
    By valour and by magnanimity:
    Your births shall be no blemish to your fame, 130
    For virtue is the fount whence honour springs,

---

125. plage] *Dyce 2;* place *O1–3, Q.*   126. bower] *O3, Q;* hower *O1–2.*
129. valour] *Oxberry;* value *O1–3, Q.*

114–21.] Ellis-Fermor relineates the prose as 'rough blank verse'; but
only two of her lines are convincing Marlovian pentameter. The prose
may be spoken in a tone of spirited jocularity, with an eye to Bajazeth's
discomfiture, breaking into the blank-verse eloquence of ll. 123 ff.

119. *Fesse*] Fez (as at l. 123 below).

125–7.] 'Tartary and Scythia were pictured by the Elizabethans as
lands of ice and snow lying to the far north. Tamburlaine's marches have
led him from North to East and from there to the tropical south' (Ellis-
Fermor, p. 154).

plage] region; Dyce's emendation has support from 'the oriental
plage' of *Two* I.i.68, and like that phrase derives from common usage of
cosmographers: Seaton, p. 397, cites 'versus orientalem plagam' and
'in orientali plaga'. For *frozen plage of heaven*, Pendry–Maxwell suggest
'?i.e. the *zona frigida*, the Arctic'.

129. *magnanimity*] fortitude, loftiness of purpose (*O.E.D.* 2, 3);
invoked again by Tamburlaine, in endowing his sons with his authority,
at *Two* V.iii.200: in both instances there is some discrepancy between
the nobility invoked so expansively and the cruelty being practised on
stage. Cf. also *Two* IV.i.85.

valour] the early texts' *value* may be seen as a variant spelling of 'valour'
or 'valure', or as a word in its own right, meaning 'worth or efficacy in
combat or warfare; manliness, valour' (*O.E.D.* 5b).

131. *virtue*] nobility and power: the word gains significant development

And they are worthy she investeth kings.

Theridamas. And since your highness hath so well
  vouchsafed,
 If we deserve them not with higher meeds
 Than erst our states and actions have retained,   135
 Take them away again and make us slaves.

Tamburlaine. Well said, Theridamas; when holy Fates
 Shall 'stablish me in strong Egyptia,
 We mean to travel to th'Antarctic Pole,
 Conquering the people underneath our feet,   140
 And be renowned as never emperors were.
 Zenocrate, I will not crown thee yet,
 Until with greater honours I be graced.   [*Exeunt.*]

[*Finis Actus quarti.*]

143. *Exeunt*] Oxberry; not in *O1–3*, Q.

---

through Tamburlaine's soliloquy in *One* V.i.165 ff., up to the announcement that 'virtue solely is the sum of glory'.

 133. *so well vouchsafed*] so graciously granted (i.e., these titles).

 134. *meeds*] merit, worth.

 135. *states*] ranks.

 137. *holy Fates*] blending Christian and pagan resonances (Ellis-Fermor, p. 155).

 140. *underneath our feet*] 'in the southern hemisphere' (Jump) is the geographical sense; but cf. *Two* III.iv.52, where Tamburlaine 'treadeth Fortune underneath his feet'.

Act V

SCENE i

[Enter] The GOVERNOR *of* DAMASCUS, *with three or four*
Citizens, *and four* Virgins *with branches of laurel in
their hands.*

Governor. Still doth this man or rather god of war
    Batter our walls and beat our turrets down;
    And to resist with longer stubbornness
    Or hope of rescue from the Soldan's power
    Were but to bring our wilful overthrow   5
    And make us desperate of our threatened lives.
    We see his tents have now been alterèd
    With terrors to the last and cruellest hue;
    His coal-black colours everywhere advanced
    Threaten our city with a general spoil;   10
    And if we should with common rites of arms
    Offer our safeties to his clemency,
    I fear the custom proper to his sword,
    Which he observes as parcel of his fame,
    Intending so to terrify the world,   15
    By any innovation or remorse
    Will never be dispensed with till our deaths.
    Therefore, for these our harmless virgins' sakes,

0.1. *Enter*] *Robinson 1; not in O1–3, Q.*

V.i.1.] Part of the sense of this line could be conveyed by punctuating
'man, or rather god, of war'.

6. *desperate*] having lost hope.

13. *proper*] peculiar.

14. *parcel*] 'an essential part of' (Ellis-Fermor, p. 156).

16.] By any change in his customs or through pity. *Remorse* associates
persistently in this scene with 'ruth' and 'pity'.

18. *harmless*] causing no harm; or, innocent.

Whose honours and whose lives rely on him,
Let us have hope that their unspotted prayers,   20
Their blubbered cheeks and hearty humble moans
Will melt his fury into some remorse,
And use us like a loving conqueror.

First Virgin. If humble suits or imprecations—
Uttered with tears of wretchedness and blood   25
Shed from the heads and hearts of all our sex,
Some made your wives, and some your children—
Might have entreated your obdurate breasts
To entertain some care of our securities
Whiles only danger beat upon our walls,   30
These more than dangerous warrants of our death
Had never been erected as they be,
Nor you depend on such weak helps as we.

Governor. Well, lovely virgins, think our country's care,
Our love of honour, loath to be enthralled   35
To foreign powers and rough imperious yokes,
Would not with too much cowardice or fear,
Before all hope of rescue were denied,
Submit yourselves and us to servitude.
Therefore, in that your safeties and our own,   40
Your honours, liberties, and lives, were weighed
In equal care and balance with our own,
Endure as we the malice of our stars,
The wrath of Tamburlaine and power of wars—

---

21. *blubbered*] flooded with tears.
hearty] heartfelt.

22. *remorse*] pity; as at l. 16 above.

23. *use ... conqueror*] (cause him to) treat us as a loving conqueror would. Tamburlaine does emerge in this way, belatedly, after the 'gentle victory' over the Soldan later in this scene.

24. *imprecations*] prayers.

27. *made*] being.

29. *securities*] safety, freedom from danger; or protection. *O.E.D.* cites the plural, as meaning simply 'the safety of more than one person', first from 1605. Cf. *Mac.*, IV.iii.29 'Let not my jealousies be your dishonours, / But mine own safeties'.

31. *warrants*] tokens, assurances (the 'coal-black colours' of l. 9 above). The word engages well with 'securities' in l. 29.

35. *enthralled*] enslaved (*O.E.D.* 1, first instance 1656).

Or be the means the overweighing heavens   45
Have kept to qualify these hot extremes,
And bring us pardon in your cheerful looks.
Second Virgin. Then here, before the majesty of heaven
And holy patrons of Egyptia,
With knees and hearts submissive we entreat   50
Grace to our words and pity to our looks,
That this device may prove propitious,
And through the eyes and ears of Tamburlaine
Convey events of mercy to his heart;
Grant that these signs of victory we yield   55
May bind the temples of his conquering head
To hide the folded furrows of his brows
And shadow his displeasèd countenance
With happy looks of ruth and lenity.
Leave us, my lord, and loving countrymen;   60
What simple virgins may persuade, we will.
Governor. Farewell, sweet virgins, on whose safe return
Depends our city, liberty, and lives.
Exeunt [all except the Virgins].

[*Enter*] TAMBURLAINE, TECHELLES, THERIDAMAS,
USUMCASANE, *with others:* TAMBURLAINE *all in black,
and very melancholy*

Tamburlaine. What, are the turtles frayed out of their nests?

63.] *after this line,* O1–3, Q *read* Actus 5. Scaena. 2.   63.1. *all* . . . Virgins] *Dyce* 1; *not in* O1–3, Q.   63.2. Enter] *Robinson* 1; *not in* O1–3, Q.

---

45. *overweighing*] 'preponderating, overruling' (Ellis-Fermor, p. 158; first instance in *O.E.D.*). The verb is used in a different sense at *One* II.i.46.

46. *qualify*] mitigate.

54. *Convey events of mercy*] suggest a merciful outcome; cf. *One* III.ii.16.

55. *signs of victory*] the branches of laurel (olive in Marlowe's sources: cf. Appendix).

58. *shadow*] 'enfold with a protecting and beneficent influence' (*O.E.D.* 2); 'screen' (Pendry–Maxwell).

59. *happy*] fortunate, propitious.

64. *turtles*] turtle-doves.
frayed] frightened; as in 'The *Massacre at Paris* Manuscript' l. 13, (*Massacre at Paris*, p. 165).

Alas, poor fools, must you be first shall feel   65
The sworn destruction of Damascus?
They know my custom: could they not as well
Have sent ye out when first my milk-white flags
Through which sweet mercy threw her gentle beams,
Reflexing them on your disdainful eyes,   70
As now when fury and incensèd hate
Flings slaughtering terror from my coal-black tents
And tells for truth submissions comes too late?
First Virgin. Most happy king and emperor of the earth,
Image of honour and nobility,   75
For whom the powers divine have made the world,
And on whose throne the holy Graces sit;
In whose sweet person is comprised the sum
Of nature's skill and heavenly majesty:
Pity our plights, O pity poor Damascus!   80
Pity old age, within whose silver hairs
Honour and reverence evermore have reigned;
Pity the marriage bed, where many a lord
In prime and glory of his loving joy
Embraceth now with tears of ruth and blood   85
The jealous body of his fearful wife,
Whose cheeks and hearts, so punished with conceit
To think thy puissant never-stayèd arm
Will part their bodies, and prevent their souls
From heavens of comfort yet their age might bear,   90
Now wax all pale and withered to the death—

---

65. *poor fools*] 'a form of address expressing pity' (Jump).
first] the first who.
68. *flags*] the 'ensigns' of Fortescue, a possible source; cf. 'colours' and
'streamers' elsewhere in the play. *Flags* lacks a main verb, but the omission assists the impression of surging anger in Tamburlaine.
70. *your*] Tamburlaine addresses the virgins here; the 'They', of l. 67
refers to the governors of Damascus.
73. *submissions*] the act of yielding (*O.E.D.* 3: singular form).
85. *tears of . . . blood*] The phrase returns at *Two* V.iii.214 to convey
Usumcasane's grief over Tamburlaine's sickness; cf. *Two* V.iii.161–2.
86. *jealous*] anxious for someone's well-being (*O.E.D.* 3); by trans-
ference, the lord fears for his lady's life (E.A.J.H.).
87. *punished with conceit*] racked with anticipation (cf. l. 158 below).
88. *never-stayèd*] never halted.
89–90. *prevent . . . From*] 'deprive . . . Of' (Woolf).

As well for grief our ruthless governor
Have thus refused the mercy of thy hand
(Whose sceptre angels kiss and Furies dread)
As for their liberties, their loves, or lives.   95
O then, for these, and such as we ourselves,
For us, for infants, and for all our bloods,
That never nourished thought against thy rule,
Pity, O pity, sacred emperor,
The prostrate service of this wretched town;   100
And take in sign thereof this gilded wreath
Whereto each man of rule hath given his hand
And wished, as worthy subjects, happy means
To be investers of thy royal brows,
Even with the true Egyptian diadem.   105
Tamburlaine. Virgins, in vain ye labour to prevent
That which mine honour swears shall be performed.
Behold my sword, what see you at the point?
Virgins. Nothing but fear and fatal steel, my lord.
Tamburlaine. Your fearful minds are thick and misty, then,   110
For there sits Death, there sits imperious Death,
Keeping his circuit by the slicing edge.
But I am pleased you shall not see him there:
He now is seated on my horsemen's spears,
And on their points his fleshless body feeds.   115
Techelles, straight go charge a few of them
To charge these dames, and show my servant Death,
Sitting in scarlet on their armèd spears.

---

97. *bloods*] 'metonymy for lives or spirits' (Ellis-Fermor, p. 160).

100. *service*] homage, obeisance.

103. *happy means*] fortunate opportunity (to crown Tamburlaine, as symbolised by the wreath).

104. *investers*] those who invest (*O.E.D.* 1, first entry).

109. *fatal*] sure to kill, deadly (*O.E.D.* 6b, first entry 1599); inevitable, of the nature of fate (*O.E.D.* 3, first entry 1605); controlling men's destinies (*O.E.D.* 4). On 'fate' and 'Fates' in the play, see Introduction, p. 50.

111–12. *Death, | Keeping his circuit*] i.e., a judge's circuit, and the swaith of a sword.

116–17.] Note the sardonic wordplay on *charge*.

117–18.] Cf. Theridamas' vision of Tamburlaine at *Two* III.iv.54–5: 'On whom Death and the Fatal Sisters wait / With naked swords and scarlet liveries'. See also *One* V.i.525 n.

Omnes. O pity us!

Tamburlaine. Away with them I say and show them Death.   120
    They [TECHELLES *and others*] *take them away.*
    I will not spare these proud Egyptians,
    Nor change my martial observations
    For all the wealth of Gihon's golden waves,
    Or for the love of Venus, would she leave
    The angry god of arms and lie with me.   125
    They have refused the offer of their lives,
    And know my customs are as peremptory
    As wrathful planets, death, or destiny.

Enter TECHELLES.

    What, have your horsemen shown the virgins Death?

Techelles. They have, my lord, and on Damascus' walls   130
    Have hoisted up their slaughtered carcasses.

Tamburlaine. A sight as baneful to their souls, I think,
    As are Thessalian drugs or mithridate.
    But go, my lords, put the rest to the sword.
            Exeunt [*all except* TAMBURLAINE].
    Ah fair Zenocrate, divine Zenocrate,   135
    Fair is too foul an epithet for thee,
    That in thy passion for thy country's love,
    And fear to see thy kingly father's harm,
    With hair dishevelled wipest thy watery cheeks;
    And like to Flora in her morning's pride,   140
    Shaking her silver tresses in the air,

120.1. TECHELLES *and others*] *Dyce 1; not in O1–3, Q.*   134.1. *all except*
TAMBURLAINE] *Dyce 1; not in O1–3, Q; Lords Oxberry.*

---

122. *observations*] observances, rituals.

123. *Gihon's golden waves*] Spenser's phrase in *Faerie Queene*, I.vii.43,
for the Eden river (see Gen. ii.13); the Nile. Perhaps among the indications that Marlowe had read this book of Spenser's poem, in print or in
manuscript. See *Two* IV.i.188 n., and Introduction, section 3.

127. *peremptory*] final, fixed, precluding all doubt or hesitation (O.E.D.
1, 2, 3: first instance of 3, 1589).

133. *Thessalian*] 'The land of witchcraft ... bore a reputation for
magic and strange drugs ... See Horace, *Odes*, I.27, 21; Ovid. *Metam.*,
vii.264, etc., and especially *Amores*, iii.7, 27' (Ellis-Fermor, p. 161).
Mithridate is an antidote against poison, and therefore rather ineptly
called 'baneful'.

Rainest on the earth resolvèd pearl in showers
And sprinklest sapphires on thy shining face
Where Beauty, mother to the Muses, sits
And comments volumes with her ivory pen,   145
Taking instructions from thy flowing eyes,
Eyes, when that Ebena steps to heaven
In silence of thy solemn evening's walk,
Making the mantle of the richest night,
The moon, the planets, and the meteors, light.   150
There angels in their crystal armours fight
A doubtful battle with my tempted thoughts
For Egypt's freedom and the Soldan's life—
His life that so consumes Zenocrate,
Whose sorrows lay more siege unto my soul   155
Than all my army to Damascus' walls;
And neither Persia's sovereign nor the Turk
Troubled my senses with conceit of foil
So much by much as doth Zenocrate.
What is beauty, saith my sufferings, then?   160
If all the pens that ever poets held
Had fed the feeling of their masters' thoughts
And every sweetness that inspired their hearts,
Their minds and muses on admirèd themes;
If all the heavenly quintessence they still   165
From their immortal flowers of poesy,
Wherein as in a mirror we perceive

157. Persia's] *Oxberry;* Perseans *O1–3, Q.*

---

142. *resolvèd*] melted.

144. *Beauty ... Muses*] 'This genealogy has been substituted by Marlowe for the more usual one that makes Mnemosyne ... mother of the Muses' (Jump).

145. *comments*] furnishes with comments, expounds (*O.E.D.* 2, earliest instance 1599).

147. *Ebena*] Night. Marlowe has coined the name from [*h*]*ebenus*, 'often applied to night and used figuratively for black or dark' (Woolf). Cf. the 'ebon sceptre' of the god of Hell, *One* IV.ii.28. Ellis-Fermor suggests that Marlowe's ear for Latin quantity would move him to write 'Ebenina'. The closing lines of the sentence here seem syntactically loose, perhaps textually corrupt.

151. *crystal*] 'clear and transparent like crystal' (*O.E.D.* 2).

158. *conceit*] anticipation; as at l. 87 above.

165. *still*] produce by distillation (*O.E.D. vb.²*, 4).

The highest reaches of a human wit—
If these had made one poem's period
And all combined in beauty's worthiness,   170
Yet should there hover in their restless heads
One thought, one grace, one wonder at the least,
Which into words no virtue can digest.
But how unseemly is it for my sex,
My discipline of arms and chivalry,   175
My nature, and the terror of my name,
To harbour thoughts effeminate and faint!
Save only that in beauty's just applause,

---

169. *period*] end to be attained, goal (*O.E.D.* 9, quoting this line; but note also *O.E.D.* 10, complete rhetorical structure).

173. *digest*] Oliver notes *degestione* in the sense 'dissolution by heat', in 'The *Massacre at Paris* Manuscript', l. 30 (*Massacre at Paris*, p. 166), and suggests this as the image here. 'Virtue' as the efficacy of a catalyst, and the imagery of distilling (l. 165), would assist this alchemical train of thought.

178–90.] These lines have been thought to be difficult because of a faulty syntax and because three lines are 'obviously corrupt'; and editors have sought to rectify the first difficulty by supplying punctuation and supporting paraphrase, and the second by emendation, without always feeling satisfied with the results in either case. For Ellis-Fermor, to read 'that' (l. 178) as a conjunction ('Save only, that . . .') leaves us with an unfinished sentence, which we would have to complete silently by such a phrase as 'lies one of the sources of valour'. Editors adopting this interpretation commonly supply a full-stop at l. 182. Alternatively, Ellis-Fermor considered that to take 'that' as referring back to 'thoughts' ('Save only *that* thought which . . .') yielded 'a strained syntax and a general effect unlike Marlowe's writing at this time'.

The sentence seems, however, to make convincing and dramatic sense if we take 'that' as a conjunction and read the main thread of Tamburlaine's meditative discourse as 'Save only that . . . I thus conceiving and subduing . . . shall give the world to note'. In this reading, the impulse to assert mastery over a troubled sensitivity to Beauty struggles through two keenly-felt parentheses which recognise that such sensitivity is indispensable to a warrior (ll. 180–2) and that Beauty itself is powerful enough to cause gods to abandon wrath in favour of human love (184–7). The syntactical complication registers Tamburlaine's perplexity in a fully dramatic fashion, and issues in his affirming a compound sense of 'virtue' as an ardent discipline of powerful feelings which are mutually opposed though they have a common stimulus: beauty incites man to valorous action, on the one hand; on the other, it dissuades him from violence, in the name of human love and pity. As an incitement, beauty has been an insistent theme in the play; as a dissuasion, it was associated with Zenocrate in *One* III.iii.122–3, and she is greeted by Tamburlaine

With whose instinct the soul of man is touched—
And every warrior that is rapt with love 180
Of fame, of valour, and of victory,
Must needs have beauty beat on his conceits—
I thus conceiving and subduing, both,
That which hath stopped the tempest of the gods,
Even from the fiery spangled veil of heaven, 185
To feel the lovely warmth of shepherds' flames
And march in cottages of strewèd weeds,
Shall give the world to note, for all my birth,
That virtue solely is the sum of glory
And fashions men with true nobility. 190
Who's within there?

Enter two or three [Attendants].

184. stopped] *O1–3, Q;* stoopt *Dyce 2, Deighton.* tempest] *O1–3, Q;* temper *Collier;* chiefest *Dyce 2;* topmost *Deighton.* 187. march] *O1–3, Q;* mask *Dyce 1.* cottages] *O1–2;* cottges *O3;* coatches *Q.* weeds] *O1–3, Q;* reeds *Dyce 2.* 191.1. *two or three*] *O1–3, Q;* ANIPPE *Ox-berry.* Attendants] *Jump;* not in *O1–3, Q.*

in the truce at the end of this Part as 'She that hath calmed the fury of my sword' (l. 438). On the conjunction of Jupiter and Venus, see *Two* III.v.79–82.

180. *rapt*] smitten.

182. *beat on*] 'impinge [on], batter' (Pendry–Maxwell).

184.] I retain *stopped the tempest* because it does make sense, and chimes with 'calm the rage of thundering Jupiter' (*One* III.iii.123). But Duthie (p. 111) argues forcibly for emending to 'stoopt the topmost', thus combining two separate emendations by Dyce and Deighton: 'Both of these emendations postulate scribal or compositorial errors of a likely enough kind. "Stopt" may be a case of accidental omission of a single letter: "tempest" may show a double misreading of a manuscript "o" as "e" (quite likely in Elizabethan script) and also a metathesis—a scribe or compositor, thinking that his copy read "tempest", might very well emend to "tempest".' For Duthie (*English Studies 1948*: see Introduction, n. 110), the emended phrase echoes an earlier allusion to Jove's love for Mnemosyne (*One* I.ii.198 n.). K. Deighton, *The Old Dramatists*.

186. *shepherds' flames*] Translating Ovid's version of the Baucis and Philemon story, Golding (p. 176) spends several lines describing the hearth and the fire on which the cottagers cook.

187. *march*] Emendation to 'mask', though not required for the line to make sense, gains some support from the word's occurrence in a related context, *One* I.ii.198: 'Jove sometimes masked in a shepherd's weed'. 'Strew green rushes for the stranger' is proverbial (Tilley, R213).
weeds] herbs.

Hath Bajazeth been fed today?

Attendant. Ay, my lord.

Tamburlaine. Bring him forth, and let us know if the town
    be ransacked.   [*Exeunt* Attendants.]   195

    Enter TECHELLES, THERIDAMAS, USUMCASANE, *and others.*

Techelles. The town is ours, my lord, and fresh supply
    Of conquest and of spoil is offered us.

Tamburlaine. That's well, Techelles, what's the news?

Techelles. The Soldan and the Arabian king together
    March on us with such eager violence   200
    As if there were no way but one with us.

Tamburlaine. No more there is not, I warrant thee, Techelles.

    They [Attendants] *bring in the Turk* [BAJAZETH *in his
        cage, and* ZABINA].

Theridamas. We know the victory is ours, my lord,
    But let us save the reverend Soldan's life
    For fair Zenocrate that so laments his state.   205

Tamburlaine. That will we chiefly see unto, Theridamas,
    For sweet Zenocrate, whose worthiness
    Deserves a conquest over every heart.
    And now, my footstool, if I lose the field,
    You hope of liberty and restitution.   210
    Here let him stay, my masters, from the tents,
    Till we have made us ready for the field.
    Pray for us, Bajazeth, we are going.

    Exeunt [*all except* BAJAZETH *and* ZABINA].

---

193. *Attendant*] *Dyce 1*; An. *O1–3*, *Q* [*possibly for* Another]; *Oxberry reads
as* Anippe.   195. *Exeunt* Attendants] *Dyce 1*; *not in O1–3*, *Q*; *Exit* An.
Oxberry.   213.1. *all* ZABINA] *Dyce 1*; *not in O1–3*, *Q*; *Exeunt Tamburlaine, Techelles, Usumcasane, and Persians. Oxberry.*   213. we]
O1–3, *Q*; *where we Pendry–Maxwell.*

192–5.] The prose is strikingly bathetic in context.

201. *no way but one*] a proverbial expression, as Jump notes (Tilley,
W148). Cf. *H5*, II.iii.16: 'I knew there was but one way'.

203–8.] Theridamas prompts Tamburlaine to reaffirm his readiness to
spare Zenocrate's father, first expressed (with conditions) at *One* IV.iv.89–
92. That Zenocrate's beauty merits this 'conquest' over him returns our
attention to the theme of 'conceiving and subduing, both' (l. 183); here,
beauty is allowed to deflect the will to destroy. But there may be irony
in the fact that Tamburlaine needs prompting to spare the Sultan, for all
the eloquence of his words about Zenocrate's grief.

Bajazeth. Go, never to return with victory!
    Millions of men encompass thee about   215
    And gore thy body with as many wounds!
    Sharp, forkèd arrows light upon thy horse!
    Furies from the black Cocytus lake
    Break up the earth, and with their firebrands
    Enforce thee run upon the baneful pikes!   220
    Volleys of shot pierce through thy charmèd skin,
    And every bullet dipt in poisoned drugs;
    Or roaring cannons sever all thy joints,
    Making thee mount as high as eagles soar!

Zabina. Let all the swords and lances in the field   225
    Stick in his breast as in their proper rooms;
    At every pore let blood come dropping forth,
    That ling'ring pains may massacre his heart
    And madness send his damnèd soul to hell!

Bajazeth. Ah fair Zabina, we may curse his power,   230
    The heavens may frown, the earth for anger quake,
    But such a star hath influence in his sword
    As rules the skies, and countermands the gods
    More than Cimmerian Styx or Destiny.
    And then shall we in this detested guise,   235
    With shame, with hunger, and with horror aye
    Griping our bowels with retorquèd thoughts,
    And have no hope to end our ecstasies.

---

218. *Cocytus*] a river of the Underworld; a lake for Marlowe here, and part of Hell's 'triple moat' at *Two* II.iv.100.

226. *proper rooms*] i.e. 'where they belong' (Jump).

233. *countermands*] goes counter to (*O.E.D.* 5, earliest entry 1590 [*sic*] *Edward II*, III.iii.4).

234. *Cimmerian Styx*] 'The chief river of the underworld . . . was the divinity by which the most solemn oaths were sworn. Marlowe's allusion may be a reminiscence of Virgil's line: "Di cuius jurare timent et fallere numen" ' (Ellis-Fermor, p. 166). For *Cimmerian*, cf. *One* III.ii.76–9 n., and *Two* V.iii.8. On Tamburlaine and Destiny, cf. *One* V.i.128.

235–7.] We may understand 'live' after 'shall we' in l. 235, if we are concerned to seek (as Marlowe habitually does) a fully articulated sentence; but an incomplete syntax expressively conveys Bajazeth's 'retorquèd thoughts'. The mood at l. 236 may be an anguished questioning, rhetorically moving Zabina towards suicide.

237. *retorquèd*] turned back on themselves; only instance in *O.E.D.*

238. *ecstasies*] extreme anguish ('beside oneself'): cf. 'ecstasy' for the anger of Barabas, *Jew of Malta*, I.ii.210.

Zabina. Then is there left no Mahomet, no God,
    No fiend, no Fortune, nor no hope of end   240
    To our infamous, monstrous slaveries?
    Gape, earth, and let the fiends infernal view
    A hell as hopeless and as full of fear
    As are the blasted banks of Erebus,
    Where shaking ghosts with ever-howling groans   245
    Hover about the ugly ferryman
    To get a passage to Elysium.
    Why should we live, O wretches, beggars, slaves,
    Why live we, Bajazeth, and build up nests
    So high within the region of the air,   250
    By living long in this oppression,
    That all the world will see and laugh to scorn
    The former triumphs of our mightiness
    In this obscure infernal servitude?
Bajazeth. O life more loathsome to my vexèd thoughts   255
    Than noisome parbreak of the Stygian snakes
    Which fills the nooks of hell with standing air,
    Infecting all the ghosts with cureless griefs!
    O dreary engines of my loathèd sight

---

243. A] *Oxberry;* As *O1–3, Q.*

---

241. *infamous*] second-syllable stress consistently in Marlowe: cf.
ll. 392, 405 below.

242. *Gape, earth*] Cf. *Dr Faustus*, xix.156. Richard dextrously deflates
Anne's recourse to this Marlovian vein in *R3*, I.ii.65.

244. *Erebus*] cf. *One* IV.i.45 n., and Tamburlaine's boast of the souls
he has sent to wait for Charon, ll. 464–5 below.

246. *ugly ferryman*] Hell and the devils are persistently 'ugly' in
Dr Faustus: e.g., vi.78. Cf. *Two* III.iv.59 n.

249–50. *build . . . air*] '?remain conspicuously and proudly alive;
?subsist on insubstantial hopes' (Pendry–Maxwell).

256. *noisome parbreak*] stinking vomit. The snakes are perhaps those
entwined in the Furies' hair. Cf. the 'filthy parbreake' of Error, *Faerie
Queene*, I.i.20. H. W. Crundell refers me to Horace, *Odes*, III.xi.17–20,
in which Cerberus appears with a hundred snakes on his head, and with
foul breath and gore at his lips. See Ovid, *Metam.*, iv.490. 'Noisome' is
found in *Lucan*, 650. The *Styx* is a river of the underworld, or a poisonous
stream in Arcadia: see *Jew of Malta*, III.iv.102 n.

258. *cureless griefs*] irremediable sufferings.

259. *engines*] 'instruments, means' (Ellis-Fermor, p. 169): the eyes.

259–62.] perhaps echoing *Faerie Queene*, I.vii.22.

That sees my crown, my honour, and my name   260
Thrust under yoke and thraldom of a thief—
Why feed ye still on day's accursèd beams,
And sink not quite into my tortured soul?
You see my wife, my queen and emperess,
Brought up and proppèd by the hand of fame,   265
Queen of fifteen contributory queens,
Now thrown to rooms of black abjection,
Smearèd with blots of basest drudgery,
And villeiness to shame, disdain, and misery.
Accursèd Bajazeth, whose words of ruth,   270
That would with pity cheer Zabina's heart
And make our souls resolve in ceaseless tears,
Sharp hunger bites upon and gripes the root
From whence the issues of my thoughts do break.
O poor Zabina, O my queen, my queen,   275
Fetch me some water for my burning breast,
To cool and comfort me with longer date,
That, in the shortened sequel of my life,
I may pour forth my soul into thine arms
With words of love, whose moaning intercourse   280
Hath hitherto been stayed with wrath and hate
Of our expressless banned inflictions.

Zabina. Sweet Bajazeth, I will prolong thy life
As long as any blood or spark of breath
Can quench or cool the torments of my grief.   285

                              She goes out.

Bajazeth. Now, Bajazeth, abridge thy baneful days
And beat thy brains out of thy conquered head,
Since other means are all forbidden me
That may be ministers of my decay.
O highest lamp of ever-living Jove,   290

---

267. *abjection*] degradation; cf. 'abject our princely minds' at *Two* V.i.140.

269. *villeiness*] servant, bondswoman: not, as cited in *O.E.D.*, 'female villain'.

282. *expressless*] inexpressible; first entry in *O.E.D.*

banned] accursed; not 'repressed, bound down' (Ellis-Fermor, p. 168).

289. *decay*] death, fall. Cf. *Faerie Queene*, II.ix.12: 'Fly fast, and save yourselves from near decay'.

290–3.] perhaps echoing *Faerie Queene*, I.vii.23.

Accursèd day, infected with my griefs,
Hide now thy stainèd face in endless night
And shut the windows of the lightsome heavens;
Let ugly darkness with her rusty coach
Engirt with tempests wrapt in pitchy clouds   295
Smother the earth with never-fading mists,
And let her horses from their nostrils breathe
Rebellious winds and dreadful thunderclaps:
That in this terror Tamburlaine may live,
And my pined soul, resolved in liquid air,   300
May still excruciate his tormented thoughts.
Then let the stony dart of senseless cold
Pierce through the centre of my withered heart
And make a passage for my loathèd life.
          He brains himself against the cage.

                    Enter ZABINA.

Zabina. What do mine eyes behold? My husband dead!   305
His skull all riven in twain, his brains dashed out!

300. air] *O3, Q;* ay *O1–2.*

---

293. *lightsome*] light-giving, luminous, radiant.
294.] See *Two* III.iv.59 n. A Virgilian–Spenserian line. Cf. the 'yron chariot' of Night in *Faerie Queene*, I.v.20, ll. 6–9, and the 'coleblacke steedes . . . / That on their rustie bits did champ'. *Hero*, Sest. II.232 has 'ugly Night', and *Lucan*, 244–5, 'old swords / With ugly teeth of black rust foully scarr'd'. Heninger (p. 62) compares *2H6*. IV.i.3–7, Night's 'jades' who 'from their misty jaws / Breathe foul contagious darkness in the air'.
300–1.] Ellis-Fermor finds (p. 169) a reference to early Greek doctrines; but we may with J. C. Maxwell think the sense simpler than this: i.e., 'his soul even when dissolved in air may still (as a part of that air, not as having any continued existence as such) torment Tamburlaine in the natural upheavals he has just described'. Maxwell refers to Lucretius, e.g. iii.455–6, for a possible source of the idea of resolving into air.
301. *excruciate*] torture.
302–3. *dart . . . centre*] Cf. the closely similar description of death at *Two* II.iv.84. Perhaps echoing *Faerie Queene*, I.vii.22.
304.1.] 'The suicide of Bajazeth is described only by Perondinus and Primaudaye, who obviously follows him' (Ellis-Fermor, p. 169); see Appendix.
305–19.] Combining verse and prose in representing madness as a derangement of remembered experience, Marlowe helps prepare for Ophelia and Lady Macbeth.

The brains of Bajazeth, my lord and sovereign!
O Bajazeth, my husband and my lord,
O Bajazeth, O Turk, O emperor—give him his liquor?
Not I. Bring milk and fire, and my blood I bring him   310
again, tear me in pieces, give me the sword with a ball
of wild-fire upon it. Down with him, down with him!
Go to my child, away, away, away. Ah, save that infant,
save him, save him! I, even I, speak to her. The sun
was down. Streamers white, red, black, here, here, here.   315
Fling the meat in his face. Tamburlaine, Tamburlaine!
Let the soldiers be buried. Hell, death, Tamburlaine,
hell! Make ready my coach, my chair, my jewels, I come,
I come, I come!
    She runs against the cage and brains herself.

[*Enter*] ZENOCRATE *with* ANIPPE.

Zenocrate. Wretched Zenocrate, that livest to see   320
    Damascus' walls dyed with Egyptian blood,
    Thy father's subjects and thy countrymen;
    Thy streets strowed with disseevered joints of men
    And wounded bodies gasping yet for life;
    But most accursed, to see the sun-bright troop   325
    Of heavenly virgins and unspotted maids,
    Whose looks might make the angry god of arms
    To break his sword and mildly treat of love,
    On horsemen's lances to be hoisted up
    And guiltlessly endure a cruel death.   330
    For every fell and stout Tartarian steed
    That stamped on others with their thund'ring hoofs,
    When all their riders charged their quivering spears
    Began to check the ground and rein themselves,

317. Let . . . Tamburlaine] *O1–2; not in O3, Q.*   319.2. *Enter*] *Q;
not in O1–3.*

---

312. *wild-fire*] incendiaries used in warfare. Cf. *Dido*, II.i.216–17,
'Myrmidons, / With balls of wildfire in their murdering paws'.
315. *streamers*] pennons.
322. *subjects . . . countrymen*] i.e., their blood.
333. *charged*] levelled.
334. *check*] stamp on. In *Hero*, Sest. II, 141–4, a horse 'Checks the
submissive ground'.

Gazing upon the beauty of their looks.   335
Ah Tamburlaine, wert thou the cause of this,
That termest Zenocrate thy dearest love—
Whose lives were dearer to Zenocrate
Than her own life, or aught save thine own love?
But see another bloody spectacle!   340
Ah wretched eyes, the enemies of my heart,
How are ye glutted with these grievous objects,
And tell my soul more tales of bleeding ruth!
See, see, Anippe, if they breathe or no.

Anippe. No breath, nor sense, nor motion in them both.   345
Ah madam, this their slavery hath enforced,
And ruthless cruelty of Tamburlaine.

Zenocrate. Earth, cast up fountains from thy entrails,
And wet thy cheeks for their untimely deaths;
Shake with their weight in sign of fear and grief.   350
Blush, heaven, that gave them honour at their birth
And let them die a death so barbarous.
Those that are proud of fickle empery
And place their chiefest good in earthly pomp—
Behold the Turk and his great emperess!   355
Ah Tamburlaine my love, sweet Tamburlaine,
That fightest for sceptres and for slippery crowns,
Behold the Turk and his great emperess!
Thou that in conduct of thy happy stars
Sleepest every night with conquest on thy brows   360
And yet wouldst shun the wavering turns of war,
In fear and feeling of the like distress
Behold the Turk and his great emperess!
Ah mighty Jove and holy Mahomet,
Pardon my love, O pardon his contempt   365

---

345. *motion*] power of movement (*O.E.D.* 2d, first entry 1603).

348.] Fountains were thought to be cast up during earthquakes by the
agency of subterranean wind (cf. Aristotle, *Met.*, Loeb, ii.368a.26–33).
Cf. *One* I.ii.50–1.

348–71.] 'The strophic movement of this speech, with its refrain, may
be compared with *Two* II.iv.1–33, V.iii.1–41, 145–58' (Ellis-Fermor,
p. 171–2); see Clemen, p. 128.

353 ff.] Zenocrate's lines as she herself nears death will echo these:
Two II.iv.42–6.

359. *in conduct*] under the guidance (Jump).

Of earthly fortune and respect of pity,
And let not conquest ruthlessly pursued
Be equally against his life incensed
In this great Turk and hapless emperess!
And pardon me that was not moved with ruth   370
To see them live so long in misery.
Ah what may chance to thee, Zenocrate?

Anippe. Madam, content yourself and be resolved
Your love hath Fortune so at his command
That she shall stay, and turn her wheel no more   375
As long as life maintains his mighty arm
That fights for honour to adorn your head.

Enter [PHILEMUS,] *a* Messenger.

Zenocrate. What other heavy news now brings Philemus?
Philemus. Madam, your father and th'Arabian king,
The first affecter of your excellence,   380
Comes now as Turnus 'gainst Aeneas did,
Armèd with lance into th'Egyptian fields,
Ready for battle 'gainst my lord the king.

Zenocrate. Now shame and duty, love and fear, presents
A thousand sorrows to my martyred soul: 385
Whom should I wish the fatal victory,
When my poor pleasures are divided thus
And racked by duty from my cursèd heart?
My father and my first betrothèd love
Must fight against my life and present love—   390
Wherein the change I use condemns my faith

377.1. PHILEMUS] *Oxberry; not in O1–3, Q.*

---

366. *respect of pity*] regard (*O.E.D. sb.* 13) for compassion (which
Tamburlaine holds in 'contempt'). Alternatively, the awkward phrasing
here could be improved by reading 'of respect and pity' (E.A.J.H.).
369. *In*] i.e. As in.
373. *resolved*] satisfied, convinced.
374–5.] Cf. *One* I.ii.174 n.
380. *affecter*] lover.
381. *Turnus 'gainst Aeneas*] Virgil, *Aen.*, Book VII. Cf. ll. 393–5 n. below.
386. *fatal*] destined, fated; cf. *Dr Faustus*, xv.22.
388. *racked*] drawn off (*O.E.D. vb.*[5] 1: earliest figurative use 1653);
extorted (*O.E.D. vb.*[4] 4).
391. *change*] changefulness, inconstancy (*O.E.D.* 4b, first entry 1600).
use] exhibit.

And makes my deeds infamous through the world.
But as the gods, to end the Trojan's toil,
Prevented Turnus of Lavinia,
And fatally enriched Aeneas' love,　　　　　395
So, for a final issue to my griefs,
To pacify my country and my love,
Must Tamburlaine, by their resistless powers,
With virtue of a gentle victory
Conclude a league of honour to my hope;　　400
Then, as the powers divine have pre-ordained,
With happy safety of my father's life
Send like defence of fair Arabia.

They sound to the battle, and TAMBURLAINE *enjoys the
victory. After,* ARABIA *enters wounded.*

Arabia. What cursèd power guides the murdering hands
Of this infamous tyrant's soldiers,　　　　　405
That no escape may save their enemies
Nor fortune keep themselves from victory?
Lie down, Arabia, wounded to the death,
And let Zenocrate's fair eyes behold
That as for her thou bearest these wretched arms　410
Even so for her thou diest in these arms,
Leaving thy blood for witness of thy love.

Zenocrate. Too dear a witness for such love, my lord.
Behold Zenocrate, the cursèd object
Whose fortunes never masterèd her griefs:　　　415
Behold her wounded in conceit for thee,
As much as thy fair body is for me.

Arabia. Then shall I die with full contented heart,
Having beheld divine Zenocrate

393–5.] The 'enrichment' of Aeneas, in gaining Lavinia, was 'fatal' to
Turnus: the allusion works itself out to Arabia's cost.

394. *Prevented*] Deprived.

398. *by . . . powers*] considering their irresistible armies.

399. *With virtue of*] In consequence of. The *gentle victory* is granted
her: cf. l. 441–3 below.

400. *to*] 'in accordance with' (Jump).

403.1. *sound to*] cf. *One* III.iii.188.1 n.

415. *fortunes*] for the plural, cf. Prologue to Part One, 8 n.

416. *conceit*] imaginative sympathy.

Whose sight with joy would take away my life,   420
As now it bringeth sweetness to my wound,
If I had not been wounded as I am.
Ah, that the deadly pangs I suffer now
Would lend an hour's licence to my tongue,
To make discourse of some sweet accidents   425
Have chanced thy merits in this worthless bondage,
And that I might be privy to the state
Of thy deserved contentment and thy love!
But making now a virtue of thy sight,
To drive all sorrow from my fainting soul,   430
Since death denies me further cause of joy,
Deprived of care, my heart with comfort dies
Since thy desirèd hand shall close mine eyes.
                    [*He dies.*]

> *Enter* TAMBURLAINE *leading the* SOLDAN; TECHELLES,
>   THERIDAMAS, USUMCASANE, *with others.*

Tamburlaine. Come, happy father of Zenocrate,
      A title higher than thy Soldan's name,   435
      Though my right hand have thus enthrallèd thee,
      Thy princely daughter here shall set thee free—
      She that hath calmed the fury of my sword,
      Which had ere this been bathed in streams of blood
      As vast and deep as Euphrates or Nile.   440
Zenocrate. O sight thrice welcome to my joyful soul,
      To see the king my father issue safe
      From dangerous battle of my conquering love!
Soldan. Well met, my only dear Zenocrate,
      Though with the loss of Egypt and my crown.   445
Tamburlaine. 'Twas I, my lord, that gat the victory;
      And therefore, grieve not at your overthrow,

433.1. *He dies*] Oxberry; *not in* O1-3, Q.

---

425. *sweet accidents*] 'unexpectedly favourable turns of fortune' (Woolf).
426. *Have*] i.e., That have.
chanced thy merits] occurred according to your high deserts; cf. *Dido*,
V.i.176: 'Which if it chance, I'll give ye burial'.
440. *Euphrates*] the first syllable accented, as at *Two* III.i.43, 54.
Cf. *Ant.*, I.ii.98.
443. *of*] with.

Since I shall render all into your hands
And add more strength to your dominions
Than ever yet confirmed th'Egyptian crown.   450
The god of war resigns his room to me,
Meaning to make me general of the world:
Jove, viewing me in arms, looks pale and wan,
Fearing my power should pull him from his throne;
Where'er I come the Fatal Sisters sweat,   455
And grisly Death, by running to and fro
To do their ceaseless homage to my sword;
And here in Afric where it seldom rains,
Since I arrived with my triumphant host
Have swelling clouds drawn from wide gasping wounds   460
Been oft resolved in bloody purple showers,
A meteor that might terrify the earth
And make it quake at every drop it drinks;
Millions of souls sit on the banks of Styx,
Waiting the back return of Charon's boat;   465
Hell and Elysium swarm with ghosts of men
That I have sent from sundry foughten fields
To spread my fame through hell and up to heaven.
And see, my lord, a sight of strange import—
Emperors and kings lie breathless at my feet: 470
The Turk and his great empress, as it seems,
Left to themselves while we were at the fight,
Have desperately despatched their slavish lives;
With them Arabia too hath left his life—
All sights of power to grace my victory;   475
And such are objects fit for Tamburlaine,

---

454. *pull . . . throne*] 'as he had pulled Saturn' (Jump). Cf. *One* II.vii.12–29 n.

455. *Fatal Sisters*] the Parcae, Tamburlaine's menials here and at *Two* III.iv.54. Cf. *Two* II.iv.99.

460–61.] Renaissance meteorology can rival Tamburlaine's vaunt, if not steal his fire: Kocher (p. 237) quotes Fulke, *A most pleasant Prospect*, 1602: 'the Sunne also from places where blood hath been spilt, draweth up great quantity of blood, and so it rayneth blood'.

464–8.] The recall of Bajazeth's and Zabina's curses and despair aptly prepares for the sight of their bodies. On the confounding of Hell in Elysium, cf. *Dr Faustus*, iii.62 n.

475. *of power to*] able to.

Wherein as in a mirror may be seen
His honour, that consists in shedding blood
When men presume to manage arms with him.

Soldan. Mighty hath God and Mahomet made thy hand,   480
Renownèd Tamburlaine, to whom all kings
Of force must yield their crowns and emperies;
And I am pleased with this my overthrow
If, as beseems a person of thy state,
Thou hast with honour used Zenocrate.   485

Tamburlaine. Her state and person wants no pomp, you see,
And for all blot of foul inchastity,
I record heaven, her heavenly self is clear.
Then let me find no further time to grace
Her princely temples with the Persian crown,   490
But here these kings that on my fortunes wait
And have been crowned for provèd worthiness
Even by this hand that shall establish them,
Shall now, adjoining all their hands with mine,
Invest her here my Queen of Persia: 495
What saith the noble Soldan and Zenocrate?

Soldan. I yield with thanks and protestations
Of endless honour to thee for her love.

Tamburlaine. Then doubt I not but fair Zenocrate
Will soon consent to satisfy us both.   500

Zenocrate. Else should I much forget myself, my lord.

Theridamas. Then let us set the crown upon her head
That long hath lingered for so high a seat.

Techelles. My hand is ready to perform the deed,
For now her marriage time shall work us rest.   505

Usumcasane. And here's the crown, my lord, help set it on.

Tamburlaine. Then sit thou down, divine Zenocrate,
And here we crown thee Queen of Persia
And all the kingdoms and dominions

---

482. *Of force*] Of necessity.
484. *beseems*] befits (cf. l. 532).
488. *record*] call to witness (*O.E.D.* 10b, sole entry); second syllable stressed.
489. *further*] more distant, further off.
491. *fortunes*] Cf. l. 415 n. above.
498. *her love*] 'your love of her' (Jump).

That late the power of Tamburlaine subdued.   510
As Juno, when the giants were suppressed
That darted mountains at her brother Jove,
So looks my love, shadowing in her brows
Triumphs and trophies for my victories;
Or as Latona's daughter bent to arms,   515
Adding more courage to my conquering mind.
To gratify thee, sweet Zenocrate,
Egyptians, Moors, and men of Asia,
From Barbary unto the Western Indie,
Shall pay a yearly tribute to thy sire;   520
And from the bounds of Afric to the banks
Of Ganges shall his mighty arm extend.
And now, my lords and loving followers,
That purchased kingdoms by your martial deeds,
Cast off your armour, put on scarlet robes,   525
Mount up your royal places of estate,
Environèd with troops of noble men,
And there make laws to rule your provinces:
Hang up your weapons on Alcides' post,

517. thee] *Dyce 2;* the [*possibly a spelling of* thee] *O1–3, Q.*

511–12.] cf. *One* II.iii.18–21 n., II.vi.2–6 n. Juno's delight at the
victory 'seems to be Marlowe's own image' (Ellis-Fermor, p. 177).

513. *shadowing*] harbouring, or depicting; cf. l. 58 n. above, and
Dr Faustus, i.127–8: 'Shadowing more beauty in their airy brows / Than
in the white breasts of the queen of love'.

515. *Latona's daughter*] Diana (Artemis), patroness of hunting.

519. *From Barbary ... Indie*] 'That is, from the northern coast of
Africa in the west to the Ganges in the east' (Ellis-Fermor, p. 177).

524. *purchased*] won; cf. 'purchase' (noun) at *One* II.v.92.

525. *scarlet robes*] The most direct association of this emblem of
peaceful lawgivers is with the image of the scarlet judge who, keeping the
circuit of Tamburlaine's sword, obediently condemns the virgins of
Damascus in *One* V.i.111–18. Tamburlaine was in scarlet, on the second
day of siege, in *One* IV.iv. J. P. Brockbank notes Plutarch, *Life of Mar-
cellus*, 'coate armor died in skarlet, which is the ordinary signe of battell'
(*Lives*, tr. North, Oxford (Blackwell), 1928, iii.95), and 'The Plot of the
Play, Called *Englands Joy*', of 1602, in which War, at the feet of Justice,
wears 'a Scarlet Roabe of peace upon his Armour' (W. W. Greg, *Dramatic
Documents*, Oxford, 1931, VIII).

529. *Alcides' post*] Bullen cites Horace, *Ep.*, I.i.4–5: 'Veianius armis /
Hercules ad postem fixis' (Veianius hangs up his arms at Hercules' door),
and comments: ' "Post" is an obvious Latinism, "postis" being the

For Tamburlaine takes truce with all the world.   530
Thy first betrothèd love, Arabia,
Shall we with honour, as beseems, entomb,
With this great Turk and his fair emperess;
Then after all these solemn exequies
We will our rites of marriage solemnise.   [*Exeunt.*]   535

Finis Actus quinti & ultimi huius primae partis.

535. our rites] *Dyce 2;* our celebrated rites *O1–3, Q.*   *Exeunt*] *Dyce 2;*
not in *O1–3, Q.*

---

door-post of the temple'. The allusion aptly caps the Herculean references
of this Part of the play.

535.1.] End of Act Five and the last Act of Part One. An unusually
formal conclusion.

THE SECOND PART OF
The bloody Conquests
of mighty Tamburlaine.

With his impassionate fury for the death of
his Lady and love, fair Zenocrate, his form
of exhortation and discipline to his three
sons, and the manner of his own death.

With . . . own death.] *O1–3; not in Q.*

PART TWO

[DRAMATIS PERSONAE

The Prologue.

ORCANES, *King of Natolia.*

GAZELLUS, *Viceroy of Byron.*

URIBASSA, *attending on Orcanes.*

SIGISMOND, *King of Hungary.*   5

FREDERICK, *lord of Buda.*

BALDWIN, *lord of Bohemia.*

CALLAPINE, *son of Bajazeth and prisoner of Tamburlaine.*

ALMEDA, *his keeper.*

TAMBURLAINE, *King of Persia.*   10

CALYPHAS ⎫
AMYRAS   ⎬ *his sons.*
CELEBINUS ⎭

THERIDAMAS, *King of Argier.*

TECHELLES, *King of Fesse.*   15

USUMCASANE, *King of Morocco.*

KING OF TREBIZOND.

---

2. *Orcanes*] a Turkish emperor of an earlier period; the name 'Orcan' occurs in Whetstone.

3. *Gazellus*] name drawn from a later period, found in Bizarus.

5. *Sigismond*] Hungarian king contemporary with Tamburlaine. Marlowe involves him unhistorically, in place of Vladislaus, in the events that led up to the battle of Varna in 1444. See p. 19 above. Whetstone has a Sigismond contemporary with 'Calapin': see Appendix, p. 320.

8. *Callapine*] historical; given his full titles in Lonicerus (see *Two* III.i.1 n.).

11, 12. *Calyphas* and *Amyras*] names adopted from a passage in Lonicerus (Seaton, 'Sources', p. 388). Whetstone mentions only *two* sons.

13. *Celebinus*] name adopted from one of the titles of Callapine, as recorded in Lonicerus.

KING OF SORIA.
KING OF JERUSALEM.
KING OF AMASIA.   20
CAPTAIN OF BALSERA.
SON *of the Captain of Balsera.*
PERDICAS.
GOVERNOR OF BABYLON.
MAXIMUS.   25
A Captain, Messengers, Attendants, Physicians, Soldiers,
   Pioners, Citizens, Lords.

ZENOCRATE, *Queen of Persia, wife of Tamburlaine.*
OLYMPIA, *wife of the Captain of Balsera.*
Turkish Concubines.]   30

Part Two DRAMATIS PERSONAE] *not in O1–3, Q; first listed, in incomplete
   form, in Oxberry.*

---

23. *Perdicas*] The name occurs in Whetstone, but the character
(distinctive, though minor) is Marlowe's creation.

Part Two

The Prologue

The general welcomes Tamburlaine received
When he arrivèd last upon our stage
Hath made our poet pen his second part,
Where death cuts off the progress of his pomp
And murd'rous Fates throws all his triumphs down.   5
But what became of fair Zenocrate,
And with how many cities' sacrifice
He celebrated her sad funeral,
Himself in presence shall unfold at large.

8. sad] *Oxberry*; said *O1–3, Q.*

Prologue. 5. *Fates*] Clotho, Lachesis, Atropos; cf. *One* I.ii.173 n.
  throws] a normal third-person plural form in Elizabethan grammar.

Act I

SCENE i

[Enter] ORCANES *King of* NATOLIA, GAZELLUS *Viceroy of*
BYRON, URIBASSA, *and their* train, *with drums and trumpets.*

Orcanes. Egregious viceroys of these eastern parts,
    Placed by the issue of great Bajazeth
    And sacred lord, the mighty Callapine,
    Who lives in Egypt prisoner to that slave
    Which kept his father in an iron cage: 5
    Now have we marched from fair Natolia
    Two hundred leagues, and on Danubius' banks
    Our warlike host in complete armour rest,
    Where Sigismond the king of Hungary
    Should meet our person to conclude a truce.   10
    What, shall we parley with the Christian,
    Or cross the stream and meet him in the field?
Gazellus King of Natolia, let us treat of peace;
    We all are glutted with the Christians' blood,
    And have a greater foe to fight against—   15
    Proud Tamburlaine, that now in Asia

0.1. *Enter*] Dyce 1; not in O1–3, Q.   0.2. URIBASSA] Oxberry; Vpibassa
O1–3, Q.   11. parley] Oxberry; parle O1–3, Q.

I.i.] On the source material for the Orcanes–Sigismond episode, see
Introduction, pp. 17–18.

0.2. *Byron*] a town not far from Babylon.

1. *Egregious*] distinguished.

6. *Natolia*] 'the whole promontory of Asia Minor' (Seaton, p. 20).

11. *parley*] See *One* I.ii.137 n.

14. *glutted . . . blood*] Cf. *Lucan*, l. 39: 'And Carthage souls be glutted
with our bloods'.

16.] 'Tamburlaine here slips easily into the place of the later Scander-
beg, whose success against the Turks at Dybra disposed Amurath II to
treat for peace' (Ellis-Fermor, p. 184).

Near Guyron's head doth set his conquering feet
And means to fire Turkey as he goes:
'Gainst him, my lord, must you address your power.

Uribassa. Besides, King Sigismond hath brought from
    Christendom   20
More than his camp of stout Hungarians,
Slavonians, Almains, Rutters, Muffs, and Danes,
That with the halberd, lance, and murdering axe
Will hazard that we might with surety hold.

Orcanes. Though from the shortest northern parallel,   25
Vast Gruntland, compassed with the frozen sea,
Inhabited with tall and sturdy men,
Giants as big as hugy Polypheme,
Millions of soldiers cut the Arctic line,
Bringing the strength of Europe to these arms,   30
Our Turkey blades shall glide through all their throats
And make this champion mead a bloody fen;
Danubius' stream, that runs to Trebizond,

---

20. *Uribassa.*] *Oxberry;* Vpibas *O1–3, Q.*   22. Almains, Rutters] *O1–3,*
Q; Almain Rutters *Collier.*   25. *Orcanes.*] *Oxberry; not in O1–3, Q.*

---

17. *Guyron*] the 'Guiron' of Ortelius's maps is a town 'not far from the
confines of Natolia, and therefore a possible outpost' (Seaton, pp. 22–3).
Marlowe could be giving the name in error to a river.

19. *address your power*] prepare, dispatch, your army.

22. *Almains*] Germans.

Rutters] cavalry: cf. 'Almain rutters', *Dr Faustus* i.124, but to read
'Almain rutters' here with Collier is unnecessary, and against the run of
the line.

Muffs] 'depreciative term for a German or Swiss' (first entry in *O.E.D.*).

24. *hazard that*] risk that which.

25. *shortest northern parallel*] the most northerly circle of latitude.

26. *Gruntland*] Grœnlandt in Ortelius (i.e. Greenland). The O3, Q,
reading 'Grantland' seems misguided. 'Marlowe or his printer has
accidentally added an infixed "t" while also anglicizing the œ to u' (Ellis-
Fermor, p. 184).

28. *Polypheme*] *Dr Faustus*, i.125, also has legendary 'Lapland giants'
in close company with 'Almain rutters', and similarly moves on to
'argosies' that carry inestimable wealth.

hugy] huge.

29. *cut the Arctic line*] 'cross the arctic circle southward' (Ellis-Fermor,
p. 185).

32. *champion mead*] open plain.

33–41.] Marlowe 'sees the waters of the Danube sweeping from the

Shall carry wrapt within his scarlet waves,
As martial presents to our friends at home,   35
The slaughtered bodies of these Christians;
The Terrene main, wherein Danubius falls,
Shall by this battle be the bloody sea.
The wand'ring sailors of proud Italy
Shall meet those Christians fleeting with the tide,   40
Beating in heaps against their argosies,
And make fair Europe, mounted on her bull,
Trapped with the wealth and riches of the world,
Alight and wear a woeful mourning weed.

Gazellus. Yet, stout Orcanes, prorex of the world,   45
Since Tamburlaine hath mustered all his men,
Marching from Cairon northward with his camp
To Alexandria and the frontier towns,
Meaning to make a conquest of our land,
'Tis requisite to parley for a peace   50
With Sigismond the king of Hungary,
And save our forces for the hot assaults
Proud Tamburlaine intends Natolia.

Orcanes. Viceroy of Byron, wisely hast thou said:

50. *parley*] Oxberry; parle *O1–3, Q.*

---

river mouths in two strong currents, the one racing across the Black Sea
to Trebizond, the other swirling southward to the Bosporus, and so
onward to the Hellespont and the Aegean. Both currents bear the
slaughtered bodies of Christian soliders, the one to bring proof of victory
to the great Turkish town, the other to strike terror to the Italian merchants cruising round the Isles of Greece' (Seaton, p. 32). Seaton cites
Oth., III.iii.457 ff., on the 'compulsive course' of the Pontick Sea, and
finds in Nicholay a possible source for this emphasis, and in Perondinus'
account of Bajazeth's defeat words that may have proved suggestive here:
'Eufrates . . . maiore sanguinis et aquaram vi ad mare Rubrum volveretur'
(Seaton, p. 33).

37. *Terrene main*] Mediterranean.

40. *fleeting*] floating.

41. *argosies*] large merchant ships.

42–3.] The abduction of Europa by Zeus is given a tone of opulence.
Ovid's account is in *Metam.*, ii.836 ff. and iv.104.

43. *Trapped*] adorned; ?playing on the sense of 'seduced', 'entrapped'.

45. *prorex*] viceroy; cf. *One* I.i.89 n. Ellis-Fermor (p. 186) finds
absurdity in its use here.

47. *Cairon*] Cairo.

50. *parley*] See *One* I.ii.137 n.

My realm, the centre of our empery,   55
Once lost, all Turkey would be overthrown;
And for that cause the Christians shall have peace.
Slavonians, Almains, Rutters, Muffs, and Danes
Fear not Orcanes, but great Tamburlaine—
Nor he, but Fortune that hath made him great.   60
We have revolted Grecians, Albanese,
Sicilians, Jews, Arabians, Turks, and Moors,
Natolians, Sorians, black Egyptians,
Illyrians, Thracians, and Bithynians,
Enough to swallow forceless Sigismond,   65
Yet scarce enough t'encounter Tamburlaine:
He brings a world of people to the field.
From Scythia to the oriental plage
Of India, where raging Lantchidol
Beats on the regions with his boisterous blows,   70

---

63. Sorians] *O1, O3, Q;* Syrians *O2.*   63–4.] *O1–2; between these two*
lines, O3, Q, insert transposed l. 118.   64. Illyrians] *O3, Q;* Illicians
O1–2.   68. plage] *O1–2;* Place *O3, Q.*

---

58. *Almains, Rutters, Muffs*] see l. 22 n. above.

59–60. *Fear*] frighten. Orcanes is awed, not by Tamburlaine, but by the
favouring Fortune to whom Tamburlaine owes his power. This view of
Tamburlaine's success recurs at *Two* III.i.28–9. It contrasts with the
insistence on Tamburlaine as controlling his own destiny (e.g. at *Two*
III.iv.52).

61. *Albanese*] inhabiting 'the district between the Caucasus and the west
coast of the Caspian Sea' (Ellis-Fermor, p. 186); '?Georgians; ?Albanians'
(Pendry–Maxwell).

62. *Sicilians*] natives of Sicily; but the octavo spelling 'Cicilians' could
be an error for 'Cilicians', inhabitants of a district of Asia Minor. See
Ovid's Elegies, xvi.39.

63. *Sorians*] 'Egyptia in Part I includes Siria, for Damascus is Egyptian;
in Part II, Egypt is distinct from Soria, and its capital is Cairo, named for
the first time' (Seaton, p. 21). Sorians may mean, alternatively, dwellers
of Zor, i.e. Tyre (F.D.H.).

64. *Illyrians*] inhabitants of part of the Balkan peninsula, extending
inland from the eastern shore of the Adriatic Sea.

Bithynians] from the north-west of Asia Minor, adjoining the Pro-
pontic, the Bosporus, and the Euxine Sea.

65. *forceless*] weak.

68. *plage*] region; cf. *One* IV.iv.125–7 n. The O3, Q, emendation perhaps bears witness to the word's relative unfamiliarity, its exotic colour.

69. *Lantchidol*] the Indian Ocean (*Lantchidol Mare* for Ortelius).

That never seaman yet discoverèd:
All Asia is in arms with Tamburlaine.
Even from the midst of fiery Cancer's tropic
To Amazonia under Capricorn,
And thence as far as Archipelago: 75
All Afric is in arms with Tamburlaine.
Therefore, viceroys, the Christians must have peace.

[*Enter*] SIGISMOND, FREDERICK, BALDWIN, *and their*
train, *with drums and trumpets.*

Sigismond. Orcanes, as our legates promised thee,
We with our peers have crossed Danubius' stream
To treat of friendly peace or deadly war.   80
Take which thou wilt, for as the Romans used
I here present thee with a naked sword:
Wilt thou have war, then shake this blade at me;
If peace, restore it to my hands again,
And I will sheathe it to confirm the same.   85
Orcanes. Stay, Sigismond, forgettest thou I am he
That with the cannon shook Vienna walls,
And made it dance upon the continent,
As when the massy substance of the earth
Quiver about the axletree of heaven?   90

77.] *after this line,* O1–3, *Q, divide Act. I. Scaena. 2.*   77.1. *Enter*]
Oxberry; *not in* O1–3, Q.

71–6.] On the geography and the punctuation, Seaton has a very
important note: refuting the provision by some editors of a full stop for
the O1 colon at the end of l. 71, she (p. 32) restores geographical sense,
and also notes the significance of the original punctuation: 'The colons at
discoured and at *Archipellago* are attractive examples of their use to
denote the "actor's pause", the rhetorical upward intonation and emphasis at the end of the line, before the drop to the end of the sense-
paragraph. . . . Here they do not imply a division of sense; that comes on
the name that tolls four strokes throughout the speech like a knell of
doom.' The geography runs from the intersection of the meridian with
the tropic of Cancer, south to *Amazonia* (in Africa, west of Mozambique),
and north again to *Archipelago*, the islands of the Aegean.

77.1.] O1 inserts a scene division here, to mark an entry, inconsistently
with its practice elsewhere: see Introduction, section 8.

88. *continent*] 'solid land' (Pendry–Maxwell).

90. *axletree of heaven*] the axis of the celestial sphere, running through
the earth at the centre. Cf. *One* IV.ii.50 n., *Two* III.iv.64.

    Forgettest thou that I sent a shower of darts
    Mingled with powdered shot and feathered steel
    So thick upon the blink-eyed burghers' heads
    That thou thyself, then County Palatine,
    The King of Boheme, and the Austric Duke   95
    Sent heralds out, which basely on their knees
    In all your names desired a truce of me?
    Forgettest thou that, to have me raise my siege,
    Waggons of gold were set before my tent,
    Stamped with the princely fowl that in her wings   100
    Carries the fearful thunderbolts of Jove?
    How canst thou think of this and offer war?
Sigismond. Vienna was besieged, and I was there,
    Then County Palatine, but now a king;
    And what we did was in extremity.   105
    But now, Orcanes, view my royal host
    That hides these plains, and seems as vast and wide
    As doth the desert of Arabia
    To those that stand on Bagdeth's lofty tower,
    Or as the ocean to the traveller   110
    That rests upon the snowy Apennines—
    And tell me whether I should stoop so low,
    Or treat of peace with the Natolian king!
Gazellus Kings of Natolia and of Hungary,
    We came from Turkey to confirm a league,   115
    And not to dare each other to the field.
    A friendly parley might become ye both.
Frederick. And we from Europe to the same intent,
    Which if your general refuse or scorn,

118.] *O1–2; transposed to between ll. 63 and 64 in O3, Q.*   117. *parley*]
Oxberry; parle *O1–3, Q.*

---

  92. *feathered steel*] arrows.

  93. *blink-eyed*] shutting their eyes continually in recoil.

  95. *Austric*] Austrian.

  100–1. *princely fowl*] eagle, 'thought to be invulnerable to lightning, and hence the armour-bearer to Jove' (Heninger, p. 85). Pendry–Maxwell suggest 'i.e. spread-eagle, emblem of (Holy) Roman Empire'.

  108–9.] 'To Marlowe, looking west in imagination from Bagdad across the Euphrates, the Arabian desert was in sight' (Ellis-Fermor, p. 189).

  109. *Bagdeth's*] Bagdad's; copytext spelling 'Badgeths'.

  117. *parley*] Cf. *One* I.ii.137 n.

Our tents are pitched, our men stand in array,   120
    Ready to charge you ere you stir your feet.
Orcanes. So prest are we, but yet if Sigismond
    Speak as a friend, and stand not upon terms,
    Here is his sword, let peace be ratified
    On these conditions specified before,   125
    Drawn with advice of our ambassadors.
Sigismond. Then here I sheathe it, and give thee my hand,
    Never to draw it out or manage arms
    Against thyself or thy confederates;
    But whilst I live will be at truce with thee.   130
Orcanes. But, Sigismond, confirm it with an oath,
    And swear in sight of heaven and by thy Christ.
Sigismond. By him that made the world and saved my soul,
    The son of God and issue of a maid,
    Sweet Jesus Christ, I solemnly protest   135
    And vow to keep this peace inviolable.
Orcanes. By sacred Mahomet, the friend of God,
    Whose holy Alcaron remains with us,
    Whose glorious body, when he left the world
    Closed in a coffin, mounted up the air   140
    And hung on stately Mecca's temple roof,
    I swear to keep this truce inviolable;
    Of whose conditions and our solemn oaths
    Signed with our hands, each shall retain a scroll
    As memorable witness of our league.   145
    Now, Sigismond, if any Christian king
    Encroach upon the confines of thy realm,

---

122. *Orcanes.*] Oxberry; Nat. *O1–3, Q.*   131. *Orcanes.*] Oxberry; Nat.
O1–3, Q.   137. *Orcanes.*] Oxberry; Nat. *O1–3, Q.*

---

122. *prest*] ready for action.

123. *stand . . . upon terms*] take too firm a line on conditions; cf. *2H4*,
IV.i.165: 'what conditions we shall stand upon'. Encouraged by Orcanes
here not to fuss over conditions of peace, Sigismond is later (II.i.49–50)
assured that ''tis superstition / To stand so strictly on dispensive faith'.

133–6.] Marlowe is availing himself of Bonfinius' account of the pact
between Amurath II and the Christians, in consequence of which
Amurath withdrew his troops to lead them against the King of Carmania
(see Introduction, section 3; and l. 161 below).

135. *protest*] swear.

138. *Alcaron*] Koran.

147. *confines*] frontiers, borders.

    Send word Orcanes of Natolia
    Confirmed this league beyond Danubius' stream,
    And they will, trembling, sound a quick retreat—   150
    So am I feared among all nations.
Sigismond. If any heathen potentate or king
    Invade Natolia, Sigismond will send
    A hundred thousand horse trained to the war
    And backed by stout lancers of Germany,   155
    The strength and sinews of th'imperial seat.
Orcanes. I thank thee, Sigismond, but when I war
    All Asia Minor, Africa, and Greece
    Follow my standard and my thund'ring drums.
    Come, let us go and banquet in our tents: 160
    I will despatch chief of my army hence
    To fair Natolia and to Trebizond,
    To stay my coming 'gainst proud Tamburlaine.
    Friend Sigismond, and peers of Hungary,
    Come banquet and carouse with us a while   165
    And then depart we to our territories.   *Exeunt.*

Scene ii

[*Enter*] CALLAPINE *with* ALMEDA, *his keeper.*

Callapine. Sweet Almeda, pity the ruthful plight
    Of Callapine, the son of Bajazeth,
    Born to be monarch of the western world,
    Yet here detained by cruel Tamburlaine.
Almeda. My lord, I pity it, and with my heart   5
    Wish your release, but he whose wrath is death,
    My sovereign lord, renownèd Tamburlaine,
    Forbids you further liberty than this.

---

157. *Orcanes.*] Oxberry; *Nat.* O1–3, Q.   *Heading.* SCENE ii] Oxberry;
Actus. I. Scaena. 3. O1–3, Q.   0.1. *Enter*] Dyce 1; not in O1–3, Q.

161. *chief*] the greater part.
163. *stay*] await.
I.ii.3.] 'The Turkish empire is "the western world" from the Asiatic
point of view' (Ellis-Fermor, p. 191).
5–7. *lord ... sovereign lord*] Almeda's double servility is pointedly
graded.

Callapine. Ah, were I now but half so eloquent
    To paint in words what I'll perform in deeds,   10
    I know thou wouldst depart from hence with me!
Almeda. Not for all Afric; therefore move me not.
Callapine. Yet hear me speak, my gentle Almeda.
Almeda. No speech to that end, by your favour, sir.
Callapine. By Cairo runs——   15
Almeda. No talk of running, I tell you, sir.
Callapine. A little further, gentle Almeda.
Almeda. Well sir, what of this?
Callapine. By Cairo runs to Alexandria Bay
    Darotes' streams, wherein at anchor lies   20
    A Turkish galley of my royal fleet,
    Waiting my coming to the river side,
    Hoping by some means I shall be released:
    Which when I come aboard will hoist up sail
    And soon put forth into the Terrene sea,   25
    Where 'twixt the isles of Cyprus and of Crete
    We quickly may in Turkish seas arrive.
    Then shalt thou see a hundred kings and more
    Upon their knees, all bid me welcome home:
    Amongst so many crowns of burnished gold   30
    Choose which thou wilt, all are at thy command.
    A thousand galleys manned with Christian slaves
    I freely give thee, which shall cut the Straits
    And bring Armadoes from the coasts of Spain,
    Fraughted with gold of rich America.   35

---

15. Cairo] *Oxberry;* Cario *O1–3, Q.*   19. Cairo] *Oxberry;* Cario *O1–3, Q.*

12–19.] Marlowe modulates pentameter into colloquial prose, then back again into set-speech verse.

15. *Cairo*] The 'Cario' of the 1590–1606 texts seems a simple printing error which it is silly to perpetuate.

20. *Darotes' streams*] Ortelius shows Darote or Derote as 'a town at the bend of the westernmost arm of the Nile delta, that is, on the river-way from Cairo to Alexandria' (Seaton, p. 28).

25. *Terrene*] Mediterranean.

33. *Straits*] Straits of Gibraltar.

34. *Armadoes*] large war-vessels, in fleets or singly. Callapine runs together the Turkish galleys (cf. *One* III.iii.47 ff.) and Elizabethan piracy of Spanish ships returning from America (cf. Ellis-Fermor, p. 192).

The Grecian virgins shall attend on thee,
Skilful in music and in amorous lays,
As fair as was Pygmalion's ivory girl
Or lovely Io metamorphosèd.
With naked negroes shall thy coach be drawn,   40
And as thou ridest in triumph through the streets,
The pavement underneath thy chariot wheels
With Turkey carpets shall be coverèd,
And cloth of arras hung about the walls,
Fit objects for thy princely eye to pierce.   45
A hundred bassoes clothed in crimson silk
Shall ride before thee on Barbarian steeds;
And when thou goest, a golden canopy
Enchased with precious stones which shine as bright
As that fair veil that covers all the world   50
When Phoebus leaping from his hemisphere
Descendeth downward to th'Antipodes—
And more than this, for all I cannot tell.

Almeda. How far hence lies the galley, say you?
Callapine. Sweet Almeda, scarce half a league from hence.   55
Almeda. But need we not be spied going aboard?
Callapine. Betwixt the hollow hanging of a hill
And crooked bending of a craggy rock,
The sails wrapt up, the mast and tacklings down,
She lies so close that none can find her out.   60
Almeda. I like that well; but tell me, my lord, if I should let
you go, would you be as good as your word? Shall I be
made a king for my labour?
Callapine. As I am Callapine the emperor,

38–9.] Two of Marlowe's many allusions to metamorphosis, fed by
Ovid: cf. *Metam.*, x.243 ff. and i.588 ff. Io was turned into a white heifer
by Jove. Venus brought to life a statue made by Pygmalion.
  44. *cloth of arras*] rich tapestry; cf. *Dr Faustus*, vi.122.
  46. *bassoes*] bashaws, pashas.
  47. *Barbarian steeds*] Barbary horses; cf. *One* III.iii.16 n.
  49. *Enchased*] set.
  50. *fair veil*] moonlight, the 'shining veil of Cynthia' (*Two* II.ii.47),
perhaps 'enchased' with stars.
  51. *Phœbus*] the sun.
  56. *need we not?*] shall we not inevitably? (Ellis-Fermor, p. 193).
  60. *close*] well concealed.

And by the hand of Mahomet I swear,   65
    Thou shalt be crowned a king and be my mate.
Almeda. Then here I swear, as I am Almeda,
    Your keeper under Tamburlaine the Great—
    For that's the style and title I have yet—
    Although he sent a thousand armèd men   70
    To intercept this haughty enterprise,
    Yet would I venture to conduct your grace
    And die before I brought you back again.
Callapine. Thanks, gentle Almeda, then let us haste,
    Lest time be past, and ling'ring let us both.   75
Almeda. When you will, my lord, I am ready.
Callapine. Even straight; and farewell, cursèd Tamburlaine!
    Now go I to revenge my father's death.   *Exeunt.*

SCENE iii

[Enter] TAMBURLAINE *with* ZENOCRATE, *and his three sons,*
CALYPHAS, AMYRAS, *and* CELEBINUS, *with drums and*
trumpets.

Tamburlaine. Now bright Zenocrate, the world's fair eye
    Whose beams illuminate the lamps of heaven,
    Whose cheerful looks do clear the cloudy air
    And clothe it in a crystal livery,
    Now rest thee here on fair Larissa plains   5

Heading. SCENE iii] *Oxberry; Actus. 1. Scaena. 4. O1–3, Q.*
0.1. *Enter*] *Oxberry; not in O1–3, Q.*

---

66. *mate*] equal.
69. *style*] official designation.
71. *haughty*] high-minded, lofty; cf. *Faerie Queene*, II.x.1: 'Who now
shall give unto me words and sound / Equall unto this haughty enterprise?'; as at *Two* IV.i.46, *Two* V.iii.30.
75. *let*] hinder.
77. *straight*] straightway.
I.iii.2. *illuminate*] light up; cf. *Paradise Lost*, vii.350–2.
5. *Larissa*] 'a sea-coast town, south of Gaza', placed by Ortelius near
the boundary between Syria and the Turkish empire (Seaton, p. 23). It
stands (Ellis-Fermor, p. 194) on 'the brook that parts / Egypt from
Syrian ground' (*Paradise Lost*, i.419–20); 'modern El Arish, S. of Gaza'
(Pendry–Maxwell).

Where Egypt and the Turkish empire parts,
Between thy sons that shall be emperors
And every one commander of a world.

Zenocrate. Sweet Tamburlaine, when wilt thou leave these
    arms
And save thy sacred person free from scathe   10
And dangerous chances of the wrathful war?

Tamburlaine. When heaven shall cease to move on both the
    poles,
And when the ground whereon my soldiers march
Shall rise aloft and touch the hornèd moon,
And not before, my sweet Zenocrate.   15
Sit up and rest thee like a lovely queen.
So, now she sits in pomp and majesty
When these my sons, more precious in mine eyes
Than all the wealthy kingdoms I subdued,
Placed by her side, look on their mother's face—   20
But yet methinks their looks are amorous,
Not martial as the sons of Tamburlaine:
Water and air, being symbolised in one,
Argue their want of courage and of wit;
Their hair as white as milk and soft as down—   25
Which should be like the quills of porcupines,
As black as jet, and hard as iron or steel—
Bewrays they are too dainty for the wars.

---

10. *scathe*] harm.

12.] Cf. the 'axletree of heaven', at *One* IV.ii.50 n.; and *Two* III.iv.
64 n.

14. *hornèd moon*] Cf. *One* III.i.10–12 n., and *Two* III.i.66–7.

21–2.] 'The misgivings of Tamburlaine and the fulfilment of his fears
in the character of Calyphas … may be traced to the accounts of the
dissolution of Tamburlaine's empire through the weakness of his successors' (Ellis-Fermor, p. 194). But Marlowe does not indicate this dissolution unequivocally at the end of the play.

23–4.] 'The moist and cold qualities of water (corresponding to the
phlegmatic humour) and the moist and hot qualities of air (corresponding
to the sanguine humour) argue ill for the temperament which is over-
balanced in these directions and lacks the firmness and fierceness due to a
just admixture of the bile and choler (earth and fire)' (Ellis-Fermor,
p. 195).

23. *symbolised*] mixed, combined; first instance in *O.E.D.*

28. *Bewrays*] Reveals.

Their fingers made to quaver on a lute,
Their arms to hang about a lady's neck,   30
Their legs to dance and caper in the air,
Would make me think them bastards, not my sons,
But that I know they issued from thy womb,
That never looked on man but Tamburlaine.

Zenocrate. My gracious lord, they have their mother's looks,   35
But when they list, their conquering father's heart.
This lovely boy, the youngest of the three,
Not long ago bestrid a Scythian steed,
Trotting the ring, and tilting at a glove,
Which when he tainted with his slender rod,   40
He reined him straight and made him so curvet
As I cried out for fear he should have fall'n.

Tamburlaine. Well done, my boy, thou shalt have shield
          and lance,
Armour of proof, horse, helm, and curtle-axe,
And I will teach thee how to charge thy foe   45
And harmless run among the deadly pikes.
If thou wilt love the wars and follow me,
Thou shalt be made a king and reign with me,
Keeping in iron cages emperors.
If thou exceed thy elder brothers' worth   50
And shine in complete virtue more than they,

29–31.] The broad contrasts of this speech, several phrases, and in particular these lines, seem to run in Shakespeare's head in *R3*, I.i.1–15.

39. *Trotting the ring*] *O.E.D.* first records this expression, used of horses taking a circular course in the schooling-ring, from 1602.

tilting] jousting at a mark—here, a glove (*O.E.D. vb.*[1] 5, first entry 1595). Cf. *Two* IV.i.204. On the chivalric element in the play, see Introduction, pp. 50–1, 56–7, etc.

40. *tainted*] touched, hit; a technical term from tilting.

41. *curvet*] an accomplished skill from the *manège*: to raise the horse's forelegs and execute a spring from the hindlegs before the forelegs reach the ground.

44. *Armour of proof*] armour of tried strength, proof-armour.
curtle-axe] a short heavy sword, cutlass.

46. *harmless*] unharmed.

49.] alluding to the imprisonment of Bajazeth in Part One, which is also recalled at *Two* V.ii.19–20.

51. *in complete virtue*] in full manliness, valour; a companion phrase for 'complete armour', as at *One* I.ii.42.

Thou shalt be king before them, and thy seed
Shall issue crownèd from their mother's womb.
Celebinus. Yes, father, you shall see me, if I live,
Have under me as many kings as you   55
And march with such a multitude of men
As all the world shall tremble at their view.
Tamburlaine. These words assure me, boy, thou art my son.
When I am old and cannot manage arms,
Be thou the scourge and terror of the world.   60
Amyras. Why may not I, my lord, as well as he,
Be termed the scourge and terror of the world?
Tamburlaine. Be all a scourge and terror to the world,
Or else you are not sons of Tamburlaine.
Calyphas. But while my brothers follow arms, my lord,   65
Let me accompany my gracious mother:
They are enough to conquer all the world,
And you have won enough for me to keep.
Tamburlaine. Bastardly boy, sprung from some coward's
  loins,
And not the issue of great Tamburlaine,   70
Of all the provinces I have subdued
Thou shalt not have a foot unless thou bear
A mind courageous and invincible:
For he shall wear the crown of Persia
Whose head hath deepest scars, whose breast most
  wounds,   75
Which, being wroth, sends lightning from his eyes,
And in the furrows of his frowning brows
Harbours revenge, war, death and cruelty;
For in a field whose superficies

---

79. superficies] *Oxberry;* superfluities O1–3, Q.

72–3. *bear . . . invincible*] cf. *Two* III.ii.143, 'to bear courageous minds';
and 'he bears a valiant mind' at *One* III.i.32.

79. *superficies*] surface. The 'superfluities' of O1–3, Q, answers to the
metre, but so, it seems, does 'superficies': at *Two* III.iv.48 it supplies the
same number of syllables. 'Marlowe may just possibly have written
"superfluities", derived from *fluere,* which is the root of the rare "superfluitance" or *that which floats on the surface.* The O.E.D. remarks, inci-
dentally, that at least once this *superfluitance* was confused with *superfluities'* (Bowers, i.224). O.E.D. earliest instance for 'superfluitance' is
1646; perhaps coined by Sir Thomas Browne.

Is covered with a liquid purple veil   80
And sprinkled with the brains of slaughtered men,
My royal chair of state shall be advanced;
And he that means to place himself therein
Must armèd wade up to the chin in blood.

Zenocrate. My lord, such speeches to our princely sons   85
Dismays their minds before they come to prove
The wounding troubles angry war affords.

Celebinus. No, madam, these are speeches fit for us,
For if his chair were in a sea of blood
I would prepare a ship and sail to it,   90
Ere I would lose the title of a king.

Amyras. And I would strive to swim through pools of blood
Or make a bridge of murdered carcasses
Whose arches should be framed with bones of Turks,
Ere I would lose the title of a king.   95

Tamburlaine. Well, lovely boys, you shall be emperors both,
Stretching your conquering arms from east to west;
And, sirrah, if you mean to wear a crown,
When we shall meet the Turkish deputy
And all his viceroys, snatch it from his head,   100
And cleave his pericranion with thy sword.

Calyphas. If any man will hold him, I will strike,
And cleave him to the channel with my sword.

Tamburlaine. Hold him and cleave him too, or I'll cleave
      thee,
For we will march against them presently.   105
Theridamas, Techelles, and Casane
Promised to meet me on Larissa plains
With hosts apiece against this Turkish crew,
For I have sworn by sacred Mahomet
To make it parcel of my empery.   110

---

101. pericranion] *Dyce 1;* Pecicranion *O1–3, Q;* pericranium *Oxberry.*

---

81. *brains of slaughtered men*] Theridamas uses the phrase at *Two*
III.iv.58, affirming this side of Tamburlaine's exercise of power.
86. *prove*] find by experience.
101. *pericranion*] the skull, in Tamburlaine's mock-pedantic jest;
technically, the pericranium is the membrane enveloping the skull.
103. *channel*] neck, throat; '?gullet' (Pendry–Maxwell).
107. *Larissa plains*] cf. l. 5 n., above.
110. *parcel*] part.

The trumpets sound, Zenocrate: they come.

Enter THERIDAMAS *and his train, with drums and trumpets.*

Welcome Theridamas, king of Argier.

Theridamas. My lord the great and mighty Tamburlaine,
    Arch-monarch of the world, I offer here
    My crown, myself, and all the power I have,   115
    In all affection at thy kingly feet.

Tamburlaine. Thanks, good Theridamas.

Theridamas. Under my colours march ten thousand Greeks,
    And of Argier and Afric's frontier towns
    Twice twenty thousand valiant men-at-arms,   120
    All which have sworn to sack Natolia;
    Five hundred brigandines are under sail,
    Meet for your service on the sea, my lord,
    That, launching from Argier to Tripoly,
    Will quickly ride before Natolia   125
    And batter down the castles on the shore.

Tamburlaine. Well said, Argier; receive thy crown again.

Enter TECHELLES *and* USUMCASANE *together.*

Kings of Moroccus and of Fesse, welcome.

Usumcasane. Magnificent and peerless Tamburlaine,
    I and my neighbour king of Fesse have brought,   130
    To aid thee in this Turkish expedition,
    A hundred thousand expert soldiers;
    From Azamor to Tunis near the sea
    Is Barbary unpeopled for thy sake,

111.] *scene division after this line in* O1–3, Q: *Actus: I. Scaena. 5.*
127.] *scene division after this line in* O1–3, Q: *Actus. I. Scaena. 6.*

111.] On the scene division here in O1–3, Q, to mark new entries, see
Introduction, p. 87.

122. *brigandines*] small pirate craft. As King of Argier, Theridamas
deploys the forces Tamburlaine saw as merciless pirates before his defeat
of Bajazeth: *One* III.iii.55.

128. *Fesse*] Fez, as at ll. 130, 140, 150 below.

127.] On the scene division here in O1–3, Q, to mark new entries, see
Introduction, p. 87.

132. *expert*] tried, proved in battle.

133. *Azamor*] 'Azimur, town on Atlantic coast of Morocco' (Pendry-
Maxwell).

134, 149. *unpeopled*] Cf. *One* III.iii.34 (of the tyrannical Bajazeth).

And all the men in armour under me,   135
Which with my crown I gladly offer thee.

Tamburlaine. Thanks, king of Moroccus; take your crown
    again.

Techelles. And mighty Tamburlaine, our earthly god,
Whose looks make this inferior world to quake,
I here present thee with the crown of Fesse,   140
And with an host of Moors trained to the war,
Whose coal-black faces make their foes retire
And quake for fear, as if infernal Jove,
Meaning to aid thee in these Turkish arms,
Should pierce the black circumference of hell   145
With ugly Furies bearing fiery flags
And millions of his strong tormenting spirits;
From strong Tesella unto Biledull
All Barbary is unpeopled for thy sake.

Tamburlaine. Thanks, king of Fesse, take here thy crown
    again.   150
Your presence, loving friends and fellow kings,
Makes me to surfeit in conceiving joy;
If all the crystal gates of Jove's high court
Were opened wide, and I might enter in
To see the state and majesty of heaven,   155
It could not more delight me than your sight.
Now will we banquet on these plains a while
And after march to Turkey with our camp,
In number more than are the drops that fall
When Boreas rents a thousand swelling clouds,   160

---

144. thee] *Oxberry;* them *O1–3, Q.*   these] *O3, Q;* this *O1–2.*

---

143. *infernal Jove*] Techelles with his black army appears in this image
as Hades (Pluto), achieving the hope Usumcasane had expressed for
Tamburlaine's followers in *One* II.vii.36–8; cf. *Two* IV.iii.32, V.i.98,
110–11.

145. *black circumference*] the phrase returns, again used of Hell, at
Two IV.ii.90.

146. *ugly Furies*] See *Two* III.iv.59.

148. *Tesella*] south of Oran.
Biledull] Ortelius's Biledulgerid, a district in north Africa.

158. *camp*] army (F.D.H.).

160. *Boreas*] the north wind; cf. *One* I.ii.205–6 n., where, as here
Boötes occurs in the immediate context, and *One* II.iv.5.

And proud Orcanes of Natolia
With all his viceroys shall be so afraid
That though the stones, as at Deucalion's flood,
Were turned to men, he should be overcome.
Such lavish will I make of Turkish blood,   165
That Jove shall send his wingèd messenger
To bid me sheathe my sword, and leave the field;
The sun, unable to sustain the sight,
Shall hide his head in Thetis' watery lap
And leave his steeds to fair Boötes' charge;   170
For half the world shall perish in this fight.
But now, my friends, let me examine ye—
How have ye spent your absent time from me?

Usumcasane. My lord, our men of Barbary have marched
Four hundred miles with armour on their backs   175
And lain in leaguer fifteen months and more:
For since we left you at the Soldan's court
We have subdued the southern Guallatia
And all the land unto the coast of Spain.
We kept the narrow Strait of Gibraltar   180
And made Canarea call us kings and lords,
Yet never did they recreate themselves
Or cease one day from war and hot alarms,
And therefore let them rest a while, my lord.

Tamburlaine. They shall, Casane, and 'tis time, i'faith.   185
Techelles. And I have marched along the river Nile

---

170. Boötes] *O3, Q;* Boetes *O1–2.*

163–4. *stones . . . turned to men*] Men were reborn from stones thrown by Deucalion and Pyrrha after the flood: cf. *Metam.*, i.318 ff.

165. *lavish*] prodigal spilling; cf. *Massacre at Paris*, xxiv.100–1: 'He loves me not that sheds most tears / But he that makes most lavish of his blood'.

168–70.] An Ovidian description: cf. *Metam.*, ii.1 ff.
Thetis] the sea goddess.
Boötes] a northern constellation, traditionally depicted as a driver of oxen; as at *One* I.ii.205–6 n.

176. *lain in leaguer*] encamped to besiege.

178. *Guallatia*] Ortelius' 'Gualata', a town and region in the west of the Libyan desert, south-west of Biledulgerid.

181. *Canarea*] the Canary Islands.

186–205.] As was first made clear by Seaton, Marlowe constructs from Ortelius a route for Techelles' conquests. He explores the Nile as far as

To Machda, where the mighty Christian priest
Called John the Great sits in a milk-white robe,
Whose triple mitre I did take by force
And made him swear obedience to my crown.   190
From thence unto Cazates did I march,
Where Amazonians met me in the field,
With whom, being women, I vouchsafed a league,
And with my power did march to Zanzibar,
The western part of Afric, where I viewed   195
The Ethiopian sea, rivers and lakes—
But neither man nor child in all the land!
Therefore I took my course to Manico,
Where, unresisted, I removed my camp.
And by the coast of Byather at last   200
I came to Cubar, where the negroes dwell,
And conquering that, made haste to Nubia;
There, having sacked Borno, the kingly seat,
I took the king, and led him bound in chains
Unto Damasco, where I stayed before.   205
Tamburlaine. Well done, Techelles. What saith Theridamas?
Theridamas. I left the confines and the bounds of Afric
    And made a voyage into Europe,
    Where by the river Tyros I subdued

Machda in Abyssinia where he subdues Prester John, who is mentioned
in a note on Ortelius' map of Africa; then he pursues the Nile's course
to Cazates, near the lake at the source; he invades the province of
Zanzibar (as distinct from the island, correctly named by Ortelius) taking
up much of southern Africa; turning north, he marches through Mani-
congo, the province of Byather, 'while above the town and province of
Guber is printed in bold type *Nigritarum Regio*' . . . 'Borno, the chief
town of Nubia, lies near the shore of *Borno lacus*, that "*Borno* Lake"
which Tamburlaine himself mentions later [*Two* V.iii.136]' (Seaton,
pp. 16–18). On *Byather*, Pendry–Maxwell note 'Biafar = ?Biafra'.

189. *triple mitre*] 'papal tiara' (Jump).

196. *Ethiopian sea*] 'S. Atlantic' (Pendry–Maxwell).

208.] We need not criticise this line for being 'metrically defective':
cf. *One* III.iii.225 n.

209–15.] 'The river Tyros (the Dneister) acts as a southern boundary
of the province Podalia; Stoko is on it, and Codemia lies to the north-
east on another stream. Partly separating Codemia from Olbia, and thus
perhaps suggesting an otherwise unnecessary sea-journey, is the thick,
green, hollow square of Nigra Silva' (Seaton, p. 29, who also explains
the great extent and ill repute of the Black Forest for early cartographers).

        Stoka, Padalia, and Codemia.   210
        Then crossed the sea and came to Oblia,
        And Nigra Silva, where the devils dance,
        Which in despite of them I set on fire;
        From thence I crossed the gulf called by the name
        Mare Magiore of th'inhabitants.   215
        Yet shall my soldiers make no period
        Until Natolia kneel before your feet.
Tamburlaine. Then will we triumph, banquet, and carouse;
        Cooks shall have pensions to provide us cates
        And glut us with the dainties of the world: 220
        Lachryma Christi and Calabrian wines
        Shall common soldiers drink in quaffing bowls—
        Ay, liquid gold when we have conquered him,
        Mingled with coral and with orient pearl.
        Come, let us banquet and carouse the whiles. *Exeunt.* 225

                    Finis Actus primi.

224. orient] *Oxberry;* orientall *O1–3, Q.*

The text's *Oblia* is a misspelling, retained here as perhaps Marlowe's
version of the place-name: cf. Belgasar, at *Two* II.i.19.

    215. *Mare Magiore*] the Black Sea.

    216. *period*] end, stop (*O.E.D.* 5c.).

    220. *glut*] This word for gratifying (or cloying) appetite is frequent with
Marlowe; cf. *One* III.iii.164 n.

    221. *Lachryma Christi*] sweet red wine of southern Italy (*O.E.D.* first
entry 1611).

    224. *orient pearl*] pearl from the Indian seas, brilliant pearl; cf., e.g.,
Dr Faustus, i.82, and *Jew of Malta,* I.i.87: 'store of Persian silks, of gold,
and orient pearl'.

Act II

[*Enter*] SIGISMOND, FREDERICK, BALDWIN, *with their* train.

Sigismond. Now say, my lords of Buda and Bohemia,
    What motion is it that inflames your thoughts
    And stirs your valours to such sudden arms?
Frederick. Your majesty remembers, I am sure,
    What cruel slaughter of our Christian bloods   5
    These heathenish Turks and pagans lately made
    Betwixt the city Zula and Danubius,
    How through the midst of Varna and Bulgaria
    And almost to the very walls of Rome
    They have, not long since, massacred our camp.   10
    It resteth now, then, that your majesty
    Take all advantages of time and power,
    And work revenge upon these infidels.
    Your highness knows for Tamburlaine's repair,
    That strikes a terror to all Turkish hearts,   15
    Natolia hath dismissed the greatest part
    Of all his army, pitched against our power

0.1. *Enter*] *Oxberry; not in O1–3, Q.*

II.i.1. *Buda*] in Hungary; cf. modern Budapest.
2. *motion*] impulse, emotion. Cf. *Massacre at Paris*, i.7: 'That kindled first this motion in our hearts'.
5. *bloods*] lives; cf. *One* V.i.97 n.
7. *Zula*] located by Seaton on Ortelius' map of Europe, 'north of the Danube, in the province of Rascia' (Seaton, p. 30).
8. *Varna*] a Bulgarian seaport, evidently taken as a region.
9. *Rome*] Seaton suggests that Marlowe was misled here by Ortelius' printing the first two syllables of 'ROMANIA' separately and with prominence north of Constantinople; she notes that 'Rome . . . may mean Constantinople', but Ortelius marks the latter as such (Seaton, p. 30).
14. *repair*] imminent arrival.
16. *Natolia*] i.e., Orcanes.

    Betwixt Cutheia and Orminius' mount,
    And sent them marching up to Belgasar,
    Acantha, Antioch, and Caesaria,   20
    To aid the kings of Soria and Jerusalem.
    Now then, my lord, advantage take hereof,
    And issue suddenly upon the rest—
    That, in the fortune of their overthrow,
    We may discourage all the pagan troop   25
    That dare attempt to war with Christians.
Sigismond. But calls not, then, your grace to memory
    The league we lately made with King Orcanes,
    Confirmed by oath and articles of peace,
    And calling Christ for record of our truths?   30
    This should be treachery and violence
    Against the grace of our profession.
Baldwin. No whit, my lord—for with such infidels,
    In whom no faith nor true religion rests,
    We are not bound to those accomplishments   35
    The holy laws of Christendom enjoin;
    But as the faith which they profanely plight
    Is not by necessary policy

---

18. *Cutheia ... Orminius' mount*] Seaton traces these forms not to Ortelius, who has 'Chiutaie' and 'Horminius', but to Lonicerus, vol. I, fol. 28; describing the location of a later battle conveniently for Marlowe's purpose, with a mention of territory 'intra Cutheiam urbem ad Orminium montem' (Seaton, 'Sources', pp. 388–9). *Cutheia* is 'modern Kütahya' (Pendry–Maxwell).

19–20. *Belgasar, Acantha*] marked by Ortelius as Beglasar and Acanta, in Natolia: see Seaton, p. 22. Cf. *Two* I.iii.209–15 n.

30. *record*] witness.

32. *profession*] In the competition among rival 'professions' in *Jew of Malta*, Marlowe elaborates these accents of hypocritical righteousness: 'It's no sin to deceive a Christian' (II.iii.311, 313 n.). The later play is rife with questions of conscience and casuistry which move between 'profession' and 'policy' (cf. l. 38). Cf. 'Ay, policy? that's their profession' (*Jew of Malta*, I.ii.163). The proverbial 'No faith with heretics' (Tilley, F33) was detested by Protestants as one aspect of Roman Catholic 'equivocation' (E.A.J.H.).

33–41.] For Marlowe's use of Bonfinius in this passage of casuistry, see Introduction, pp. 17–18.

35. *accomplishments*] fulfilments of promises (Jump).

38. *policy*] prudent statecraft—the 'Machiavellian' cant for political cunning and treachery. It is shared in *Tamburlaine* only by Mycetes, in

To be esteemed assurance for ourselves,
So what we vow to them should not infringe   40
Our liberty of arms and victory.

Sigismond. Though I confess the oaths they undertake
Breed little strength to our security,
Yet those infirmities that thus defame
Their faiths, their honours, and their religion,   45
Should not give us presumption to the like.
Our faiths are sound, and must be consummate,
Religious, righteous, and inviolate.

Frederick. Assure your grace, 'tis superstition
.   To stand so strictly on dispensive faith: 50
And should we lose the opportunity
That God hath given to venge our Christians' death
And scourge their foul blasphemous paganism?
As fell to Saul, to Balaam and the rest

---

47. consummate] *Dyce 2;* consinuate *O1–3, Q;* continuate *Oxberry.*

One II.iv.10, in his absurd attempt to hide his crown during battle. Note
Guise, in *Massacre at Paris,* ii.62: 'My policy hath fram'd religion'.

39. *assurance*] trustworthy pledge, guarantee. Cf. *Tw. N.,* IV.iii.26.

47. *consummate*] *O.E.D.* does not record the 'consinuate' of O1–3, Q,
and the word scans ill, though just conceivably Marlowe's sharp ear for
the litigious could have coined it: ?'subtly woven together'. 'Robinson's
emendation, approved by Broughton, of "continuate" retains the letters
uate and is acceptable in meaning, as *continued intact, without a break,* or
lasting, long-continued. Yet Dyce 2's emendation *consummate* for his
original acceptance of *continuate* has several advantages. In secretary
hand the confusion of *um* as *inu* is perhaps easier to account for than that
of *t* for *s;* and though *continuate* is acceptable metrically, the couplet here
perhaps requires regularity in both its lines as provided by *consumate.*
Finally, although "consumate" as *complete, perfect, of highest degree or
quality,* is a shade more strained, its association to "religious" and
"righteous" is perhaps less tautological than that of "inviolate" to "continuate" ' (Bowers, i.224–5). *Massacre at Paris,* i.19–20, has the verb
form in a broadly related context: 'consummate / The rest with hearing
of a holy mass'.

50. *dispensive*] subject to dispensation (*O.E.D.* earliest entry).

53. *scourge*] In seeking to act as a scourge of the Christian god, Frederick
recalls Tamburlaine's, and the play's, first appeal to the concept, at *One*
III.iii.44.

54. *Saul ... Balaam*] 'See I *Samuel* xv and *Numbers* xxii and xxiii'
(Ellis-Fermor, p. 207), with the comment that 'Balaam's position is the
converse of Sigismund's': Balaam kept faith with God; Saul spared the
Amalekites from destruction, against God's will.

That would not kill and curse at God's command,   55
So surely will the vengeance of the Highest,
And jealous anger of His fearful arm,
Be poured with rigour on our sinful heads
If we neglect this offered victory.

Sigismond. Then arm, my lords, and issue suddenly,   60
Giving commandment to our general host
With expedition to assail the pagan
And take the victory our God hath given.   *Exeunt.*

SCENE ii

[*Enter*] ORCANES, GAZELLUS, URIBASSA, *with their* train.

Orcanes. Gazellus, Uribassa, and the rest,
Now will we march from proud Orminius' mount
To fair Natolia, where our neighbour kings
Expect our power and our royal presence,
T'encounter with the cruel Tamburlaine   5
That nigh Larissa sways a mighty host,
And with the thunder of his martial tools
Makes earthquakes in the hearts of men and heaven.

Gazellus. And now come we to make his sinews shake
With greater power than erst his pride hath felt: 10
An hundred kings by scores will bid him arms,
And hundred thousands subjects to each score—
Which, if a shower of wounding thunderbolts
Should break out of the bowels of the clouds
And fall as thick as hail upon our heads   15
In partial aid of that proud Scythian,
Yet should our courages and steelèd crests
And numbers more than infinite of men
Be able to withstand and conquer him.

Uribassa. Methinks I see how glad the Christian king   20

0.1. *Enter*] *Oxberry; not in* O1–3, Q.

62. *expedition*] haste.
II.ii.2. *Orminius' mount*] See *Two* II.i.18 n.
4. *Expect . . . power*] Await . . . army.
6. *Larissa*] Cf. *Two* I.iv.5 n., *Two* I.iv.107.
16. *partial*] biased.

Is made for joy of your admitted truce,
That could not but before be terrified
With unacquainted power of our host.

Enter a Messenger.

Messenger. Arm, dread sovereign and my noble lords!
 The treacherous army of the Christians,   25
 Taking advantage of your slender power,
 Comes marching on us, and determines straight
 To bid us battle for our dearest lives.
Orcanes. Traitors, villains, damnèd Christians!
 Have I not here the articles of peace   30
 And solemn covenants we have both confirmed,
 He by his Christ, and I by Mahomet?
Gazellus. Hell and confusion light upon their heads
 That with such treason seek our overthrow
 And cares so little for their prophet, Christ.   35
Orcanes. Can there be such deceit in Christians,
 Or treason in the fleshly heart of man,
 Whose shape is figure of the highest God?
 Then if there be a Christ, as Christians say—
 But in their deeds deny him for their Christ— 40
 If he be son to everliving Jove
 And hath the power of his outstretched arm,
 If he be jealous of his name and honour
 As is our holy prophet Mahomet,
 Take here these papers as our sacrifice   45

---

21. *admitted*] permitted, granted.

23. *unacquainted*] unfamiliar, unexampled.

24–6.] The contrast is sharp with Tamburlaine's assault on Cosroe's army immediately after joining forces with him: 'We will not steal upon him cowardly, / But give him warning and more warriors' (*One* II.v.102–103).

29 ff.] For Marlowe's close use of Bonfinius' account of the battle of Varna see Introduction, section 3.

38. *figure*] likeness, image. Cf. *Two* IV.iii.25. The governing recall is of Gen. i.26.

40.] Kocher, p. 101, cites Titus i.16: 'They profess that they know God; but in works they deny him'.

42–3.] Kocher, p. 101, cites Exodus vii.5 and xx.5, in tracing the scriptural overtones here.

And witness of Thy servant's perjury!
> [*He tears to pieces the articles of peace.*]

Open, thou shining veil of Cynthia,
And make a passage from th'empyreal heaven,
That he that sits on high and never sleeps
Nor in one place is circumscriptible,   50
But everywhere fills every continent
With strange infusion of his sacred vigour,
May in his endless power and purity
Behold and venge this traitor's perjury.
Thou Christ that art esteemed omnipotent,   55
If thou wilt prove thyself a perfect God
Worthy the worship of all faithful hearts,
Be now revenged upon this traitor's soul
And make the power I have left behind
(Too little to defend our guiltless lives)   60
Sufficient to discomfit and confound
The trustless force of those false Christians.
To arms, my lords, on Christ still let us cry—
If there be Christ, we shall have victory.   [*Exeunt.*]

[SCENE iii]

Sound to the battle, and SIGISMOND *comes out wounded.*

Sigismond. Discomfited is all the Christian host,

46.1] *Robinson; not in O1–3, Q.*   64. *Exeunt.*] *Dyce 1; not in O1–3, Q;*
Alarums.—They go out. Oxberry.   *Heading.* SCENE iii] *Dyce 1; not in*
O1–3, Q.

---

47. *shining veil of Cynthia*] 'moonlit sky [?'barrier to (mortal) perception)' (Pendry–Maxwell). Cf. *Two* I.ii.50 n.

48. *empyreal heaven*] the empyrean; see *One* II.vii.15 n.

49–50.] Kocher, pp. 97–100, amply illustrates the orthodox currency of these views of God and the leading phrases: e.g. Daniel vii.9: 'I beheld till the thrones were cast down, and the Ancient of days did sit', and Augustine's 'Deus . . . solus incircumscriptus'. *O.E.D.* quotes Bale, 1550: 'God is a sprete, how can ye than prove him circumscriptible or locall?' Cf. *Dr Faustus*, v.122–3, turning 'circumscriptible' to account in evoking Hell: 'Hell hath no limits, nor is circumscrib'd / In one self place, but where we are is hell'.

62. *trustless*] treacherous.

II.iii.18–23.] Koran, xxxvii.60–4, mediated through Lonicerus, fol. 64v, as Seaton has shown ('Sources', pp. 386–7).

And God hath thundered vengeance from on high
For my accursed and hateful perjury.
O just and dreadful punisher of sin,
Let the dishonour of the pains I feel   5
In this my mortal well-deservèd wound
End all my penance in my sudden death;
And let this death wherein to sin I die
Conceive a second life in endless mercy.   [*He dies.*]

Enter ORCANES, GAZELLUS, URIBASSA, *with others.*

Orcanes. Now lie the Christians bathing in their bloods,   10
    And Christ or Mahomet hath been my friend.
Gazellus. See here the perjured traitor Hungary,
    Bloody and breathless for his villainy!
Orcanes. Now shall his barbarous body be a prey
    To beasts and fowls, and all the winds shall breathe   15
    Through shady leaves of every senseless tree
    Murmurs and hisses for his heinous sin.
    Now scalds his soul in the Tartarian streams
    And feeds upon the baneful tree of hell,
    That Zoacum, that fruit of bitterness,   20
    That in the midst of fire is ingraft,
    Yet flourisheth as Flora in her pride,
    With apples like the heads of damnèd fiends.
    The devils there in chains of quenchless flame
    Shall lead his soul through Orcus' burning gulf   25
    From pain to pain, whose change shall never end.
    What sayest thou yet, Gazellus, to his foil,
    Which we referred to justice of his Christ
    And to His power, which here appears as full

9. *He dies.*] Oxberry; not in *O1–3, Q.*

---

22. *Flora . . . pride*] echoing *One* V.i.140.

24. *quenchless*] Cf. *Two* III.v.27, the 'quenchless fire' of hell. *O.E.D.*
cites Tottel, 1557: 'These hellish houndes, with paines of quenchlesse
fyre'.

24–6. *quenchless flame . . . never end*] 'It may be noticed that, the specific
quotation from Lonicerus ended, Orcanes' hell becomes now that of the
Christians (ll. 24, 26), now that of the Greeks (l. 25)' (Ellis-Fermor, p.
211).

25. *Orcus*] Hell; cf. 'Orcus' gulf', *One* III.i.65.

27. *foil*] overthrow; disgrace (*O.E.D. sb.*² 2b, first entry 1599).

As rays of Cynthia to the clearest sight?   30
Gazellus. 'Tis but the fortune of the wars, my lord,
    Whose power is often proved a miracle.
Orcanes. Yet in my thoughts shall Christ be honourèd,
    Not doing Mahomet an injury,
    Whose power had share in this our victory: 35
    And since this miscreant hath disgraced his faith
    And died a traitor both to heaven and earth,
    We will both watch and ward shall keep his trunk
    Amidst these plains for fowls to prey upon.
    Go, Uribassa, give it straight in charge.   40
Uribassa. I will, my lord.

              Exit URIBASSA [*and others, with the body*].

Orcanes. And now, Gazellus, let us haste and meet
    Our army, and our brother of Jerusalem,
    Of Soria, Trebizond, and Amasia,
    And happily with full Natolian bowls   45
    Of Greekish wine now let us celebrate
    Our happy conquest, and his angry fate.   *Exeunt.*

SCENE iv

The arras is drawn, and ZENOCRATE *lies in her bed of state,*

43. brother] *O1–3, Q;* brothers *Oxberry.*   Heading. SCENE iv] *Actus 2.*
Scaena vltima O1–2; Actus I. Scaena vltima O3, Q.

---

32. *proved a miracle*] offered as a demonstration of miraculous agency.
    36. *miscreant*] heretic, misbeliever, as at *One* III.iii.236, in a similar
context; if in the generalised sense of 'villain', antedates *O.E.D.* 2, first
entry 1590.
    38. *will both watch and ward*] decree that continuous look-out and
guard. Cf. *Faerie Queene*, I.ii.9: 'Still, when she slept, he kept both
watch and ward'.
    42–3. *meet | Our army*] Orcanes had sent the greater part of his army
ahead against Tamburlaine, to aid Soria and Jerusalem (*Two* II.i.16–21).
    43. *brother*] *O.E.D.* records this plural form up to *c.* 1400, and the
plural *brether* till as late as 1875. The octavo reading may be an error for
'brothers'.
    44. *Amasia*] 'a province in northern Asia Minor' (Jump); cf. *Two*
III.i.4, 51.
    II.iv.0.1 *The arras is drawn*] i.e. across the discovery space, or across a
removable curtained booth (cf. A. Gurr, *The Shakespearean Stage*,
London, 1970, p. 100).

TAMBURLAINE *sitting by her; three* Physicians *about her bed, tempering potions.* THERIDAMAS, TECHELLES, USUM-CASANE, *and the* three sons [CALYPHAS, AMYRAS, CELEBINUS].

Tamburlaine. Black is the beauty of the brightest day;
          The golden ball of heaven's eternal fire
          That danced with glory on the silver waves
          Now wants the fuel that inflamed his beams,
          And all with faintness and for foul disgrace   5
          He binds his temples with a frowning cloud,
          Ready to darken earth with endless night.
          Zenocrate, that gave him light and life,
          Whose eyes shot fire from their ivory bowers
          And tempered every soul with lively heat,   10
          Now by the malice of the angry skies,
          Whose jealousy admits no second mate,
          Draws in the comfort of her latest breath
          All dazzled with the hellish mists of death.
          Now walk the angels on the walls of heaven,   15
          As sentinels to warn th'immortal souls
          To entertain divine Zenocrate.
          Apollo, Cynthia, and the ceaseless lamps
          That gently looked upon this loathsome earth,
          Shine downwards now no more, but deck the heavens   20
          To entertain divine Zenocrate.
          The crystal springs whose taste illuminates

0.3. *tempering*] concocting, mixing.

1–37.] See Introduction, p. 40. There is a significant congruity in rhetorical mode and sentiment with the opening of *1H6*, e.g. 1–5; 'Hung be the heavens with black, yield day to night! / Comets, importing change of times and states, / Brandish your crystal tresses in the sky / And with them scourge the bad revolting stars / That have consented unto Henry's death!'

9. *bowers*] eye-sockets (E.A.J.H.).

10. *tempered*] refreshed, gave health to (cf. the sentiment of ll. 44–5 below); 'melt; make well-disposed' (Pendry–Maxwell). The word carries a sense of alchemical mystery; cf. *Two* IV.ii.63 n.

11–12.] a reference to the legendary jealousy of Juno (E.A.J.H.).

12. *mate*] companion.

17. *entertain*] receive, welcome.

22. *crystal springs*] Kocher (p. 94) cites the 'river of life' from Rev.

 Refinèd eyes with an eternal sight,
 Like trièd silver runs through Paradise
 To entertain divine Zenocrate.   25
 The cherubins and holy seraphins
 That sing and play before the King of Kings
 Use all their voices and their instruments
 To entertain divine Zenocrate.
 And in this sweet and curious harmony   30
 The god that tunes this music to our souls
 Holds out his hand in highest majesty
 To entertain divine Zenocrate.
 Then let some holy trance convey my thoughts
 Up to the palace of th'empyreal heaven,   35
 That this my life may be as short to me
 As are the days of sweet Zenocrate.
 Physicians, will no physic do her good?
Physician. My lord, your majesty shall soon perceive—
 And if she pass this fit, the worst is past.   40
Tamburlaine. Tell me, how fares my fair Zenocrate?
Zenocrate. I fare, my lord, as other empresses,
 That, when this frail and transitory flesh

---

24. runs] *O1–3, Q;* run *Ellis-Fermor.*   35. th'empyreal] *This ed.;*
th'imperiall *O1–3, Q.* 42. empresses] *O2, Q;* Emperesses *O1, O3.*

---

xxii.1. On ll. 22–4, Ellis-Fermor (p. 213) comments: 'Lines again
characteristic of Marlowe, the river "the streams whereof make glad the
city of God" mingling with the waters of Aganippe'.

 illuminates] lights. Cf. *Two* I.iii.2, in a context which bears other comparison with this speech.

 24. *trièd*] purified, refined. The springs of vision which purge mortal
sight are crystal, like Zenocrate herself in love's eyes, and they share
beneficent virtue with the pure fire of her spirit (ll. 9–10), and with the
paradisal music—metaphysical and actual—which is tuned to the human
spirit. Harmony, beauty, 'measure', health, are all in creative relation:
cf. ll. 49–50, and see Introduction, pp. 48, 71.

 30. *curious*] exquisite, elaborately wrought, associating with the 'enchased' gems and embroideries of actual and metaphoric artistry. The
metaphor moves aptly into the actual music that composes Zenocrate's
dying, ll. 77–95 below.

 35. *empyreal heaven*] the empyrean. Cf. *One* II.vii.15 n.

 40. *fit*] severe period of illness; crisis (*O.E.D. sb.*[2] 2, 3).

 42.] Zenocrate's lines recall her sorrowful musing on mortality in the
death of Bajazeth and his 'great emperess', in *One* V.i.353 ff.

Hath sucked the measure of that vital air
That feeds the body with his dated health,   45
Wanes with enforced and necessary change.
Tamburlaine. May never such a change transform my love,
In whose sweet being I repose my life,
Whose heavenly presence, beautified with health,
Gives light to Phoebus and the fixèd stars,   50
Whose absence makes the sun and moon as dark
As when, opposed in one diameter,
Their spheres are mounted on the serpent's head
Or else descended to his winding train.
Live still, my love, and so conserve my life,   55
Or, dying, be the author of my death.
Zenocrate. Live still, my lord, O let my sovereign live,
And sooner let the fiery element
Dissolve, and make your kingdom in the sky,
Than this base earth should shroud your majesty: 60
For should I but suspect your death by mine,
The comfort of my future happiness
And hope to meet your highness in the heavens,
Turned to despair, would break my wretched breast,
And fury would confound my present rest.   65
But let me die, my love, yet let me die,
With love and patience let your true love die:
Your grief and fury hurts my second life.
Yet let me kiss my lord before I die,
And let me die with kissing of my lord.   70
But since my life is lengthened yet a while,

---

51. makes] *O3, Q;* make *O1–2.*   56. author] *Q;* anchor *O1–3.*

44.] Cf. *One* II.vi.25.

45. *dated*] having a fixed date or term. Cf. *One* II.vi.37.

52–4.] A standard description of lunar eclipse. The two points at which such eclipses occurred were, northward and southward, 'caput draconis' and 'cauda draconis'. Kocher adds (p. 228): 'When [Marlowe] calls the sun dark during an eclipse of the moon he may be taken to mean that it is invisible, though still radiant, since it is on the other side of the earth from the observer of the eclipse'.

56. *author*] the 'anchor' of *O1–3* yields poor sense.

58–9. *let . . . sky*] 'may the sphere of fire, which encloses the regions of the air, . . . come to an end, and may you make your kingdom among the heavenly spheres which lie beyond it' (Jump).

Let me take leave of these my loving sons
And of my lords, whose true nobility
Have merited my latest memory:
Sweet sons farewell, in death resemble me,   75
And in your lives your father's excellency.
Some music, and my fit will cease, my lord.

They call music.

Tamburlaine. Proud fury and intolerable fit
That dares torment the body of my love
And scourge the scourge of the immortal God!   80
Now are those spheres where Cupid used to sit,
Wounding the world with wonder and with love,
Sadly supplied with pale and ghastly death
Whose darts do pierce the centre of my soul.
Her sacred beauty hath enchanted heaven,   85
And had she lived before the siege of Troy,
Helen, whose beauty summoned Greece to arms
And drew a thousand ships to Tenedos,
Had not been named in Homer's Iliads—
Her name had been in every line he wrote;   90
Or had those wanton poets, for whose birth
Old Rome was proud, but gazed a while on her,
Nor Lesbia nor Corinna had been named—
Zenocrate had been the argument
Of every epigram or elegy.   95

The music sounds, and she dies.

What, is she dead? Techelles, draw thy sword,
And wound the earth, that it may cleave in twain,
And we descend into th'infernal vaults
To hale the Fatal Sisters by the hair

90. *Her*] This ed. ital.; Her *O1–3, Q.*

---

81. *those spheres*] i.e. her eyes—but the scale of the metaphor is in-dispensable.

84. *darts ... pierce the centre*] recalling the rhetoric of Bajazeth just before his suicide, *One* V.i.302–4. The *centre* of the universe is the earth: cf. 'Affection! thy intention stabs the centre', *Wint.,* I.ii.138.

87–8.] recalled in Faustus's praise of Zenocrate's inferior rival: *Dr Faustus,* xviii.99–100.

93. *Lesbia ... Corinna*] in the 'wanton' poetry of Catullus and Ovid.

99. *Fatal Sisters*] Atropos, Clotho, Lachesis, the 'Fates' of *One* I.ii.173. Cf. *One* V.i.455 n. For the Herculean exploit, cf. *One* I.ii.159–60.

And throw them in the triple moat of hell   100
For taking hence my fair Zenocrate.
Casane and Theridamas, to arms!
Raise cavalieros higher than the clouds,
And with the cannon break the frame of heaven,
Batter the shining palace of the sun   105
And shiver all the starry firmament,
For amorous Jove hath snatched my love from hence,
Meaning to make her stately queen of heaven.
What god soever holds thee in his arms,
Giving thee nectar and ambrosia,   110
Behold me here, divine Zenocrate,
Raving, impatient, desperate and mad,
Breaking my steelèd lance with which I burst
The rusty beams of Janus' temple doors,
Letting out death and tyrannising war,   115
To march with me under this bloody flag—
And if thou pitiest Tamburlaine the Great,
Come down from heaven and live with me again!

Theridamas. Ah, good my lord, be patient, she is dead,
And all this raging cannot make her live.   120
If words might serve, our voice hath rent the air;
If tears, our eyes have watered all the earth;
If grief, our murdered hearts have strained forth blood.
Nothing prevails, for she is dead, my lord.

Tamburlaine. For she is dead! Thy words do pierce my soul.   125
Ah, sweet Theridamas, say so no more—
Though she be dead, yet let me think she lives,
And feed my mind that dies for want of her:

---

100. *triple moat*] Cf. *Two* III.ii.12–13, for Hades 'Compassed with Lethe, Styx, and Phlegethon'. See *Aeneid* vi.548–51.

103. *cavalieros*] high earthworks forming fortifications.

107.] Cf. Theridamas at *Two* IV.ii.18–19.

114. *rusty*] Cf. the 'rusty coach' of darkness at *One* V.i.294, and the 'rusty gates of hell' at *Two* V.i.96.

Janus' temple doors] 'The temple of Janus, the guardian of gates and doors, was a bronze shrine in the Forum, with doors on its eastern and western sides. The doors stood open in time of war and were closed in time of peace' (Woolf). Cf. *Aeneid* vii.607 ff.

114–18.] Marlowe is skilfully balancing what is true and what is indulgent and impotent in the hyperboles of theatrical grief.

Where'er her soul be, thou shalt stay with me,
Embalmed with cassia, ambergris and myrrh,   130
Not lapt in lead but in a sheet of gold,
And till I die thou shalt not be interred.
Then in as rich a tomb as Mausolus'
We both will rest and have one epitaph
Writ in as many several languages   135
As I have conquered kingdoms with my sword.
This cursèd town will I consume with fire
Because this place bereft me of my love:
The houses, burnt, will look as if they mourned,
And here will I set up her statua   140
And march about it with my mourning camp,
Drooping and pining for Zenocrate.

                                    The arras is drawn.

[*Finis Actus secundi.*]

140. statua] *Broughton, conj. Dyce 1;* stature *O1–2;* Statue *O3, Q.*
142.2. *Finis Actus secundi.*] *This ed.; not in O1–3, Q.*

---

129. *her ... thou*] a telling shift of focus, as Tamburlaine turns to address his dead Queen.

130. *cassia*] fragrant shrub or plant: *O.E.D.*, deriving the rhetorical-poetic sense of the word from classical sources and from Psalm xlv.8, cites Milton, Dryden, and Keats, but its first instance is from Greene in 1590.

133. *Mausolus'*] the tomb of Mausolus, King of Caria, fourth century B.C.; one of the seven wonders of the world.

140. *statua*] effigy. Cf. *One* IV.ii.105–6 n., *One* I.ii.243. The form 'statua' is recorded in English from *c.* 1400 (*O.E.D.*, which defends emendation to 'statua' in Shakespearean texts, 'as a trisyllable is required, and there is no evidence of trisyllabic pronunciation of *statue*').

Act III

SCENE i

Enter the Kings of TREBIZOND *and* SORIA, *one bringing a sword, and another a sceptre; next,* [ORCANES *of*] NATOLIA *and* JERUSALEM *with the imperial crown; after,* CALLAPINE, *and after him other* Lords [*and* ALMEDA.] ORCANES *and* JERUSALEM *crown him* [CALLAPINE], *and the other give him the sceptre.*

Orcanes. Callapinus Cyricelibes, otherwise Cybelius, son and
   successive heir to the late mighty emperor Bajazeth, by
   the aid of God and his friend Mahomet Emperor of
   Natolia, Jerusalem, Trebizond, Soria, Amasia, Thracia,
   Illyria, Carmonia, and all the hundred and thirty king-   5
   doms late contributory to his mighty father: long live
   Callapinus, Emperor of Turkey!
Callapine. Thrice worthy kings of Natolia, and the rest,
   I will requite your royal gratitudes
   With all the benefits my empire yields;   10
   And were the sinews of th'imperial seat
   So knit and strengthened as when Bajazeth
   My royal lord and father filled the throne,
   Whose cursèd fate hath so dismembered it,
   Then should you see this thief of Scythia,   15
   This proud usurping king of Persia,

0.4. *and* ALMEDA] *Dyce 1; not in O1–3, Q.*

III.i.o.6. *other*] others.
  1. *Callapinus Cyricelibes ... Cybelius*] titles as given in Lonicerus (Seaton, 'Sources', p. 388).
  4. *Amasia*] as at *Two* II.iii.44 n., *Two* III.i.51.
  5. *Carmonia*] Carmania, on the borders of Natolia and Syria.
  11. *th'imperial*] see *One* II.vii.15 n.

Do us such honour and supremacy,
Bearing the vengeance of our father's wrongs,
As all the world should blot our dignities
Out of the book of base-born infamies.   20
And now I doubt not but your royal cares
Hath so provided for this cursèd foe
That, since the heir of mighty Bajazeth
(An emperor so honoured for his virtues)
Revives the spirits of true Turkish hearts   25
In grievous memory of his father's shame,
We shall not need to nourish any doubt
But that proud Fortune, who hath followed long
The martial sword of mighty Tamburlaine,
Will now retain her old inconstancy   30
And raise our honours to as high a pitch
In this our strong and fortunate encounter:
For so hath heaven provided my escape
From all the cruelty my soul sustained,
By this my friendly keeper's happy means,   35
That Jove, surcharged with pity of our wrongs,
Will pour it down in showers on our heads,
Scourging the pride of cursèd Tamburlaine.
Orcanes. I have a hundred thousand men in arms—
Some that, in conquest of the perjured Christian,   40
Being a handful to a mighty host,
Think them in number yet sufficient
To drink the river Nile or Euphrates,
And, for their power, enow to win the world.
Jerusalem. And I as many from Jerusalem,   45

---

17. *Do us ... supremacy*] acknowledge us with honour as supreme: an interesting usage, not found in *O.E.D.*

19–20.] i.e. 'So that the world would delete our exalted names from the roll of infamy' (on which Bajazeth's ill-usage had inscribed them).

28–9.] The commonplace that 'fortune is only constant in inconstancy' may be traced to Ovid, *Trist.*, V.viii.18 (cf. Tilley, F605). On Tamburlaine as Fortune's creature, cf. *Two* I.i.60 n.

32. *fortunate*] engineered by Fortune; a stronger sense than our 'lucky' (F.D.H.).

40–1.] The small army that scourged Sigismond in *Two* II.iii.

44. *enow*] enough.

45–6. *Jerusalem ... Scalonia's bounds*] 'The king of Jerusalem naturally

Judaea, Gaza, and Scalonia's bounds,
That on mount Sinai with their ensigns spread
Look like the parti-coloured clouds of heaven
That show fair weather to the neighbour morn.
Trebizond. And I as many bring from Trebizond,   50
Chio, Famastro, and Amasia,
All bord'ring on the Mare-Major sea,
Riso, Sancina, and the bordering towns,
That touch the end of famous Euphrates:
Whose courages are kindled with the flames   55
The cursèd Scythian sets on all their towns,
And vow to burn the villain's cruel heart.
Soria. From Soria with seventy thousand strong,
Ta'en from Aleppo, Soldino, Tripoly,
And so unto my city of Damasco,   60
I march to meet and aid my neighbour kings,
All which will join against this Tamburlaine
And bring him captive to your highness' feet.
Orcanes. Our battle, then, in martial manner pitched,
According to our ancient use shall bear   65
The figure of the semicircled moon,
Whose horns shall sprinkle through the tainted air

---

46. Scalonia's] *This ed.;* Scalonians *O1–3;* Sclauonians *Q;* Sclavonian *Oxberry;* Sclavonia's *Robinson.*

---

raises his [army] from "*Iudaea, Gaza* and *Scalonians* bounds"; that the town of Ascalon appears in the map as Scalona effectively disposes of the 1605 Quarto's absurd change to *Sclauonians,* apparently a confused reminiscence of the earlier enumeration of Sigismund's composite army of "Slauonians, Almains, Rutters, Muffes, and Danes" ' (Seaton, p. 30). Jump reads 'Scalonians' bounds'; but it seems merely sensible to emend to 'Scalonia's'.

52–4. *from Trebizond ... Euphrates*] 'For the king of Trebizond, Marlowe's finger traces from west to east the northern seaboard of Asia Minor: Chia, Famastro, Riso, Sanƚina' (Seaton, p. 30). The *Mare-Major* is the Black Sea. *Euphrates* has an accented first syllable, as at *One* V.i.440.

58–60.] 'For the king of Soria, he passes from Aleppo south-westward to the sea-coast near Cyprus, and chooses Soldino and Tripoli, and so inland again to Damasco' (Seaton, p. 30).

66.] This figure recalls the metaphor in Bajazeth's vaunt of his army's size in *One* III.i.11–12. Kocher (p. 242 n.) finds a source in Paulus Jovius. Cf. also *Two* I.iii.14.

    The poisoned brains of this proud Scythian.

Callapine. Well then, my noble lords, for this my friend
    That freed me from the bondage of my foe,   70
    I think it requisite and honourable
    To keep my promise and to make him king,
    That is a gentleman, I know, at least.

Almeda. That's no matter, sir, for being a king,
    For Tamburlaine came up of nothing.   75

Jerusalem. Your majesty may choose some 'pointed time,
    Performing all your promise to the full:
    'Tis nought for your majesty to give a kingdom.

Callapine. Then will I shortly keep my promise, Almeda.

Almeda. Why, I thank your majesty.   *Exeunt.*   80

Scene ii

[*Enter*] TAMBURLAINE *with* USUMCASANE, *and his three*
sons [CALYPHAS, AMYRAS, CELEBINUS]; *four* [Soldiers]
bearing the hearse of ZENOCRATE, *and the drums sounding*
a doleful march, the town burning.

Tamburlaine. So, burn the turrets of this cursèd town,
    Flame to the highest region of the air
    And kindle heaps of exhalations
    That, being fiery meteors, may presage
    Death and destruction to th'inhabitants.   5

74–5.] *verse in O1–3, Q; prose in Ellis-Fermor.*   *Heading.* SCENE ii]
Oxberry; Actus. 2. Scaena 2. *O1–3, Q.*   0.1. *Enter*] *Robinson; not in*
O1–3, Q.

68.] This description of Tamburlaine has the more force for the recent
spectacle of his rage, in *Two* II.iv.112 ff.

74–80.] The skilfully phased decline into banality and prosaic rhythms
recalls aptly the scenes featuring Mycetes in Part One. Ellis-Fermor
needlessly suggests that Almeda's interjection is an interpolated actor's
gag, and prints it as prose (which it very nearly is, in effect).

III.ii.0.4. *the town burning*] on the staging of this, see Introduction,
p. 25.

2–8.] The *exhalations*, lighter than 'vapours', are in standard Renaissance meteorology drawn up to the highest region of the element of fire, and ignited by the
neighbouring element of fire, and manifest themselves to the eye as
dragons, spears, etc. Cf. *Two* IV.i.201–5. Aristotle, *Met.*, Loeb, 341b.1.,
isolates burning flames, shooting stars, and torches.

Over my zenith hang a blazing star
That may endure till heaven be dissolved,
Fed with the fresh supply of earthly dregs,
Threat'ning a death and famine to this land.
Flying dragons, lightning, fearful thunderclaps,   10
Singe these fair plains, and make them seem as black
As is the island where the Furies mask
Compassed with Lethe, Styx, and Phlegethon,
Because my dear Zenocrate is dead.

Calyphas. This pillar placed in memory of her,   15
Where in Arabian, Hebrew, Greek, is writ,
This town being burnt by Tamburlaine *the Great*
Forbids the world to build it up again.

Amyras. And here this mournful streamer shall be placed,
Wrought with the Persian and Egyptian arms   20
To signify she was a princess born
And wife unto the monarch of the East.

Celebinus. And here this table as a register
Of all her virtues and perfections.

Tamburlaine. And here the picture of Zenocrate   25
To show her beauty which the world admired:
Sweet picture of divine Zenocrate
That, hanging here, will draw the gods from heaven
And cause the stars fixed in the southern arc,

9. death] *O1–3, Q;* dearth Dyce 1.

---

6. *zenith*] 'point of dominant (astrological) influence' (Pendry–Maxwell).

7. *till heaven be dissolved*] Cf. the despair of the younger Spencer over Edward's departure in *Edward II*, IV.vi.101–2: 'Rent, sphere of heaven, and, fire, forsake thy orb, / Earth, melt to air'. See *Two* V.iii.251.

8. *earthly dregs*] Cf. the 'massy dregs of earth' which are replenished in Tamburlaine's murder of his own son at *Two* IV.i.123.

9.] To emend 'death' to 'dearth', with Dyce, achieves only tautology.

12. *mask*] lurk unseen; cf. *One* IV.iv.17.

13.] Hades' three rivers form its 'triple moat' at *Two* II.iv.100.

19. *streamer*] pennon. Cf. the streamers in Zabina's mad outcry at *One* V.i.315, and the 'black streamers' of *Two* V.iii.49.

22. *the monarch of the East*] recalling the phrase from *One* I.ii.184.

23. *table*] memorial tablet.

29–32. *the stars ... hemisphere*] 'The southern stars, through their desire to see the portrait of Zenocrate, will move into the northern latitudes' (Ellis-Fermor, p. 223). Kocher (p. 229) points out that stars

Whose lovely faces never any viewed   30
That have not passed the centre's latitude,
As pilgrims travel to our hemisphere
Only to gaze upon Zenocrate.
Thou shalt not beautify Larissa plains,
But keep within the circle of mine arms;   35
At every town and castle I besiege
Thou shalt be set upon my royal tent,
And when I meet an army in the field
Those looks will shed such influence in my camp
As if Bellona, goddess of the war,   40
Threw naked swords and sulphur balls of fire
Upon the heads of all our enemies.
And now, my lords, advance your spears again;
Sorrow no more, my sweet Casane, now;
Boys, leave to mourn—this town shall ever mourn,   45
Being burnt to cinders for your mother's death.

Calyphas. If I had wept a sea of tears for her,
It would not ease the sorrow I sustain.

Amyras. As is that town, so is my heart consumed
With grief and sorrow for my mother's death.   50

Celebinus. My mother's death hath mortified my mind,
And sorrow stops the passage of my speech.

Tamburlaine. But now, my boys, leave off and list to me
That mean to teach you rudiments of war:
I'll have you learn to sleep upon the ground,   55
March in your armour thorough watery fens,

---

39. Those] *Dyce 1;* Whose *O1–3, Q.*   56. thorough] *O2–3, Q;* throwe *O1.*

in the southern polar circle are not visible from the northern hemisphere.
    the centre's latitude] 'the equator, the middle line of latitude' (Ellis-Fermor, p. 223).
    41. *sulphur balls of fire*] 'may here refer to Greek fire or to the primitive sixteenth-century hand-grenades described in military text-books such as Paul Ive's *Practise of Fortification*' (Ellis-Fermor, p. 224). Cf. 'wild-fire', *One* V.i.312.
    55–92.] Marlowe draws directly on the technical information in Paul Ive's *Practise of Fortification*, 1589. In the National Theatre production of 1976, this densely technical speech was given authentic human point by its being spoken very rapidly, up to a moment of breathlessness, as if known by heart and now spoken to divert Tamburlaine himself from grief over the death of Zenocrate.

Sustain the scorching heat and freezing cold,
Hunger and thirst, right adjuncts of the war.
And after this, to scale a castle wall,
Besiege a fort, to undermine a town,   60
And make whole cities caper in the air.
Then next, the way to fortify your men:
In champion grounds what figure serves you best;
For which the quinque-angle form is meet,
Because the corners there may fall more flat   65
Whereas the fort may fittest be assailed,
And sharpest where th'assault is desperate.
The ditches must be deep, the counterscarps
Narrow and steep, the walls made high and broad,
The bulwarks and the rampiers large and strong,   70
With cavalieros and thick counterforts,
And room within to lodge six thousand men.
It must have privy ditches, countermines,
And secret issuings to defend the ditch;
It must have high argins and covered ways   75

58. thirst] *Q;* cold *O1–3.*   64. which] *Robinson;* with *O1–3, Q.*

61. *caper*] i.e., having been blown up (E.A.J.H.).

63. *champion*] level and open; cf. *One* II.ii.40, *Two* I.i.32.

figure] cf. the Turkish 'figure of the semicircled moon' at *Two* III.i.66.

64–7.] i.e. in country *other than* level and open, where the quinque-angle is best suited because its strong and weak points (the obtuse and the sharp angles) may be placed so as to take advantage of the inequalities of the terrain, which render some sections more assailable than others (Kocher, p. 254).

66. *Whereas*] Where.

68–9. *counterscarps | Narrow and steep*] The 'outermost ring of defence' (Kocher, p. 253); detailed in l. 75 below: the earthworks are *steep*, the covered way *narrow*.

70. *bulwarks*] earthworks projecting outward from the fort at each angle as artillery bases.

rampiers] ramparts supporting the walls from behind.

71. *cavalieros*] commanding artillery platforms within a fortification.

counterforts] braces strengthening the walls on the inside.

73. *privy ditches*] deeper ditches set into the main ditch.

countermines] 'an underground tunnel as far as possible beneath the ditch and circling the walls, from which the enemy's mining operations could be detected and intercepting tunnels dug' (Kocher, p. 252).

74. *secret issuings*] small doorways to permit defensive sallies 'to drive out any besiegers who might effect an entry' (Kocher, p. 252).

75. *argins*] earthworks shielding ('covering') infantry (Kocher, p. 252).

To keep the bulwark fronts from battery,
And parapets to hide the musketeers,
Casemates to place the great artillery,
And store of ordnance, that from every flank
May scour the outward curtains of the fort,   80
Dismount the cannon of the adverse part,
Murder the foe and save the walls from breach.
When this is learned for service on the land,
By plain and easy demonstration
I'll teach you how to make the water mount,   85
That you may dry-foot march through lakes and pools,
Deep rivers, havens, creeks, and little seas,
And make a fortress in the raging waves,
Fenced with the concave of a monstrous rock,
Invincible by nature of the place.   90
When this is done, then are ye soldiers,
And worthy sons of Tamburlaine the Great.

Calyphas. My lord, but this is dangerous to be done:
We may be slain or wounded ere we learn.

Tamburlaine. Villain, art thou the son of Tamburlaine,   95
And fearest to die, or with a curtle-axe
To hew thy flesh and make a gaping wound?
Hast thou beheld a peal of ordnance strike
A ring of pikes, mingled with shot and horse,

---

82. the walls] *Oxberry;* their walles *O1–3, Q.*

---

77. *parapets*] formed by the difference in height between wall and rampart.

78. *Casemates*] 'chambers in the walls and bulwarks down near the bottom of the ditch which came into play after the enemy had succeeded in entering the ditch' (Kocher, p. 251).

79. *ordnance*] the spelling of the octavo, 'ordinance', reminds us that the metre sometimes requires three syllables.

80. *curtains*] fortified walls.

81. *Dismount*] throw down from their carriage.
adverse part] enemy.

82. *Murder*] perhaps alluding to the *murderer*, a small cannon (*O.E.D.* 2; no entry for vb. *murder* in this sense): E.A.J.H.

85. *mount*] rise.

96. *curtle-axe*] cutlass, broadsword.

99.] an orthodox military disposition: a defensive ring of pikemen, supported by infantry with small firearms, and closely flanked by cavalry (Kocher, pp. 246–7).

Whose shattered limbs, being tossed as high as heaven,   100
Hang in the air as thick as sunny motes—
And canst thou, coward, stand in fear of death?
Hast thou not seen my horsemen charge the foe,
Shot through the arms, cut overthwart the hands,
Dyeing their lances with their streaming blood,   105
And yet at night carouse within my tent,
Filling their empty veins with airy wine
That, being concocted, turns to crimson blood—
And wilt thou shun the field for fear of wounds?
View me, thy father, that hath conquered kings   110
And with his host marched round about the earth
Quite void of scars and clear from any wound,
That by the wars lost not a dram of blood,
And see him lance his flesh to teach you all.

                                    He cuts his arm.

A wound is nothing, be it ne'er so deep,   115
Blood is the god of war's rich livery.
Now look I like a soldier, and this wound
As great a grace and majesty to me
As if a chair of gold enamellèd,
Enchased with diamonds, sapphires, rubies,   120
And fairest pearl of wealthy India,
Were mounted here under a canopy,
And I sat down, clothed with the massy robe
That late adorned the Afric potentate
Whom I brought bound unto Damascus' walls.   125
Come, boys, and with your fingers search my wound
And in my blood wash all your hands at once,

111. marched] *O3, Q;* march *O1–2.*

---

104. *overthwart*] across. Cf. Malory, *Morte Darthur*, ed. Vinaver, xxi, ll. 25–6: 'al Englond overthwart and endelonge'.

107–8.] an elaboration of the commonplace 'Good wine makes good blood' (Tilley, W461).

airy] '?effervescent [the *element* air is the equivalent of the 'humour' blood, both being hot and moist]' (Pendry–Maxwell).

concocted] digested.

114. *lance*] gash.

120. *Enchased*] set.

124. *the Afric potentate*] Bajazeth, conqueror of Africa, brought as a caged prisoner to the siege of Damascus in *One* V.i.

  While I sit smiling to behold the sight—
  Now, my boys, what think you of a wound?
Calyphas. I know not what I should think of it;   130
  Methinks 'tis a pitiful sight.
Celebinus. 'Tis nothing: give me a wound, father.
Amyras. And me another, my lord.
Tamburlaine. Come, sirrah, give me your arm.
Celebinus. Here, father, cut it bravely as you did your own. 135
Tamburlaine. It shall suffice thou darest abide a wound:
  My boy, thou shalt not lose a drop of blood
  Before we meet the army of the Turk—
  But then run desperate through the thickest throngs,
  Dreadless of blows, of bloody wounds and death; 140
  And let the burning of Larissa walls,
  My speech of war, and this my wound you see,
  Teach you my boys to bear courageous minds
  Fit for the followers of great Tamburlaine.
  Usumcasane, now come let us march 145
  Towards Techelles and Theridamas
  That we have sent before to fire the towns,
  The towers and cities of these hateful Turks,
  And hunt that coward, faint-heart, runaway,
  With that accursèd traitor Almeda, 150
  Till fire and sword have found them at a bay.
Usumcasane. I long to pierce his bowels with my sword
  That hath betrayed my gracious sovereign,
  That cursed and damnèd traitor Almeda.
Tamburlaine. Then let us see if coward Callapine 155
  Dare levy arms against our puissance,
  That we may tread upon his captive neck
  And treble all his father's slaveries.   *Exeunt.*

---

 135. *bravely*] well.
 143.] echoing Tamburlaine's insistence from *Two* I.iii.72–3.
 149. *coward, faintheart, runaway*] so punctuated in O1–3, Q; *coward*, it seems, is a noun here as in *Two* IV.i.89. The character referred to is Callapine.
 151. *at a bay*] at bay.
 156. *puissance*] trisyllabic.

Scene iii

[*Enter*] TECHELLES, THERIDAMAS, *and their* train
[Soldiers *and* Pioners].

Theridamas. Thus have we marched northward from
    Tamburlaine
    Unto the frontier point of Soria;
    And this is Balsera, their chiefest hold,
    Wherein is all the treasure of the land.
Techelles. Then let us bring our light artillery,   5
    Minions, falc'nets, and sakers, to the trench,
    Filling the ditches with the walls' wide breach,
    And enter in to seize upon the gold.
    How say ye, soldiers, shall we not?
Soldiers. Yes, my lord, yes, come let's about it.   10
Theridamas. But stay a while; summon a parley, drum:
    It may be they will yield it quietly,
    Knowing two kings, the friends to Tamburlaine,
    Stand at the walls with such a mighty power.

    Summon the battle. [*Enter above*] Captain *with his wife*
        [OLYMPIA] *and* son.

Captain. What require you, my masters?   15
Theridamas. Captain, that thou yield up thy hold to us.
Captain. To you! Why, do you think me weary of it?
Techelles. Nay, captain, thou art weary of thy life
    If thou withstand the friends of Tamburlaine.
Theridamas. These pioners of Argier in Africa   20

Heading. SCENE iii] *Robinson;* Actus. 3. Scaena. 1. *O1–3, Q.*   0.1. *Enter*]
Oxberry; not in O1–3, Q.   0.2. Soldiers *and* Pioners] *Jump; not in O1–3,*
Q.   13. friends] *O3, Q;* friend *O1–2.*   14.1. *Enter above*] *Oxberry.*
[Captain *appears on the walls.*]; *not in O1–3, Q.*

III.iii.3. *Balsera*] Plotting the northward march across Soria to its
northern border with Natolia, Marlowe seems to have misread Ortelius'
'Passera', printed with its first 's' long (Seaton, p. 24). Ortelius does have
a 'Balsara' not far from modern Basra, and this (though not 'northward')
may have caught Marlowe's eye.
    hold] fortress, stronghold.
    6. *Minions, falc'nets, and sakers*] small cannon of various types and sizes.
    7.] Cf. ll. 25–6 below.
    11. *parley*] Cf. *One* I.ii.137.
    20. *pioners*] sappers.

Even in the cannon's face shall raise a hill
Of earth and faggots higher than thy fort,
And over thy argins and covered ways
Shall play upon the bulwarks of thy hold
Volleys of ordnance till the breach be made   25
That with his ruin fills up all the trench—
And when we enter in, not heaven itself
Shall ransom thee, thy wife, and family.

Techelles. Captain, these Moors shall cut the leaden pipes
That bring fresh water to thy men and thee,   30
And lie in trench before thy castle walls,
That no supply of victual shall come in,
Nor any issue forth but they shall die:
And therefore, captain, yield it quietly.

Captain. Were you that are the friends of Tamburlaine   35
Brothers to holy Mahomet himself,
I would not yield it: therefore do your worst—
Raise mounts, batter, intrench, and undermine,
Cut off the water, all convoys that can,
Yet I am resolute; and so, farewell.   *Exeunt* [*above*].   40

Theridamas. Pioners, away, and where I stuck the stake
Intrench with those dimensions I prescribed;
Cast up the earth towards the castle wall,
Which till it may defend you, labour low,
And few or none shall perish by their shot.   45

Pioners. We will, my lord.   *Exeunt* [*Pioners*].

Techelles. A hundred horse shall scout about the plains
To spy what force comes to relieve the hold.
Both we, Theridamas, will intrench our men,
And with the Jacob's staff measure the height   50

---

33. any] *Oxberry; not in O1–3, Q.*   39. can] *O1–3, Q; come Oxberry.*
40. *Exeunt above*] *after Oxberry.* [*Captain, Olympia, and their Son, retire from the Walls.*]; *not in O1–3, Q.*   46. Pioners] *Oxberry; not in O1–3, Q.*

---

22. *faggots*] bundles of tree-branches.
23. *argins and covered ways*] See *Two* III.ii.75 n., 78 n.
24. *bulwarks*] Cf. *Two* III.ii.70 n.
26. *ruin*] falling (*O.E.D.* 1).
38. *mounts*] earthworks; a technical military term.
39. *that can*] that you can.
50. *Jacob's staff*] a gunner's quadrant, used for range-finding (Kocher, p. 257).

    And distance of the castle from the trench,
    That we may know if our artillery
    Will carry full point-blank unto their walls.
Theridamas. Then see the bringing of our ordnance
    Along the trench into the battery,   55
    Where we will have gabions of six foot broad
    To save our cannoneers from musket shot,
    Betwixt which shall our ordnance thunder forth,
    And with the breach's fall, smoke, fire, and dust,
    The crack, the echo, and the soldiers' cry,   60
    Make deaf the air, and dim the crystal sky.
Techelles. Trumpets and drums, alarum presently,
    And soldiers, play the men; the hold is yours! [*Exeunt.*]

[SCENE iv]

Enter the Captain *with his wife* [OLYMPIA] *and* son.

Olympia. Come, good my lord, and let us haste from hence
    Along the cave that leads beyond the foe:
    No hope is left to save this conquered hold.
Captain. A deadly bullet gliding through my side
    Lies heavy on my heart; I cannot live.   5
    I feel my liver pierced, and all my veins
    That there begin and nourish every part
    Mangled and torn, and all my entrails bathed
    In blood that straineth from their orifex.
    Farewell, sweet wife! Sweet son, farewell! I die.   10
                           [*He dies.*]
Olympia. Death, whither art thou gone, that both we live?

56. gabions] *conj. Broughton, Cunningham;* Galions *O1–2;* Gallions *O3, Q.*
63. hold] *O3, Q;* holds *O1–2.*   *Exeunt*] *Oxberry; not in O1–3, Q.*
Heading. SCENE iv] *Dyce 1; not in O1–3, Q.*   10.1. *He dies.*] *Oxberry;*
not in O1–3, Q.

    56. *gabions*] shields made of 'earth packed into a circle of stakes set in
the ground and bound with osier twigs or similar materials' (Kocher, p.
258). The 'galions' or 'gallions' of the 1590–1606 texts does not make
sense.
    58–62.] directing stage presentation, or offstage effects.
    III.iv.9. *orifex*] orifice, wound.
    11–12.] Olympia's wish not to outlive the Captain recalls Tambur-
laine's feelings about Zenocrate in *Two* II.iv.55–6.

Come back again, sweet Death, and strike us both!
One minute end our days, and one sepulchre
Contain our bodies: Death, why comest thou not?
Well, this must be the messenger for thee—   15
Now, ugly Death, stretch out thy sable wings,
And carry both our souls where his remains.
Tell me, sweet boy, art thou content to die?
These barbarous Scythians, full of cruelty,
And Moors in whom was never pity found,   20
Will hew us piecemeal, put us to the wheel,
Or else invent some torture worse than that—
Therefore die by thy loving mother's hand,
Who gently now will lance thy ivory throat,
And quickly rid thee both of pain and life.   25

Son. Mother, despatch me, or I'll kill myself:
For think ye I can live, and see him dead?
Give me your knife, good mother, or strike home—
The Scythians shall not tyrannise on me.
Sweet mother, strike, that I may meet my father.   30

She stabs him.

Olympia. Ah sacred Mahomet, if this be sin,
Entreat a pardon of the God of heaven,
And purge my soul before it come to thee!

Enter THERIDAMAS, TECHELLES, *and all their* train.

Theridamas. How now, Madam, what are you doing?
Olympia. Killing myself, as I have done my son,   35
Whose body with his father's I have burnt,
Lest cruel Scythians should dismember him.
Techelles. 'Twas bravely done, and like a soldier's wife.
Thou shalt with us to Tamburlaine the Great
Who, when he hears how resolute thou wert,   40

---

29. *tyrannise on me*] Cf. *Edward II*, I.ii.3: 'tyrannise upon the church'.
31.] Olympia's stabbing of her son, in extremity, will be recalled when Tamburlaine executes 'war's justice' on Calyphas (*Two* IV.i.120).

33.] Bowers introduces a stage direction 'Burns the bodies'. One reading is that Olympia, having hidden the bodies, lies about having burnt them in an attempt to keep them from outrage, though she speaks of the flame at ll. 70–1. In the 1976 National Theatre production, they were burned in a pit.

Will match thee with a viceroy or a king.

Olympia. My lord deceased was dearer unto me
    Than any viceroy, king, or emperor.
    And for his sake here will I end my days.

Theridamas. But lady, go with us to Tamburlaine,   45
    And thou shalt see a man greater than Mahomet,
    In whose high looks is much more majesty
    Than from the concave superficies
    Of Jove's vast palace, th'empyreal orb,
    Unto the shining bower where Cynthia sits   50
    Like lovely Thetis in a crystal robe;
    That treadeth Fortune underneath his feet
    And makes the mighty god of arms his slave;
    On whom Death and the Fatal Sisters wait
    With naked swords and scarlet liveries;   55
    Before whom, mounted on a lion's back,
    Rhamnusia bears a helmet full of blood
    And strews the way with brains of slaughtered men;
    By whose proud side the ugly Furies run,
    Hearkening when he shall bid them plague the world;   60
    Over whose zenith, clothed in windy air,
    And eagle's wings joined to her feathered breast,
    Fame hovereth, sounding of her golden trump,

48–51.] i.e. from the surface of the empyrean through the eight moving spheres to the innermost, the moon's bower. After 'Than' (l. 48) we understand some such expression as 'can be seen'. See *One* II.vii.15 n. on altering the original spelling 'imperiall'.

52. *That*] i.e., Tamburlaine. Cf. 'I hold the Fates fast bound in iron chains', *One* I.ii.173.

54. *the Fatal Sisters*] Cf. *Two* III.iv.54 n., *One* I.ii.174, V.i.455.

54–5.] We may recall *One* V.i.117–18, where Tamburlaine spoke of 'my servant Death, Sitting in scarlet on their armèd spears'.

57. *Rhamnusia*] Nemesis; cf. *One* II.iii.37.

58. *brains . . . men*] a phrase recalled from an equally sanguinary vision in *Two* I.iv.81.

59. *ugly Furies*] *ugly* in the sense of occasioning dread or horror; cf. *Two* I.iii.146. Cf. Surrey, *Aeneid*, iv.626: Agamemnon's son . . . 'That sitting found within the temples porche / The uglie furies his slaughter to revenge' (*The Aeneid of Henry Howard Earl of Surrey*, ed. Florence H. Ridley, Berkeley, Calif., 1963, p. 141).

61. *zenith*] the highest point in his career (first *O.E.D.* instance 1610); or, possibly, course towards the zenith (only *O.E.D.* instance *Paradise Lost*, x.329).

That to the adverse poles of that straight line
Which measureth the glorious frame of heaven   65
The name of mighty Tamburlaine is spread—
And him, fair lady, shall thy eyes behold. Come.

Olympia. Take pity of a lady's ruthful tears,
That humbly craves upon her knees to stay
And cast her body in the burning flame   70
That feeds upon her son's and husband's flesh.

Techelles. Madam, sooner shall fire consume us both
Than scorch a face so beautiful as this,
In frame of which nature hath showed more skill
Than when she gave eternal chaos form,   75
Drawing from it the shining lamps of heaven.

Theridamas. Madam, I am so far in love with you
That you must go with us—no remedy.

Olympia. Then carry me I care not where you will,
And let the end of this my fatal journey   80
Be likewise end to my accursèd life.

Techelles. No, madam, but the beginning of your joy;
Come willingly, therefore.

Theridamas. Soldiers, now let us meet the general,
Who by this time is at Natolia,   85
Ready to charge the army of the Turk.
The gold, the silver, and the pearl ye got
Rifling this fort, divide in equal shares:
This lady shall have twice so much again
Out of the coffers of our treasury.   *Exeunt.*   90

SCENE V

[*Enter*] CALLAPINE, ORCANES, JERUSALEM, TREBIZOND,
SORIA, ALMEDA, *with their* train. [*To them enter a*
Messenger.]

Messenger. Renownèd emperor, mighty Callapine,

0.1. Enter] Oxberry; not in O1–3, Q.
0.2. To . . . Messenger] Oxberry (To them a MESSENGER); not in O1–3,
Q.

---

64. *that straight line*] the celestial diameter, heaven's 'axletree' (cf.
One IV.ii.50, *Two* I.i.90, I.iii.12 n.).
80. *fatal*] decreed by fate.

God's great lieutenant over all the world:
Here at Aleppo with an host of men
Lies Tamburlaine, this king of Persia—
In number more than are the quivering leaves   5
Of Ida's forest, where your highness' hounds
With open cry pursues the wounded stag—
Who means to girt Natolia's walls with siege,
Fire the town and overrun the land.

Callapine. My royal army is as great as his,   10
That from the bounds of Phrygia to the sea
Which washeth Cyprus with his brinish waves,
Covers the hills, the valleys and the plains.
Viceroys and peers of Turkey, play the men,
Whet all your swords to mangle Tamburlaine,   15
His sons, his captains, and his followers—
By Mahomet, not one of them shall live!
The field wherein this battle shall be fought
For ever term the Persians' sepulchre
In memory of this our victory.   20

Orcanes. Now he that calls himself the scourge of Jove,
The emperor of the world, and earthly god,
Shall end the warlike progress he intends
And travel headlong to the lake of hell
Where legions of devils, knowing he must die   25
Here in Natolia by your highness' hands,
All brandishing their brands of quenchless fire,
Stretching their monstrous paws, grin with their teeth
And guard the gates to entertain his soul.

Callapine. Tell me, viceroys, the number of your men,   30

III.v.3. *Here*] i.e. to the south of the Turks, who are in Asia Minor:
cf. ll. 11–12 below.

6. *Ida*] 'presumably Mt. Ida near Troy' (Jump).

8. *Natolia*] Asia Minor, as commonly; here confusingly referred to as
a city.

11. *Phrygia*] 'an inland country in western Asia Minor' (Jump).

18. *The field wherein*] identified as 'Asphaltis' by Tamburlaine at *Two*
IV.iii.5: i.e., the bituminous lake near Babylon. Cf. 'Limnasphaltis',
Two V.i.17.

27. *quenchless*] Cf. the 'quenchless flame' of Hell at *Two* II.iii.24. See
One I.ii.22 n.

29. *entertain*] receive. The malevolent counterpart of *Two* II.iv.17.

And what our army royal is esteemed.

Jerusalem. From Palestina and Jerusalem,
  Of Hebrews three score thousand fighting men
  Are come since last we showed your majesty.

Orcanes. So from Arabia desert, and the bounds   35
  Of that sweet land whose brave metropolis
  Re-edified the fair Semiramis,
  Came forty thousand warlike foot and horse
  Since last we numbered to your majesty.

Trebizond. From Trebizond in Asia the Less,   40
  Naturalized Turks and stout Bithynians
  Came to my bands full fifty thousand more
  That, fighting, knows not what retreat doth mean,
  Nor e'er return but with the victory,
  Since last we numbered to your majesty.   45

Soria. Of Sorians from Halla is repaired,
  And neighbour cities of your highness' land,
  Ten thousand horse and thirty thousand foot
  Since last we numbered to your majesty:
  So that the army royal is esteemed   50
  Six hundred thousand valiant fighting men.

Callapine. Then welcome, Tamburlaine, unto thy death.
  Come, puissant viceroys, let us to the field—
  The Persians' sepulchre—and sacrifice
  Mountains of breathless men to Mahomet,   55
  Who now with Jove opens the firmament
  To see the slaughter of our enemies.

  [*Enter*] TAMBURLAINE *with his three* sons [CALYPHAS,
  AMYRAS, CELEBINUS], USUMCASANE, *with other* [Soldiers].

Tamburlaine. How now, Casane! See, a knot of kings,

---

43. *knows*] *O1–3, Q;* know *Oxberry.*   47.] *O1–3; not in Q.*   57.] *after
this line, early texts have scene divisions:* Actus 2. Scaena. I. *O1;* ACTUS II.
SCAENA II. *O2;* Actus 4 Scena I. *O3, Q.*   57.1. *Enter*] *Oxberry; not
in O1–3, Q.*

---

34. *showed*] i.e. showed our lists(?), gave our numbers (E.A.J.H.).
36–7.] The legendary Semiramis rebuilt Babylon. See *Two* V.i.69–70 n.
43. *knows*] Oxberry alters the Elizabethan plural form to the modern
'know'.
46. *Halla*] to Ortelius, a town south-east of Aleppo (Seaton, p. 30).

Sitting as if they were a-telling riddles.

Usumcasane. My lord, your presence makes them pale and
    wan: 60

Poor souls, they look as if their deaths were near.

Tamburlaine. Why, so he is, Casane, I am here;

But yet I'll save their lives and make them slaves.

Ye petty kings of Turkey, I am come

As Hector did into the Grecian camp   65

To overdare the pride of Graecia,

And set his warlike person to the view

Of fierce Achilles, rival of his fame—

I do you honour in the simile:

For if I should, as Hector did Achilles   70

(The worthiest knight that ever brandished sword),

Challenge in combat any of you all,

I see how fearfully ye would refuse,

And fly my glove as from a scorpion.

Orcanes. Now thou art fearful of thy army's strength,   75

Thou wouldst with overmatch of person fight.

But, shepherd's issue, base-born Tamburlaine,

Think of thy end: this sword shall lance thy throat.

Tamburlaine. Villain, the shepherd's issue, at whose birth

Heaven did afford a gracious aspect   80

And joined those stars that shall be opposite

Even till the dissolution of the world,

65–8. *As Hector ... fame*] 'For this episode, we look in vain in the
Iliad. It belongs to the post-Homeric Troy tale. It might well be familiar
to Marlowe from any one of several repetitions of the Trojan story, such
as Lydgate's *Troy Book*, in which (Bk. III, ll. 3755 *seq.*) it is treated at
length' (Ellis-Fermor, p. 238).

66. *overdare*] 'To surpass in or overcome by daring; to daunt' (*O.E.D.*
2: first entry).

74. *scorpion*] L. and E. Feasey (p. 419) see an echo of the locusts like
scorpions of Rev. ix.10.

75–6.] 'Now that you fear your army is not strong enough, you seek to
rely on your superiority in single combat'.

78. *lance*] slash.

80. *a gracious aspect*] favourable astrological conjunction; the 'gracious
stars' of *One* I.ii.92 n.

81. *those stars*] Jupiter and Venus.

82. *the dissolution ... world*] Cf. *Two* III.ii.7 n. On this idea, cf. *Dr
Faustus*, II.i.125–7, *Edward II*, IV.vi.101–2. See Kocher, p. 223.

And never meant to make a conqueror
So famous as is mighty Tamburlaine,
Shall so torment thee and that Callapine 85
That like a roguish runaway suborned
That villain there, that slave, that Turkish dog,
To false his service to his sovereign,
As ye shall curse the birth of Tamburlaine.

Callapine. Rail not, proud Scythian, I shall now revenge 90
My father's vile abuses and mine own.

Jerusalem. By Mahomet, he shall be tied in chains,
Rowing with Christians in a brigandine
About the Grecian isles to rob and spoil,
And turn him to his ancient trade again: 95
Methinks the slave should make a lusty thief.

Callapine. Nay, when the battle ends, all we will meet
And sit in council to invent some pain
That most may vex his body and his soul.

Tamburlaine. Sirrah Callapine, I'll hang a clog about your 100
neck for running away again, you shall not trouble me
thus to come and fetch you.
But as for you, viceroy, you shall have bits
And, harnessed like my horses, draw my coach;
And when ye stay, be lashed with whips of wire. 105
I'll have you learn to feed on provender
And in a stable lie upon the planks.

Orcanes. But, Tamburlaine, first thou shalt kneel to us
And humbly crave a pardon for thy life.

Trebizond. The common soldiers of our mighty host 110
Shall bring thee bound unto the general's tent.

---

87. *that villain*] i.e., Almeda.

88. *false*] break, violate.

91. *abuses*] ill-usage, injuries.

93. *brigandine*] small pirate craft; the 'pilling brigandines' of *One* III.iii.248. Tamburlaine was outraged by Bajazeth's use of Christians as galley-slaves in *One* III.iii.47 ff.

99. *vex*] afflict, distress (*O.E.D.* vb. 2, 3).

100. *clog*] heavy weight designed to impede motion (*O.E.D.* 2).

for] 'as a precaution against' (Jump).

100–2.] The prose passage sits ill before the blank-verse lines, but here and elsewhere prose is an effective vehicle of grim humour and savagery.

Soria. And all have jointly sworn thy cruel death,
  Or bind thee in eternal torment's wrath.
Tamburlaine. Well, sirs, diet yourselves; you know I shall
  have occasion shortly to journey you.   115
Celebinus. See, father, how Almeda the jailor looks upon us.
Tamburlaine. Villain, traitor, damnèd fugitive,
  I'll make thee wish the earth had swallowed thee!
  Seest thou not death within my wrathful looks?
  Go, villain, cast thee headlong from a rock,   120
  Or rip thy bowels and rend out thy heart
  T'appease my wrath, or else I'll torture thee,
  Searing thy hateful flesh with burning irons
  And drops of scalding lead, while all thy joints
  Be racked and beat asunder with the wheel: 125
  For if thou livest, not any element
  Shall shroud thee from the wrath of Tamburlaine.
Callapine. Well, in despite of thee he shall be king.
  Come, Almeda, receive this crown of me:
  I here invest thee king of Ariadan,   130
  Bordering on Mare Roso near to Mecca.
Orcanes. What, take it, man!
Almeda. Good my lord, let me take it.
Callapine. Dost thou ask him leave? Here, take it.
Tamburlaine. Go to, sirrah, take your crown, and make up the   135
  half dozen.
  So, sirrah, now you are a king you must give arms.
Orcanes. So he shall, and wear thy head in his scutcheon.
Tamburlaine. No, let him hang a bunch of keys on his stan-
  dard, to put him in remembrance he was a jailor, that,   140

112–13. The second line is awkward if read as describing an alternative
torment to that in the first. E.A.J.H. suggests reading 'them' for 'thee'
taking l. 113 as the terms of the soldiers' oath.

115. *journey*] drive (*O.E.D. vb.* 3, first entry).

130–1. *Ariadan . . . Mecca*] 'This exactly describes the position in the
map of Africa of this unimportant town that Marlowe arbitrarily selected;
it appears again in *Turcicum Imperium*, but much less conspicuous, and
the sea there is not called *Mar Rosso*' (Seaton, p. 28).

133.] The comic byplay recalls the scene between Tamburlaine and the
cowardly Mycetes in *One* II.iv, a parallel recalled explicitly in ll. 155–7
below.

137. *arms*] punning on 'alms'.

when I take him, I may knock out his brains with them,
and lock you in the stable when you shall come sweating
from my chariot.

Trebizond. Away, let us to the field, that the villain may be
slain.   145

Tamburlaine [*To a soldier.*] Sirrah, prepare whips, and bring
my chariot to my tent: for as soon as the battle is done,
I'll ride in triumph through the camp.

Enter THERIDAMAS, TECHELLES, *and their* train.

How now, ye petty kings—lo, here are bugs
Will make the hair stand upright on your heads,   150
And cast your crowns in slavery at their feet.
Welcome, Theridamas and Techelles both—
See ye this rout, and know ye this same king?

Theridamas. Ay, my lord, he was Callapine's keeper.

Tamburlaine. Well, now you see he is a king, look to him,   155
Theridamas, when we are fighting, lest he hide his crown
as the foolish king of Persia did.

Soria. No, Tamburlaine, he shall not be put to that exigent,
I warrant thee.

Tamburlaine. You know not, sir.   160
But now, my followers and my loving friends,
Fight as you ever did, like conquerors;
The glory of this happy day is yours:
My stern aspect shall make fair Victory,
Hovering betwixt our armies, light on me,   165
Loaden with laurel wreaths to crown us all.

Techelles. I smile to think how when this field is fought
And rich Natolia ours, our men shall sweat
With carrying pearl and treasure on their backs.

Tamburlaine. You shall be princes all immediately.   170

---

146. *To a soldier*] *This ed.; not in O1–3, Q.*

---

149. *bugs*] bugbears, bogeys: objects of terror, with Tamburlaine
sarcastically treating the kings as scared children. Cf. *3H6*, V.ii.2:
'Warwick was a bug that fear'd us all'.

155–7.] Ellis-Fermor's disposition to find prose suspect whenever it
occurred in the play led her to think this back reference to Part One an
interpolation; but a similar recall occurs, in verse, at *Two* I.iii.49.

164. *aspect*] countenance, expression.

Come fight, ye Turks, or yield us victory.
Orcanes. No, we will meet thee, slavish Tamburlaine.

Exeunt [severally].

[*Finis Actus tertii.*]

172.1. *severally*] *Dyce 1; not in O1–3, Q.*   172.2. *Finis Actus tertii.*]
This ed.; not in O1–3, Q.

Act IV

Alarm: AMYRAS *and* CELEBINUS *issue from the tent where*
CALYPHAS *sits asleep.*

Amyras. Now in their glories shine the golden crowns
    Of these proud Turks, much like so many suns
    That half dismay the majesty of heaven.
    Now, brother, follow we our father's sword
    That flies with fury swifter than our thoughts   5
    And cuts down armies with his conquering wings.
Celebinus. Call forth our lazy brother from the tent,
    For if my father miss him in the field,
    Wrath kindled in the furnace of his breast
    Will send a deadly lightning to his heart.   10
Amyras. Brother, ho! What, given so much to sleep
    You cannot leave it when our enemies' drums
    And rattling cannons thunder in our ears
    Our proper ruin and our father's foil?
Calyphas. Away, ye fools, my father needs not me,   15
    Nor you, in faith, but that you will be thought
    More childish valorous than manly wise:
    If half our camp should sit and sleep with me,
    My father were enough to scare the foe;
    You do dishonour to his majesty   20
    To think our helps will do him any good.

0.1. *issue*] Oxberry; *issues O1–3, Q.*   6. conquering] *O2–3, Q;* conquerings *O1;* conquering's *Kirschbaum.*   19. scare] Oxberry; *scar O1–3, Q.*

IV.i.6. *conquering wings*] possibly 'conquering's wings', which retains
the O1 reading ['conquerings wings'] but at the cost of introducing an
un-Marlovian construction.

8–10.] Cf. such Biblical *loci* as Psalm xviii.8.

14. *proper*] own.

foil] defeat.

Amyras. What, darest thou then be absent from the fight,
    Knowing my father hates thy cowardice
    And oft hath warned thee to be still in field
    When he himself amidst the thickest troops   25
    Beats down our foes, to flesh our taintless swords?
Calyphas. I know, sir, what it is to kill a man—
    It works remorse of conscience in me.
    I take no pleasure to be murderous,
    Nor care for blood when wine will quench my thirst.   30
Celebinus. O cowardly boy! Fie, for shame, come forth.
    Thou dost dishonour manhood and thy house.
Calyphas. Go, go, tall stripling, fight you for us both,
    And take my other toward brother here,
    For person like to prove a second Mars.   35
    'Twill please my mind as well to hear both you
    Have won a heap of honour in the field
    And left your slender carcasses behind,
    As if I lay with you for company.
Amyras. You will not go, then?   40
Calyphas. You say true.
Amyras. Were all the lofty mounts of Zona Mundi
    That fill the midst of farthest Tartary
    Turned into pearl and proffered for my stay,
    I would not bide the fury of my father   45
    When, made a victor in these haughty arms,

---

24. *still*] constantly (*O.E.D. adv.* 3).

26. *to flesh our taintless swords*] to christen our unstained swords, i.e. kill for the first time (assisted by Tamburlaine's bravery): 'flesh', *O.E.D.* 3, first entry.

30.] The contrast is sharp with the idea invoked by Tamburlaine that wine, in heroic carousals, turns to blood: *Two* III.ii.107–8.

32. *house*] family, race (*O.E.D. sb.*[1] 6).

33. *tall*] bold, valiant. Ellis-Fermor quotes *Rom.*, II.iv.30, for a similar mocking use of the term. Marlowe uses it elsewhere without disparagement: *Two* IV.iii.70.

34. *toward*] promising, forward.

35. *like*] likely.

42–3. *Zona Mundi ... Tartary*] 'In Ortelius' maps of *Europe* and *Russia*, the range of *Zona mundi montes*, or *Orbis Zona montes*, runs southwards through northernmost Tartary from the coast near Waygatz and Petsora, in the coloured maps most obviously "farthest Tartary" ' (Seaton, p. 28).

46. *haughty*] courageous, exalted.

He comes and finds his sons have had no shares
In all the honours he proposed for us.

Calyphas. Take you the honour, I will take my ease;
My wisdom shall excuse my cowardice.   50
I go into the field before I need?

> *Alarm, and* AMYRAS *and* CELEBINUS *run in.*

The bullets fly at random where they list,
And should I go and kill a thousand men
I were as soon rewarded with a shot,
And sooner far than he that never fights.   55
And should I go and do nor harm nor good
I might have harm, which all the good I have,
Joined with my father's crown, would never cure.
I'll to cards: Perdicas!

[*Enter* PERDICAS.]

Perdicas. Here my lord.   60
Calyphas. Come, thou and I will go to cards to drive away
the time.
Perdicas. Content, my lord, but what shall we play for?
Calyphas. Who shall kiss the fairest of the Turks' concubines
first, when my father hath conquered them.   65
Perdicas. Agreed, i'faith.

> *They play* [*in the open tent*].

Calyphas. They say I am a coward, Perdicas, and I fear as
little their *taratantaras*, their swords, or their cannons, as
I do a naked lady in a net of gold, and for fear I should be

---

51. need?] *O1–3, Q;* need! *Ellis-Fermor.*   59.1. *Enter* PERDICAS.] *Dyce
1; not in O1–3, Q.*   62.] *They retire to the open tent. Jump (after l.
62); not in O1–3, Q.*   66.1. *in the open tent*] *This ed., after Jump (see l.
62 n.); not in O1–3, Q.*   68. *taratantaras*] *Oxberry; tara, tantaras
O1–3, Q.*

67–81.] Tamburlaine's expression 'tickle ... with desire' ironically
reverses Calyphas' prurient savouring of the kind of battle *he* prefers. In
more general terms, Calyphas has separated out, at once incisively and
corruptly, Romance motifs from Heroic, or rather, the venereal from the
foolhardy.
68. *taratantaras*] bugle-calls.
69. *net*] veil, gown of fine mesh; perhaps with a suggestion of 'snare'.
and] The sense requires 'who', but Calyphas' lecherous fantasy out-
runs grammar.

afraid, would put it off and come to bed with me.   70
Perdicas. Such a fear, my lord, would never make ye retire.
Calyphas. I would my father would let me be put in the front
    of such a battle once, to try my valour!   *Alarm.*
    What a coil they keep! I believe there will be some hurt
    done anon amongst them.   75

    Enter TAMBURLAINE, THERIDAMAS, TECHELLES,
USUMCASANE, AMYRAS, CELEBINUS, *leading the* Turkish
    Kings [ORCANES *of* NATOLIA, JERUSALEM, TREBIZOND,
        SORIA; *and* Soldiers].

Tamburlaine. See now, ye slaves, my children stoops your
      pride
    And leads your glories sheep-like to the sword.
    Bring them, my boys, and tell me if the wars
    Be not a life that may illustrate gods,
    And tickle not your spirits with desire   80
    Still to be trained in arms and chivalry?
Amyras. Shall we let go these kings again, my lord,
    To gather greater numbers 'gainst our power,
    That they may say, it is not chance doth this
    But matchless strength and magnanimity?   85
Tamburlaine. No, no, Amyras, tempt not Fortune so;
    Cherish thy valour still with fresh supplies,
    And glut it not with stale and daunted foes.
    But where's this coward, villain, not my son,
    But traitor to my name and majesty?   90
        He goes in and brings him [CALYPHAS] *out.*
    Image of sloth and picture of a slave,

75.4. *and* Soldiers] *Dyce 1; not in O1–3, Q.*

---

    74. *coil they keep*] noisy fuss they make.
    76. *stoops*] humiliate, subdue.
    79. *illustrate*] shed lustre on. Second syllable stressed. Cf. 'illuminates',
Two I.iii.2, II.iv.22.
    85. *magnanimity*] courage; also invoked, by Tamburlaine, at *One*
IV.iv.129 and *Two* V.iii.200.
    88. *glut*] Cf. *One* III.iii.164 n.
    89. *not my son*] echoing *Two* I.iii.32, where Tamburlaine tempered the
phrase to compliment Zenocrate: 'not my sons, / But that I know they
issued from thy womb'.

The obloquy and scorn of my renown,
How may my heart, thus firèd with mine eyes,
Wounded with shame and killed with discontent,
Shroud any thought may hold my striving hands   95
From martial justice on thy wretched soul?
Theridamas. Yet pardon him I pray your majesty.
Techelles and Usumcasane. Let all of us entreat your
        highness' pardon.

                        [*They kneel.*]
Tamburlaine. Stand up, ye base unworthy soldiers!
Know ye not yet the argument of arms?   100
Amyras. Good my lord, let him be forgiven for once,
And we will force him to the field hereafter.
Tamburlaine. Stand up, my boys, and I will teach ye arms
And what the jealousy of wars must do.
O Samarcanda, where I breathèd first,   105
And joyed the fire of this martial flesh,
Blush, blush, fair city, at thine honour's foil,
And shame of nature, which Jaertis' stream,
Embracing thee with deepest of his love,
Can never wash from thy distainèd brows!   110

---

98. *They kneel.*] *This ed.; not in* O1–3, Q.   108. which] *Oxberry; with*
O1–3, Q.

92. *obloquy*] reproach, disgrace (*O.E.D.* 2, first entry 1589).

95. *Shroud*] harbour, shelter: relatively infrequent without implication
of secrecy (*O.E.D.*).

100. *argument of arms*] Ellis-Fermor suggests 'course or nature of
military life', drawing metaphorically on 'the argument in which is set
down the lines along which a play or story is destined to proceed' (p. 245).
More exactly, Tamburlaine is appealing to a code of justice implied in
military conduct. Cf. 'argument of art', *Two* V.iii.97.

104. *jealousy of wars*] zeal or vehemence of feeling for military
values.

106. *joyed*] delighted in.

107. *foil*] disgrace, stigma.

108. *Jaertis' stream*] 'undoubtedly the Jaxartes which appears in
Ortelius' *Persicum Regnum* as "Chesel fl[umen] olim Iaxartes" and runs
from Tartary due west into the Caspian Sea. But Samarchand in this
map is marked to the south of the Iaxartes, on one of the headwaters of
the Amu' (Ellis-Fermor, p. 246). Perondinus places the city on the river.
Cf. *Two* IV.iii.107–8.

110. *distainèd*] dishonoured.

Here, Jove, receive his fainting soul again,
A form not meet to give that subject essence
Whose matter is the flesh of Tamburlaine,
Wherein an incorporeal spirit moves,
Made of the mould whereof thyself consists,   115
Which makes me valiant, proud, ambitious,
Ready to levy power against thy throne,
That I might move the turning spheres of heaven:
For earth and all this airy region
Cannot contain the state of Tamburlaine.   120

                              [*Stabs* CALYPHAS.]

By Mahomet thy mighty friend I swear,
In sending to my issue such a soul,
Created of the massy dregs of earth,
The scum and tartar of the elements,
Wherein was neither courage, strength, or wit,   125
But folly, sloth, and damnèd idleness,
Thou hast procured a greater enemy
Than he that darted mountains at thy head,

120.1. *Stabs* CALYPHAS] *Robinson [after l. 135]; not in O1–3, Q.*

115.] Gen. i.26 is being provocatively applied to man as sharing the qualities of a warring God.

111–15.] 'Here Jove receive again the soul of Calyphas, a spirit (i.e. "form" almost in the sense of "idea") not worthy to be the immortal part (essence) of that subject whose mortal part (matter) is derived from the flesh of Tamburlaine—in whom moves an immortal spirit of the same mould as thine own', etc. (Ellis-Fermor, p. 246, noting the Aristotelian provenance of the terms. The alchemist's application of the terms is found at *Two* IV.ii.62 (F.D.H.).

111–20.] Kocher (p. 84) notes the relation of this invocation of Jove as aspiring and violent to *One* II.vii.12–29.

118.] Cf. *One* IV.ii.8 n.

119–20.] Kocher, pp. 84–5, notes the 'fitting appropriation' of 1 Kings viii.27 to Tamburlaine's purpose: 'But will God indeed dwell on the earth? Behold, the heaven, and heaven of heavens cannot contain Thee.' And cf. Orcanes, 'Nor in one place is circumscriptible', *Two* II.ii.50.

121. *thy*] Still addressing Jove (l. 111).

122. *to my issue*] to be my child (E.A.J.H.).

123–6.] Cf. *One* II.vii.31–3 n.

124. *tartar*] bitartrate of potash, deposited in the process of fermentation, and adhering to the sides of the wine-cask in the form of a hard crust: *O.E.D. sb.*[1] 1d, first instance of figurative use.

128. *he that darted mountains*] echoing the allusion to the war of the Titans on Jove in *One* V.i.511–12.

Shaking the burden mighty Atlas bears,
Whereat thou trembling hiddest thee in the air,   130
Clothed with a pitchy cloud for being seen.
And now, ye cankered curs of Asia,
That will not see the strength of Tamburlaine
Although it shine as brightly as the sun,
Now you shall feel the strength of Tamburlaine,   135
And by the state of his supremacy
Approve the difference 'twixt himself and you.

Orcanes. Thou showest the difference 'twixt ourselves and
    thee
In this thy barbarous damnèd tyranny.

Jerusalem. Thy victories are grown so violent   140
That shortly heaven, filled with the meteors
Of blood and fire thy tyrannies have made,
Will pour down blood and fire on thy head,
Whose scalding drops will pierce thy seething brains
And with our bloods revenge our bloods on thee.   145

Tamburlaine. Villains, these terrors and these tyrannies
(If tyrannies war's justice ye repute)
I execute, enjoined me from above,
To scourge the pride of such as Heaven abhors—
Nor am I made arch-monarch of the world,   150
Crowned and invested by the hand of Jove,
For deeds of bounty or nobility:
But since I exercise a greater name,
The scourge of God and terror of the world,
I must apply myself to fit those terms,   155
In war, in blood, in death, in cruelty,
And plague such peasants as resist in me
The power of heaven's eternal majesty.

---

157. resist in] *conj. Broughton, Dyce 1;* resisting *O1–3, Q.*   158. The]
O1–3, Q; [Resist] the *Oxberry.*

---

131. *for being seen*] 'to avoid being seen' (Ellis-Fermor, p. 247).
137. *Approve*] see demonstrated.
141–5.] As in *One* V.i.460–1, Marlowe draws on Renaissance meteorology: the bloody rain caused by Tamburlaine's cruelty to his victims,
including the Turkish kings themselves, will inflict a scalding retribution
on him. See *One* IV.ii.51–2 n.
157. *resist*] perhaps recalling Romans xiii.2. See pp. 73–4 above.

Theridamas, Techelles, and Casane,
Ransack the tents and the pavilions   160
Of these proud Turks, and take their concubines,
Making them bury this effeminate brat,
For not a common soldier shall defile
His manly fingers with so faint a boy.
Then bring those Turkish harlots to my tent,   165
And I'll dispose them as it likes me best.
Meanwhile, take him in.

Soldiers. We will, my lord.

          [*Exeunt* Soldiers *with the body of* CALYPHAS.]

Jerusalem. O damnèd monster, nay, a fiend of hell—
  Whose cruelties are not so harsh as thine,   170
  Nor yet imposed with such a bitter hate!

Orcanes. Revenge it, Rhadamanth and Aeacus,
  And let your hates, extended in his pains,
  Expel the hate wherewith he pains our souls!

Trebizond. May never day give virtue to his eyes,   175
  Whose sight, composed of fury and of fire,
  Doth send such stern affections to his heart!

Soria. May never spirit, vein, or artier feed
  The cursèd substance of that cruel heart,
  But, wanting moisture and remorseful blood,   180
  Dry up with anger and consume with heat!

Tamburlaine. Well, bark, ye dogs! I'll bridle all your
      tongues
  And bind them close with bits of burnished steel
  Down to the channels of your hateful throats,
  And with the pains my rigour shall inflict   185
  I'll make ye roar, that earth may echo forth

168.1. *Exeunt . . .* CALYPHAS] *Dyce 1; not in* O1–3, Q.

---

  172. *Rhadamanth and Aeacus*] sons of Zeus and judges of the dead.
  175. *virtue*] power.
  177. *affections*] feelings.
  178. *artier*] artery; cf. *One* II.vii.10 n.
  180. *remorseful*] compassionate: *O.E.D.* 2, first entry 1591. The King of Soria's curse anticipates precisely the affliction from which Tamburlaine actually dies. See *Two* V.iii.83 ff.
  182. *bridle*] L. and E. Feasey find a relation to Isaiah xxxvii.29.
  186–91.] perhaps echoing *Faerie Queene*, I.viii.11.

The far-resounding torments ye sustain,
As when an herd of lusty Cimbrian bulls
Run mourning round about the females' miss,
And stung with fury of their following   190
Fill all the air with troublous bellowing.
I will, with engines never exercised,
Conquer, sack, and utterly consume
Your cities and your golden palaces,
And with the flames that beat against the clouds   195
Incense the heavens and make the stars to melt,
As if they were the tears of Mahomet
For hot consumption of his country's pride;
And till by vision or by speech I hear
Immortal Jove say 'Cease, my Tamburlaine',   200
I will persist a terror to the world,
Making the meteors that, like armèd men,
Are seen to march upon the towers of heaven,
Run tilting round about the firmament
And break their burning lances in the air   205
For honour of my wondrous victories.
Come, bring them in to our pavilion.   *Exeunt.*

---

188. *Cimbrian bulls*] recalling an image from *Faerie Queene*, I.viii.11:
'as when in Cymbrian plaine / An heard of Bulles, whom kindly rage
doth sting, / Do for their milky mothers want complaine'. See p. 19
above. The Cimbri were a Teutonic tribe.

189. *the females' miss*] loss or lack of females; cf. 'I should have a heavy
miss of thee', *1H4*, V.iv.105.

190. *their following*] following them.

196. *Incense*] set on fire, consume with fire. Kocher (p. 233) points out
that this violates Renaissance meteorology, in which 'fire blazed immediately under the moon's sphere without damaging it'.

200.] Possibly recalling 1 Chron. xxi.15, 2 Sam. xxiv.16. See p. 76
above.

202–5.] the fiery impression of 'burning spears', formed by the kindling
of an exhalation in the highest region of Air (Heninger, pp. 91–3):
portents transformed into signs which Tamburlaine has occasioned in
honour of his own victories. Cf. *Two* III.ii.2–8 n., *Dido* IV.iv.117,
Lucan 530.

204. *tilting*] jousting; cf. *Two* I.iii.39 n.

Scene ii

OLYMPIA [*discovered*] *alone.*

Olympia. Distressed Olympia, whose weeping eyes
 Since thy arrival here beheld no sun,
 But closed within the compass of a tent
 Hath stained thy cheeks, and made thee look like death,
 Devise some means to rid thee of thy life   5
 Rather than yield to his detested suit
 Whose drift is only to dishonour thee.
 And since this earth, dewed with thy brinish tears,
 Affords no herbs whose taste may poison thee,
 Nor yet this air, beat often with thy sighs,   10
 Contagious smells and vapours to infect thee,
 Nor thy close cave a sword to murder thee,
 Let this invention be the instrument.

Enter THERIDAMAS.

Theridamas. Well met, Olympia, I sought thee in my tent,
 But when I saw the place obscure and dark   15
 Which with thy beauty thou wast wont to light,
 Enraged, I ran about the fields for thee,
 Supposing amorous Jove had sent his son,
 The winged Hermes, to convey thee hence—
 But now I find thee, and that fear is past.   20
 Tell me, Olympia, wilt thou grant my suit?
Olympia. My lord and husband's death, with my sweet
  son's,
 With whom I buried all affections
 Save grief and sorrow which torment my heart,
 Forbids my mind to entertain a thought   25

Heading. SCENE ii] *Dyce 1;* Actus. 4. Scaena. 3, *O1–3, Q.*   0.1.] *Oxberry;* Olympia alone. *O1–3, Q.*

 IV.ii.4. *Hath*] The antecedent would seem to be 'eyes', and that is
tolerable in Elizabethan grammar; but the verb also associates with
'Olympia' in this address by the character to herself.
 7. *drift*] purpose.
 12. *close*] secret.
 18–19.] Theridamas borrows Tamburlaine's conceit from *Two*
II.iv.107.
 23. *affections*] emotions, feelings.

That tends to love, but meditate on death,
A fitter subject for a pensive soul.

Theridamas. Olympia, pity him in whom thy looks
Have greater operation and more force
Than Cynthia's in the watery wilderness,   30
For with thy view my joys are at the full,
And ebb again as thou departest from me.

Olympia. Ah, pity me, my lord, and draw your sword,
Making a passage for my troubled soul,
Which beats against this prison to get out   35
And meet my husband and my loving son.

Theridamas. Nothing but still thy husband and thy son?
Leave this, my love, and listen more to me:
Thou shalt be stately queen of fair Argier,
And, clothed in costly cloth of massy gold,   40
Upon the marble turrets of my court
Sit like to Venus in her chair of state,
Commanding all thy princely eye desires;
And I will cast off arms and sit with thee,
Spending my life in sweet discourse of love. .   45

Olympia. No such discourse is pleasant in mine ears,
But that where every period ends with death
And every line begins with death again:
I cannot love, to be an empress.

Theridamas. Nay, lady, then if nothing will prevail, 50
I'll use some other means to make you yield.
Such is the sudden fury of my love,
I must and will be pleased, and you shall yield—
Come to the tent again.

---

49. *love, to*] Oxberry; *love to* O1–3, Q.

29. *operation*] efficacy, 'virtue'. Cf. *Two* II.iv.24 n., and Introduction, p. 51.

30.] i.e., the moon's influence on tides.

34–5.] The metaphors here enforce recall of Bajazeth's extremity, beating against his literal prison to 'make a passage for my loathèd life': *One* V.i.286–304.

47. *period*] sentence.

49.] Olympia seems to be saying that she could not love Theridamas even for the sake of becoming an empress. The absence of a comma after 'love' in O1 does not weigh against this reading of the line; without a comma, the sense is weaker.

Olympia. Stay, good my lord, and will you save my honour,   55
    I'll give your grace a present of such price
    As all the world cannot afford the like.
Theridamas. What is it?
Olympia. An ointment which a cunning alchemist
    Distillèd from the purest balsamum   60
    And simplest extracts of all minerals,
    In which the essential form of marble stone,
    Tempered by science metaphysical
    And spells of magic from the mouths of spirits,
    With which if you but 'noint your tender skin,   65
    Nor pistol, sword, nor lance can pierce your flesh.
Theridamas. Why, madam, think ye to mock me thus
    palpably?
Olympia. To prove it, I will 'noint my naked throat
    Which when you stab, look on your weapon's point,
    And you shall see't rebated with the blow.   70
Theridamas. Why gave you not your husband some of it if
    you loved him, and it so precious?
Olympia. My purpose was, my lord, to spend it so,
    But was prevented by his sudden end.
    And for a present easy proof hereof,   75
    That I dissemble not, try it on me.
Theridamas. I will, Olympia, and will keep it for
    The richest present of this eastern world.
                    She 'noints her throat.

71–2. *as prose in* O1–3, *Q; as verse* (it, / If) *Oxberry.*   76–7. *between
these two lines,* O3 *interposes Two* IV.iii.28–85 *(two pages).*

---

59 ff.] On the source in Ariosto, cf. Introduction, pp. 18–19 above.

60. *balsamum.*] *O.E.D.*'s earliest entry for the sense 'healthful pre-
servative essence' under *balsamum* is dated 1631.

61. *simplest extracts*] 'What alchemy terms the elements, or elemental
parts, of the minerals' (Ellis-Fermor, p. 252).

62. *form*] determinant principle, creative quality: to marble as soul is
to body. Cf. *Two* IV.i.111–15 n.

63. *Tempered*] brought to a proper consistency. Cf. *Two* II.iv.0.3.
science metaphysical] knowledge of agencies beyond the natural or
physical; the 'metaphysics of magicians' of *Dr Faustus*, i.48.

70. *rebated*] blunted.

71–2.] The 1590–1606 prose lineation may be accidental, but it sorts
well with Theridamas' prosaic lines elsewhere in the scene (e.g. 67, 54).

Olympia. Now stab, my lord, and mark your weapon's point,
That will be blunted if the blow be great.   80
Theridamas. Here then, Olympia—

                                        [*Stabs her.*]

What, have I slain her? Villain, stab thyself!
Cut off this arm that murderèd my love,
In whom the learned Rabbis of this age
Might find as many wondrous miracles   85
As in the theoria of the world!
Now hell is fairer than Elysium;
A greater lamp than that bright eye of heaven.
From whence the stars do borrow all their light,
Wanders about the black circumference,   90
And now the damnèd souls are free from pain,
For every Fury gazeth on her looks:
Infernal Dis is courting of my love,
Inventing masks and stately shows for her,
Opening the doors of his rich treasury   95
To entertain this queen of chastity;
Whose body shall be tombed with all the pomp
The treasure of my kingdom may afford.

                                Exit, taking her away.

81.1. *Stabs her.*] *Oxberry; not in O1–3, Q.*   87. Elysium] *Oxberry;*
Elisian *O1–2;* Elizian *O3, Q.*

---

81 ff.] Ariosto lends plausibility to the episode by having Isabel's suitor
'overlayed / With wine, that in his idle braine did worke' (Book xxix,
st. 26). A producer of *Tamburlaine* could achieve much by introducing a
spirit of playfulness, in tune with the incredulity expressed at l. 67, and
by having Olympia herself virtually thrust the blade home.
    84. *Rabbis*] sages (in a generalised sense).
    86. *theoria*] 'contemplation, survey?' (*O.E.D.*, citing only this instance).
Ellis-Fermor quotes 'the true theory of death' from Browne, *Religio
Medici,* i. §45.
    90. *black circumference*] recalling *Two* I.iii.145.
    93. *Dis*] Hades, ruler of the underworld; as at *One* II.vii.37. Elsewhere,
'infernal Jove' (e.g., *Two* I.iii.143). Virgil's Juppiter Stygius.
    96. *entertain*] receive, welcome. The affinity of this speech to Tambur-
laine's lament as Zenocrate dies is focused in the close recall of the refrain
'To entertain divine Zenocrate' (*Two* II.iii.17 ff.).

Scene iii

[*Enter*] TAMBURLAINE, *drawn in his chariot by* TREBI-
ZOND *and* SORIA *with bits in their mouths, reins in his left
hand, in his right hand a whip, with which he scourgeth
them.* TECHELLES, THERIDAMAS, USUMCASANE, AMYRAS,
CELEBINUS; [ORCANES *of*] NATOLIA *and* JERUSALEM *led
by with five or six common* Soldiers.

Tamburlaine. Holla, ye pampered jades of Asia!
What, can ye draw but twenty miles a day,
And have so proud a chariot at your heels,
And such a coachman as great Tamburlaine?
But from Asphaltis, where I conquered you,   5
To Byron here where thus I honour you?
The horse that guide the golden eye of heaven
And blow the morning from their nostrils,
Making their fiery gait above the clouds,
Are not so honoured in their governor   10
As you, ye slaves, in mighty Tamburlaine.
The headstrong jades of Thrace Alcides tamed,
That King Aegeus fed with human flesh

Heading. SCENE iii] *Dyce 1;* Actus: 4. Scaena. 4. *O1–3, Q.*   o.1. *Enter*]
Robinson; not in O1–3, Q.

IV.iii.o.1. *drawn in his chariot*] Cf. *One* IV.ii.78 n.

1. *pampered jades*] Marlowe draws the phrase from Golding's Ovid,
'pampered Jades of Thrace' (ix.238): see *P.M.L.A.,* LII (1937), 902–5,
and l. 12 below. The phrase is also found in George Gascoigne, *The
Steele Glas,* 1576 (Leonard Nathanson, *N.&Q.,* CCIII (1958), 53–4).

5. *Asphaltis*] the bituminous lake near Babylon; cf. *Two* III.v.18. The
'Limnasphaltis' of *Two* V.i.17 n. Pendry–Maxwell suggest '?somewhere
near Aleppo'.

6. *Byron*] a town near Babylon.

7. *horse*] This was common as the plural form until the seventeenth
century (*O.E.D. sb.* 1b).

7–10.] Tamburlaine returns to the comparison in *Two* V.iii.230–5; cf.
Aeneid, xii.114 f.

8. *nostrils*] trisyllabic, as the 1590–1606 texts' spelling 'nosterils'
indicates.

12–14.] Not Aegeus, father of Theseus, but King Diomedes of Thrace
was the owner of the savage mares, fed on human flesh, which Hercules
subdued as his eighth labour. Marlowe has perhaps let his attention stray
to the fifth labour, the cleansing of the stables of Augeias, King of Elis.

And made so wanton that they knew their strengths,
Were not subdued with valour more divine   15
Than you by this unconquered arm of mine.
To make you fierce, and fit my appetite,
You shall be fed with flesh as raw as blood
And drink in pails the strongest muscadel;
If you can live with it, then live, and draw   20
My chariot swifter than the racking clouds;
If not, then die like beasts, and fit for nought
But perches for the black and fatal ravens.
Thus am I right the scourge of highest Jove,
And see the figure of my dignity   25
By which I hold my name and majesty.

Amyras. Let me have coach, my lord, that I may ride
And thus be drawn with these two idle kings.

Tamburlaine. Thy youth forbids such ease, my kingly boy:
They shall tomorrow draw my chariot   30
While these their fellow kings may be refreshed.

Orcanes. O thou that swayest the region under earth,
And art a king as absolute as Jove,
Come as thou didst in fruitful Sicily,
Surveying all the glories of the land—   35
And as thou tookest the fair Proserpina,
Joying the fruit of Ceres' garden plot,
For love, for honour, and to make her queen,
So for just hate, for shame, and to subdue
This proud contemner of thy dreadful power,   40

28–85.] *interposed between Two* IV.ii.76 *and* 77 *in O3.*

14. *wanton*] skittish, refractory (*O.E.D.* 1b.).

19. *muscadel*] or muscatel, a strong sweet wine.

21. *racking*] moving before the wind; a suggestive secondary meaning, 'galloping at full stretch', is possible: Robert Cockcroft, *Renaissance and Modern Studies*, viii (1968), 37.

23. *fatal*] ominous (*O.E.D.* 4c, first entry).

24. *right*] properly, altogether, aright.

25. *figure*] image, emblem; as at *Two* II.ii.38. Pendry–Maxwell suggest 'i.e. his whip'.

32–8.] 'For the story of the rape of Persephone and the wanderings of Ceres, see *Metam.*, V.385 ff.' (Ellis-Fermor). The 'king' invoked is Dis (Pluto): cf. *Two* IV.ii.93 n.

40. *contemner*] despiser.

Come once in fury and survey his pride,
Haling him headlong to the lowest hell!
Theridamas. Your majesty must get some bits for these,
To bridle their contemptuous cursing tongues
That like unruly never-broken jades   45
Break through the hedges of their hateful mouths,
And pass their fixèd bounds exceedingly.
Techelles. Nay, we will break the hedges of their mouths
And pull their kicking colts out of their pastures.
Usumcasane. Your majesty already hath devised   50
A mean as fit as may be to restrain
These coltish coach-horse tongues from blasphemy.

               [CELEBINUS *bridles* ORCANES.]

Celebinus. How like you that, sir king? Why speak you not?
Jerusalem. Ah cruel brat, sprung from a tyrant's loins,
How like his cursèd father he begins   55
To practise taunts and bitter tyrannies!
Tamburlaine. Ay Turk, I tell thee, this same boy is he
That must, advanced in higher pomp than this,
Rifle the kingdoms I shall leave unsacked
If Jove, esteeming me too good for earth,   60
Raise me to match the fair Aldebaran
Above the threefold astracism of heaven

52.1.] *This ed.; not in O1–3, Q.*

44–52.] The gloating, strained wordplay is aptly crude, recalling the
bantering torture of Bajazeth in *One* IV.iv.

50–2.] Cf. 'They will talk still, my lord, if you do not bridle them'
(*Two* V.i.146). Marlowe may have found a hint for this passage in Whetstone's account of an exchange between Tamburlaine and a Genoese
merchant: see Appendix, p. 319.

61–2.] *Aldebaran* is the bright red eye in the constellation Taurus. To
match it would be to provide Taurus with an equally bright second eye,
perhaps, its present one being a far dimmer star. The *threefold astracism*
may well be the three prominent stars which stand out among the Hyades
to form a nose below Aldebaran (Woolf). *Astracism* is a form of 'asterism'
(constellation): *O.E.D.* has one other instance, from 1695. Kocher (p. 227)
explains 'threefold' in terms either of a received division of the constellations or of the ascending levels of the cosmos in Renaissance terms.
Pendry–Maxwell suggest 'division of cosmos into earth, planets and stars'.
H. W. Crundell refers me to the 'fiery Trigon' of *2H4*, II.iv.255: a
conjunction of Aries, Leo, and Sagittarius. Woolf's explanation seems the
most convincing.

Before I conquer all the triple world.
Now fetch me out the Turkish concubines:
I will prefer them for the funeral   65
They have bestowed on my abortive son.
                        The Concubines *are brought in.*
Where are my common soldiers now that fought
So lion-like upon Asphaltis' plains?

Soldiers. Here, my lord.

Tamburlaine. Hold ye, tall soldiers, take ye queens apiece—   70
I mean such queens as were kings' concubines—
Take them, divide them and their jewels too,
And let them equally serve all your turns.

Soldiers. We thank your majesty.

Tamburlaine. Brawl not, I warn you, for your lechery,   75
For every man that so offends shall die.

Orcanes. Injurious tyrant, wilt thou so defame
The hateful fortunes of thy victory,
To exercise upon such guiltless dames
The violence of thy common soldiers' lust?   80

Tamburlaine. Live content then, ye slaves, and meet not me
With troops of harlots at your slothful heels.

Concubines. O pity us, my lord, and save our honours!

Tamburlaine. Are ye not gone, ye villains, with your spoils?
                        They [Soldiers] *run away with the* Ladies.

Jerusalem. O merciless, infernal cruelty!   85

Tamburlaine. Save your honours! 'Twere but time indeed,
Lost long before you knew what honour meant.

Theridamas. It seems they meant to conquer us, my lord,

---

81. content] *O1–3, Q;* continent *Oxberry.*

---

63. *the triple world*] the world as known in Tamburlaine's time, comprising Europe, Asia, and Africa. See *One* IV.iv.77–84 n.

65. *prefer*] promote, advance.

66. *abortive*] produced by abortion; useless, imperfect (*O.E.D.* 2, earliest instance 1593).

70. *tall*] bold, valiant; as at *Two* IV.i.33, but without sarcasm here.
queens] punning on 'queans', harlots.

78. *fortunes*] Cf. Prologue to Part One, 8 n.

81. *content*] There seems no need to emend to 'continent', as editors have done since Oxberry, purely out of preference for its more precise meaning.

And make us jesting pageants for their trulls.

Tamburlaine. And now themselves shall make our pageant,   90
And common soldiers jest with all their trulls.
Let them take pleasure soundly in their spoils
Till we prepare our march to Babylon,
Whither we next make expedition.

Techelles. Let us not be idle, then, my lord,   95
But presently be prest to conquer it.

Tamburlaine. We will, Techelles—forward then, ye jades!
Now crouch, ye kings of greatest Asia,
And tremble when ye hear this scourge will come
That whips down cities and controlleth crowns,   100
Adding their wealth and treasure to my store.
The Euxine Sea, north to Natolia;
The Terrene, west; the Caspian, north-north-east;
And on the south, Sinus Arabicus—
Shall all be loaden with the martial spoils   105
We will convey with us to Persia.
Then shall my native city Samarcanda
And crystal waves of fresh Jaertis' stream,
The pride and beauty of her princely seat,
Be famous through the furthest continents,   110
For there my palace royal shall be placed
Whose shining turrets shall dismay the heavens
And cast the fame of Ilion's tower to hell.
Thorough the streets with troops of conquered kings
I'll ride in golden armour like the sun,   115
And in my helm a triple plume shall spring,
Spangled with diamonds dancing in the air,
To note me emperor of the threefold world:

---

89. *pageants*] See p. 28.
trulls] strumpets.
94. *expedition*] haste.
96. *prest*] ready.
100. *controlleth crowns*] holds sway over kings.
102. *Euxine Sea*] Black Sea.
103. *Terrene*] the Mediterranean.
104. *Sinus Arabicus*] the Red Sea.
107–8.] Cf. *Two* IV.i.108 n.
113. *Ilion*] Troy.
118. *three-fold world*] Cf. l. 63 n. above.

Like to an almond tree ymounted high
Upon the lofty and celestial mount   120
Of ever-green Selinus, quaintly decked
With blooms more white than Herycina's brows,
Whose tender blossoms tremble every one
At every little breath that thorough heaven is blown.
Then in my coach like Saturn's royal son,   125
Mounted his shining chariot, gilt with fire,
And drawn with princely eagles through the path
Paved with bright crystal and enchased with stars,
When all the gods stand gazing at his pomp—
So will I ride through Samarcanda streets   130
Until my soul, dissevered from this flesh,
Shall mount the milk-white way and meet him there.
To Babylon, my lords, to Babylon!   *Exeunt.*

Finis Actus quarti.

121. ever-green] *Robinson;* every greene *O1–3, Q.*   126. chariot] *Dyce 1;* chariots *O1–3, Q.*

119–24.] adapted from *Faerie Queene*, I.vii.32. The alexandrine at 124, and some descriptive niceties, identify Marlowe, not Spenser, as the borrower. See p. 19 above.

121. *Selinus*] Sicilian town, alluded to in *Aeneid*, iii.705; site of a temple of Jupiter.

122. *Herycina*] Venus, so called after Mount Eryx in Sicily, the site of a shrine to her: cf. Ovid, *Metam.*, v.363, Horace, *Odes*, I., and 'Erycine' in *Volpone*, III.iv.204.

125–8.] The *path* is the Milky Way, highway to the palace of Jove, *Saturn's royal son*. See Heninger, p. 106, who also refers us from the 'milk-white way' of l. 132 to the 'milk-white paths, whereon the gods might trace / To Jove's high court', *Hero*, i.298.

128. *enchased*] Cf. *One* IV.ii.9.

131. *soul dissevered from this flesh*] Cf. *Two* V.iii.168–9.

Act V

Scene i

Enter the GOVERNOR OF BABYLON *upon the walls with*
[MAXIMUS *and*] *others.*

Governor. What saith Maximus?
Maximus. My lord, the breach the enemy hath made
    Gives such assurance of our overthrow
    That little hope is left to save our lives
    Or hold our city from the conqueror's hands.   5
    Then hang out flags, my lord, of humble truce,
    And satisfy the people's general prayers
    That Tamburlaine's intolerable wrath
    May be suppressed by our submission.
Governor. Villain, respects thou more thy slavish life   10
    Than honour of thy country or thy name?
    Is not my life and state as dear to me,
    The city and my native country's weal,
    As any thing of price with thy conceit?
    Have we not hope, for all our battered walls,   15
    To live secure and keep his forces out,
    When this our famous lake of Limnasphaltis
    Makes walls afresh with every thing that falls
    Into the liquid substance of his stream,
    More strong than are the gates of death or hell?   20
    What faintness should dismay our courages
    When we are thus defenced against our foe
    And have no terror but his threat'ning looks?

0.1. MAXIMUS *and*] Oxberry; *not in O1–3, Q.*

V.i.0.1. *upon the walls*] On staging, see Introduction, section 4.
14.] as anything that you think valuable.
17. *Limnasphaltis*] the bituminous lake near Babylon; cf. 'Asphaltis'
where Tamburlaine had defeated Orcanes, *Two* IV.iii.5 n.

Enter another [Citizen *above*], *kneeling to the* GOVERNOR.

Citizen. My lord, if ever you did deed of ruth
 And now will work a refuge to our lives,   25
 Offer submission, hang up flags of truce,
 That Tamburlaine may pity our distress
 And use us like a loving conqueror.
 Though this be held his last day's dreadful siege
 Wherein he spareth neither man nor child,   30
 Yet are there Christians of Georgia here
 Whose state he ever pitied and relieved,
 Will get his pardon, if your grace would send.
Governor. How is my soul environèd,
 And this eternised city Babylon   35
 Filled with a pack of faint-heart fugitives
 That thus entreat their shame and servitude!

[*Enter another* Citizen.]

Second Citizen. My lord, if ever you will win our hearts,
 Yield up the town, save our wives and children:
 For I will cast myself from off these walls   40
 Or die some death of quickest violence
 Before I bide the wrath of Tamburlaine.
Governor. Villains, cowards, traitors to our state,
 Fall to the earth and pierce the pit of hell,
 That legions of tormenting spirits may vex   45
 Your slavish bosoms with continual pains!
 I care not, nor the town will never yield
 As long as any life is in my breast.

Enter THERIDAMAS *and* TECHELLES, *with other* Soldiers.

Theridamas. Thou desperate governor of Babylon,

23.1. Citizen] *Oxberry; not in O1–3, Q.* *above*] *Dyce 1; not in O1–3, Q.*
24. Citizen] *Oxberry; not in O1–3, Q.* 37.1.] *Dyce 1; not in O1–3, Q.*
38. *Second* Citizen.] *Oxberry* [CIT.]; *Another O1–3, Q.* 49. *Therida-*
mas] *Oxberry; not in O1–3, Q.*

24. *ruth*] pity.
31–3.] a return to the concept of Tamburlaine as the scourge of the
Christian God: cf. *One* III.iii.44 n.
34.] Among nineteenth-century editors' suggestions for supplying two
syllables here are 'Alas' to open the line and 'with cares' to close it.
35. *eternised*] everlastingly famous. Cf. *One* I.ii.72, *Two* V.ii.54.

To save thy life, and us a little labour,   50
Yield speedily the city to our hands,
Or else be sure thou shalt be forced with pains
More exquisite than ever traitor felt.

Governor. Tyrant, I turn the traitor in thy throat,
And will defend it in despite of thee.   55
Call up the soldiers to defend these walls.

Techelles. Yield, foolish governor—we offer more
Than ever yet we did to such proud slaves
As durst resist us till our third day's siege.
Thou seest us prest to give the last assault,   60
And that shall bide no more regard of parley.

Governor. Assault and spare not; we will never yield.

Alarm; and they scale the walls. [Exeunt above.]

Enter TAMBURLAINE [*all in black, drawn in his chariot by*
TREBIZOND *and* SORIA], *with* USUMCASANE, AMYRAS *and*
CELEBINUS, *with others; the two spare kings* [ORCANES *of*
NATOLIA, *and* JERUSALEM].

Tamburlaine. The stately buildings of fair Babylon
Whose lofty pillars, higher than the clouds,
Were wont to guide the seaman in the deep,   65
Being carried thither by the cannon's force,
Now fill the mouth of Limnasphaltis' lake
And make a bridge unto the battered walls.
Where Belus, Ninus, and great Alexander
Have rode in triumph, triumphs Tamburlaine,   70
Whose chariot wheels have burst th'Assyrians' bones,

56–112.] *leaf missing from Bodleian copy of O1.*   62.1. *Exeunt above*]
Jump; not in O1–3, Q.   62.2. *all in black*] *This ed.; not in O1–3, Q.*
drawn . . . SORIA] after Dyce 1; not in O1–3, Q.   62.4.] *after* kings
Dyce 1 has led by soldiers; *not in O1–3, Q.*

---

53. *exquisite*] excruciating (*O.E.D.* 3b, first entry 1603).
60. *prest*] ready.
69–70.] 'The three successive masters of Babylon here come before
Tamburlaine: Belus, the legendary founder, himself the son of Poseidon;
Ninus, the hardly less legendary founder of the empire of Nineveh, whose
queen, Semiramis, built the famous walls of Babylon; and Alexander of
Macedon, who overcame the then effete Babylonian empire in 331 B.C.'
(Ellis-Fermor, pp. 262–3).
71. *burst*] broken, shattered.

Drawn with these kings on heaps of carcasses.
Now in the place where fair Semiramis,
Courted by kings and peers of Asia,
Hath trod the measures, do my soldiers march;   75
And in the streets, where brave Assyrian dames
Have rid in pomp like rich Saturnia,
With furious words and frowning visages
My horsemen brandish their unruly blades.

Enter THERIDAMAS *and* TECHELLES, *bringing the* GOVERNOR
of BABYLON.

Who have ye there, my lords?   80
Theridamas. The sturdy governor of Babylon,
That made us all the labour for the town
And used such slender reckoning of your majesty.
Tamburlaine. Go, bind the villain—he shall hang in chains
Upon the ruins of this conquered town.   85
Sirrah, the view of our vermilion tents,
Which threatened more than if the region
Next underneath the element of fire
Were full of comets and of blazing stars
Whose flaming trains should reach down to the earth,   90
Could not affright you—no, nor I myself,
The wrathful messenger of mighty Jove,
That with his sword hath quailed all earthly kings,
Could not persuade you to submission,
But still the ports were shut: villain, I say,   95
Should I but touch the rusty gates of hell,

---

72. *with*] by.
73. *Semiramis*] See ll. 69–70 n. above, and *Two* III.v.36–7.
75. *measures*] grave or stately dances.
76. *brave*] finely-dressed, grand.
77. *Saturnia*] Juno.
86. *vermilion tents*] see Introduction, pp. 24–6.
87–90.] In received Aristotelian theory, a comet was an ignited mass of exhalations at the uppermost limits of the earth's atmosphere. Cf. Heninger, pp. 87, 90.
93. *quailed*] overpowered; daunted, caused to quail. Cf. *Lucan*, 311. The common modern usage is found at l. 126 below.
95. *ports*] gates; cf. *One* II.i.42.

The triple-headed Cerberus would howl
And wake black Jove to crouch and kneel to me;
But I have sent volleys of shot to you,
Yet could not enter till the breach was made.   100
Governor. Nor, if my body could have stopt the breach,
Shouldst thou have entered, cruel Tamburlaine.
'Tis not thy bloody tents can make me yield,
Nor yet thyself, the anger of the Highest,
For, though thy cannon shook the city walls,   105
My heart did never quake, or courage faint.
Tamburlaine. Well now I'll make it quake. Go draw him up,
Hang him in chains upon the city walls
And let my soldiers shoot the slave to death.
Governor. Vile monster, born of some infernal hag,   110
And sent from hell to tyrannise on earth,
Do all thy worst: nor death, nor Tamburlaine,
Torture, or pain, can daunt my dreadless mind.
Tamburlaine. Up with him then, his body shall be scarred.
Governor. But Tamburlaine, in Limnasphaltis' lake   115
There lies more gold than Babylon is worth,
Which when the city was besieged I hid—
Save but my life and I will give it thee.
Tamburlaine. Then, for all your valour, you would save
        your life?
Whereabout lies it?   120
Governor. Under a hollow bank, right opposite
Against the western gate of Babylon.
Tamburlaine. Go thither some of you and take his gold;
        [*Exeunt* Soldiers.]
The rest, forward with execution!
Away with him hence, let him speak no more: 125

123.1. *Exeunt* Soldiers] *after Dyce 1; not in O1-3, Q.*

97.] Cf. the 'triple-headed dog' of *One* I.ii.160; both passages carrying
Herculean suggestions.
98. *black Jove*] Pluto. Invoked in vengeance against Tamburlaine by
Orcanes at *Two* IV.iii.32 ff. Cf. *One* II.vii.36-38, *Two* I.iii.143.
110-11.] Note that Tamburlaine is in black—which also gives extra
point to l. 98 above.
115-22.] The episode does not occur in Marlowe's sources, though
Ellis-Fermor (p. 264) notes a parallel in one account of Timur.

I think I make your courage something quail.
                [GOVERNOR *is taken away by* Soldiers.]
When this is done, we'll march from Babylon,
And make our greatest haste to Persia.
These jades are broken-winded, and half tired:
Unharness them, and let me have fresh horse.   130
        [Soldiers *unharness* TREBIZOND *and* SORIA.]
So, now their best is done to honour me,
Take them, and hang them both up presently.

Trebizond. Vile tyrant, barbarous, bloody Tamburlaine!

Tamburlaine. Take them away, Theridamas, see them
    despatched.

Theridamas. I will, my lord.   135
    [*Exit* THERIDAMAS *with the Kings of* TREBIZOND *and*
                          SORIA.]

Tamburlaine. Come, Asian viceroys, to your tasks a while
And take such fortune as your fellows felt.

Orcanes. First let thy Scythian horse tear both our limbs
Rather than we should draw thy chariot
And like base slaves abject our princely minds   140
To vile and ignominious servitude.

Jerusalem. Rather lend me thy weapon, Tamburlaine,
That I may sheathe it in this breast of mine:
A thousand deaths could not torment our hearts
More than the thought of this doth vex our souls.   145

Amyras. They will talk still, my lord, if you do not bridle
    them.

Tamburlaine. Bridle them, and let me to my coach.

They bridle them. [*The* GOVERNOR *of* BABYLON *appears
    hanging in chains. Re-enter* THERIDAMAS.]

Amyras. See now, my lord, how brave the captain hangs!

126.1. GOVERNOR . . . Soldiers] *after Dyce 1; not in* O1–3, Q.   130.1.
Soldiers . . . SORIA] *after Dyce 1; not in* O1–3, Q.   133. Vile] O1–3,
Q (all Vild); Wild *Oxberry.*   135.1. *Exit* . . . SORIA] *Robinson; not in*
O1–3, Q.   147.1–2 *The* GOVERNOR . . . THERIDAMAS.] *Dyce 1; not in*
O1–3, Q.

---

    132. *presently*] immediately.
    140. *abject*] degrade, debase.
    148, 149. *brave*] excellent(ly) (Jump); also, sarcastically, courageous
in l. 148.

Tamburlaine. 'Tis brave indeed, my boy, well done!
      Shoot first, my lord, and then the rest shall follow.   150
Theridamas. Then have at him to begin withal.

                                                  THERIDAMAS *shoots.*

Governor. Yet save my life, and let this wound appease
      The mortal fury of great Tamburlaine.
Tamburlaine. No, though Asphaltis' lake were liquid gold
      And offered me as ransom for thy life,   155
      Yet shouldst thou die. Shoot at him all at once.

                                                  They shoot.

      So, now he hangs like Bagdeth's governor,
      Having as many bullets in his flesh
      As there be breaches in her battered wall.
      Go now, and bind the burghers hand and foot,   160
      And cast them headlong in the city's lake:
      Tartars and Persians shall inhabit there,
      And to command the city, I will build
      A citadel, that all Africa,
      Which hath been subject to the Persian king,   165
      Shall pay me tribute for, in Babylon.
Techelles. What shall be done with their wives and children,
      my lord?
Tamburlaine. Techelles, drown them all, man, woman, and
      child;
      Leave not a Babylonian in the town.   170
Techelles. I will about it straight; come, soldiers.

                              Exeunt [TECHELLES *with* Soldiers].

Tamburlaine. Now, Casane, where's the Turkish Alcaron
      And all the heaps of superstitious books
      Found in the temples of that Mahomet
      Whom I have thought a god? They shall be burnt.   175
Usumcasane. Here they are, my lord.
Tamburlaine. Well said; let there be a fire presently.

171.1. *with* Soldiers] *Oxberry; not in O1-3, Q.*

---

      157. *Bagdeth*] Bagdad, 'equated with Babylon' (Pendry–Maxwell).
      171.1. Exeunt . . . *Soldiers*] I owe the revised stage direction to F.D.H.
      172. *Alcaron*] Koran.
      172 ff.] The historical Timur was, as (for instance) Perondinus insists,
a devout Mahommedan.

[*They light a fire.*]

In vain, I see, men worship Mahomet:
My sword hath sent millions of Turks to hell,
Slew all his priests, his kinsmen, and his friends,   180
And yet I live untouched by Mahomet.
There is a God full of revenging wrath,
From whom the thunder and the lightning breaks,
Whose scourge I am, and him will I obey.
So Casane, fling them in the fire.   185

[*They burn the books.*]

Now, Mahomet, if thou have any power,
Come down thyself and work a miracle;
Thou art not worthy to be worshippèd
That suffers flames of fire to burn the writ
Wherein the sum of thy religion rests.   190
Why sendest thou not a furious whirlwind down,
To blow thy Alcaron up to thy throne
Where men report thou sittest by God himself—
Or vengeance on the head of Tamburlaine
That shakes his sword against thy majesty   195
And spurns the abstracts of thy foolish laws?
Well, soldiers, Mahomet remains in hell;
He cannot hear the voice of Tamburlaine.
Seek out another godhead to adore,
The God that sits in heaven, if any god,   200
For he is God alone, and none but he.

177.1. *They . . . fire.*] Dyce *1; not in* O1–3, Q.   185.1.] Dyce *1; not in*
O1–3, Q.

---

182. *a God full of revenging wrath*] the power that 'thundered vengeance'
at the cost of Sigismond, *Two* II.iii.2. L. and E. Feasey refer to the God
of Psalm xviii.7–14.

186–7.] It is possible that Marlowe refers provocatively to the challenge
to Christ on the Cross (cf. Matt. xxvii.40): Kocher, p. 88.

191–2. *a furious whirlwind . . . throne*] Mahomet, if he were to do so,
would not violate Aristotelian meterology: cf. *Mete.*, III.i.371a (Loeb,
p. 237).

200–1.] Kocher, p. 87, notes Scriptural parallels in Deut. xxxii.39, and
iv.35: 'the Lord he is God, and there is none else beside him'. But
Kocher needlessly isolates the phrase 'if any God' as part of 'Marlowe's
war against Christianity' (pp. 89–90).

[*Re-enter* TECHELLES]

Techelles. I have fulfilled your highness' will, my lord:
      Thousands of men, drowned in Asphaltis' lake,
      Have made the water swell above the banks,
      And fishes fed by human carcasses,   205
      Amazed, swim up and down upon the waves
      As when they swallow asafoetida,
      Which makes them fleet aloft and gasp for air.
Tamburlaine. Well then, my friendly lords, what now
            remains
      But that we leave sufficient garrison   210
      And presently depart to Persia,
      To triumph after all our victories?
Theridamas. Ay, good my lord, let us in haste to Persia,
      And let this captain be removed the walls
      To some high hill about the city here.   215
Tamburlaine. Let it be so; about it, soldiers—
      But stay, I feel myself distempered suddenly.
Techelles. What is it dares distemper Tamburlaine?
Tamburlaine. Something, Techelles, but I know not what;
      But forth, ye vassals: whatsoe'er it be,   220
      Sickness or death can never conquer me.   *Exeunt.*

SCENE ii

Enter CALLAPINE, AMASIA, [Captain, Soldiers,] *with drums
and trumpets.*

Callapine. King of Amasia, now our mighty host

201.1. *Re-enter* TECHELLES.] *Oxberry; not in O1–3, Q.*   205. fed] *Ox-
berry;* feed *O1–3, Q.*   207. asafoetida] *Oxberry* (Assafoetida)*; Assafitida
O1–3, Q.*   *Heading.* SCENE ii] *Robinson;* Actus. 5. Scaena. 4. *O1–3,
Q;* SCENE IV *Oxberry.*   0.1. Captain] *Dyce 2; not in O1–3, Q.*
Soldiers] *Oxberry; not in O1–3, Q.*

205.] 'Marlowe's imagination misled him slightly when he introduced
fishes into the bituminous lake of Babylon' (Ellis-Fermor, p. 268).
      207. *asafoetida*] a resinous gum with a strong smell, used in medicine.
      208. *fleet*] float; as in *Dido*, IV.iv.134, *Edward II*, I.iv.49.
      217.] The onset of illness can be taken variously, as a punishment for
impiety or as coincidental with it. Marlowe may not intend us to resolve
the question; and Tamburlaine's defiance of Mahomet was itself in the
name of another God-figure.

Marcheth in Asia Major, where the streams
Of Euphrates and Tigris swiftly runs,
And here may we behold great Babylon
Circled about with Limnasphaltis' lake,   5
Where Tamburlaine with all his army lies,
Which being faint and weary with the siege,
We may lie ready to encounter him
Before his host be full from Babylon,
And so revenge our latest grievous loss   10
If God or Mahomet send any aid.

Amasia. Doubt not, my lord, but we shall conquer him:
The monster that hath drunk a sea of blood
And yet gapes still for more to quench his thirst,
Our Turkish swords shall headlong send to hell,   15
And that vile carcass drawn by warlike kings
The fowls shall eat, for never sepulchre
Shall grace that base-born tyrant Tamburlaine.

Callapine. When I record my parents' slavish life,
Their cruel death, mine own captivity,   20
My viceroys' bondage under Tamburlaine,
Methinks I could sustain a thousand deaths
To be revenged of all his villainy.
Ah sacred Mahomet, thou that hast seen
Millions of Turks perish by Tamburlaine,   25
Kingdoms made waste, brave cities sacked and burnt,
And but one host is left to honour thee,
Aid thy obedient servant Callapine
And make him, after all these overthrows,
To triumph over cursèd Tamburlaine.   30

Amasia. Fear not, my lord, I see great Mahomet
Clothèd in purple clouds, and on his head
A chaplet brighter than Apollo's crown,
Marching about the air with armèd men
To join with you against this Tamburlaine.   35

Captain. Renownèd general, mighty Callapine,

---

36. *Captain.*] Dyce 2; *not in* O1–3, Q.

V.ii.9. *full from Babylon*] i.e., back to full strength after the siege; cf.
l. 58 below.
    19. *record*] call to mind.

Though God himself and holy Mahomet
Should come in person to resist your power,
Yet might your mighty host encounter all
And pull proud Tamburlaine upon his knees   40
To sue for mercy at your highness' feet.

Callapine. Captain, the force of Tamburlaine is great,
His fortune greater, and the victories
Wherewith he hath so sore dismayed the world
Are greatest to discourage all our drifts;   45
Yet when the pride of Cynthia is at full
She wanes again, and so shall his, I hope,
For we have here the chief selected men
Of twenty several kingdoms at the least,
Nor ploughman, priest, nor merchant stays at home: 50
All Turkey is in arms with Callapine.
And never will we sunder camps and arms
Before himself or his be conquerèd.
This is the time that must eternise me
For conquering the tyrant of the world.   55
Come, soldiers, let us lie in wait for him,
And if we find him absent from his camp
Or that it be rejoined again at full,
Assail it and be sure of victory.   *Exeunt.*

SCENE iii

[*Enter*] THERIDAMAS, TECHELLES, USUMCASANE.

Theridamas. Weep, heavens, and vanish into liquid tears!
Fall, stars that govern his nativity,
And summon all the shining lamps of heaven

---

45. *drifts*] purposes; cf. *One* I.ii.69.
51.] The line echoes the description of Tamburlaine's host at *Two*
I.i.72, 76.
54. *eternise*] immortalize.
58. *Or that*] Before.
rejoined] reassembled.
V.iii.1–9.] The lines have affinities with the opening of *1H6*.

To cast their bootless fires to the earth
And shed their feeble influence in the air;   5
Muffle your beauties with eternal clouds,
For hell and darkness pitch their pitchy tents
And Death with armies of Cimmerian spirits
Gives battle 'gainst the heart of Tamburlaine.
Now, in defiance of that wonted love   10
Your sacred virtues poured upon his throne
And made his state an honour to the heavens,
These cowards invisibly assail his soul
And threaten conquest on our sovereign;
But if he die, your glories are disgraced,   15
Earth droops and says that hell in heaven is placed.

Techelles. O then, ye powers that sway eternal seats
And guide this massy substance of the earth,
If you retain desert of holiness,
As your supreme estates instruct our thoughts,   20
Be not inconstant, careless of your fame,
Bear not the burden of your enemies' joys
Triumphing in his fall whom you advanced;
But as his birth, life, health, and majesty
Were strangely blest and governèd by heaven,   25
So honour, heaven, till heaven dissolvèd be,
His birth, his life, his health, and majesty.

Usumcasane. Blush, heaven, to lose the honour of thy name,
To see thy footstool set upon thy head,
And let no baseness in thy haughty breast   30
Sustain a shame of such inexcellence,
To see the devils mount in angels' thrones

---

4. *bootless*] unavailing.

7.] See *One* I.ii.22 n.

8. *Cimmerian*] 'Of or belonging to the Cimmerii, a people fabled by the ancients to live in perpetual darkness. Hence, proverbially used as a qualification of dense darkness' (*O.E.D.*, first instance 1598). Used earlier in the play, of clouds at *One* III.ii.77, and of the Styx, *One* V.i.234.

19. *desert of holiness*] worthiness of religious worship.

20. *estates*] station, rank.

25. *governèd*] cared for.

29.] 'A reminiscence of Psalm cx.1' (Ellis-Fermor, p. 271). See *One* IV.ii.14 n.

31. *inexcellence*] sole instance in *O.E.D.*

And angels dive into the pools of hell.
And though they think their painful date is out
And that their power is puissant as Jove's,   35
Which makes them manage arms against thy state,
Yet make them feel the strength of Tamburlaine,
Thy instrument and note of majesty,
Is greater far than they can thus subdue,
For if he die, thy glory is disgraced,   40
Earth droops and says that hell in heaven is placed.

>   [*Enter* TAMBURLAINE, *drawn by the captive kings*
>   ORCANES *of* NATOLIA *and* JERUSALEM; AMYRAS,
>   CELEBINUS, *and* Physicians.]

Tamburlaine. What daring god torments my body thus
    And seeks to conquer mighty Tamburlaine?
    Shall sickness prove me now to be a man
    That have been termed the terror of the world?   45
    Techelles and the rest, come take your swords
    And threaten him whose hand afflicts my soul;
    Come let us march against the powers of heaven
    And set black streamers in the firmament
    To signify the slaughter of the gods—   50
    Ah friends, what shall I do? I cannot stand.
    Come, carry me to war against the gods,
    That thus envy the health of Tamburlaine.
Theridamas. Ah, good my lord, leave these impatient words,
    Which add much danger to your malady.   55
Tamburlaine. Why shall I sit and languish in this pain?
    No, strike the drums, and, in revenge of this,

41.1–3.] *after Dyce 1; not in O1–3, Q.*

---

34. *they . . . out*] they (the devils) think their allotted period of suffering
is over.

36. *thy*] i.e., heaven's. Tamburlaine had invoked Jove as precedent
inciting him to 'manage arms against thy [Cosroe's] state' in *One* II.vii.16.

38. *note*] mark, sign.

41.1–2.] Dyce 1 conjectures '*perhaps the poet intended that Tamburlaine
should enter at the commencement of this scene*'.

49. *streamers*] pennons; recalling the 'mournful streamer' set up in
memory of Zenocrate, *Two* III.ii.19, and the 'streaming colours' of *One*
IV.iii.o.1.

Come, let us charge our spears and pierce his breast
Whose shoulders bear the axis of the world,
That if I perish, heaven and earth may fade.   60
Theridamas, haste to the court of Jove:
Will him to send Apollo hither straight
To cure me, or I'll fetch him down myself.

Techelles. Sit still, my gracious lord, this grief will cease,
And cannot last, it is so violent.   65

Tamburlaine. Not last, Techelles? No, for I shall die:
See where my slave, the ugly monster Death,
Shaking and quivering, pale and wan for fear,
Stands aiming at me with his murdering dart
Who flies away at every glance I give,   70
And when I look away comes stealing on.
Villain, away, and hie thee to the field!
I and mine army come to load thy bark
With souls of thousand mangled carcasses—
Look where he goes! but see, he comes again   75
Because I stay! Techelles, let us march,
And weary Death with bearing souls to hell.

Physician. Pleaseth your majesty to drink this potion
Which will abate the fury of your fit
And cause some milder spirits govern you.   80

Tamburlaine. Tell me, what think you of my sickness now?

Physician. I viewed your urine, and the hypostasis,
Thick and obscure, doth make your danger great;

82. hypostasis] *Robinson;* Hipostates *O1–3, Q.*

---

58. *charge*] level.
his] i.e. Atlas'. Tamburlaine was seen as an Atlas figure in *One* II.i.9–
11.

62. *Apollo*] 'As the god who warded off evil, he came to be regarded as
a god of medicine' (Jump).

64. *grief*] pain, suffering; cf. l. 162 below.

64–5.] For the proverbial idea, cf. Tilley, N321, and *Jew of Malta*,
I.i.130. Cf. *Two* IV.i.140–5.

67–71.] For a portent similar to this, perhaps known to Marlowe,
Seaton refers to André Thevet, *Cosmographie Universelle*, 1575, I, fol.
308 (Seaton, 'Sources', pp. 398–9).

73. *thy bark*] Cf. the loading of 'Charon's boat', *One* V.i.464–5.

82. *hypostasis*] sediment. On the diagnosis from this evidence, see Parr,
pp. 12–13.

83. *doth*] Ellis-Fermor and some other editors wrongly read 'both'.

Your veins are full of accidental heat
Whereby the moisture of your blood is dried: 85
The humidum and calor, which some hold
Is not a parcel of the elements
But of a substance more divine and pure,
Is almost clean extinguishèd and spent,
Which, being the cause of life, imports your death.   90
Besides, my lord, this day is critical,
Dangerous to those whose crisis is as yours:
Your artiers, which alongst the veins convey
The lively spirits which the heart engenders,
Are parched and void of spirit, that the soul,   95
Wanting those organons by which it moves,
Cannot endure, by argument of art.
Yet if your majesty may escape this day,
No doubt but you shall soon recover all.
Tamburlaine. Then will I comfort all my vital parts   100
And live in spite of death above a day.

                              Alarm within.

[*Enter a* Messenger.]

Messenger. My lord, young Callapine that lately fled your

101.2.] Oxberry; not in *O1–3*, Q.

---

84. *accidental*] inessential, abnormal (Pendry–Maxwell).

84–90.] Tamburlaine's passions have caused an excess of 'accidental heat', which 'parches his arteries and dries up in his blood the radical moisture (*humidum*) which is necessary for the preservation of his natural heat (*calor*). The depletion of his *humidum* and *calor* (whose admixture in the blood gives rise to the *spirits*) prevents his soul's functions, stops his bodily activities, and thereby causes his death' (Parr, p. 19). The sickness, in one view, fulfils Soria's curse on Tamburlaine (*Two* IV.i.178–81).

91–2. *critical . . . crisis*] the physician has in mind the unfavourable days in Tamburlaine's horoscope. J. C. Maxwell suggested that *crisis* might be a misprint for *crasis*, 'constitution, blend of elements or humours': its technical nature suits the context, and it avoids a lame repetition, though *O.E.D.* first records it in 1602 (*T.L.S.*, 4 January 1947).

93. *alongst*] parallel to. On *veins* and *artiers*, cf. *One* II.vii.10 n., and *Two* IV.i.178–9.

96. *organons*] 'subtle highly-refined substances or fluids formerly supposed to permeate the blood and chief organs of the body' (*O.E.D.* 1).

97. *argument of art*] i.e., the logic of medicine.

100. *comfort*] cheer, console, husband.

    majesty, hath now gathered a fresh army, and, hearing
    your absence in the field, offers to set upon us presently.

Tamburlaine. See, my physicians, now, how Jove hath sent   105
    A present medicine to recure my pain:
    My looks shall make them fly, and, might I follow,
    There should not one of all the villain's power
    Live to give offer of another fight.

Usumcasane. I joy, my lord, your highness is so strong,   110
    That can endure so well your royal presence
    Which only will dismay the enemy.

Tamburlaine. I know it will, Casane. Draw, you slaves!
    In spite of death I will go show my face.

     Alarm. TAMBURLAINE *goes in, and comes out again with
       all the rest.*

Tamburlaine. Thus are the villains, cowards, fled for fear,   115
    Like summer's vapours vanished by the sun.
    And could I but a while pursue the field,
    That Callapine should be my slave again.
    But I perceive my martial strength is spent:
    In vain I strive and rail against those powers   120
    That mean t'invest me in a higher throne,
    As much too high for this disdainful earth.
    Give me a map, then let me see how much
    Is left for me to conquer all the world,
    That these my boys may finish all my wants.   125
                      One brings a map.
    Here I began to march towards Persia,
    Along Armenia and the Caspian Sea,
    And thence unto Bithynia, where I took
    The Turk and his great empress prisoners;
    Then marched I into Egypt and Arabia,   130

---

104. *offers*] makes as if.
106. *present*] ready.
    recure] cure.
110. *joy*] rejoice.
111. *endure*] indurate, harden (*O.E.D.* 1).
112. *only*] i.e., Tamburlaine's royal presence is capable in itself of dis-
maying his opponents; or, nothing but that will dismay them; or, again,
his fortitude in sickness will do so.
116. *vanished*] caused to disappear.

And here, not far from Alexandria,
Whereas the Terrene and the Red Sea meet,
Being distant less than full a hundred leagues,
I meant to cut a channel to them both,
That men might quickly sail to India;   135
From thence to Nubia near Borno lake,
And so along the Ethiopian sea,
Cutting the tropic line of Capricorn
I conquered all as far as Zanzibar;
Then by the northern part of Africa   140
I came at last to Graecia, and from thence
To Asia, where I stay against my will—
Which is from Scythia, where I first began,
Backward and forwards near five thousand leagues.
Look here, my boys, see what a world of ground   145
Lies westward from the midst of Cancer's line
Unto the rising of this earthly globe,
Whereas the sun, declining from our sight,
Begins the day with our Antipodes:
And shall I die, and this unconquered?   150
Lo here, my sons, are all the golden mines,
Inestimable drugs and precious stones,
More worth than Asia and the world beside;
And from th'Antarctic Pole eastward behold
As much more land which never was descried,   155

131–5.] 'The first canal linking the Mediterranean to the Red Sea was attributed by Pliny to the legendary Pharaoh Sesostris' (Woolf). Tamburlaine's dream anticipates the Suez Canal, as he does the Panama Canal at *One* III.iii.252 ff.

136. *Borno lake*] Lake Chad (Pendry–Maxwell); cf. *Two* I.iii.186–205 n.

146.] 'In Ortelius the meridian 0° cuts the Tropic of Cancer just off the coast of north-west Africa. Tamburlaine traces the map westward from this point' (Woolf). *the midst ... line*] 'i.e. where the meridian intersects the tropic, close to Canary Islands [on Ortelius' map]' (Pendry–Maxwell).

149. *our Antipodes*] 'here, the dwellers in the Western Hemisphere, and the southern half of it (that is, South America, the source of Spanish gold and the riches of the fabulous El Dorado)' (Ellis-Fermor, p. 276).

150, 158. *unconquered*] A speaker of these poignant lines may prefer the abrupt trisyllabic stress.

154–5. *from th'Antarctic ... descried*] Australasia, 'never yet "descried" but already the subject of vague rumour' (Ellis-Fermor, p. 276).

Wherein are rocks of pearl that shine as bright
As all the lamps that beautify the sky:
And shall I die, and this unconquered?
Here, lovely boys, what death forbids my life,
That let your lives command in spite of death.   160
Amyras. Alas, my lord, how should our bleeding hearts,
    Wounded and broken with your highness' grief,
    Retain a thought of joy, or spark of life?
    Your soul gives essence to our wretched subjects
    Whose matter is incorporate in your flesh.   165
Celebinus. Your pains do pierce our souls; no hope survives,
    For by your life we entertain our lives.
Tamburlaine. But sons, this subject, not of force enough
    To hold the fiery spirit it contains,
    Must part, imparting his impressions   170
    By equal portions into both your breasts:
    My flesh, divided in your precious shapes,
    Shall still retain my spirit though I die,
    And live in all your seeds immortally.
    Then now remove me, that I may resign   175
    My place and proper title to my son:
[*To Amyras.*] First take my scourge and my imperial crown,
    And mount my royal chariot of estate,
    That I may see thee crowned before I die—
    Help me, my lords, to make my last remove.   180
Theridamas. A woeful change, my lord, that daunts our
    thoughts

177. *To Amyras*] This ed.; not in *O1–3, Q.*

---

162. *grief*] pain.

164–5, 168–74.] 'The soul of Tamburlaine has imparted to his sons the spirit that animates them, their bodies being similarly part of his flesh. Tamburlaine replies that he himself, however ("this subject"), is not strong enough to hold any longer the fiery spirit it contains and must divide the power of that spirit ("his impressions") between his two sons, who are thus the inheritors alike of his body and of his soul' (Ellis-Fermor, p. 277, remarking the Aristotelianism of the terms used). Cf. *Two* IV. i.112–15.

167. *entertain*] maintain.

170.] See *One* I.ii.22 n.

176, 182. *proper*] own.

178.] The echo of *One* V.i.526 ('Mount up your royal places of estate') points up the comparison of the two endings.

More than the ruin of our proper souls.

Tamburlaine. Sit up, my son, let me see how well
    Thou wilt become thy father's majesty.

                                    They crown him.

Amyras. With what a flinty bosom should I joy   185
    The breath of life and burden of my soul,
    If not resolved into resolvèd pains
    My body's mortifièd lineaments
    Should exercise the motions of my heart,
    Pierced with the joy of any dignity!   190
    O father, if the unrelenting ears
    Of death and hell be shut against my prayers,
    And that the spiteful influence of heaven
    Deny my soul fruition of her joy,
    How should I step or stir my hateful feet   195
    Against the inward powers of my heart,
    Leading a life that only strives to die,
    And plead in vain unpleasing sovereignty?

Tamburlaine. Let not thy love exceed thine honour, son,
    Nor bar thy mind that magnanimity   200
    That nobly must admit necessity:
    Sit up, my boy, and with those silken reins
    Bridle the steelèd stomachs of those jades.

Theridamas. My lord, you must obey his majesty
    Since fate commands, and proud necessity.   205

Amyras. Heavens witness me, with what a broken heart
    And damnèd spirit I ascend this seat—
    And send my soul, before my father die,
    His anguish and his burning agony!

Tamburlaine. Now fetch the hearse of fair Zenocrate: 210

185–90.] 'How hard a heart I should have if I could enjoy my life and the possession of my soul and if my body were not dissolved in extreme pain (l. 187) and sympathetically afflicted (l. 188) and could still direct the movements of a heart that was touched to joy by such things as earthly dignities' (Ellis-Fermor, p. 278). On such involved language, see pp. 51–4.

200. *magnanimity*] recalling *One* IV.iv.129 n., and *Two* IV.i.85.

207. *damnèd*] doomed (*O.E.D.* 1b); an implication of eternal suffering (*O.E.D.* 4) may be present, especially if the pain of l. 209 is posthumous.

208. *send*] i.e., may Heaven send.

Let it be placed by this my fatal chair
And serve as parcel of my funeral.

Usumcasane. Then feels your majesty no sovereign ease,
Nor may our hearts, all drowned in tears of blood,
Joy any hope of your recovery?   215

Tamburlaine. Casane, no, the monarch of the earth
And eyeless monster that torments my soul
Cannot behold the tears ye shed for me,
And therefore still augments his cruelty.

Techelles. Then let some god oppose his holy power   220
Against the wrath and tyranny of Death,
That his tear-thirsty and unquenchèd hate
May be upon himself reverberate.

They bring in the hearse [*of* ZENOCRATE].

Tamburlaine. Now, eyes, enjoy your latest benefit,
And when my soul hath virtue of your sight,   225
Pierce through the coffin and the sheet of gold
And glut your longings with a heaven of joy.
So, reign, my son, scourge and control those slaves,
Guiding thy chariot with thy father's hand.
As precious is the charge thou undertakest   230
As that which Clymen's brain-sick son did guide
When wandering Phoebe's ivory cheeks were scorched
And all the earth, like Aetna, breathing fire.
Be warned by him, then, learn with awful eye

223.1. *of* ZENOCRATE] *Dyce 1; not in* O1–3, Q.   231. Clymen's] O2;
Clymeus O1, O3, Q.

***

211. *fatal chair*] the chair he is doomed to die in.

212. *parcel*] part.

214. *tears of blood*] Cf. *One* V.i.85 n.

225.] 'The implication in this line is the familiar stoic belief that the
body and its senses clog the spirit, which will exercise finer spiritual
senses when it is freed from the body. When Tamburlaine's soul is
freed and has the power of vision now vested only in the eyes of his body,
he will see the spirit of Zenocrate' (Ellis-Fermor, p. 279).

227. *glut*] Cf. *One* III.iii.164 n., and *Dr Faustus*, xviii.91; 'To glut the
longing of my heart's desire'.

231. *Clymen's brain-sick son*] Phaethon, child of Apollo and Clymene.
The phrase recalls *One* IV.ii.49; and cf. Tamburlaine's comparison of his
chariot with the sun's in *Two* IV.iii.7–10.

232. *Phoebe*] the moon; cf. *One* III.ii.19.

234. *awful*] awe-inspiring.

To sway a throne as dangerous as his: 235
For if thy body thrive not full of thoughts
As pure and fiery as Phyteus' beams,
The nature of these proud rebelling jades
Will take occasion by the slenderest hair
And draw thee piecemeal like Hippolytus   240
Through rocks more steep and sharp than Caspian clifts.
The nature of thy chariot will not bear
A guide of baser temper than myself,
More than heaven's coach the pride of Phaeton.
Farewell my boys, my dearest friends farewell,   245
My body feels, my soul doth weep to see
Your sweet desires deprived my company,
For Tamburlaine, the scourge of God, must die.
                                                          [*He dies.*]
Amyras. Meet heaven and earth, and here let all things end,
For earth hath spent the pride of all her fruit,   250
And heaven consumed his choicest living fire.
Let earth and heaven his timeless death deplore,
For both their worths will equal him no more. [*Exeunt.*]

FINIS.

248.1. *He dies.*] Oxberry [*Dies.*]; *not in* O1–3, Q.   253. *Exeunt*] Dyce 2;
not in O1–3, Q.

---

237. *Phyteus*] after φύτιος, 'generative', listed in one authority as an
appellation of 'the sun or Zeus'; B. P. Fisher, *N.&Q.*, XXII (1975),
247–8; cf. C. Brennan, 'Marlowe', *Beiblatt zur Anglia*, xvi (1905), p. 207.
    238. *jades*] the notorious 'pampered jades' of *Two* IV.iii.1.
    239. *take . . . hair*] Cf. Tilley, T311: 'Take Time (occasion) by the
forelock, for she is bald behind'. Cf. Spenser's Occasion, *Faerie Queene*,
II.iv.4.
    240. *Hippolytus*] dragged to death by his chariot horses; cf. *Aeneid*,
vii.761 ff.
    241. *clifts*] cliffs.
    251.] In *Two* III.ii.6–7, Tamburlaine wished his zenith to be marked
with a 'blazing star / That may endure till heaven be dissolved'.
    252. *timeless*] untimely.

Source Material

Note: u/v, i/j, and long s have been modernised, and contractions expanded. Marginal headings in Whetstone, referring to major occurrences, sources, etc., have been omitted.

George Whetstone, *The English Myrror*, 1586

I. *from* Book I, Chapter 3:

Envy originall of warre, and capitall cause of the destruction of the first Monarchies

... discontented (or rather dissentious) persons (how soever the power of a settled Prince, keepe them under) uppon a chaunge, will discover their seditious hartes, as fyre hid in ashes, by the sprinkeling of Gunpowder bewrayeth the heate. To quell which cunning daungerous people though *Machyvell* prescribe a pollicy, unseeming a Christian Prince, who is to referre hidden trespasses to the vengeaunce of God, and not to punishe with death an intent, without an attempt of evill: For untimely death, onely appertayneth either to Gods secreat vengeaunce, to open and lawfull conviction of justice, or in lawfull wayes to the sworde of the souldiour, for what humaine bloud is otherwise shedde, is tyrannye in a Prince, and punishable in a private person: yet Princes to brydle suche close enemies, of publicke peace: maye safelye without reproch of tyranny, follow the counsell of a *Geneowe* marchant, who was somtimes familiarly favoured of *Tamberlayne* the Great, surnamed *flagellum dei*, who worthy the name of vengeance, at what time as he after two assaults was peaceably possessed of a fayre city, the citizens with their chiefe Magistrates, wives and Children cloathed all in white having Olive braunches in their handes, as assuraunces of peace: uppon their knees humbly beseeching him of grace: Notwithstanding, commaunded his souldiers to kill them all like dogges. This *Genowa* mooved with pitty to see this outrage, besought Tamburlaine, to spare his crueltie for such, as he conquered by force. And (quoth he) if yee feare, that these dogs will another day bite, strike out their teeth. Their countenances if need be, will helpe to scare Wolves, meaning that he should spoyle them of their armour, and if occasion served, he might make them fight, as kinge *Astiages* did his cowardly souldiers, either with enemies in their faces, or friendes at their backes. Which good counsell *Tamberlaine* in his fury regarded not: Yet other Princes that have their passions more temperate, may thereby learne how to keep under their owne suspected subjects without dispeopling of their realmes, to animate forraine enemies.

II. *from* Book I, Chapter 11:
The contention that envie set betweene the Emperour of Constantinople, the Lord of Bulgarie, and other Princes, was the first grounde and sure foundation of the great TURKES Empire

Amurat left 2. sons, *Soliman* and *Bajazet, Bajazet* slew his brother *Soliman,* and made himself King: in the beginning of his raigne, he prepared great wars against the Christians, to revenge the death of his father: and with a great armie, he incountred in battaile with *Marke* L. of *Bulgaria,* and with the greatest part of the nobilitie of *Bulgaria* and *Servia,* whom he slew and utterly defeated. 3. yeeres after this victorie, he returned a newe upon the Christians in *Hungarie,* but chiefely in *Albania* and *Valaschia* and from thence sente many Christians slaves into *Turkie,* and being possessed of the greatest parte of *Greece,* to wit, of the ancient countries of *Athens, Boetia* and *Arcania,* he laid siege unto the great Citie of *Constantinople,* which drave the Emperor in proper person to desire aid of the westerne Princes: in which behalfe K. *Charles* the 7. succoured him with *2000.* launces: among whome there were two french gentlemen of great expectation, who joyned with *Sigismond* K. of *Hungarie* and afterwards Emperour, who for the same purpose raised a great armie: with whome also joyned the grandmaster of the *Rhodes,* the *Despos* of *Servia,* and a great number of other christian Princes: whereupon Bajazet leaving his siege at *Constantinople* sodeinly with 300000 men set upon the Christians, who were about a *100000.* men, betweene whom there was a most bloudy battaile: in fine the Christians were overthrowne, and the greater part slaine: the

King of *Hungarie* and the grandmaster of *Rhodes* hardely escaped by flight, and the *Frenchmen* were neere all slaine or taken: this battell was *Anno 1395.* upon *Michaelmas* even. After which victorie *Bajazet* returned againe to his former siege of *Constantinople*, and had surely won the same, if the newes of *Tamberlaines* entrie into his countrey, and that he had already gained many townes, cities and provinces, constrained him to trusse up his baggage, and with his full power to go finde his enemie in *Asia*: now two of the mightiest princes of the world, encountered eache other in battaile, where *Bajazet* was overcome and taken, who endured the most vile and hard prisonment that ever was heard of: for *Tamberlain* still carried him with his armie in an iron cage, and alwayes when he mounted upon his horse, he set his foot upon his shoulders: moreover, at meales he tyed him under his boorde, and like a dog fedde him with fragments: in this sorte ended this Prince his life, who had bene the most adventrous, the most renowmed and the most feared Prince of his time. The sons of *Bajazet* which escaped the battaile where their father was overthrowne, in their flight taken upon the seas by certaine galleis of the Christians, and certainely at that instant a faire occasion was offered the Christians, to have kept under for ever their capitall enemie the Turke, but their sinnes forbad so precious a blessing. The one of *Bajazets* sonnes named *Calapin* was delivered, who seeing the incapacities and contention of *Tamberlaines* sonnes, and taking withal other advantages that time offered, proclaimed himselfe Lord of his fathers Empire, and by strong hand kept *Greece* and *Thracia*. The Emperour *Sigismond*, both to keepe *Calapin* under, and to be avenged of the overthrowe which his father gave him, offered him battaile, in which *Sigismond* was overthrowne, & narrowly escaped by flight: *Calapin raigned 6.* yeeres, and dyed, leaving behind him two sonnes, the eldest named *Orcan*, and the other *Mahomet*.

III. *from* Book I, Chapter 12:

> *The wonderfull conquest of Tamberlaine, reconquered and his large kingdom overthrowne by the envy and discord of his two sonnes*

Amonge the illustrous Captaines *Romaines*, and *Grecians*, none of all their martiall acts, deserve to be proclaimed with more renown, then the conquest and millitarie disciplines of *Tamber-*

laine: but such was the injury of his fortune as no worthye writers undertooke his historye at large: although *Baptista Fulgosius* in his collection *Campinus florintin*, in his history of the *Turkes*: make some mention thereof: about the year of the Lorde *1390*. *Tamberlaine* being a poore labourer, or in the best degree a meane souldiour, descended from the *Partians*: notwithstanding the povertye of his parents: even from his infancy he had a reaching and an imaginative minde, the strength and comelinesse of his body, aunswered the hautines of his hart. This *Tamberlaine* as *Fulgosius* reporteth, keeping beasts among other youthes of his condition his companions in a meriment chose him for their king: whereupon *Tamberlaine* (having a ruling desire) after an othe of obedience, commanded every man to sell his cattaile: and to contemn their meane estate, and to follow him as their captaine: and in smal time, he assembled *500.* heardmen, and laborers, whose first act was to rob the marchants that passed that way: he parted the spoyle continually among his companions, and intertayned them with such faithfulnes and love, as the rumour thereof dayly increased his strength: the king of *Partia* understanding these matters, sent one of his captaines with a thousand horse to take him: but *Tamberlaine* so behaved him selfe, as he won this captaine to be his companion and assistant with al his strength who thus joined, did things of greater importance then before: these matters in question, envy had sowen discord between the king of *Persia* and his brother. *Tamberlaine* joyned with the kings brother: and so valiantly behaved him self, that he overthrew the king and seated his brother in the kingdom: the new king created *Tamberlaine*, chiefe captaine of his army: who under colour to inlarge his kingdom, raised many people, and found the means to make them revolt from their obedience, and so deposed the new king, whom he lately ayded to the kingdom: and then made him selfe king of *Persia*: redeeming (by this industry and dexterity in armes) his countrey from the servitude of the *Sarizens* and kinges of *Persia*. *Tamberlayne* having a puissaunt armye: in processe of time, conquered *Siria*, *Armenia*, *Babylon*, *Mesopotamia*, *Scitia*, *Asia*, *Albania*, and other provinces, with many goodly and invincible Cities: it is pittie his pollicies be not largely written, which in these conquestes could not but be famous: but of his militarie discipline thus much wryters commend, in his armye was never found mutine: he

was wise, liberall, and rewarded every souldiour with his desert:
there is no remembrance of a greater army then his: his government and order was such, that his campe seemed a goodly City,
wherein every necessary office was found, marchants without
feare of robbing, or spoyling repayred thither, with all maner of
necessary provision for his army: the reason was he suffered no
theft unpunished, and as lovingly honored, praised, and payed
the vertuous and valiaunt souldiour, which favour joyned with
justice, made him both feared and loved: he ledde a greater army
then king *Darius*, or *Xerxes*: for writers affirme, that he had had
foure hundred thousand horsemen, and 6. hundred thousand
foot men, the which he ledde to conquer the lesse *Asia*. *Bajazet*
the great *Turke* (of whose worthinesse, and wonderfull prowes is
sufficiently spoken in the former chapter) advertised of *Tamber-
laynes* proceedings: was driven to leave his siege to *Constantinople*: and with all expedition, to inlarge his power to the utter-
most: to incounter with *Tamberlayne*, by estimation he had as
manye horse men as *Tamberlayne*, and a great number of foot
men: these two puissant captaines in whom wanted neither
vallour, pollicye, nor anye advauntage of war, with equall
courages, mutuallye consented to abide the fortune of battaile:
and so incountring on the confines of *Armenia*: at the dawning of
the daye with all their power they beganne the fiercest battaile
that in any age was foughten, which by the huge number of
people, and the experience of their captains may be lawfully
supposed: the slaughter continued of both parties, and the
victorye doubtfull all the whole dayes. In fine the *Turkes* of whom
two hundred thousand were slaine: vanquished by the multitude
of their enemies tourned their backes: which *Bajazet* perceiving:
to incourage his army, with an unappauled spirite resisted the
furye of his enemies. But such was Gods will, for lacke of rescue,
by the overcharge of foes, he was taken prisoner, and presented
to *Tamberlaine*, who closed this great Emperour in an Iron cage,
and as a dog fed him onely with the fragments that fell from his
table (as in the former chapter is showne) a notable example of
the incertaintye of worldly fortunes: *Bajazet*, that in the morning was the mightiest Emperor on the earth, at night, was driven
to feede among the dogs, and which might most grieve him,
he was thus abased, by one that in the beginning was but a
poore sheepheard. *Tamberlaine* thus possessed of *Asia minor*,

which was before in the possession of the *Turke*, he speeded into *Aegypt*, and by the way raised all *Siria*, *Phenice*, and the *Palestine*, he tooke manye famous Cities and among others *Smirna*, *Antioch*, *Tripoli*, *Sebastian* and *Damas*: In *Aegypt* he encountred with the *Souldan*, and the king of *Arabia*, and overthrew them: he was ever best at ease when he found a stout resistance in his enemy: that his pollicie and prowesse might be the better knowne: as appeared at the city of *Damas*, which after he had taken, the principle and most valiaunt men retyred unto a tower, which was thought impregnable, afterwards they offered him composition, but he refused unlesse they would fight, or yeelde unto his mercy: and with diligence beyond expectation, he raysed a tower level with theirs: from whence he battred them in such sort as they were unable to resist: it is sayde, that in his batteries and assaultes, he used the firste daye to raise a white tent, which gave knowledge that if that daye the Citizens yeelded: they should have both their goods, lives, and liberty: the seconde daye he raysed a red tent, which signified, that if they did that daye yeeld, he would save all, but the maisters and chiefe of every house: the third day he raised a blacke tent, which signified that the gates of compassion were closed, and all that were that day, and afterwardes subjected, were slaine without respect of man woman or childe: it is written that *Tamberlaine* besieged a strong city, which withstood the *1*. and *2*. daies assault, the *3*. day the people fed with a vaine hope of mercy, set open the gates, and with their wives and children cloathed all in white, having Olive branches in their handes, they humbly beseeched grace, but *Tamberlaine* in place of compassion caused his squadrons of horsemen to tread them under their feete, and not to leave a mothers child a live, and afterwardes he leviled the city with the ground. At that time there was a marchaunt of *Genowa*, somewhat favored of Tamberlaine: pittying the cruelty; boldly demanded why he shewed such cruelty to those, that yeelded and beseeched pardon, whom *Tamberlaine* (with a countenance fiered with fury) answered: thou supposest that I am a man, but thou art deceived, for I am no other than the ire of God, and the destruction of the world: and therfore see thou come no more in my sight, least I chasten thy over proud boldnes. The marchant made speed away, and was never afterwards seene in the campe. And in truth *Tamberlain* although he was endued with many excellencies and vertues: yet it seemed by his cruelty, that God raysed him to chasten the kings and proud people of the earth. In the ende this great personage, without disgrace of fortune, after sundry great victories, by the course of nature died, and left behind him two sons, every way far unlike their father: between whom envy sowed such dissention, that through their incapacities to govern the conquests of their Father, the children of *Bajazet*, whom they kept prisoners, stole into *Asia*, and so won the people to disobedience, as they recovered the goods and possessions that their father lost. The like did other kings and princes, whom *Tamberlaine* had spoyled, in so much as in small time this Empire was so abased, that many dayes agoe, there was no remembrance left, either of him or his linage: save that *Baptista Ignatius* a great searcher of antiquities saith, that the successors of *Tamberlaines* sons: possessed the provinces conquered by him about the river of *Euphrates*, until the time of king *Usancasan*, and according to the opinion of some writers, of the heyres of this *Usancasan*, was chosen the first Sophy, who to this day (to the benefit of all christendom) maintaineth mortall wars against the great *Turk*.

Petrus Perondinus, *Magni Tamerlanis Scythiarum Imperatoris Vita*, 1553

I. Chapter IX (bis):
   De dedecore ac vilissimo suplicii genere quibus Baiazitem affecit, et de eiusdem morte

Nondum victoris Tamerlanis dirus exaturatus satiatusque animus videbatur caede cladeque Turcarum copiis miserabili modo illatis, nisi reliquum suae feritatis in Baiazithem quoque omnium miserrimum effudisset, quippe eo procumbente, non sine ludibrio eius tergo pedem imponens, solitus erat equum conscendere: prandenti vero et comessanti, quo magis ridiculo foret et despicatui, micas et frustilla sub mensa tripodi alligatus, canis in modum comedere cogebatur. Reliquum vero temporis ferrea in cavea bestiarum more conclusus degebat ad admirandum humanarum rerum spectaculum, exemplumque fortunae, nusquam fidae miserandum, quin vel uxor eius, quam una cum ipso captivam traxerat, crepidulis tantum calciata, sagoque perbrevissimo induta militari, denudatis obscoenis dedecorose ante

Baiazithis oculos Scytharum proceribus una discumbentibus pocula ministrare cogebatur: imitatus in hoc Tartarus Tamerlanes Tiberium Romanorum Imperatorem, nudis non nisi puellis ministrantibus coenantem. quod indignissime ferens Baiazithes, ira percitus, moeroreque confectus, tanta oneratus ignominia, mortem sibimet dire imprecabatur: qui nulla via voti compos quum evassiset, animum inexorabili obstinatione despondens, vita excessit, capite numerosis ictibus ferreis caveae clathris perfracto, illisoque cerebro, suo ad id misero funestoque fato compulsus, quod iam regem summum Asiae turpiter cohercendum, regnoque avito et patrio spoliandum opilioni quondam praebuerit, atque tanta res suas calamitate insigniverit: alter vero ex adverso ab illa ipsa rerum humanarum domina fortuna, ad tam summum Ethnearchiae fastigium evectus fuerit, ut bellum ingens ac tetrum regi antea invicto et praepotenti multisque victoriis et opibus clarissimo inferre potuerit, mira felicitate conficere, eundemque et uxorem sordidatos tandem in vincula abripere, ac ingenti cum praeda gloriabundus in terram patriam reverti.

Modern English version of the above (see Preface for acknowledgments):

   Of the disgraceful and most vile manner of punishment with which he afflicted Bajazeth, and of Bajazeth's death

Not yet did the cruel spirit of the victor Tamburlaine appear replete and sated with blood and slaughter after the appalling attack on the Turkish forces, until he had spent the rest of his savagery on Bajazeth, the most wretched of mankind, for he was wont to use the prostrate Bajazeth's back as a footstool when mounting his horse, mocking the Turk as he did so. Indeed, so that he might be more of an object of ridicule and contempt to Tamburlaine while he was eating his meals and carousing, Bajazeth was made to eat crumbs and crusts under the table like a dog, tied to a stool. As for the rest of the time, he spent it in an iron cage, shut up like a beast, affording a wondrous and lamentable example of the fickleness of fortune in human affairs. For, to crown all, his wife, who had been dragged away with him as a prisoner of war, was compelled to hand round goblets to the reclining Scythian chiefs, clad only in sandals and the briefest of military cloaks, her privy parts exposed disgracefully under the very eyes of Bajazeth. The Tartar Tamburlaine imitated in this the Roman Emperor Tiberius, who only dined to the ministrations of nude girls. Bajazeth, bearing this most indignantly, excited with anger and overcome with grief under the load of so much ignominy, grimly prayed for death for himself. When he had by no means managed to gain his prayer, steeling his spirit with inexorable resolution, he killed himself, striking his head with numerous blows on the iron bars of his cage and dashing out his brains. He was driven to this by his own miserable and deadly fate, in as much as he had allowed a one-time shepherd disgracefully to imprison the supreme king of Asia and rob him of his ancestral and paternal kingdom, branding his affairs with so great a calamity—while the other had been elevated from adversity by fortune, that mistress of human affairs, to so supreme a summit of the Ethnearchia, that he was able to wage war on a king hitherto unconquered, a very powerful king and very famous in his many victories and his wealth, to execute it with wonderful success, and finally to throw that same Bajazeth and his wife, vilely clad, into chains, and to return glorious with great booty into his fatherland.

II. Chapter XXI:

De statura Tamerlanis, et moribus eius

Statura fuit procera, et eminenti, barbatus, latus, ac humeris et pectore, caeterisque membris aequalis et congruens, integra valetudine, excepto altero pede, quo non perinde valebat, ut inde claudicare ac deformiter incedere prospiceretur, oris truculenti atque obductae suae frontis oculi introrsus recedentes praeferocis animi sui saevitiem spirantes, intuentibus terrorem et formidinem incutiebant. valida erat usque adeo nervorum compage, ut validissimum quemque e Scythis in palaestra prosterneret, ac Parthici ingentis arcus chordam lacertosis brachiis ultra aurem facile posset extendere, aeneumque mortarium excussi iaculi spiculo transfodere. Fuit igitur Tamerlanes corpore et moribus Cartaginiensi Hannibali simillimus, quantum scripta veterum edocent, ostenduntque numismata ingenio callido, atroci, perfido, nihilque pensi habente, usu postulante truci, in reprimendis hominum latrociniis castigandaque militum licentia saeviore, ut metu poenae oculos, nedum manus ab auro gazaque omni diripienda cohibere didicissent, ut ipse ibi solus fortasse

omnia vindicasset, cunctaque pro arbitrio diripuisset. in caeteris
vero plerumque connivebat. at quod mirum videri possit, quae-
rebat atrox bellorum exantlator indefesse tanquam eximium
virtutis opus, quibus cum bellum gereret, aut quos semper
turbulentissimis bellorum procellis, agitaret, vel qui incorrupta
libertate fruentibus saeve iugum imponeret.

Modern English version of the above:
  Of the stature of Tamburlaine and his character
He had a tall and lofty stature, was bearded, and broad across the
shoulders and chest, and he was equally well-proportioned and
robust in all his limbs, with the exception of one foot, where he
was not so strong, and it was apparent that this caused him to
limp, with a mis-shapen gait. He had a fierce countenance, and
the deep-set eyes in the knitted brow expressed the savagery of
his warlike spirit, striking fear and terror into onlookers. So very
strong were his muscles, that he could throw the strongest of the
Scythians on the wrestling-floor, and he could easily bend the
string of a huge Parthian bow with his brawny arms past his ear,
and pierce a brazen mortar with the point of a javelin. Tamburlaine was, then, in physique and character very like Cartha-
ginian Hannibal, so far as the ancient writers show, and the
images on coins reveal him to be shrewd, savage, treacherous in
mind, and lacking any scruples, (but) when necessity required
cruelty, he was exceedingly brutal in curbing brigandage and
punishing the license of the soldiery, with the result that men
had learned through fear of penalty to keep their eyes, not to
speak of hands, away from plundering all gold and treasure,
while he, though but one man, appropriated virtually everything
to himself, and plundered everything by virtue of his power.
Indeed, for the most part he overlooked other things, but what
may seem extraordinary is that this fierce veteran of wars sought
indefatigably, as though it were a wonderful work of virtue, for
people he might wage war on, or for people to harry constantly
with tempestuous raids, or for people enjoying complete freedom,
so that he could impose on them a savage yoke.

III. Chapter XXII:
  De disciplina eius circa rem militarem
Sub benigna quadam insignium conspiratione siderum felicis-

simoque eximiae magnitudinis stellarum concursu natum atque in lucem editum fuisse Tamerlanem, existimare fas est. mirum siquidem monstrosumque videri potest, quod obscuris ortum parentibus, ac vili gentilium suorum pago genitum, nullis educatum moribus, aut disciplinis imbutum, quibus ad perennem laudis et virtutis gloriam iter prosterni solet, usque adeo ingenti animo et pertinaci spiritu Martis munera obivisse viderint homines, ut ad summum bellicae virtutis apoclima profectum et acclamatum Imperatorem Scytharum proceres salutarent: quippe res omnes, quae in summo duce inesse oportere existimantur, in Tamerlane non dubie effulsisse audivimus, rei militaris scientiam, auctoritatem, felicitatem, ingenii acumen, laboris tolerantiam, rebusque maximis aggrediendis audaciam: hae identidem et aliae praeclarae, cum corporis, tum animi dotes, quae in ipso explenduerunt, magnum et admirabilem continuo praestitere: sic ut cunctis suspiciendus mortalium ingeniis, et summis efferendus princeps adoreis laudibus, nulla unquam temporis longinquitate minuendam aut abolendam gloriam Tartaris, et nullis ante seculis visum iubar Scythiae attulisse videatur.

Modern English version of the above:
Of his training in regard to soldiering
It is right to suppose that Tamburlaine was born and came forth into the light under a favourable harmony of distinguished constellations and the lucky conjunction of stars of uncommon magnitude. For it may be regarded as wondrous and portentous that mankind should have beheld a man born of obscure parents and in an insignificant village of his nation, a man moreover untrained in those qualities of character or skills which normally pave the way for undying distinction and commendation for valour, undertake the duties of Mars with so prodigious a courage and so persevering a spirit that he scaled the supreme peak of military excellence and was hailed and acclaimed as emperor by the Scythian chiefs. Indeed, we have heard that all the qualities regarded as requisite in a leader of genius blazed out unequivocally in Tamburlaine: knowledge of the art of warfare, authority, good fortune, sharpness of wit, the ability to endure toil, and boldness in undertaking the greatest enterprises. The combinations of these and other remarkable endowments of mind and body distinguishing him at once rendered him a great

man and one worthy of admiration. Consequently, as a man to be esteemed by every human intelligence and as a prince to be praised to the skies for his supreme renown, he may be thought to have conferred upon the Tartars a glory that no lapse of time, however long, can dim or obliterate, and to have irradiated Scythia with a splendour never beheld in any previous age.

Glossarial Index to the Commentary

Words and phrases are listed in the form in which they appear in the text. An asterisk before a word indicates that the note contains information which may supplement that given in *O.E.D.* This index also lists Biblical allusions and proverbs or proverbial phrases, under 'Biblical allusions' and 'Proverbs'. I have included only a selection from the proper names on which there are notes.

330